WOOD TOYS AND PLAYHOUSES

Popular Science Books offers a wood identification kit
that includes 30 samples of cabinet woods. For details on
ordering, please write: Popular Science Books, P.O. Box
2033, Latham, N.Y. 12111.

Wood Toys

AND PLAYHOUSES

Peter Stevenson

CHILTON BOOK COMPANY / RADNOR, PENNSYLVANIA

Library of Congress Cataloging in Publication Data
Stevenson, Peter, 1941-
  Wood toys and playhouses.
  Includes index.
  1. Wooden toy making. 2. Playhouses, Children's.
I. Title.
TT174.5.W6S74   1984   745.592   83-43302
ISBN 0-8019-6762-7 (pbk.)

1 2 3 4 5 6 7 8 9 0   4 3 2 1 0 9 8 7 6 5

CONTENTS

WOOD TOYS AND PLAYHOUSES

INTRODUCTION

About ten years ago we put together our first book on how to create handcrafted wooden toys. It was received kindly: The publisher seemed pleased, we were pleased and, apparently, the kids were pleased. Things have changed, however, so we are bringing out a new book and are hoping for the same results.

In the years following the first toy book, a lot of the materials on the market have changed, making finding substitutes a challenge to the builder's ingenuity. In addition, we've learned a thing or two about making projects easier for the builder to understand as well as to construct. And, although we'll go along with those who feel that playthings shouldn't be labeled as boys' toys or girls' toys, we *are* including a few more toy themes that seem especially suited to girls.

There are certain aspects of toy building that haven't changed and may never change. We still follow these principles when designing our toys. We will pass along these thoughts behind our toys, so that if you get the urge to veer off into new directions, you'll know how we arrived at our ideas. Since these are the same specifications we used when we wrote the first book, the basic principles will be repeats (at the risk of boring those who followed our train of thought the first time).

Toymaking involves a basic set of values. Children are a receptive audience, but they're not dummies. Some things are important in toy design; others aren't. We took a hard look at the components of a toy over the years to try to separate one group from the other. We rated the reception of a toy on the children's reactions; both at the first presentation (did it light up their eyes, or was it received with a polite "That's nice"?) and in terms of enduring use (was it shelved after the first flurry of interest, or was it lovingly worn out and rebuilt over the years?).

Naturally, the ideal toy is received gleefully on first presentation and goes on to become a member of the family, but these are rare toys in anybody's catalogue. We've come to think that both short-term and long-term reactions are worthwhile. Some toys are admired more than they are used, whereas others slowly grow in importance as the child gets acquainted with what they can do. Both categories are highly valued, so it takes a while to prove that a toy is a "winner" or a "dud". And then, too, one kid's excite-

ment is another kid's boredom. This is where your own judgment of what your children are interested in, and what they'll never be interested in, becomes a factor.

Over the years we've come to believe that a toy's true value is discovered when the user has grown up and the parent is clearing out the room, deciding which toys to give away to the younger kids down the street. The results of this "test" are sometimes surprising. Some toys that were hardly touched can be given away only on threat of family lawsuits, whereas others that the parent always thought were big attention-getters are passed on without a whimper. We've come to realize that toys have value long past the time that they're put away on a shelf. There seems to be a solid continuity to growing up when you can look forward and back at the same time and know the same old faithful toys will be there when you're ready to pass them on to your own kids. So we're taking a long view of toys this time and are now judging them with a little more time under our belts.

The most important feature of any toy is the fact that you made it. The toy, no matter how ragged, beat-up, or even basically ugly to begin with, stands as permanent evidence of hours that you spent creating something for your children. And even though the initial response to a toy you made especially for them may not stand up to some electronic gimmick they've been pining for, check in a couple of decades (or years, or months) and see which one they'd rather part with. The effort put into a toy, reminding the recipient of good times with somebody close, is what adds to the value of the toy as the years pass. You can forget every other rule of design here and that will still hold true.

The fact that you built it is important; the finish isn't, because toys should take a beating. And the more they're used, the more beating they'll get. If you've poured a lot of hours into the finish, you're going to cringe every time your children set the toy on its side in the gravel. An overfinished toy will be pampered, and that's not good fun when a child really wants to get down to heavy playing. So we favor putting the effort into the basic concept and constructing the toys from rough-and-ready materials that can gain appeal the more beat-up they get. Once in a while, you'll come across a design for a toy that has to be shiny and glistening— one that needs to be treated right. But for the most part, we prefer the kind of rustic finish that hides its scars, or even looks better for them.

Although finish isn't that important, basic proportions are if you want to build a classic toy. When designing the toys in these books, we first went to find the real thing—the real airplane or steam shovel—as a starting point. Once your eye is trained to recognize the basic proportions of the subject, you can start to modify it into toy shape. We looked at other similar toys after becoming familiar with the porportions of the real thing to see where we agreed with the other toy-makers' versions and where we didn't. It became obvious which toymakers actually researched their subjects and which simply copied others' toy designs.

It's always difficult to recall the proportions of objects we see every day when we start trying to reproduce them. A learning-dynamics psychologist will tell you that it's easy to recognize goofs but hard to reconstruct anything without errors, so you have to put in more effort than your critics do to get the job done. You may *think* you know what a bicycle

looks like, but chances are you can't draw an accurate picture of a bike frame without a model. We design toys the easy way and find photographs of the real thing. If we're creating a representative airplane or locomotive, we find several styles, take the features we like best from each, and combine them, so long as they make some sort of sense. (Nobody should put a World War I biplane tail on a jet fuselage.) So long as the models are from the same era, you can take a tail from one, a nose from another, and a wing configuration from a third and end up with a representative design for that basic subject.

Next comes proportioning, and here's where the fun comes in. Our theory in the first book was that toys shouldn't be miniatures. Miniatures, especially highly detailed models, are fascinating and fun to look at, but their very accuracy stunts play fun. If something's extremely real-looking, how do you explain the fact that it's driving down a road that curves around an enormous flower pot? But if the toy is an abstract and obviously not real, imagination comes into play: The flower pot can become a casino building where all the spies on your island congregate, or maybe a football stadium about to be taken over by invaders. Play changes as a child gets used to viewing things more closely and demands more complete detailing and more logical settings. Detailing can be included while an abstract design is not maintained; and this is how some of the most satisfactory toy designs have come about. Take a look at some turn-of-the-century toy locomotives and ships and you'll see a wealth of details combined with abstract proportioning, which resulted in appealing toys with lasting play value.

We still stick by our early ideas about abstract proportioning: that something is

"cute" and "appealing" when its basic proportions are shortened and the details are slightly enlarged. Our guess is that this comes from our association of "cuteness" with baby animals, which almost always have shortened limbs and trunks with proportionally large heads and eyes. Change the porportions of almost any machine (and most toys represent machines or structures) in the same way and you'll end up with a "cute" or "appealing" locomotive or semitrailer truck (or submachine gun, for that matter). Most toymakers seem to believe that the younger the age group for whom the toy is designed, the more you foreshorten. After a certain point, foreshortening no doubt looks "cute" only to the adult buying it. Therefore, we stick with a moderate shortening for all ages.

In addition, some testing that showed that perception of color intensity fades as an individual gets older got us to thinking about color. If perception of color fades with time, then the only ones who are impressed by the super-bright primary colors seen on toys are adults. Toddlers must find these hues garish. We ran several unofficial tests and are convinced that in order to please the sensitive eyes of a child, one should use muted, sensible colors that are seen in the real world, not circus-approved, full-saturation primary hues. One of the appeals of wooden toys is the subtle combining of browns, tans, and blacks, which makes a rich, satisfying object to study and handle. There may be a reason why children would rather play with Daddy's walnut desk set than with a new, multihued robot.

The basic components of "good taste" as defined by many different cultures are remarkably similar. Maybe the principles of taste are included in the information we're given at birth. Whatever the case,

we vote to give the kids a chance to follow their instincts when it comes to toys, and we've found by experimenting that what they like turns out to be in such good taste that it would put a lot of executive clubs' interior designers to shame.

When we design a new toy, after pouring over photographs of the real thing (and looking over the actual object, if possible), we sit down and make a little sketch, usually a three-quarter front view and a side view, and revise it until we think it's perfect. Then we pin this up someplace where we'll come across it several times a day without thinking about it. Usually this brings about a lot of changes, as "perfect" is transformed into "really perfect." Next, we'll start cutting wood (or whatever other material we are going to use), following the proportions that we have specified as carefully as possible.

When we cut, we try to remember two rules: (1) Take your time. It takes only a few seconds per cut. Just because the saw is loud is no reason to rush it. (2) Follow the lines that you draw. We stick closely to the design that we've created. Then we assemble the parts temporarily, blocking them up into position or taping them together for easy disassembly.

We put the assembled parts in a place where we're likely to happen upon them without thinking, just as we do with the initial sketches, and then make careful note of our reaction. Another test is to use a hand mirror to look at the creation from all angles. It's a good idea to leave a pencil and notebook next to the parts to jot down your ideas for changes and to mark the parts for subsequent cutting. We rarely alter a project until we've had some time to think about it. It's easy to cut, but it's sometimes impossible to relengthen.

When trying to set the length or height of something, we stretch out the design until it's obviously too long or too high and mark this point. Then we compress the pattern until it's obviously too short or too low and mark this point as well. That gives us a field of choice with which to begin. Then we can try the midpoint between the two limits as a starting measurement and use this in a mock-up of the parts for our initial tests.

Before we get into the actual building steps for the toys, keep in mind some rules we've learned about tools, fasteners, and materials in general.

■ TOOLS

To keep the projects within reach of the average household electric-tool kit, we try to avoid bench tools. All the toys can be made with a $\frac{1}{4}''$ electric drill, a hand-held circular saw (or Skilsaw), and an electric saber saw. A basic tool kit includes a hammer, a screwdriver (a push-type Yankee screwdriver comes in handy), channel-lock pliers, a crescent wrench, a wood chisel about 1" across, and a Surform serrated wood shaper. This tool makes toymaking fun because it allows faster and more precise rounding and shaping than we've ever been able to get with a traditional plane or rasp. (The shorter, one-hand model is better at getting into tight spots than the two-hand model.) Other hand tools and attachments for a power drill will be needed here and there, such as a grinding wheel, an alignment jig, and a hole saw.

Several power tools revolutionize the speed and quality of toymaking. One is the band saw. It's expensive and falls in the category of a permanent-shop bench tool, but it's fun to use and makes a

clean, precise cut. Because it allows you to make and finish toys fast, we recommend it if you have the space and your budget allows only one bench tool. (It's our *only* one). Another tool that's not absolutely necessary, but one that will allow you to put out more finished work in a short time, is a belt sander. If you work only with small toys, a bench-mounted one is the obvious choice. But if you find yourself working on many household projects, choose the hand-held style, which can be clamped in a vise and used as a bench sander, then taken out to do other jobs as well. With a band saw and a belt sander, chances are you'll find yourself all of a sudden considering more ambitious projects.

We prefer to use screws in our projects where some people would use nails. The reason: Every time we nail a project together, the first nails are usually pounded loose by the time the last ones are hammered in. With screws, you get a precise, strong bond of parts without destruction-testing the parts that have already been attached. One advantage of screws is that they can be removed without marring the surface if you must reposition parts.

Whenever driving screws, first drill a pilot hole with a combination drill bit/countersink attachment in a power drill, sized to match the size of the screw, to make the driving easy and prevent wood splitting. With the right size drill/countersink, the screw can be driven in easily but can still get a strong grip.

Woodworkers continue to argue over whether Phillips-head screws or slot-head screws are easier to drive. We've gone back and forth ourselves over this issue. It's good to learn a few facts about both styles, especially if you drive a lot of screws with a Yankee screwdriver or a power-drill attachment.

Regardless of the type of screw, it's important to have an unworn screwdriver tip if you're using a power-drill attachment. Phillips-head screws can be driven faster, and you don't have to push as hard to maintain contact with the screw. It's also easier to line up the driver tip. But you may tend to ease up on the pushing until the driver tip slips. One slip with a regular slot-head driver and the screw will not be damaged. In fact, you can ruin the screw and the reverse side of the slot will still be brand new. One slip with the easier-to-drive Phillips-head screws and the screw is in trouble. Two slips and it's ruined, both for driving *and* for backing out, so you can end up with a half-driven screw that has to be yanked with a hammer, chiseled, or removed with pliers.

■ GLUE

We use yellow squeeze-bottle-style aliphatic glue (Elmer's or Wilhold, for example) in the final assembly of all inside projects. For boats or exterior house projects that are subject to immersion, we use Wilhold Plastic Resin boat glue (a powdered, water-mix glue that has proved itself economical and dependable over the years). But for toys, even toys that get left outside, we use the yellow squeeze-bottle glue, making sure that the joints are well painted or varnished to keep out moisture.

■ WOODS

When building toys that will be varnished to show wood grain, we often vary the grain and color or contrast a dark grain against a blonde wood. One of the nicest-

to-work-with woods that is well suited to toys is redwood. It's light, stronger than most people think, and it shapes well and resists splitting. The only drawbacks are that it's soft and can get scarred (an advantage if you want a weathered and worn look), and its resin is poisonous. That's why a redwood fence post is impervious to insects.

If you think your craftsmanship will leave potential splinters, or if the toy may be gnawed upon, use another wood wherever we have used redwood in the prototypes. Pine is easy to work with, but its grain is dull and almost invisible. When you varnish it, it takes on very little color, and it's almost impossible to stain with good results. It has great shaping and cutting qualities and resists splitting, but it doesn't hold a screw well for structural use.

Fir is tougher than pine and has good screw-holding qualities, looks good varnished to a reddish gold, takes a stain well (there is almost too much contrast in the grain pattern), and shapes well. Its chief drawback is that it can split just at the wrong time in assembly. Spruce is a good all-around wood with all of the attributes of fir as well as a little more strength and less propensity to split. Its color is grayer and more subdued, and its grain pattern is just about invisible.

We rarely use any of the harder-to-get, harder-to-work, harder-to-pay-for woods like oak and walnut because of the cost and the tools needed to shape and round them. Because the woods are hard and require skill to cut, a beginner may end up with a toy that looks like a woodshop cutting exercise rather than a family heirloom. Walnut is beautiful wood, but it's expensive. And oak, in our opinion, is much overrated both in strength and in looks. It can, and usually does, split if it's not regularly oiled or varnished.

Mahogany is a great wood for toys, but it's also expensive. It shapes well, holds a screw well, has a beautiful amber grain when varnished, and is strong. But it's hard to find in the standard lumber sizes used for the projects here. So most of our projects are built of fir, pine, and, redwood; the old standbys.

☐ General Wood Finishing

For small wood projects like toys, the Surform serrated wood shaper works best. In looking over toys built by other toymakers from our first book, we've found that almost everybody can saw out the toys correctly, but not everybody shapes them correctly. We think this is the result of technique. The most common mistake we've seen in wood shaping is that telltale squared look with just the corners rounded off, rather than a smooth curve. This symptom has one cause and that's switching to a finer sandpaper too soon. Often the builder begins by trying to round off a curved shape with too fine a sandpaper. Then, after getting nowhere, he or she becomes frustrated and switches to a fine sandpaper to create a smooth (but not well-rounded) surface, just to get a feeling of accomplishment. We know how it works because we've done it ourselves many times. To get a well-shaped toy that doesn't look like a high-school shop project, the secret is to leave the finish-sanding to the very end. When shaping with the Surform, you'll find that even when you're moving the shaper in the direction of the grain, moving it one way will tend to lift the grain and remove large quantities of wood, whereas moving it the other way smooths

the grain but doesn't shave off as much wood.

When beginning to shape a toy, we try to clamp the piece so that we can shape it against the grain (not across it), the direction that removes the most wood but leaves the surface well roughed up. Next, we change directions 180 degrees and continue to shape down to the desired contour, moving with the grain to prevent the surface from becoming too rough. Then we use rough sandpaper of 60 or even 40 grit. Garnet paper is better, of course, because it remains abrasive longer.) Sandpaper this coarse will rough up the surface again, but chances are this will show where we missed some flat spots and hollows with the shaper. Coarse sandpaper is a great shaping tool for softer woods and the key to getting that sculptured look. Once you are happy with the shape, it's time to bring in the 80-grit paper, then the 150-grit, to create a truly smooth, well-shaped surface. Skipping the coarse-paper step usually results only in smoothed off lumps.

On all wood projects that are to be painted (and even on some that are varnished), we use catalyzed polyester autobody putty for filler. It's tough, a good bonder, easy to work with, quick to finish, and cheap compared with wood fillers, which take forever to dry, crack if they're applied too thickly, and are hard to shape. Brand names vary, so read the label to make sure you're not getting a hard finishing putty like "Snow White." "Cuz," "Bondo," or any other medium-hard polyester filler will do. Even though it smells like fiberglass, it's not nearly so temperamental. A few rules of the game will make the job more fun.

The first step is to mix the putty in the can well with a stick. Next, find a smooth, clean plywood, metal, or, better yet, Masonite palette. Any dirt or shavings in the putty will leave grooves when you smooth it on with a knife. You'll need one stick to ladle the putty out of the can and onto the palette, another stick for mixing, and a putty knife for applying it. Keep the mixing stick and ladling stick separate. Don't mix with the putty knife because it's too easy to end up with unmixed putty on the knife, which invariably gets applied later on.

Depending on the size of the job, ladle out a dollop of putty about $2\frac{1}{2}''$ square and $\frac{1}{2}''$ high. Then squeeze out a circle of catalyst paste about the size of a quarter. Keep all work from here on out of direct sunlight as much as possible because sunlight will cause the putty to harden. Warmth also speeds hardening, so if you have to work in the hot sun, don't mix in as much catalyst.

Mix in the catalyst quickly and thoroughly with a figure-8 movement of the mixing stick, making sure there are no little spots that remain gray and uncatalyzed. Some catalysts are brick red; others are blue. Whatever the hue, the routine is the same, and the mixed batch will be a gray base. Adding too much catalyst will cause the putty to harden before you can work it. If there is too little catalyst in the basic gray, it will never harden. A little practice will teach you how to judge the right amount of catalyst to squeeze out.

Once the batch is mixed, you must work quickly. Fill the biggest holes or gaps first. We apply lots of putty to the gaps, building up a lump larger than the final contour if possible in the first application. Then we fill the smaller holes as the chemical hardening slowly starts to take effect. Small holes surrounded by a smooth surface can be filled with the

putty knife, but usually we try to overfill the indents because the putty shrinks on hardening; and if you catch it right, the putty is easy to shape down with the Surform shaper. On the second application, all air bubbles or uneven spots left in the first application after shaping can be filled and smoothed with the putty knife.

About five minutes after the putty starts to lump and resemble cottage cheese, it will start to get rubbery. At this point, it has very few adhesion properties, so clean off the palette, the putty knife, and the mixing stick.

As soon as the putty has hardened enough to leave a white line where you scratch it with your fingernail, you can start to shape it with the Surform. You'll have ten minutes or so, depending on the temperature, when the putty will grate like cheese, allowing a lot of material to be shaved away in a little amount of time. Then it will start to take on its final hardness. You can still shape hardened Bondo with a Surform, but it takes more elbow grease and Surform blades. After it's hard, it sands well without gumming up the sandpaper.

■ PAINTS AND VARNISHES

We have two basic rules about paint: (1) Stale paint that's been sitting on the store shelf (or on your garage shelf) can cause problems, so try to buy where the volume turnover is good, like a discount paint store. (2) Whenever using more than one can of paint of the same color, intermix them to assure an even color between cans.

It's hard to convince people of this (we believed it ourselves only after repeated disasters), but applying many thin coats of paint is better than trying to make one, two, or even three coats cover. This depends on the paint of course, but we have yet to see a true one-coat paint.

The first coat of paint (especially spray paint) will largely disappear into the woods. The next coat, if you read the label and give the paint ample time to dry, will usually dry faster than the first coat. The oils in the wood slow drying time, so the first coat takes longest.

Much of the finish-sanding can be done after the first coat. Before applying each coat, sand lightly with fine sandpaper to remove drips, paint-brush bristles, or other dust or debris that could cause holes in the next coat. We usually fine-sand the latest coat just before adding the next to prevent any moisture from accumulating on the surface if, say, we leave the part overnight before painting.

With spray paints, always follow the label directions about time between coats. Some spray paints must dry thoroughly; others are not supposed to. The usual penalty for not reading the labels about drying time is that the next coat will curdle. With brush-painted enamel, four or five coats will provide a glossy protection to keep the wood from cracking as a result of changes in temperature and humidity. With spray paint, six to eight coats will provide a glossy, professional gleam. With satin-finish varnish, two to three coats are necessary before you begin to see less improvement with each new coat.

Take your time and work carefully, and the whole project will go much faster with surprisingly few crises.

THE PEUGEOT

■ MATERIALS LIST

$1\frac{1}{2}''$ × $1\frac{5}{8}''$ × $7\frac{1}{2}''$ fir 2 × 3 or 2 × 4 stock
18″ length of pine 1 × 3 stock
$2\frac{1}{2}''$ length of $1\frac{1}{4}''$ dowel
$1\frac{3}{8}''$ length of $\frac{7}{8}''$ dowel
10″ length of $\frac{5}{16}''$ dowel
1″ length of $\frac{1}{2}''$ dowel
Roll of $\frac{1}{2}''$ Scotch tape
$1\frac{3}{8}''$-diameter wooden drawer-pull knob
Three $1\frac{1}{2}''$ finishing nails
Two $1\frac{1}{2}''$ #8 flathead wood screws
3″ #12 roundhead wood screw
Thumbtack
$7\frac{1}{2}''$ length of heavy, round black electrical
    cord ($\frac{3}{8}''$ O.D.)

☐ *See color insert for completed project.*

We'll start off with something simple, with a minimum of shaping and freehand sculpturing, just to get the tools warmed up. The simple racer shown here is made of pine and fir for a subtle contrast of wood tones. It is loosely based on that very successful Edwardian race car, the Peugeot, a milestone car of its day, with double overhead cams, knock-off center-lock wheels, and a light construction. It was a true giant killer, snatching victory after victory away from the monstrous engines of the typical race cars of the time. But back to woodworking.

■ CUTTING

The first step is to cut five wooden wheels from the 1″-thick (actually $\frac{3}{4}''$-thick) pine stock using a $2\frac{1}{4}''$-diameter hole-saw attachment for the power drill. Cheap, adjustable hole saws actually cut soft woods better than the more expensive ones. To cut the wheels, drill $\frac{1}{4}''$ holes for the centers through the 1″ stock. A square or an alignment jig will keep the hole drilling square to prevent wheel wobble. Next, using the $1\frac{3}{4}''$ blade and the hole as a guide, cut circles into the wood about $\frac{1}{8}''$ deep on each side. Then change to a $2\frac{1}{4}''$ blade and cut out the wheel, drilling halfway in from each side to leave the burr at the wheel's center.

The next step is to cut out the chassis platform from 1″ pine stock, marking the $\frac{3}{8}''$ axle holes carefully on both sides of the chassis, as shown in Figure 1–1. Use a $\frac{3}{8}''$ wood-spade bit to drill the axle holes squarely through the edge of the chassis board from both sides.

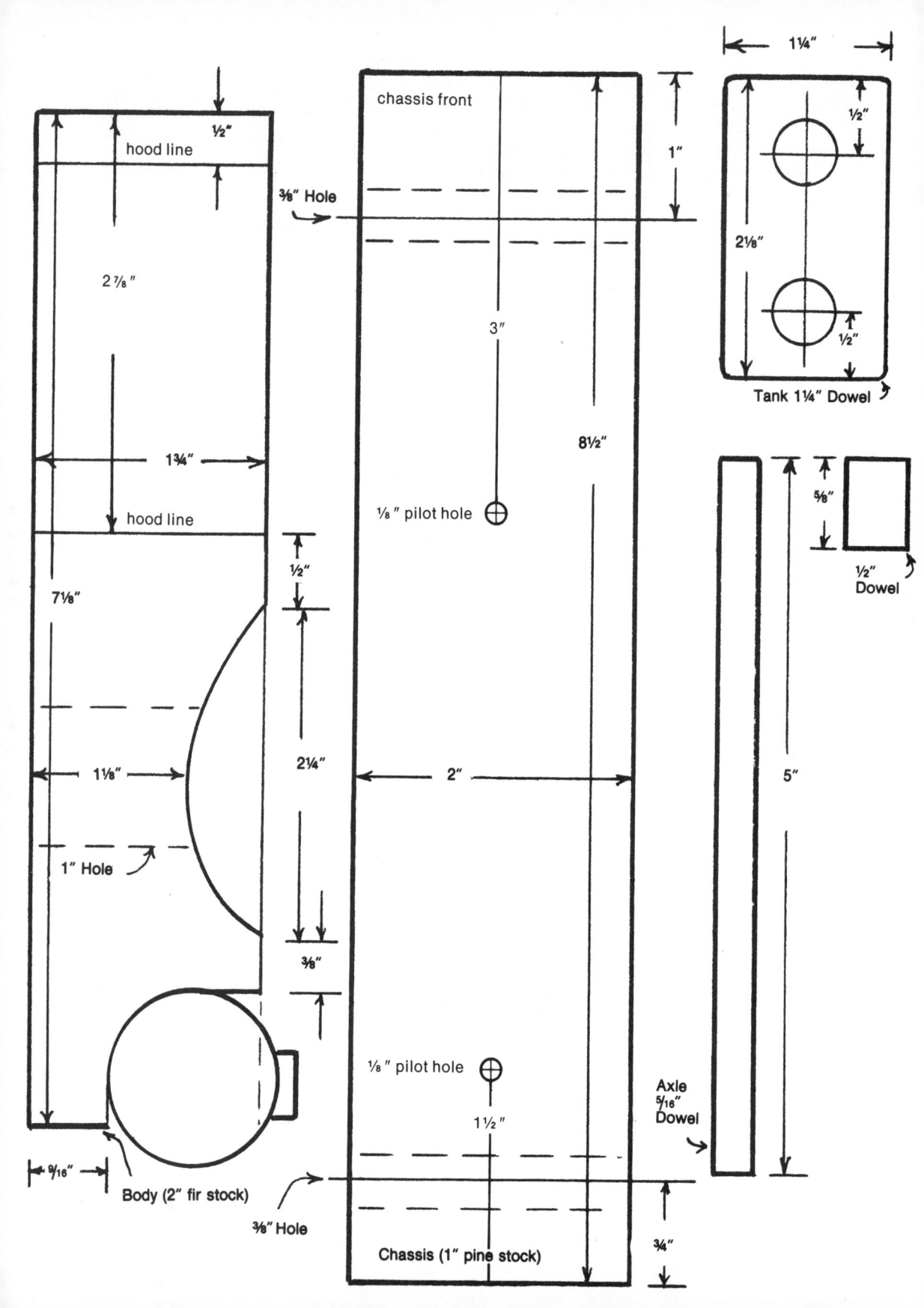

For the body, draw the side view onto a length of $2'' \times 4''$ fir stock. A circular saw can be used to cut the straight outlines, and the cockpit curve and gas-tank-mount curve can be cut with a saber saw, although a band saw will perform all the cuts well.

Cut the gas tank from the $1\frac{1}{4}''$ dowel. Next, drill the $\frac{3}{16}''$ screw-mounting hole (to hold the spare tire) through the center of the tank dowel, then the two gas-cap holes on the top of the tank, as shown, spacing the holes $\frac{1}{2}''$ from the ends of the tank and drilling with a $\frac{1}{2}''$ spade bit to a depth of about $\frac{3}{8}''$. Cut lengths of the $\frac{1}{2}''$ dowel to fit into these holes so that the tops are about $\frac{1}{4}''$ up from the tank.

Cut the axles from the $\frac{5}{16}''$ dowel to a length of $5''$. Make the exhaust pipe from the $7\frac{1}{2}''$ length of heavy, round black electric cord. To finish the shaping of the body, draw the hood lines and mark (without drilling) the placement of the $\frac{3}{8}''$ exhaust-pipe hole in the left side of the hood and the $1''$ hole that goes into the center of the cockpit. Round the top corners of the hood slightly with the Surform shaper. Use a hacksaw (or a band saw) to cut the hood lines to about $\frac{1}{8}''$ deep up the sides and over the top.

For the driver's body, cut a $1\frac{3}{8}''$ length of the $\frac{7}{8}''$ diameter dowel. Then, for the head, drill a $\frac{1}{16}''$ hole through the top of a $1\frac{3}{8}''$-diameter round wooden drawer-pull knob. Nail the knob head to one end of the dowel body, which rests in the cockpit hole when in use.

■ SHAPING

Use the Surform to round the outer corners of the five wheels, the end edges of

the tank, the tops of the $\frac{1}{2}''$ dowels used for gas caps, and the edges of the chassis platform. Drill the exhaust hole about $\frac{3}{4}''$ deep, angling the hole back at about 45 degrees. Finally, sand all parts with 80-grit, then 150-grit, sandpaper.

■ ASSEMBLY

Place the body on the top of the chassis platform, set in from each side equally, with the rear end of the body flush with the rear of the chassis. Mark its position and place the assembly upside down on the hood top. Coat the bottom of the body with glue and drive two $1\frac{1}{2}''$ screws through the pilot holes to fasten the chassis to the body, as shown in Figure 1–2.

Next, position the gas tank on the curve at the back of the body. Center the tank with the $\frac{1}{2}''$ holes for the gas caps pointing upward and the center hole showing at the rear. Insert $\frac{1}{8}''$ drill through the hole in the tank and drill a hole into the rear of the body about $\frac{1}{2}''$. Drive a $3''$ #12 round-head screw in through the spare tire and the rear of the gas tank, then into the pilot hole in the rear of the body. Squirt a drop or two of glue in the gas-tank-cap holes and tap the $\frac{1}{2}''$ dowels into them.

To mount the wheels, tap the $\frac{5}{16}''$ axles into the center holes until they stick out the other side a little less than $\frac{1}{8}''$. If the axle won't insert easily into the hole, round its end a little with sandpaper. Next, neatly wrap the axle next to the wheel with $\frac{1}{2}''$-wide Scotch tape until the tape is about $\frac{1}{8}''$ thick and provides a straight side edge to run against the side of the chassis around the axle hole. Then insert the other end of the axle through

FIGURE 1–1 *Measurements for the Peugeot body, chassis, gas tank, and axles.*

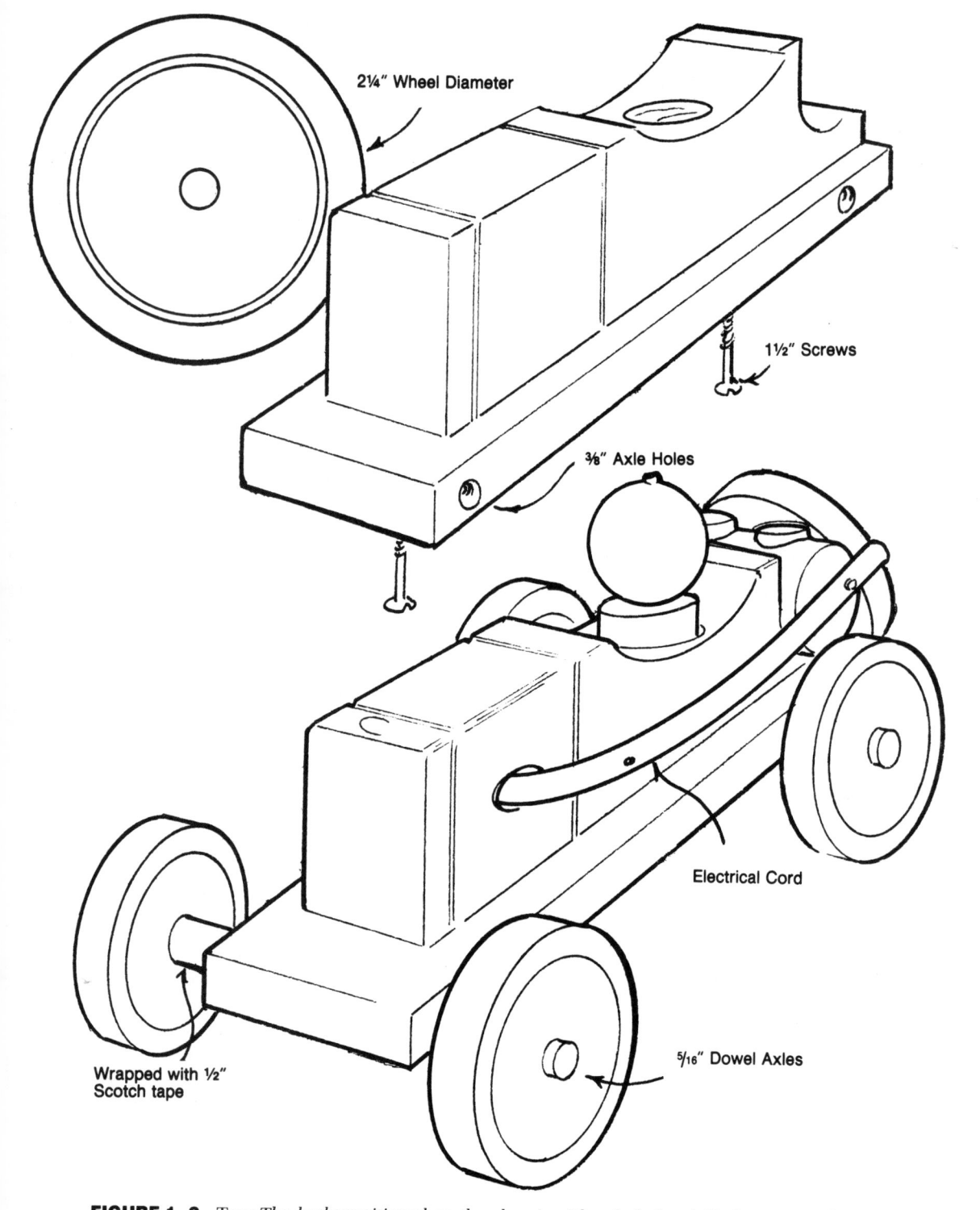

FIGURE 1–2 Top: *The body positioned on the chassis with axle holes drilled.* Bottom: *The wheels positioned on the axles; the driver's body and head attached and inserted in the cockpit; and the exhaust pipe attached.*

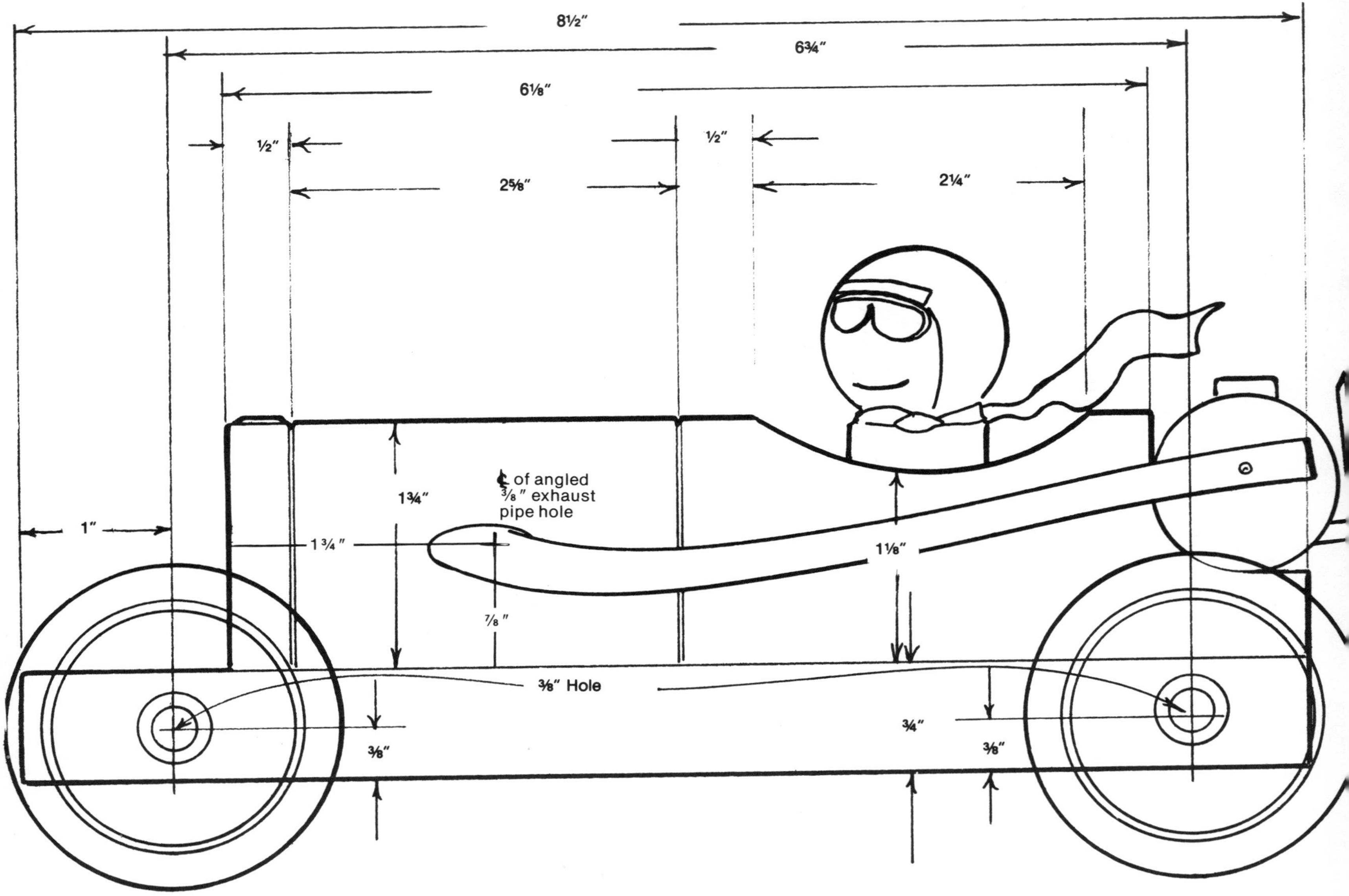

FIGURE 1-3 *The finished dimensions of the Peugeot.*

1"

½"

1¾"

1¾"

⅜"

⅞"

⅜" Hole

₵ of angled
⅜" exhaust
pipe hole

2⅝"

6⅛"

8½"

½"

6¾"

2¼"

1⅛"

¾"

⅜"

the axle hole. You may want to oil it first for maximum performance.

Place another wheel on a firm surface and tap the end of the axle through it. Wrap the Scotch tape around the axle just inside the wheel, allowing about $\frac{1}{8}''$ lateral play for the axle on the chassis. Repeat these steps to attach the front wheels to the chassis.

■ FINISHING

The whole car will need a fine sanding and about three coats of satin-finish varnish. Draw the driver's face on the drawer pull with pen and then varnish it as well. After the car is dry, insert the electrical-cord exhaust pipe into the hole in the side of the hood. Bend it back along the hood side to curve down a little, then back up at the rear, as shown in Figure 1–3. Next, with a $\frac{1}{8}''$ bit, drill one hole through the exhaust pipe just in back of the rear hood line. Drill a second hole through the pipe and into the gas tank. Tap $1\frac{1}{2}''$ finishing nails through the holes in the exhaust pipe and into the car. Tap a thumbtack into the center of the hood between the hood front and the forward hood line for a radiator cap. Tie a scarf around the driver's neck and the car is ready for action.

THE JET

■ MATERIALS LIST

14″ length of redwood (or soft wood) 2 × 3 or 2 × 4 stock

3″ length of $1\frac{1}{4}$″ dowel

$1\frac{3}{4}$″ length of $\frac{7}{8}$″ dowel

12″ length of redwood (or soft wood) 1 × 3 stock

$1\frac{3}{8}$″-diameter wooden drawer-pull knob

5″ × 12″ scrap of $\frac{3}{8}$″ or $\frac{1}{4}$″ plywood

3″ × 12″ scrap of $\frac{1}{4}$″ plywood

Six $1\frac{1}{2}$″ finishing or ribbed paneling nails

Two $\frac{5}{8}$″ × 3″ × $\frac{1}{8}$″ galvanized-iron corner brackets

Three $\frac{1}{8}$″ × 1″ roundhead bolts (with 9 nuts)

Six $1\frac{1}{2}$″ #8 flathead wood screws

☐ *See color insert for completed project.*

The jet is an example of a composite toy design. The plane itself doesn't represent any specific fighter jet, but we went to the real-life machines to come up with an easy-to-build representative of fighter jets in general taking a fuselage from one, a wing plan from another. This plane is a cross between a Navy Skyhawk and a F–4 Phantom.

■ CUTTING AND SHAPING

For color contrast, we used a darker redwood fuselage against the fir-plywood wing and tail section empennage and the pine-dowel windshield.

The first step is to draw the outline of the fuselage on the side of the 14″ length of redwood (Fig. 2–1). Then draw the two engines (Fig. 2–2) on the 1″-thick (actually $\frac{3}{4}$″-thick) redwood stock. Draw the main wing plan on the $\frac{3}{8}$″ plywood stock ($\frac{1}{4}$″ will also work), then draw the elevator and rudder on the $\frac{1}{4}$″ plywood stock (Fig. 2–3).

You can use a band saw or a saber saw to cut out all wood parts. With a Surform, round off the top of the fuselage behind the cockpit, then gradually taper back to a flat top at the tail, rounding only at the corners. Round off the fuselage bottom, behind the wing only at the corners, and leave it essentially flat on the bottom. The bottom in front of the wing starts off flat but tapers into a rounded point at the front. The top front is also rounded, tapering back to a squared corner at the rear of the cockpit.

The two engines are shaped to make an opposing pair rounded off on the top,

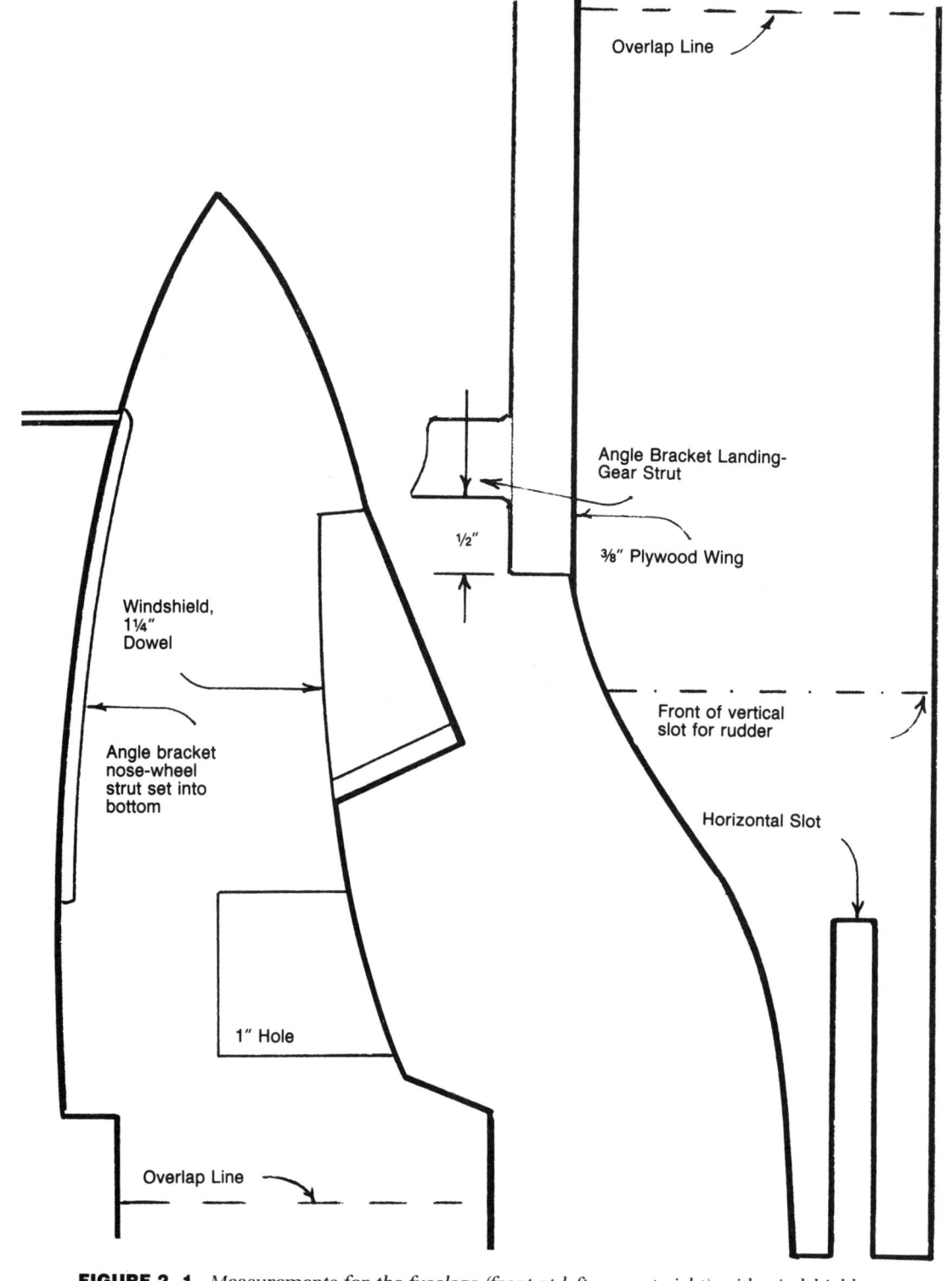

Overlap Line

Angle Bracket Landing-Gear Strut

3/8" Plywood Wing

1/2"

Windshield,
1¼"
Dowel

Angle bracket
nose-wheel
strut set into
bottom

Front of vertical
slot for rudder

Horizontal Slot

1" Hole

Overlap Line

FIGURE 2–1 *Measurements for the fuselage (front at left, rear at right), with windshield attached, showing landing-gear-strut attachments.*

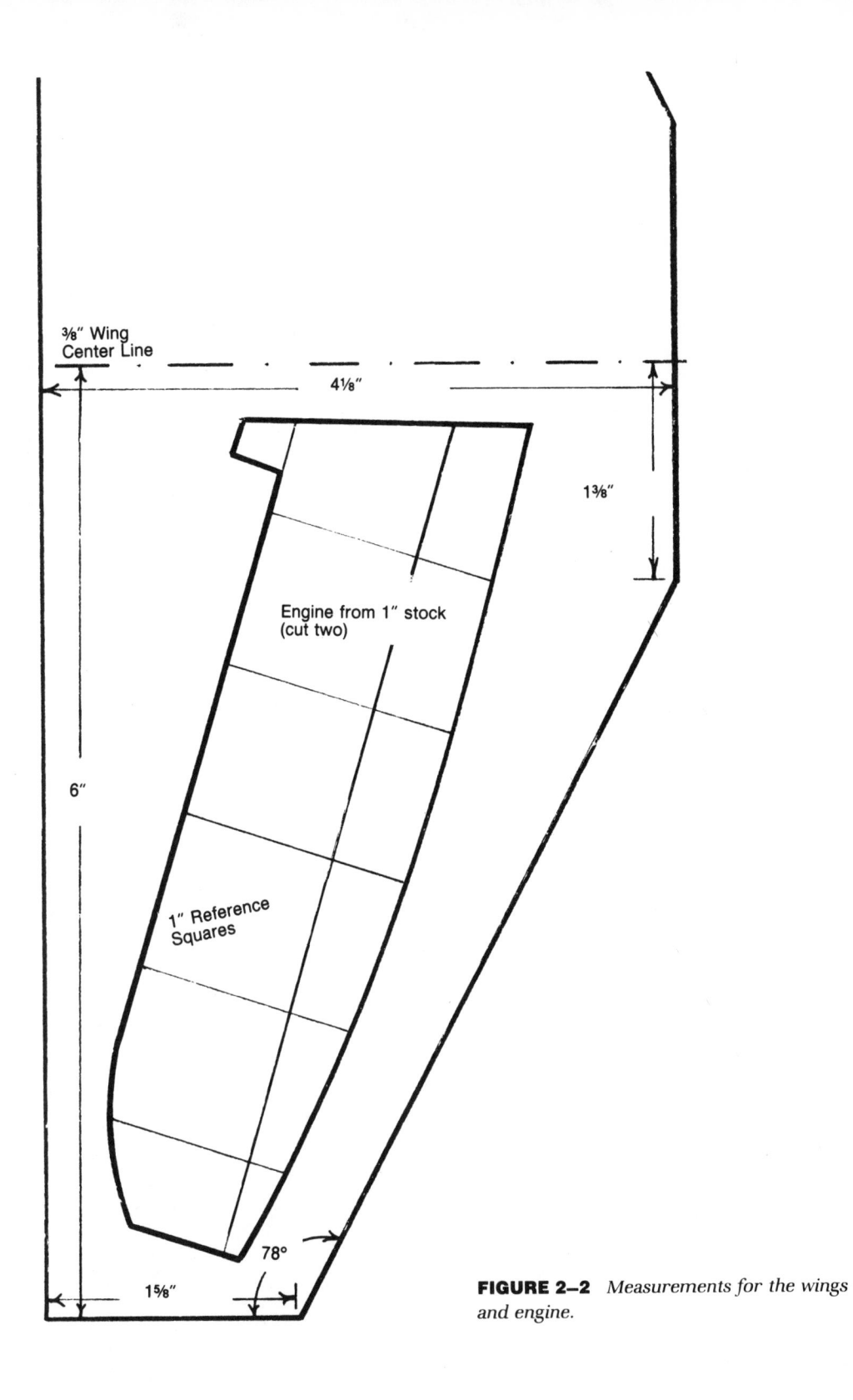

³⁄₈" Wing
Center Line

4¹⁄₈"

1³⁄₈"

Engine from 1" stock
(cut two)

6"

1" Reference
Squares

78°

1⁵⁄₈"

FIGURE 2–2 *Measurements for the wings and engine.*

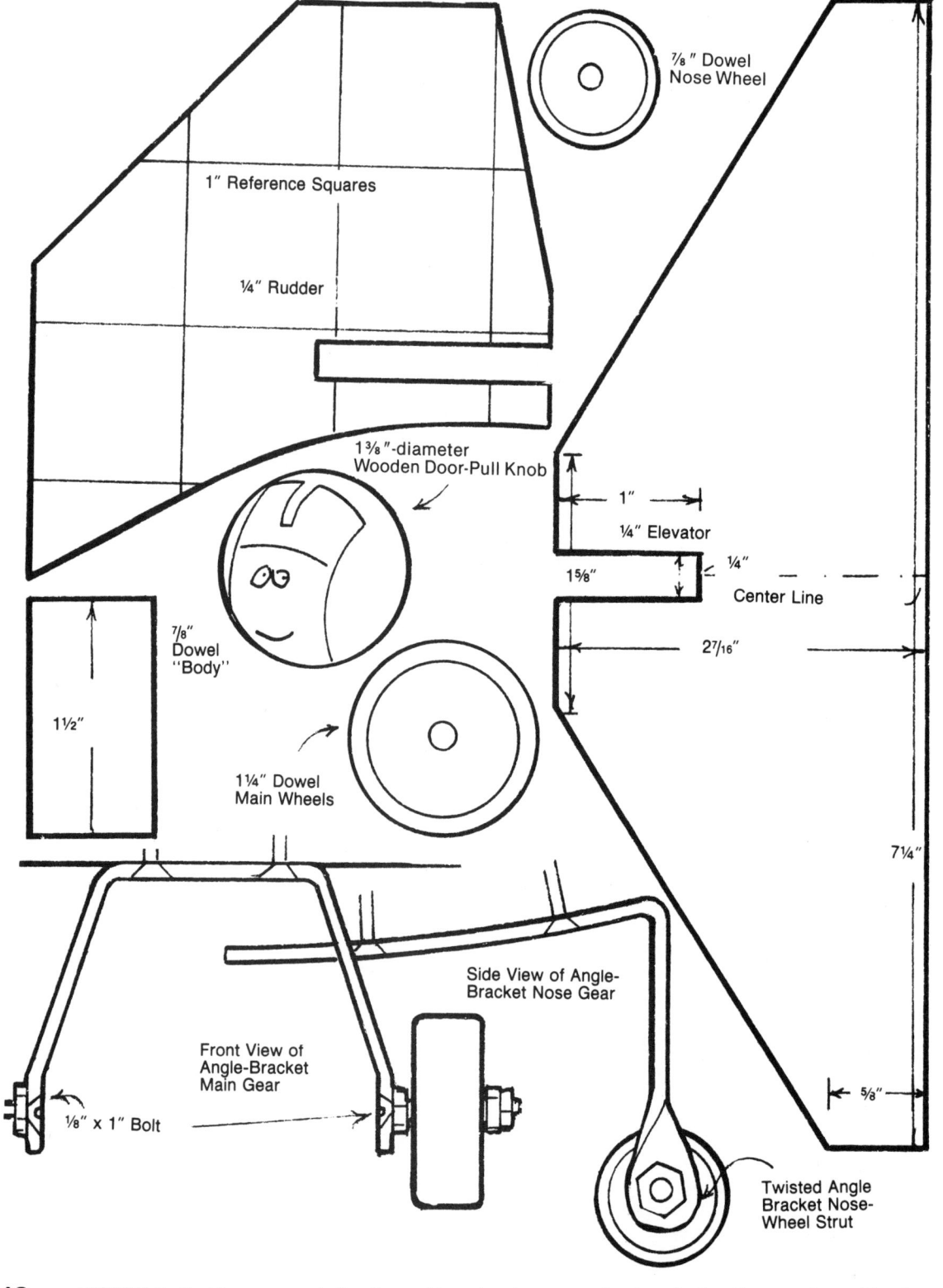

7/8" Dowel
Nose Wheel

1" Reference Squares

1/4" Rudder

1 3/8"-diameter
Wooden Door-Pull Knob

1" Elevator

1/4"

1/4" Elevator

1 5/8"

Center Line

7/8"
Dowel
"Body"

1 1/2"

2 7/16"

1 1/4" Dowel
Main Wheels

7 1/4"

Side View of Angle-
Bracket Nose Gear

Front View of
Angle-Bracket
Main Gear

1/8" x 1" Bolt

5/8"

Twisted Angle
Bracket Nose-
Wheel Strut

18   **FIGURE 2–3** *Measurements for the rudder, elevator, nose wheel, and pilot.* Bottom: *Assembly of the landing gear.*

outside corner and bottom outside corners behind and in front of the wing. Round the inside corners of the engines a little just for the front and rear inch or so, both on the top and on the bottom.

Round the leading and trailing edges of all plywood wing and tail surfaces where they stick out of the fuselage. We made no real airfoil; instead, we just rounded off the corners with a Surform and 80-grit sandpaper to prevent splintering.

Slice the wedge-shaped windshield from the $1\frac{1}{4}''$ dowel. Drill two pilot holes angling down through its rear so that you can drive $1\frac{1}{2}''$ #8 flathead wood screws down through the rear of the windshield and into the top of the cockpit cutout. If set in flush, the screw heads can represent dial faces in the cockpit.

■ ASSEMBLY

Screw the windshield down and shape its front and sides at the bottom with the Surform. Remove it and score a line over the top with a hacksaw, about $\frac{1}{8}''$ forward of the rear end of the windshield wedge. Then replace the windshield.

Sand all parts with 80-grit, than 150-grit sandpaper. Then drive $1\frac{1}{2}''$ finishing nails into the sides of the engines, approximately in the positions shown in Figure 2–4. Align, then glue, the engine to the side of the fuselage. Make sure that the wing cutouts are flush. Drive the nails into the fuselage, wipe away the excess glue, and attach the other engine.

To attach the tail, insert the rudder into the vertical slot at the rear of the fuselage. Next, insert the elevator into the horizontal slot and drill $\frac{1}{16}''$ pilot holes for the $1\frac{1}{2}''$ finishing nails, which will be driven up through the fuselage bottom about 2" forward of the rear tip. The nails

should angle up so that they pass through the elevator near the front of its slot. If you want a colored rudder, spray-paint it before inserting it into the fuselage slot. Squirting glue into the slots during the final assembly will help keep the tail surfaces from rattling.

Attach the main wing to the fuselage bottom and center it in the wing cutout with two $1\frac{1}{2}''$ #8 flathead wood screws spaced about 2" apart along the center line.

The landing gear is made of two galvanized-iron corner brackets, $\frac{5}{8}''$ wide and 3" long on each corner arm. It's a good idea to pound the bracket for the rear wheels into a straight line in a vise, then rebend it, as shown in Figure 2–3. Screw it to the wing bottom, centered and $\frac{5}{8}''$ in front of the trailing edge. Twist one arm of the front bracket, as shown, 90 degrees using a vise and a pair of vise-grip or channel-lock pliers, so the twist takes place about $1\frac{1}{4}''$ below the 90-degree bend in the bracket. The bracket can be twisted in either direction to get the same effect. Next, cut off the twisted arm of the bracket 2" below the 90-degree corner angle. Round this cut tip and drill a $\frac{1}{8}''$ hole through it about $\frac{1}{4}''$ up from the bottom.

Cut off $\frac{1}{4}''$-thick slices of $1\frac{1}{4}''$-diameter dowel ($1\frac{1}{8}''$ will do) and a $\frac{3}{8}''$ slice of $\frac{7}{8}''$ dowel to form the wheels. Drill $\frac{1}{8}''$ holes through the center, twisting the bit a little after drilling to enlarge the center hole. The center holes can be oiled to provide easier rolling later on.

We bent the front bracket slightly to follow the bottom curve of the fuselage from $\frac{3}{4}''$ in front of the wing to $3\frac{3}{4}''$ in front of the wing. Center this arm against the bottom, then draw the outline of the arm onto the fuselage. We used a chisel to gouge out the wood inside this outline to allow the bracket to be recessed flush.

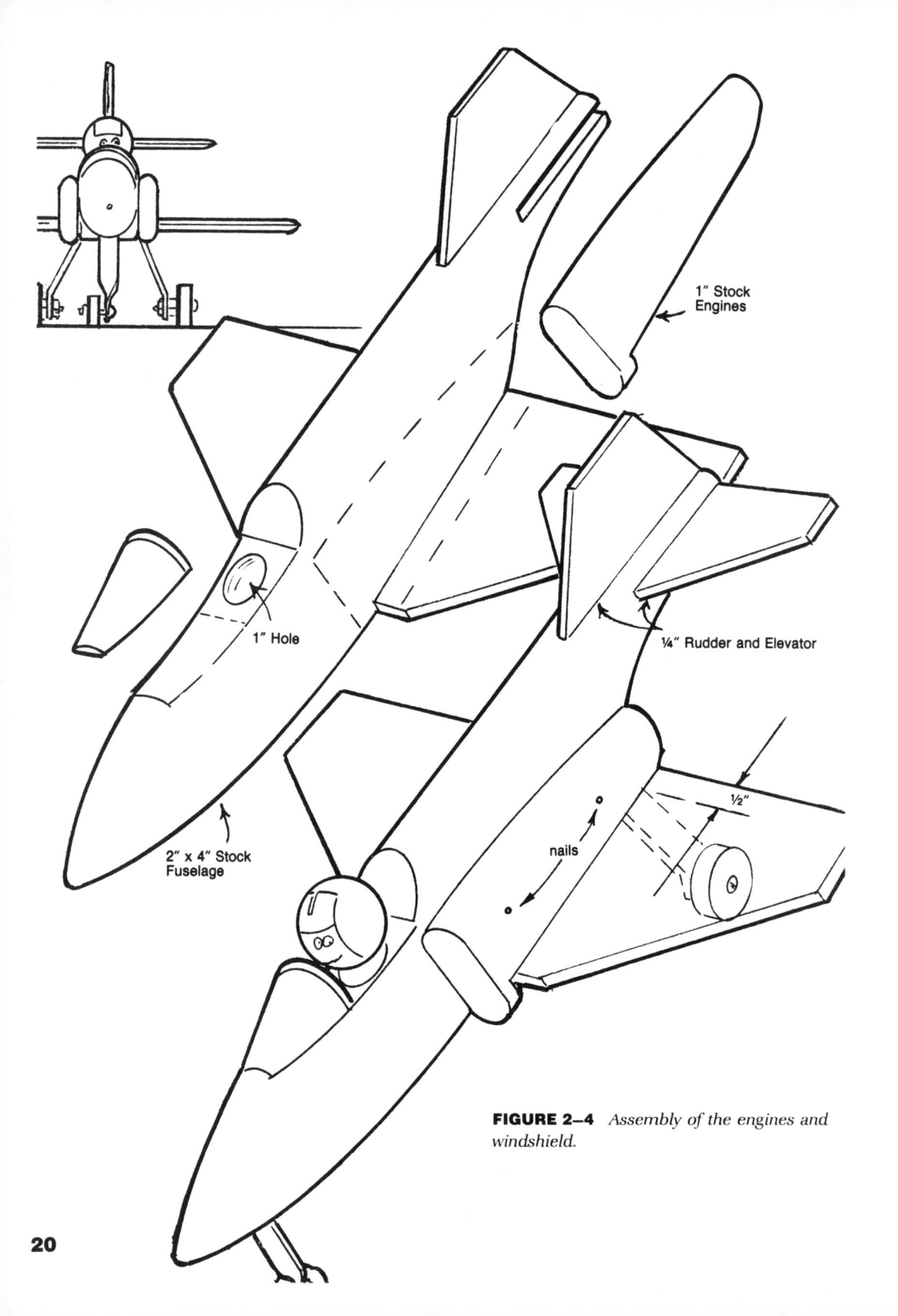

1" Stock
Engines

1" Hole

¼" Rudder and Elevator

2" x 4" Stock
Fuselage

nails

½"

FIGURE 2–4 *Assembly of the engines and windshield.*

Drive pilot holes for $1\frac{1}{2}''$ #8 screws in through the screw holes in the bracket; drive in screws to secure the front wheel bracket to the fuselage bottom.

Insert the roundhead bolts through the holes near the bottom of all three landing-gear arms. Then run nuts all the way on and tighten them securely against the landing-gear brackets. Straighten the bolts with pliers as necessary so that they are parallel with the wing trailing edge, both from the front and from the top. Run all three wheels onto the bolts, then put on a nut and locknut for each bolt end. Tighten the bolts, but make sure that the wheels turn freely. Cut off any excess bolt threads beyond the locknut with a hacksaw.

To insert the pilot in the cockpit, drill a 1"-diameter hole straight down into the cockpit center line, $\frac{5}{8}''$ forward of the rear, to a depth of about $\frac{7}{8}''$. For the pilot's body, use a $1\frac{1}{4}''$ length of $\frac{7}{8}''$ diameter dowel. For the pilot's head, use a $1\frac{3}{8}''$-diameter wooden drawer pull. Drill a $\frac{1}{16}''$ hole in the top of the head and nail it to the body.

■ FINISHING

At this stage, sand the whole plane and the pilot with 150-grit or finer paper and apply two to three coats of satin-finish varnish.

Since one side of a piece of plywood is usually of a better grade than the other, paint the vertical rudder with glass enamel, using the same color for the pilot's helmet. Then use a contrasting plastic tape to lay down a checkerboard pattern on the tail and trim it with a razor knife. Use the same tape to create a jagged-lightening pattern on the pilot's helmet. You can, of course, use any squadron design you like for the tail and any pattern on the helmet. We used a black El Marko pen to fill in the pilot's visor and blacken the tires because it has better weather-resistance than other pens we have tried. Paint a confident smile on the pilot's face, add 20-20 eyes, and the plane is ready for its first scramble.

3

THE RYAN S-T

■ MATERIALS LIST

$1\frac{1}{4}'' \times 2\frac{1}{2}'' \times 12''$ redwood or soft wood
   2×4 stock
$\frac{3}{4}'' \times 3'' \times 20''$ redwood (clear)
$5'' \times 7''$ scrap of $\frac{1}{4}''$ plywood or Masonite
$\frac{5}{8}''$ model-airplane spinner
$3''$ finishing nail
Three $2''$ finishing nails
$\frac{7}{8}''$-diameter wooden drawer-pull knob
Forty-two $1''$ #8 flathead wood screws
Two $1\frac{1}{2}''$ #8 flathead wood screws
One cup of catalyzed auto-body putty

☐ *See color insert for completed project.*

If you want to make a classic aircraft and don't mind doing a little sculpting with the Surform wood shaper, the Ryan S-T project is a good prospect. After a few years, any toy designer's house can start to look like a toy store, but no matter how many toys vie for attention, the Ryan S-T always stands out in the crowd. It's based on a pre–World War II Ryan trainer/pursuit plane made in the mid-1930s that looks like a toy in real life, so very little needed to be changed to maintain its toy appeal.

A band saw is handy for building this toy. The cuts can all be made with hand saws, but if you can borrow a band saw for a half-hour or so, the job will go faster and more smoothly.

■ CUTTING AND SHAPING

The first step is to draw the side view of the fuselage on one side of the redwood or pine 2 × 4 and cut it out (Figs. 3–1 and 3–2). Draw a center line down the bottom edge and draw the top view profile on the bottom, cutting it out with the coping saw or band saw. If you use a saber saw, make the cuts slowly and keep checking to make sure the blade is square to the saw base and not bent off to one side.

The next step is to draw the front profile of the wings onto the edge of a length of 1″ × 4″ redwood or pine (Fig. 3–3). After cutting the profile with the band saw or coping saw, draw the bottom profile and cut with a saber saw or band saw.

Draw the landing-gear parts (Figs. 3–2 and 3–3) on the scraps of 1″ redwood or pine stock and put them in a vise for rough-cut shaping from the front.

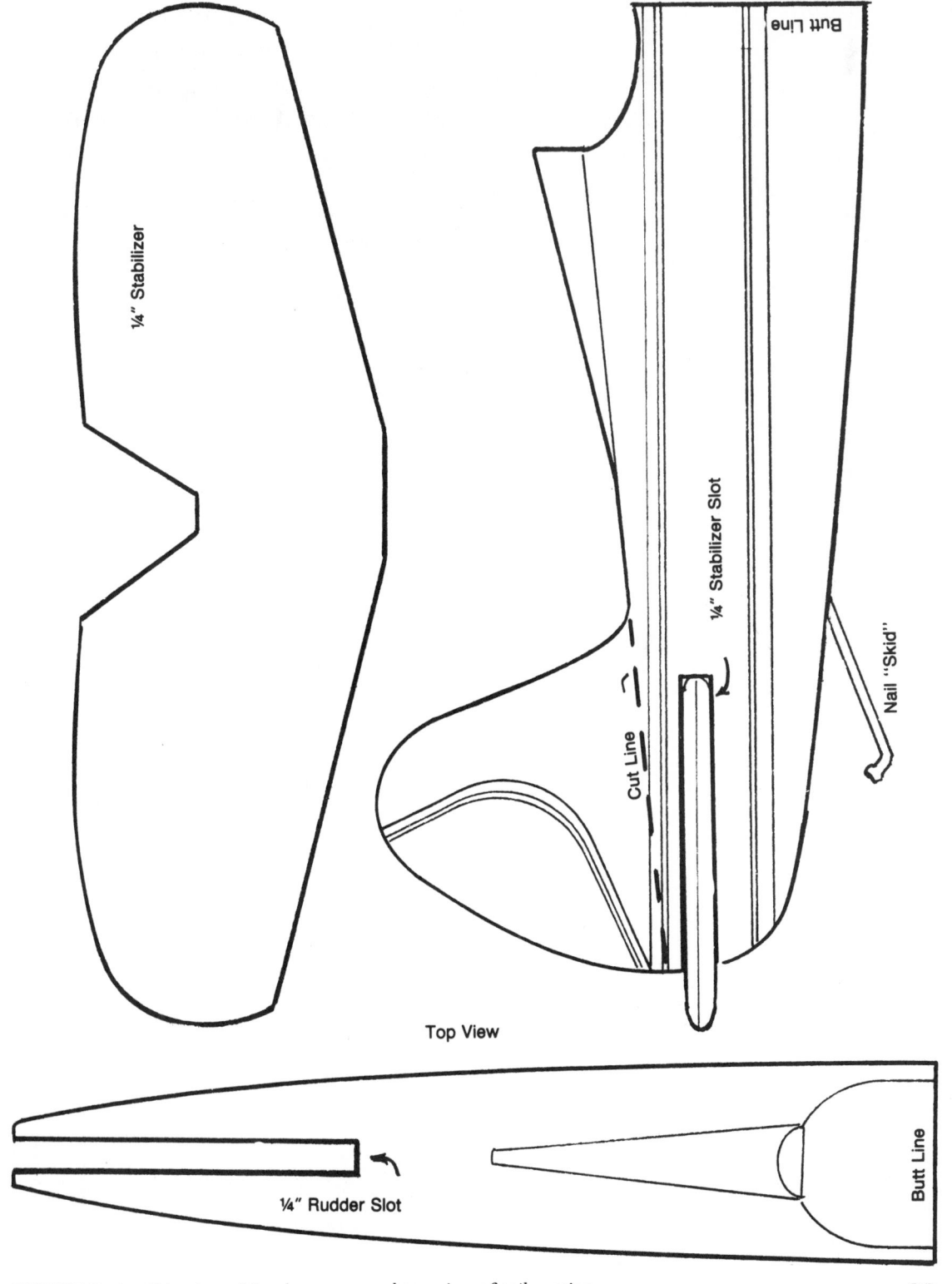

FIGURE 3–1 *Side view of fuselage rear and top view of tail section.*

23

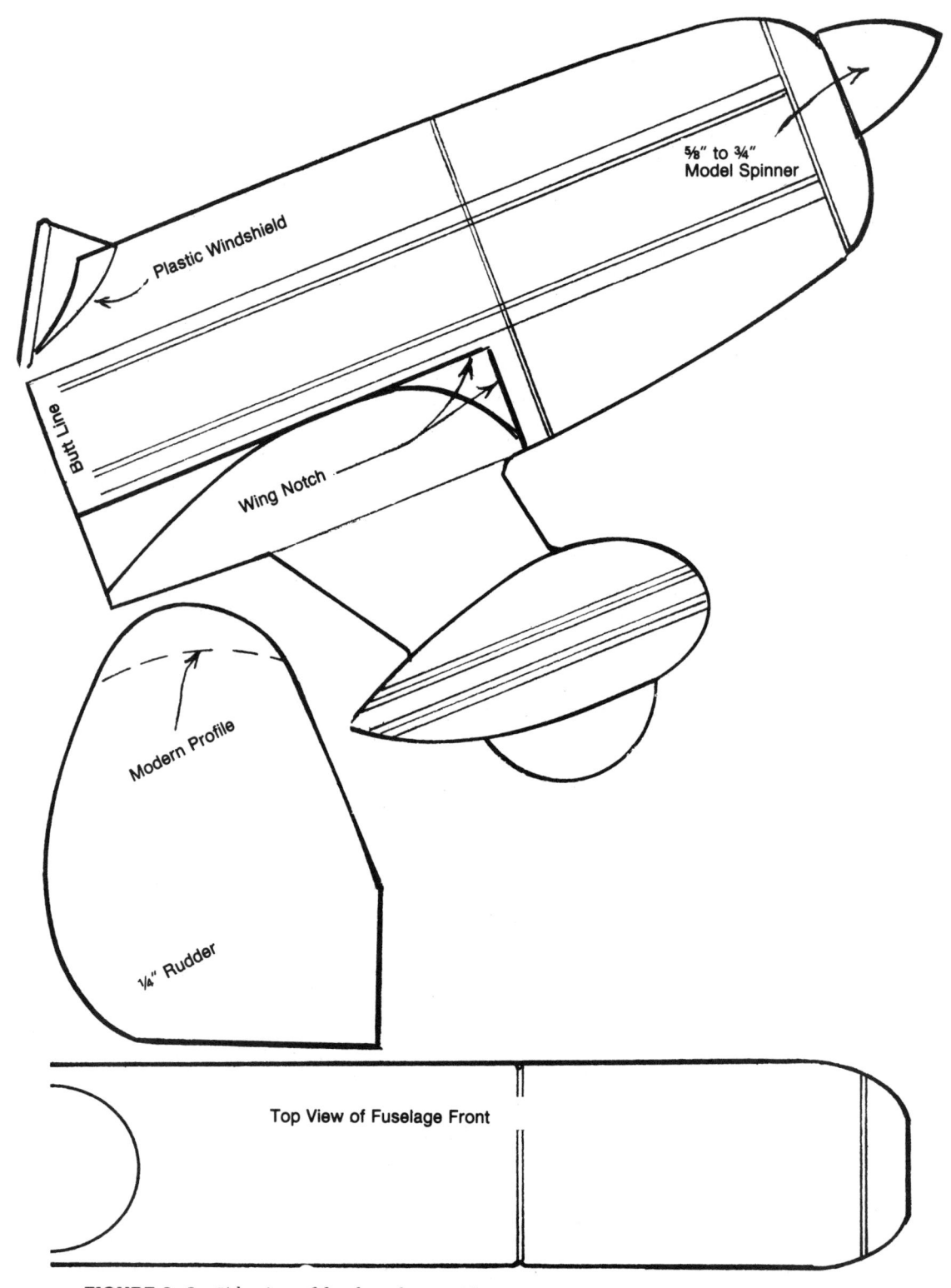

FIGURE 3–2 *Side view of fuselage front, with spinner attached to nose, windshield in place, and landing gear attached. Bottom: Top view of fuselage front.*

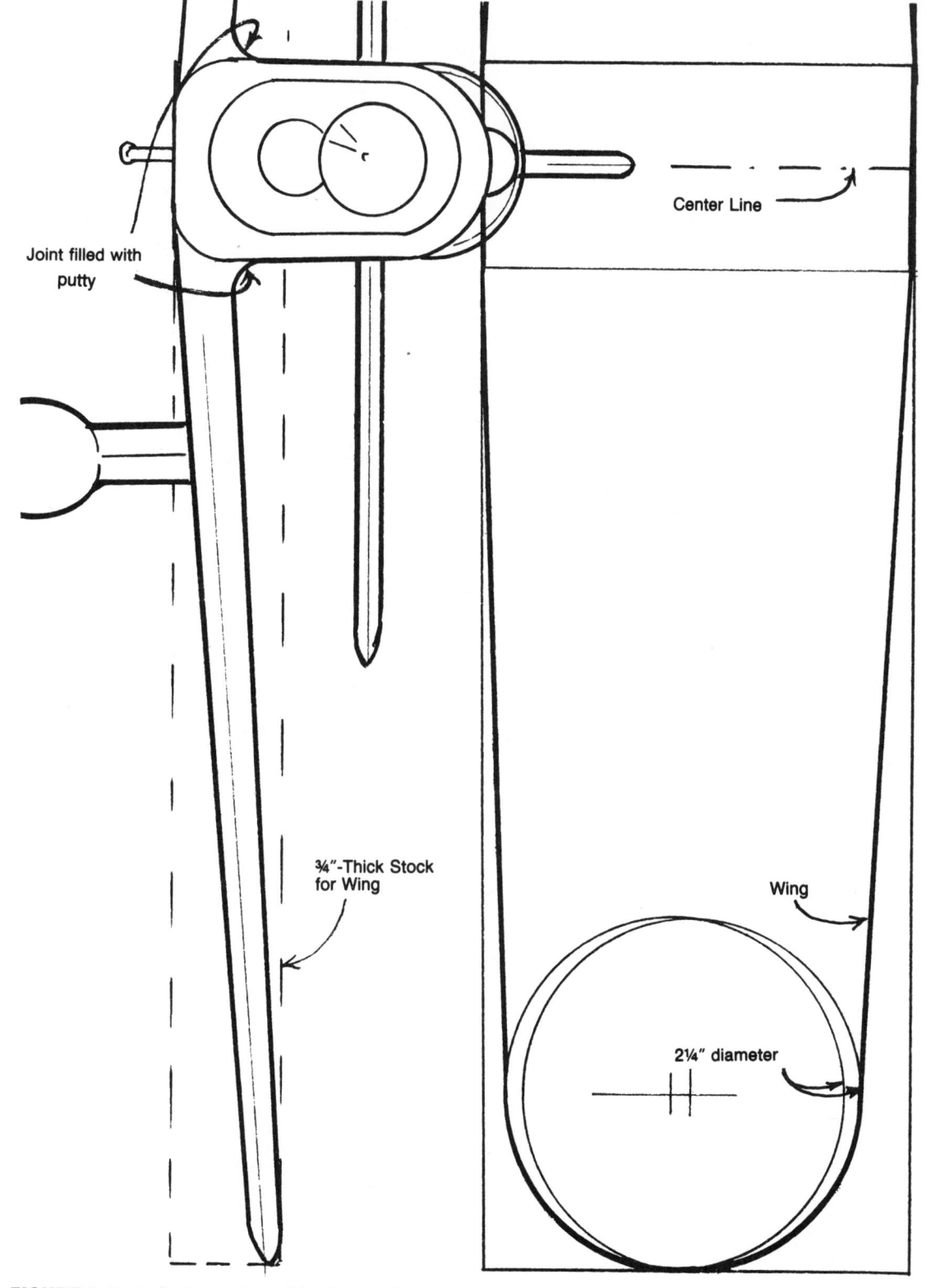

Joint filled with
putty

Center Line

¾"-Thick Stock
for Wing

Wing

2¼" diameter

FIGURE 3–3 Left: *Front view of fuselage with wings and landing gear attached.* Right: *Pattern for the wing.*

25

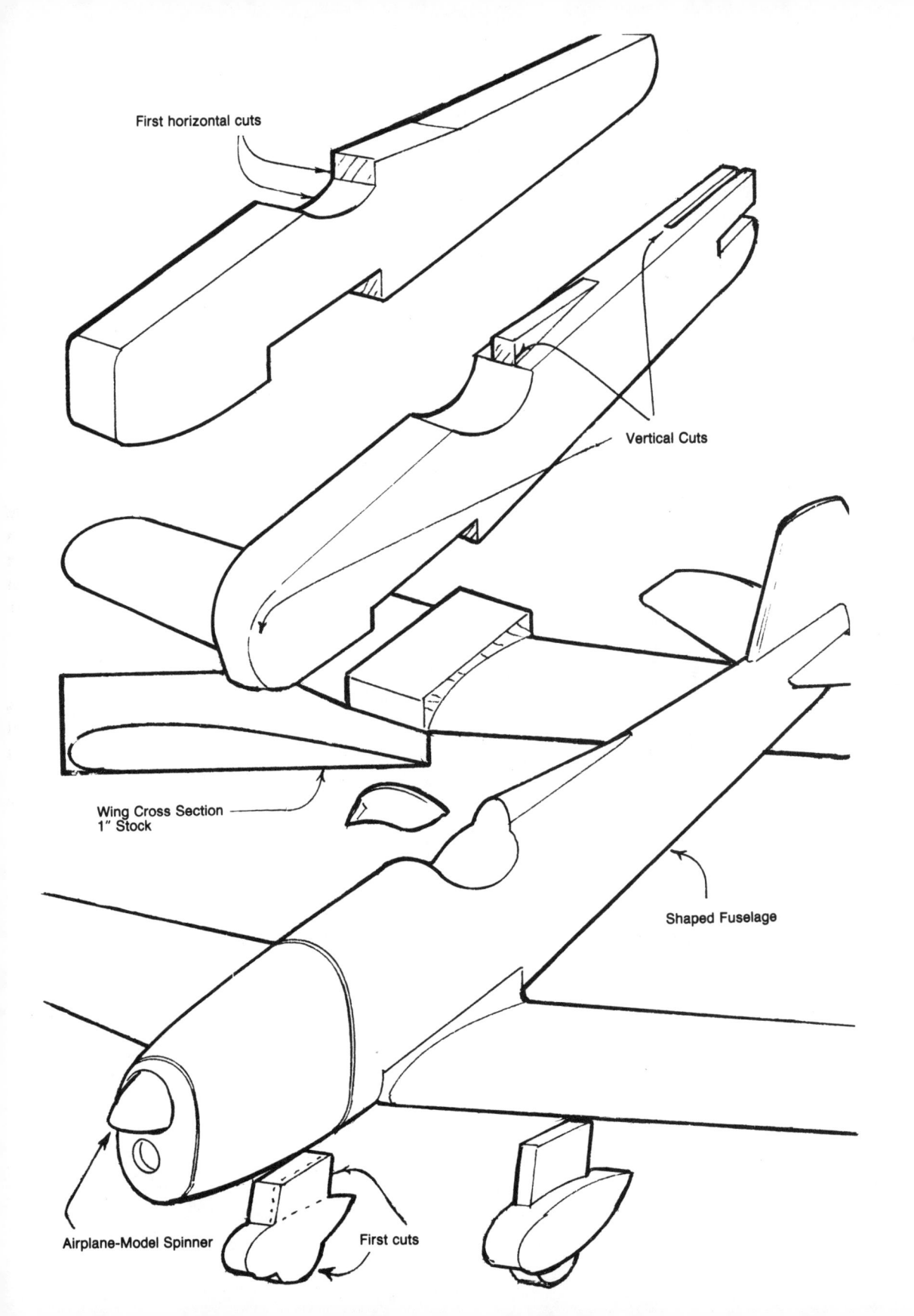

First horizontal cuts

Vertical Cuts

Wing Cross Section
1″ Stock

Shaped Fuselage

Airplane-Model Spinner

First cuts

Cut the rudder and stabilizer from scraps of $\frac{1}{4}''$ paneling stock (or from $\frac{1}{4}''$ plywood). Cut away the top of the fuselage, squarely down both sides of the head rest, then use the Surform wood shaper to round down the head rest. Round off the upper and lower corners of the fuselage so that it's roughly oval when viewed from the front. Next, use the Surform shaper to form an approximation of an airfoil shape. Then taper the exposed edges of the tail surfaces. To finish the ends of the fuselage, cut the horizontal and vertical cuts for the stabilizer and rudder to the thickness of the stock. Use a $\frac{3}{8}''$ spade bit to drill the intake hole in the nose as shown in Figure 3–4. Mark the engine panel lines around the nose and cut them with a hacksaw.

To make a spinner, shape the end of a $\frac{3}{4}''$ dowel to a convex cone for the last $\frac{7}{8}''$ of the dowel (Fig. 3–4). Cut it off and drill a $\frac{1}{16}''$ hole through its center. Glue the spinner to the nose and drive a 2″ finishing nail through the center of the spinner and into the nose. To save time, use a $\frac{5}{8}''$ model-airplane spinner.

Shape and round with a Surform and with extra-coarse sandpaper. Round off the nose to an oval-bullet form, as shown in Figure 3–4.

■ ASSEMBLY

To assemble the Ryan, center the wing board under the notch in the bottom of the fuselage. To attach the wing board, drill two pilot holes for $1\frac{1}{2}''$ screws about $1\frac{1}{2}''$ apart along the center line through the bottom of the wing and into the bottom of the fuselage.

Next, mix a blob of catalyzed polyester auto-body putty (or "Bondo") and apply it in the tail slots. Insert the rudder and stabilizer into the slots, squeezing out the putty that was smoothed off, cleanly fairing the base of the tail surfaces into the fuselage. Before the putty starts to harden, apply a blob of it to the joint of the wing root and fuselage and smooth it with your thumb.

Mark the placement of the landing-gear struts on the bottom of the wing. Hold them firmly in place and drill 1″ pilot holes through the wing $1\frac{1}{8}''$ out from the fuselage on both sides and $\frac{7}{8}''$ back from the leading edge of the wing. The bit should go down through the wing and into the tops of the struts.

Screw the struts in place, aligning them parallel with the center line of the fuselage, using glue. Drill a $\frac{1}{16}''$ pilot hole for a 2″ finishing nail into the bottom of the fuselage beneath the tail on the angle shown in Figure 3–1, then drive the nail in on the angle, with its bottom end bent up as shown.

Sand off the putty and wood parts with coarse paper. Mix another, smaller batch of putty and apply it over the landing-gear screws, around the landing-gear joint with the wing bottom, and into any gaps missed by the first puttying. When the parts are assembled and shaped, switch to medium, then fine, sandpaper.

■ FINISHING

After assembly, give the plane about five or six coats of spray gloss enamel (we used a colonial ivory). Paint the cockpit (to a little less than $\frac{1}{8}''$ inside the edges of

FIGURE 3–4 *Cutouts of the fuselage and wings.*

the fuselage) and tires black (or use an El Marko marking pen).

The orange trim can be painted on, but it's just about impossible to get accurate edge lines with two-tone paint schemes, so we used plain Contact paper, which has stood up well over the years. In fact, the plane was a number of years old when finally photographed for the book. The straight stripes for the side of the fuselage were cut with a paper cutter and applied to the side of the plane from front to back and trimmed at the ends with a razor knife. The curved shapes on the wings and tail were outlined and cut as solid shapes. Then a $\frac{1}{8}$"-wide strip was trimmed off evenly and set aside. Another $\frac{1}{8}$"-wide strip was trimmed off the curve and thrown away. The backing was peeled off and the curved shape was smoothed onto the wing. Finally, the trimmed strip was peeled and applied $\frac{1}{8}$" to the outside of the curved shape to simulate a sport plane.

For the windshield, a strip of plastic can be cut to the shape shown, then glued, using push pins to hold in the tips while drying. Make the pilot from a $\frac{7}{8}$"-diameter wooden drawer-pull knob. Draw on the face with marker pens and paint on the wind cap or color it with colored markers. Drill a $\frac{1}{16}$" hole through the top of the knob, nail the head into the cockpit with a 2" finishing nail. A coat of wax to smooth off any dust or hair caught on the paint surface, and the Ryan S-T is ready for action.

THE MASERATI 250F

■ MATERIALS LIST

$3\frac{1}{4}'' \times 2\frac{3}{4}'' \times 13\frac{1}{2}''$ piece of redwood or soft
    wood 4×4 stock
$2\frac{1}{2}''$ length of $\frac{1}{2}''$ dowel
$2''$ length of $\frac{7}{8}''$ dowel
$1\frac{3}{8}''$-diameter wooden drawer-pull knob
$2''$ finishing nail
$3''$-diameter plastic drinking glass
$12''$ length ($\frac{3}{32}$ or $\frac{1}{8}''$) of spring-steel wire
Four model-airplane axle ends
Four $2\frac{3}{8}''$-diameter model-airplane wheels
$3''$ length of $\frac{1}{8}''$ plastic or metal tubing
Eight $\frac{1}{8}''$ washers
Two rubber bands
$\frac{5}{8}''$ chair-leg-bottom button
Three $\frac{1}{8}''$ screw eyes
Wire coat hanger
$17''$ length of soft copper or brass $\frac{1}{4}''$ O.D.
    tubing
$25''$ of braided nylon string

☐ *See color insert for completed project.*

In our first toy book we included some "sling racers," heavy wooden cars with tethers attached to their sides so the person running the car can apply a little pull and have the car make a smooth circle around him. A good deal of skill is necessary to keep the car from crashing, and

the action can get fast and exciting, especially if you run two cars at once. So we couldn't resist putting a sling racer into this book as well. This one is a new-generation sling racer that's capable of far greater speeds than the earlier cars we made.

Ironically, the Maserati sling racer is faster than the racers in the first book for mostly the same reason that the actual Maserati 250F was faster than the 1930s car—and that's because of the faster handling that results from the better chassis springs and suspension design. This Maserati stands out as one of the most beautifully tuned road machines ever made. It was modeled after the one driven by five-times world Grand Prix champion Juan Fangio in his last victory at the Nurburgring in Germany in 1957. In his mid-fifties, Fangio was understandably anxious to wrap up his last championship against fierce competition from the emerging young British drivers. He could have played out the season picking up a few points here and there, or he could go out and blast every one off the track in one last finale, and this is just what he did. The car is now at the Briggs Cunningham Museum in Costa Mesa, California, and we happened to be there when enthusi-

asts flew Fangio from Argentina for a reunion with this historic car. Making his way straight through the collection, Fangio gave the car one of his athletic hugs.

The secret of the toy's high speed lies in the soft rubber tires and simple suspension of axles hung by rubber bands. The soft ride keeps the car from flying up, and the cushion ride allows it to coast farther and faster than a solid, hard-riding vehicle.

■ CONSTRUCTION NOTE

Before making the Maserati, it's necessary to take a trip to an official model-airplane shop. You will need four soft airplane wheels and tires, $2\frac{1}{4}''$ to $2\frac{3}{8}''$ overall diameter, with metal wheels. There are two basic types: Those with small wheels and large tires (meant to be scale wheels for model private planes) and those with larger wheels (scale wheels for World War II bombers or other military planes). The larger wheels look more like car wheels, so these are the ones you want.

You will also need two 6" lengths of spring-steel landing-gear wire (about $\frac{3}{32}''$ diameter to fit the wheels), twelve small brass washers, a 4" length of brass tubing ($\frac{1}{8}''$ I.D.), and four end nuts for landing gears (aluminum caps that fit over the landing-gear wire with lock screws on one side). If the store carries $\frac{1}{4}''$ O.D. soft copper tubing, pick up some for the exhaust pipes. Otherwise, look in the plumbing section of a lumber and supply yard for toilet-tank filler tubes. You will need two 10" lengths.

■ CUTTING AND DRILLING

The first step in building the Maserati is to draw the side profile on a 14" length of 4" × 4" redwood stock (Figs. 4–1 and 4–2). You can cut it out with a coping saw, although using a band saw would be faster. (Since the toy will be painted rather than varnished, and gaps filled with polyester autobody putty, sawing mistakes can be corrected easily.)

The next step is crucial to the final performance, so take the time to do it right. The job is to drill the axle holes so that they're straight. To do this, carefully mark the top and bottom positions of the front and rear axle holes on one side of the body (see Figs. 4–1 and 4–2). The position of the bottom holes will determine how the body sits, so drill them carefully and as squarely as possible. A drafting square can be used when drilling to help hold the drill perpendicular to the side of the board (or simpler yet, just use a drill press with an $\frac{1}{8}''$ bit).

Drill a top and bottom hole, and use a square to draw a line straight down the side. With the square, draw an extension of this line straight across the bottom, then up the other side to mark the positions of the top and bottom axle holes on the opposite side. Drill in at these holes, angling them to join with the holes from the first side. Then angle the drill vertically to cut away the wood between the top and bottom holes to join them into a vertical slot.

■ SHAPING

The next step is to draw a center line down the top of the car and mark the top profile on the wood. Cut the side curves, then shape the car into a flattened oval at the hood, extending back to a more rounded cross section at the tail, with the Surform shaper. After the extended egg-shaped body is rounded down, rough-

sand it and then sand again with medium-grit paper.

Draw hood lines and gas-tank-strap lines squarely across the center line of the body. Next, make a cut about $\frac{1}{8}''$ deep with a hacksaw or coping saw, then sand smooth with a folded edge of 150-grit paper in the grooves. Cut the air scoop from a scrap of $\frac{5}{8}''$-diameter dowel. Use the shaper to flatten the area where the scoop is to be attached. Then drill two $\frac{1}{16}''$ pilot holes and nail the wedge-shaped scoop in place with glue. Drill two $\frac{1}{4}''$ holes into the hood in the positions shown in Figure 4–2 angling them back at about 30 degrees. Drill a 1″ hole about $1\frac{1}{4}''$ deep into the center of the cockpit with a spade wood bit.

The next step is to smooth down the body in preparation for painting. First use the Surform, then coarse, medium, and fine sandpaper. Fill any cracks, gaps, or holes with auto-body putty. We gave the car six coats of blood-red gloss enamel, sanding between coats. The cockpit, the very front of the car, and the front of the air scoop were painted satin black. We brushed yellow paint on the band around the nose, in front of the forward hood line and onto the border around the front of the car about $\frac{1}{8}''$ in from the edge.

■ ASSEMBLY

To assemble the car, insert each exhaust tube into its hole through the hood and bend them gently down toward the rear to avoid kinking them at the tight bend at the front (see Fig. 4–3). Give the pipes a smooth curve up toward the rear, then cut them off. The bottom pipe should end at the front gas-tank-strap line, and the top pipe should be cut about $\frac{1}{8}''$ in front of that.

Open a screw eye with a pair of pliers and drill a $\frac{1}{16}''$ pilot hole into the rear, about $\frac{1}{2}''$ to the rear of the cockpit and level with the rear corner of the cockpit. Drive in the opened screw eye up to the base of the eye with the opening facing down. With a pair of pliers, close the eye over the two side-by-side pipes.

For a gas cap, drive a chrome $\frac{5}{8}''$-diameter chair-leg-bottom button with a hammer in the center and $\frac{1}{4}''$ to the rear of the cockpit.

For a windshield, use the lip of a disposable plastic drinking glass, cut on the angle shown in Figure 4–1. (A flat piece of clear plastic can also be cut and bent to shape.) Then cut a piece of red plastic tape and tape the windshield to the rear of the hood. If necessary, to hold the plastic in place while the adhesive sets, push thumbtacks in at both bottom and the rear corners of the windshield.

For the driver, cut a $1\frac{1}{4}''$ length of $\frac{7}{8}''$-diameter dowel, then drill a $\frac{1}{16}''$ hole through a $1\frac{3}{8}''$ diameter wooden drawer-pull knob. Make a cut into one side of the knob at the angle shown. Cut a helmet visor from cardboard or plastic and slip it into the cut. Drive a 2″ finishing nail through the hole in the center of the knob and the visor and into the center of one end of the dowel. We painted the driver's helmet a dull brick red; the goggles and ear protection were painted black with a marker pen.

Depending on how roughly the car will be treated, the dowel driver body can be wrapped with tape to fit firmly in the cockpit hole to prevent the driver from popping out at top speed.

Drive screw eyes (like those used on wire hook latches) into $\frac{1}{16}''$ pilot holes in the positions shown in the side view in Figures 4–1 and 4–2. To make a sling bridle, bend the wire coat hanger to the

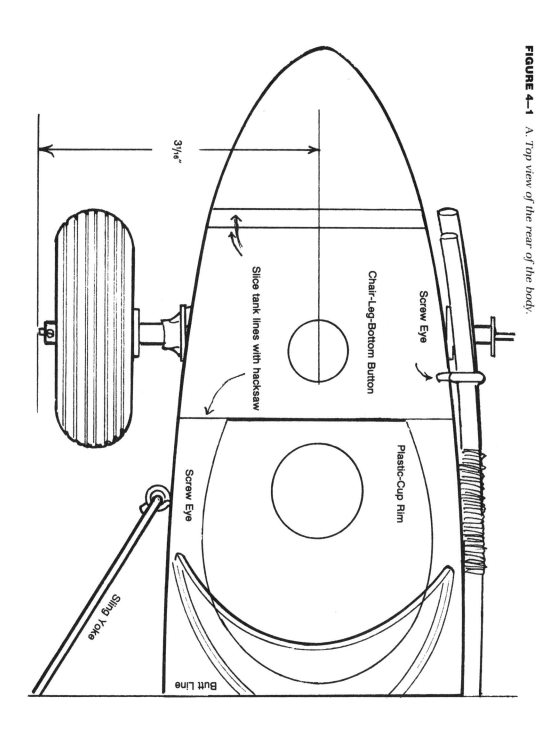

FIGURE 4–1   A. Top view of the rear of the body.

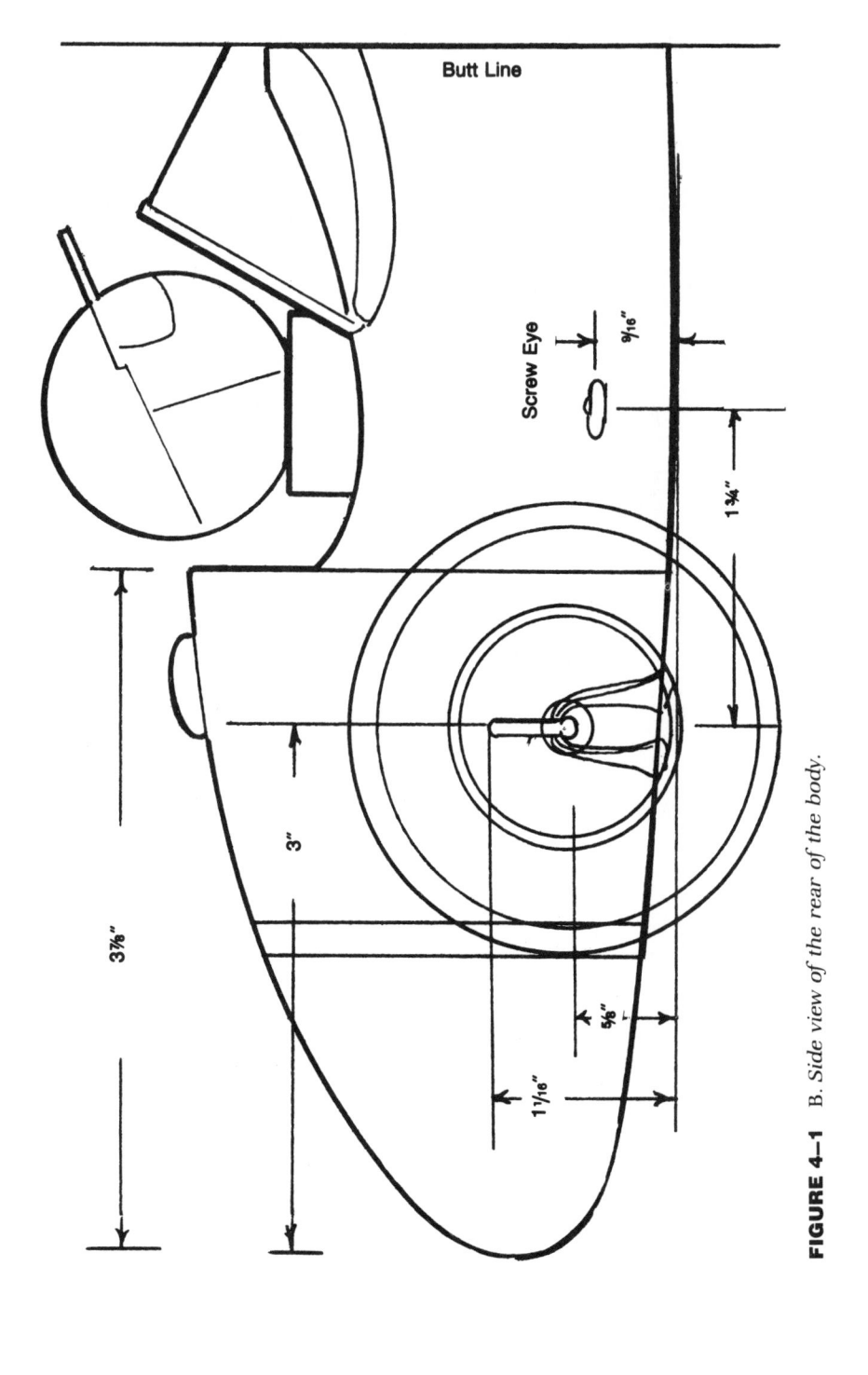

Butt Line

Screw Eye

9/16"

1¾"

3"

3⅞"

5/8"

1¹/16"

FIGURE 4—1 B. *Side view of the rear of the body.*

THE MASERATI 250F **33**

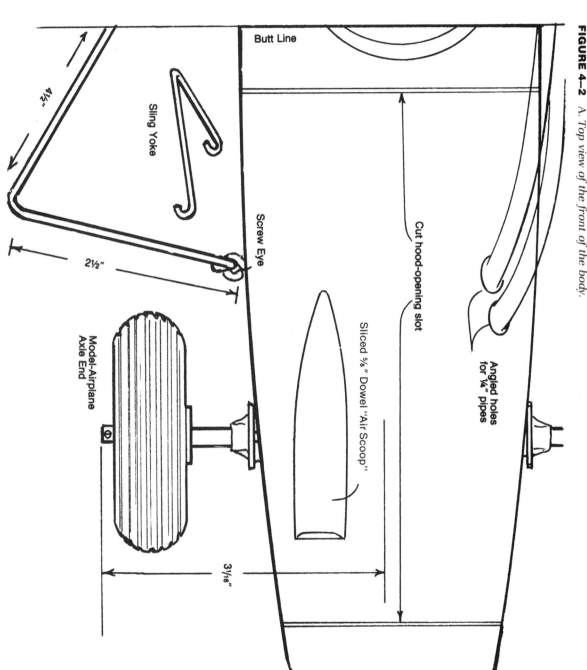

Butt Line

Sling Yoke

4½"

2½"

Screw Eye

Model-Airplane
Axle End

Sliced ⅝" Dowel "Air Scoop"

Cut hood-opening slot

Angled holes
for ¼" pipes

3¹¹/₁₆"

FIGURE 4–2 A. Top view of the front of the body.

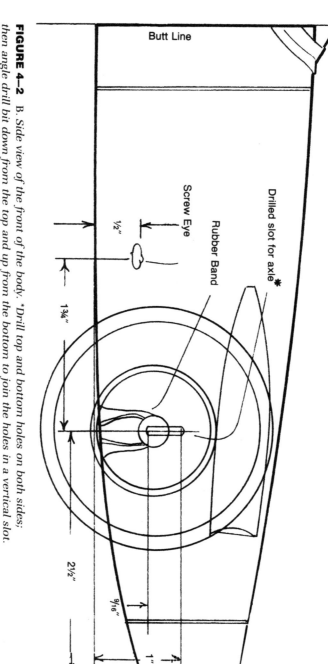

Butt Line

Drilled slot for axle ✳

Screw Eye

Rubber Band

½"

1¾"

2½"

9/16"

1"

FIGURE 4–2 B. *Side view of the front of the body.* *Drill top and bottom holes on both sides; then angle drill bit down from the top and up from the bottom to join the holes in a vertical slot.*

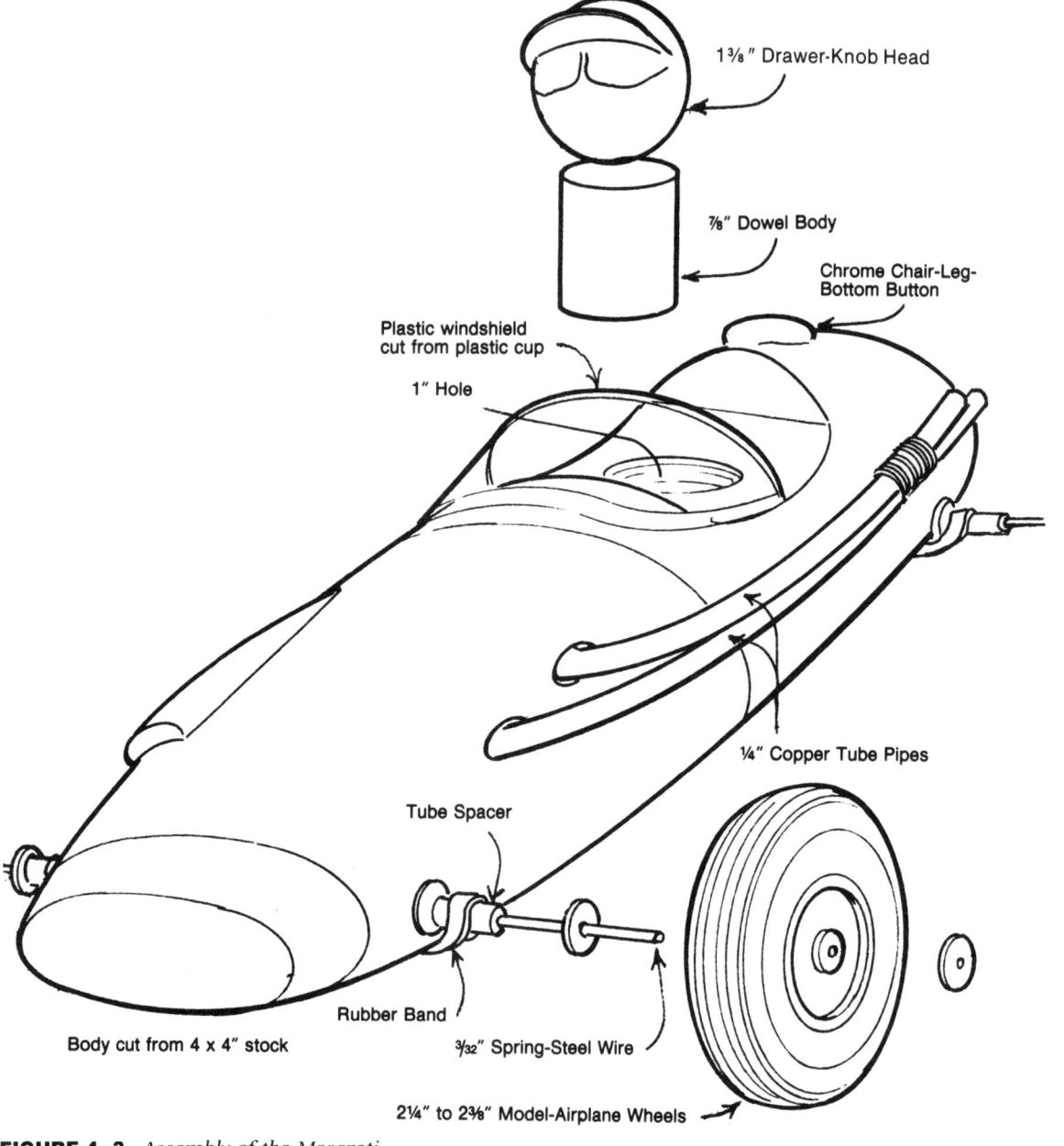

1 3/8 " Drawer-Knob Head

7/8" Dowel Body

Chrome Chair-Leg-Bottom Button

Plastic windshield cut from plastic cup

1" Hole

1/4" Copper Tube Pipes

Tube Spacer

Rubber Band

Body cut from 4 x 4" stock

3/32" Spring-Steel Wire

2 1/4" to 2 3/8" Model-Airplane Wheels

FIGURE 4—3 *Assembly of the Maserati.*

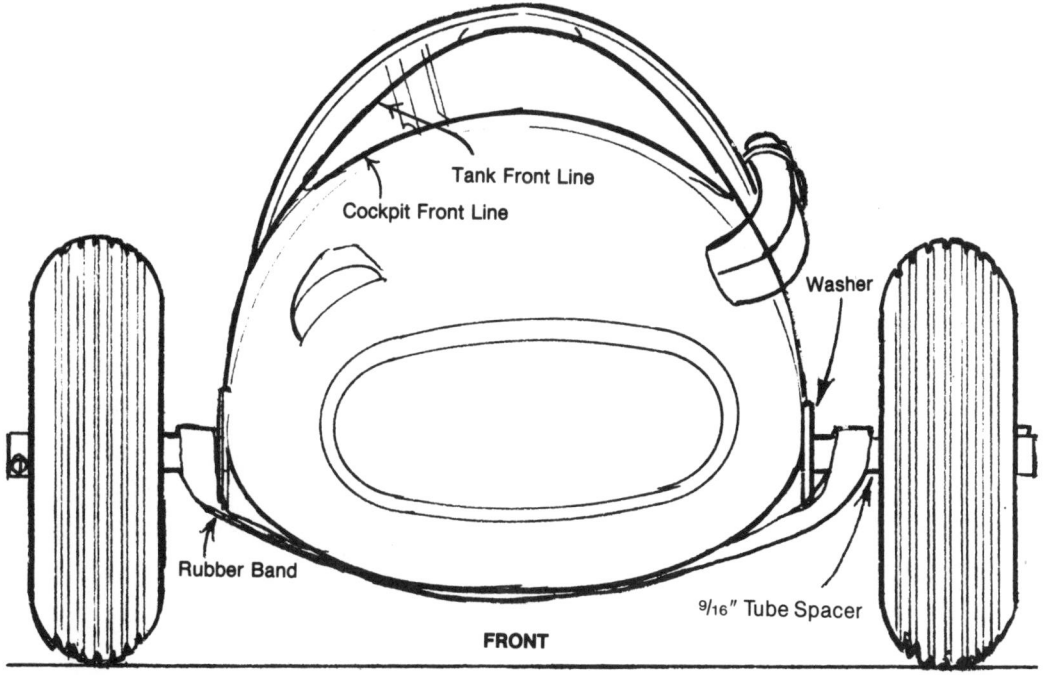

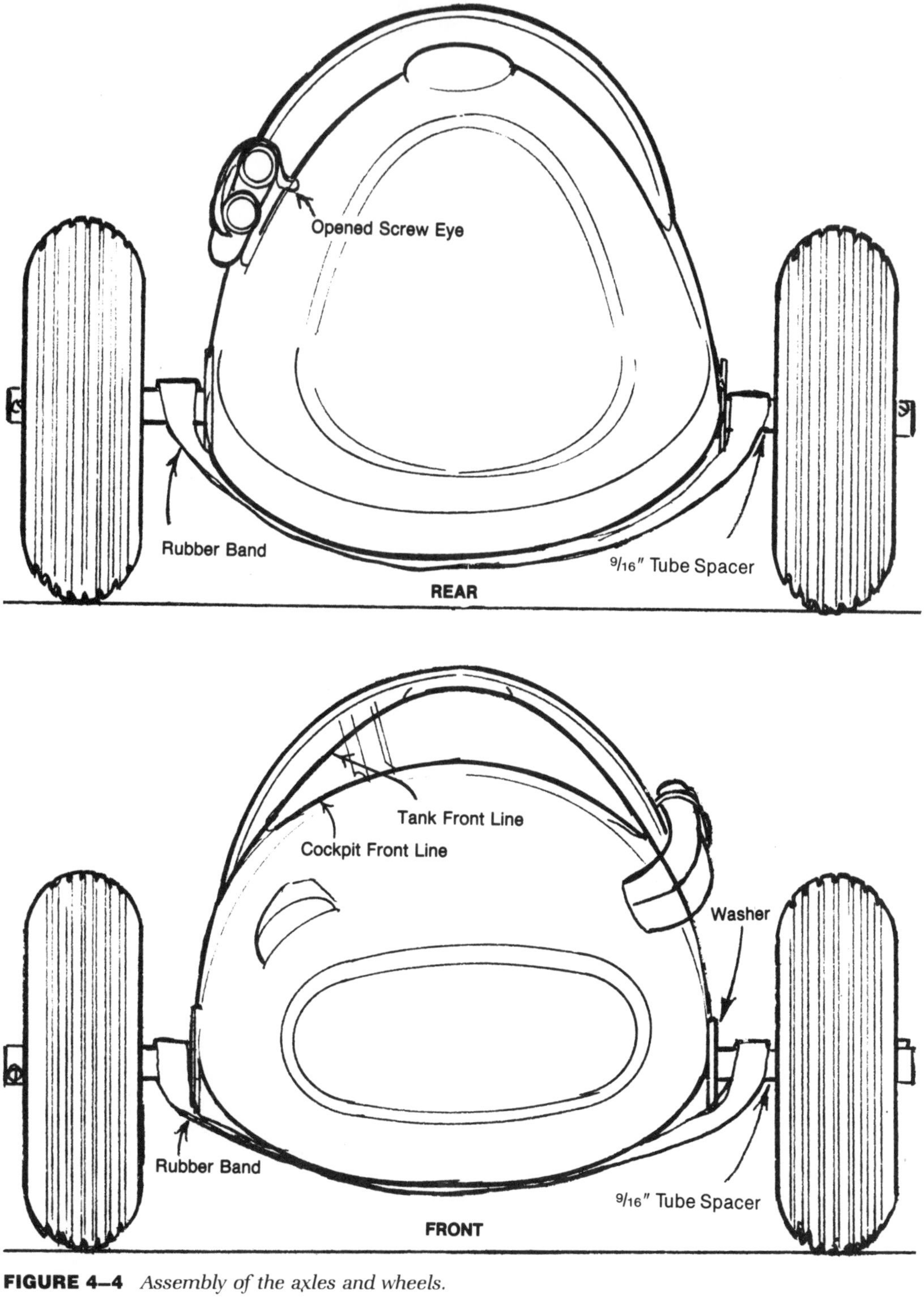

FIGURE 4—4 *Assembly of the axles and wheels.*

shape shown so that each end can be looped down through the screw eyes. Tie a 25″ length of braided nylon string to the apex of the bridle and wrap it around a dowel for a handle.

To get things rolling, attach one axle end to both 6″ axle rods. Insert the other ends of the rods through a washer, through the outer side of a wheel, and through the other washer. Cut four $\frac{9}{16}$″ lengths of the copper or brass tubing with a hacksaw. Insert the end of both axles through one of these lengths of tubing, then through a washer, and finally through the axle holes in the body.

Put a washer on each end of the axles. Then place a $\frac{9}{16}$″-long tube spacer, another washer, a wheel, another washer, and finally the landing-gear-wire end cap (Figs. 4–3 and 4–4). Use $\frac{1}{4}$″-wide by about $1\frac{1}{2}$″-diameter rubber band on each axle to provide spring. (If you don't have this standard size handy, one can be tied in a circle the same size from about a 6″ length of $\frac{1}{4}$″-wide-rubber powered airplane banding, or use several smaller bands on each axle). You may have to experiment before you find the best springing action for the car on the track you intend to use. To hook up the rubber band to spring, slip the band over one tire, stretch it, and loop it under the body and over the opposite wheel so that both ends of the band rest on a spacer tube. Oil all the wheels and the car is ready to be track-tested.

■ OPERATING THE CAR ON A TRACK

A smooth tennis court makes a great track. Speeds will be high, so make sure that you use strong tether string. Pad any solid obstructions with cardboard boxes. Place the car on the court near one edge so that it can rotate counterclockwise, then take the end of the tether to the center, start walking in small counter clockwise circles while pulling a little on the string, and get ready for action. By releasing the tension on the string for a moment in a turn, the car can be put into a two-wheel drift, then brought out of it with a tug on the tether.

Two cars more than double the action. You can let them pass each other on either side and get into some horrifying accidents. This Maserati (see color insert) has been through a number of end-over-end crowd pleasers, and it still looks presentable, except around the grill and the driver's helmet. (Fangio's helmet was famous for being beat-up, however, so it just adds to the authenticity.) The one thing the car doesn't like is a head-on collision with a tennis-net post, so we recommend that you cushion the posts.

THE DUMP TRUCK

■ MATERIALS LIST

4' length of redwood 2 × 6 stock
2' length of fir 2 × 6 stock
1' length of #2 pine 1 × 10 stock
6' length of #2 pine 1 × 6 stock
18" of $\frac{3}{4}$" dowel
Forty-eight 1$\frac{1}{2}$" #8 flathead wood screws
Six 1$\frac{1}{2}$" finishing nails
Two 2" butt hinges
Two 10" lengths of $\frac{1}{2}$" galvanized pipe
Four 4" lengths of $\frac{1}{2}$" galvanized pipe
One 3" length of $\frac{1}{2}$" galvanized pipe
Three 2" lengths of $\frac{1}{2}$" galvanized pipe
Three galvanized T-fittings
90-degree ell fitting
Six end caps for pipes
Two $\frac{7}{8}$"-diameter plastic chair-leg-bottom
　　caps

☐ *See color insert for completed project.*

After the Great Depression, when the bottom had dropped out of the market for toys, play automobiles became as elaborate as the real cars of the day. You no longer pushed a toy truck over to a toy steam shovel and turned the shovel over to dump in the dirt. Instead, you sat on the top of the truck and drove it over to

the shovel. Then you sat on the shovel and pulled the levers to do the dumping. And that's the way it is with this Dump Truck and the Steam Shovel that follows it.

We took many of the same lines that were used in the ride 'em toys of the 1930s, translated them into wood for easy building, mixed in some lumberyard hardware to make them work, and there we had them: a Mack-style dump truck and a full-control steam shovel for moving dirt to construct sandbox freeways.

The driver sits on the cab of the Dump Truck, steers with a T-bar coming up through the radiator, and dumps with a lever just outside the cab, like the tailgate release on the real thing.

■ CONSTRUCTION NOTE

For the Dump Truck and for the Steam Shovel in the following chapter, we used screws to assemble most of the wood parts because it's a good, permanent way of assembling components on small projects like these without causing more damage than construction, as with nails. Plus, you can reposition parts if they're

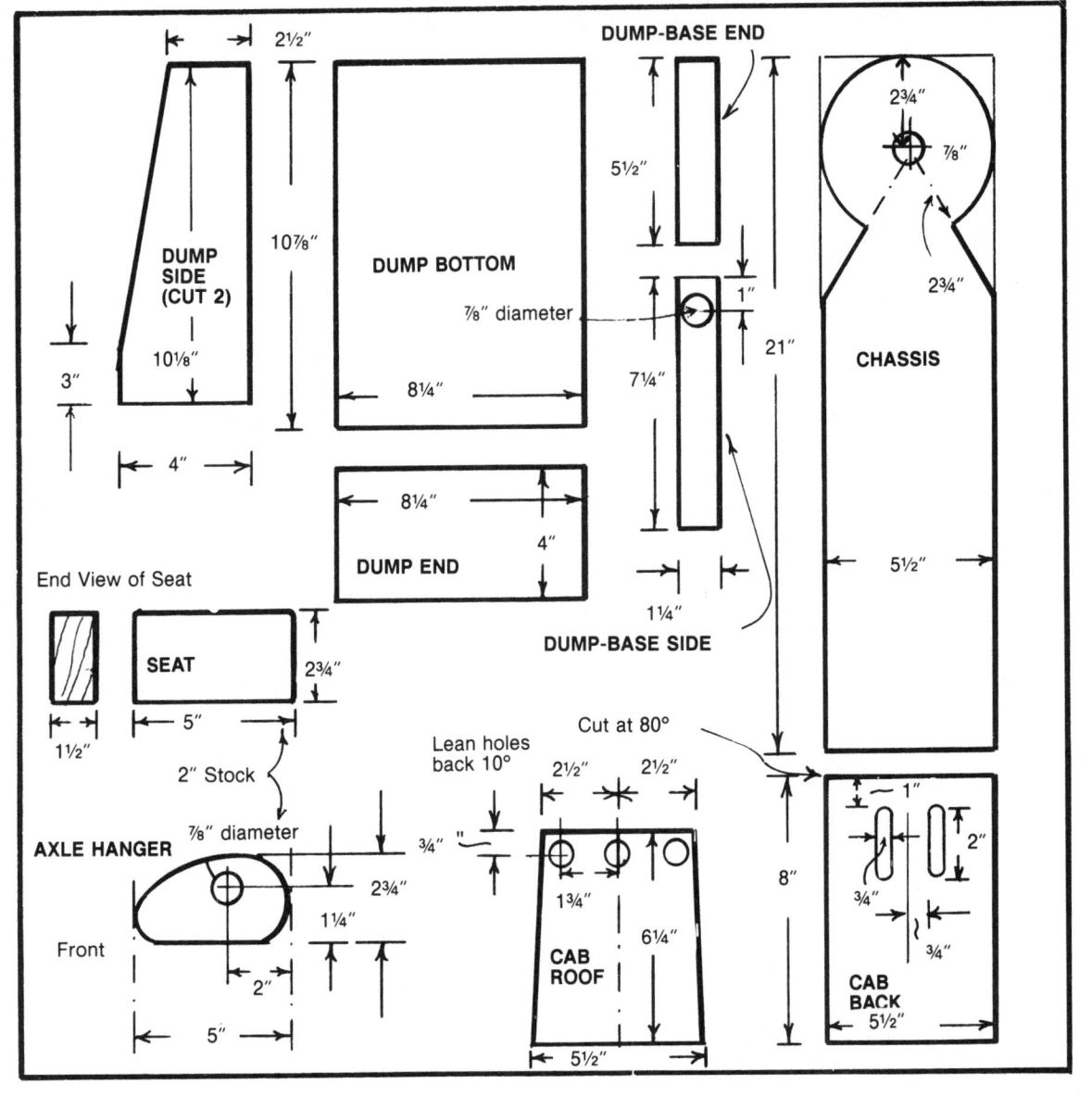

FIGURE 5–1 *Dump Truck components.*

screwed together, while nailed parts are harder to keep in alignment and are difficult to get apart again to reposition. Whenever driving in screws, use a combination drill bit/countersink to bore the pilot holes for the screws through the aligned parts. We use $1\frac{1}{2}''$ #8 plated flat-head wood screws whenever joining 1" stock (actually $\frac{3}{4}''$ net thickness), along with yellow or white squeeze-bottle glue to join surfaces, except where noted.

■ CUTTING AND DRILLING

To make the truck, start by cutting out all the 1"-stock parts with a circular saw (or with a saber saw or hand saw). Cut the chassis, bed bases, dump-bed bottom, bed front, bed sides, cab rear, and cab roof from pine or any light soft to medium wood (Fig. 5–1). Cut the parts from 2" stock ($1\frac{1}{2}''$ net thickness) with a saber saw, and check to make sure that the blade is at a 90-degree angle to the base. If you have a band saw, you can cut out the parts in short order.

Cut the cab seat and the rear axle hangers (see Fig. 5–5) and the dashboard (Fig. 5–2) from fir or pine stock. Cut the two hood layers and the radiator shell (Fig. 5–2) and the wheels (Fig. 5–3) from redwood or other dark-grained wood. For the wheels, draw a line down the center of one side of a 2' length of 2×6 clear redwood. (Redwood splinters *can* lead to infection, so if you think the operators will pick up splinters from the equipment after it's been sanded and varnished, use another dark wood, or use pine or fir and stain it dark.)

Next, with a square, draw a line straight across the piece of redwood 3" from one end. Mark three more lines across the board, spacing the lines 6" apart, starting

with the line you just marked. Set the tips of a compass $2\frac{1}{2}''$ apart and draw four $5\frac{1}{4}''$ circles for the wheels, using the cross points of the lines marked on the board as the center points (Fig. 5–3, top left). Then measure out from the centers of all wheels along all four lines $1\frac{1}{2}''$ and mark them. Use a 1"- or $1\frac{1}{8}''$-diameter spade wood bit to bore holes at these four points on each wheel to a depth of about $\frac{1}{4}''$ (see Fig. 5–3). Drill through the centers of the four wheels with a $\frac{7}{8}''$-diameter spade bit, keeping the drill as perpendicular to the board surface as possible. An alignment jig in a power drill or a drill press comes in handy for this.

Mark and drill a $\frac{7}{8}''$ hole through the chassis and through the 2"-stock axle hangers, as shown in Figure 5–1. Then drill $\frac{7}{8}''$ holes through each side of the bed base. Mark the center point of the top of the radiator grill, as well as the center point of its base, and drill down through the top and up through the base of the radiator shell with the $\frac{7}{8}''$ bit, making sure the holes are aligned inside so that a length of $\frac{1}{2}''$ I.D. galvanized pipe can be inserted through the radiator and turned freely.

Next, mark a center line over the top of the dashboard, mark the center point of this line, then mark points on this line $1\frac{3}{4}''$ out toward each side and drill into the three points about 1" deep with a $\frac{3}{4}''$ spade bit.

■ ASSEMBLY
□ Mounting the Wheels

To mount the rear wheels, place the chassis on the two axle carriers, with the bottom of the chassis on the flat top of the carriers, as shown in Figure 5–5. Next, drill pilot holes and drive two $1\frac{1}{2}''$ screws

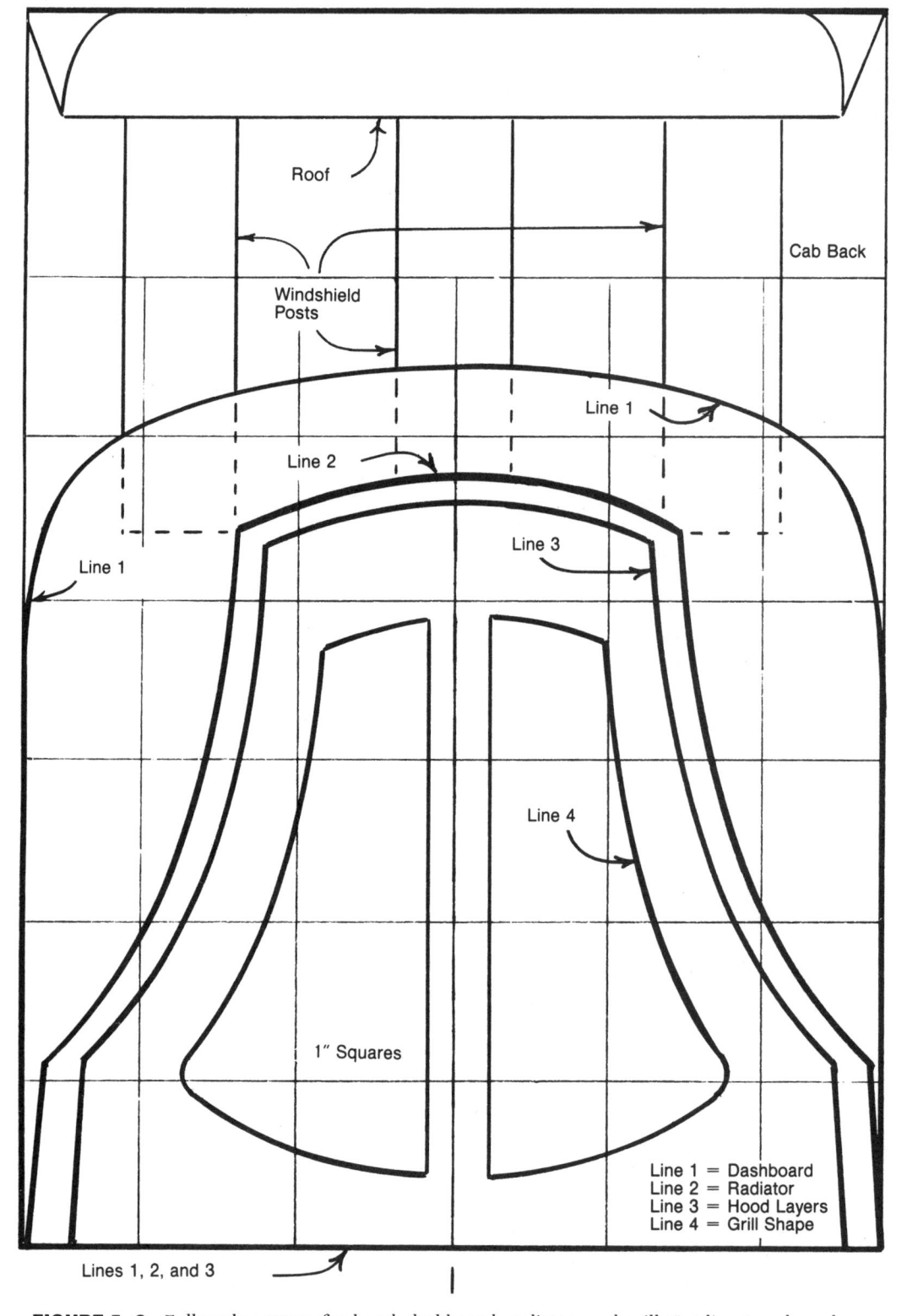

FIGURE 5–2 *Full-scale pattern for hood, dashboard, radiator, and grill. Cut line 1 and mark dashboard; cut line 2 and mark radiator; cut line 3 and mark the two hood layers; cut line 4 and mark the two grill shapes on the radiator.*

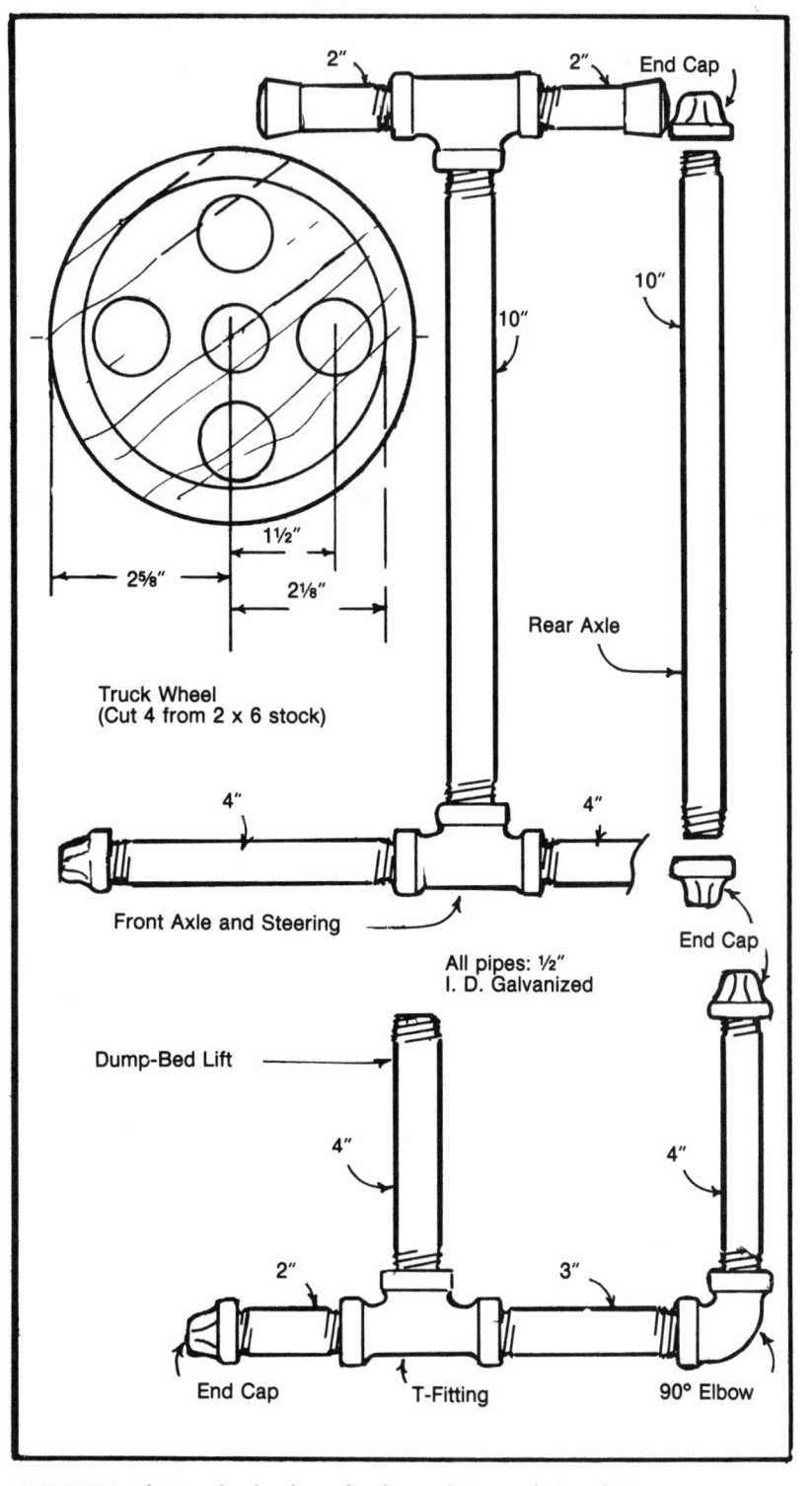

FIGURE 5–3 *Truck wheels and axles and internal pipe fittings.*

through the chassis and into each carrier with its outer side flush with the side of the chassis. Run a $\frac{1}{2}''$ galvanized pipe cap onto the 10" length of $\frac{1}{2}''$ pipe and insert it through the center of a wheel through the axle carriers. Slip on another wheel and thread on another cap finger tight (to be tightened with a wrench in the final assembly).

To attach the front wheels, thread 4" lengths of the $\frac{1}{2}''$ galvanized pipe into the ends of a $\frac{1}{2}''$ T-fitting (see Fig. 5–4). Then thread a 10" length into the arm of the T and tighten all pipes firmly. Insert the 10" length up through the hole in the chassis, and slip the wheels over the axle ends and end caps, threading them finger tight.

□ The Hood Assembly

To make the hood assembly, first round the top and side edges of the grill front slightly with a Surform shaper. Then place the radiator shell face down on a firm surface and place a hood part down over this, flush with the bottom edge of the grill but set in from the sides and top equally (about $\frac{3}{16}''$). Drive in $\frac{1}{2}''$ to $\frac{3}{4}''$ countersink holes for the screws about 1" to either side of the center line of the part and about midway down, to a depth of about $\frac{3}{4}''$. Drill pilot holes for screws through the centers of these countersink holes and into the radiator shell underneath. Spread glue onto the joining surfaces and screw the parts to the back side of the front hood part the same way, mounting the screws about 1" farther down to miss the first screws driven in through the front hood part. All sides of the front and rear hood parts should be flush.

Round off the top and side edges of the dashboard with the Surform shaper. Then

screw it to the back side of the rear hood part, first making sure that it's flush with the bottom and centered; it should overlap equally on both sides. Mount the screws about 1" higher than the rear hood part to clear its mounting screws.

Position the hole in the grill over the 10" length of pipe sticking up in front and make any adjustments needed in the hole so that the base of the hood lies flat on the chassis. The pipe should turn freely. Drive four $1\frac{1}{2}''$ screws up through the chassis and into the center of the bottoms of the grill shell piece and dashboard. Each screw should be about 1" in from each edge of the chassis. The dashboard should be flush with the sides of the chassis.

With a hand saw, slice out a wedge just over the notched outside of the chassis and about $\frac{1}{4}''$ to the outside of the sides of the notch so that the wheels will clear the sides of the hood when the steering wheel is turned hard to either side (see Fig. 5–4). (A chisel can be used to cut away the base of the hood edge to clear the wheels, while leaving more of the hood intact.)

□ The Bed Lift and Bed Base

To assemble the bed lift onto the bed, thread a 4" and a 3" length of pipe into a $\frac{1}{2}''$ L-fitting and tighten them with wrenches (see Fig. 5–4). Slip the hole in one of the bed-base sides over the 3" pipe length and thread a $\frac{1}{2}''$ T-fitting end hole onto this. Thread a 4" length into the side hole of the T and a 2" length into the other end hole. Tighten the T-fitting onto the assembly with pipe wrenches so that when the 4" length in the T-fitting lies down flat on the chassis, the first 4" length used as a handle sticks up, leaning forward about 20 degrees.

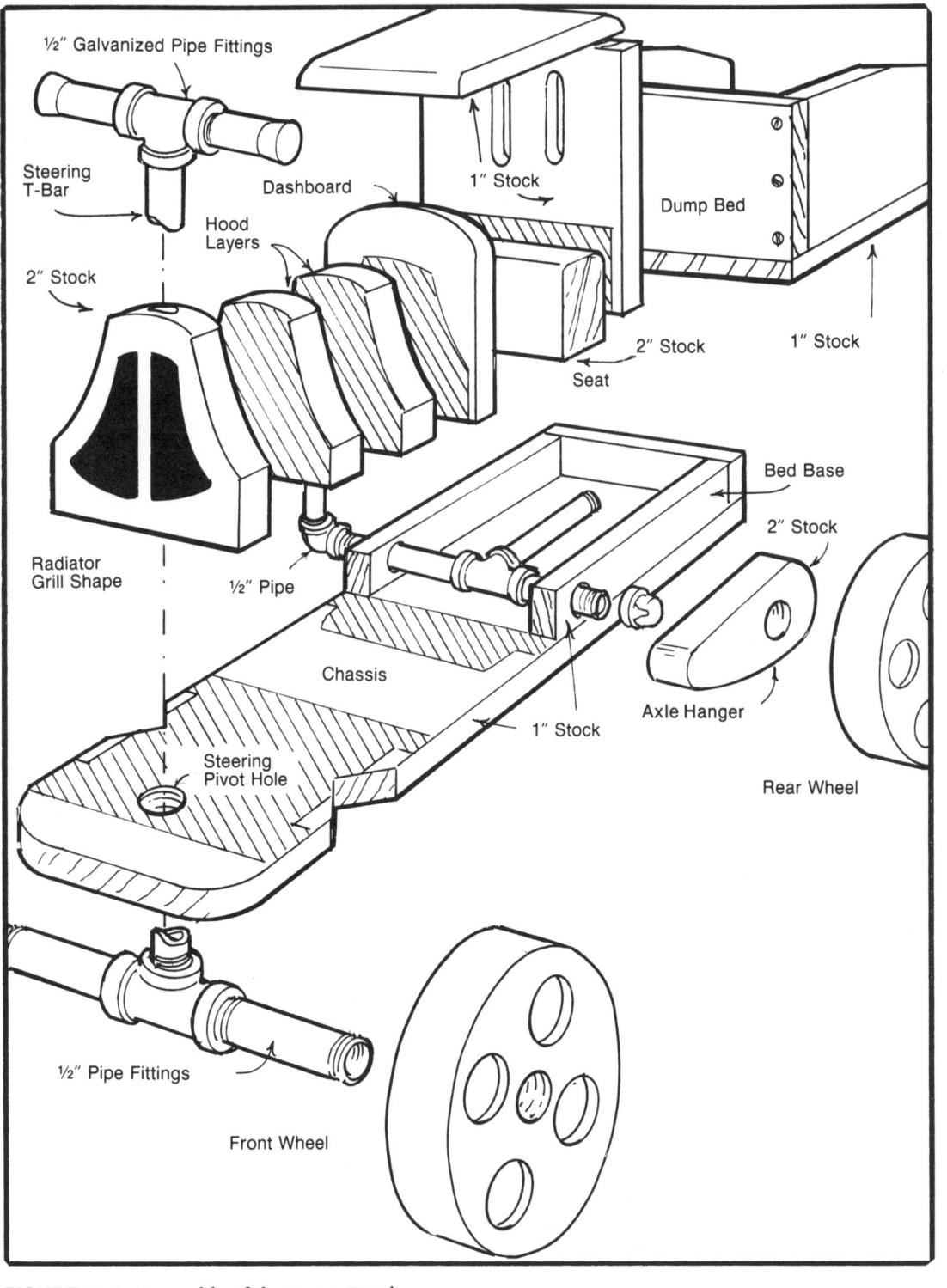

FIGURE 5–4 *Assembly of the Dump Truck.*

45

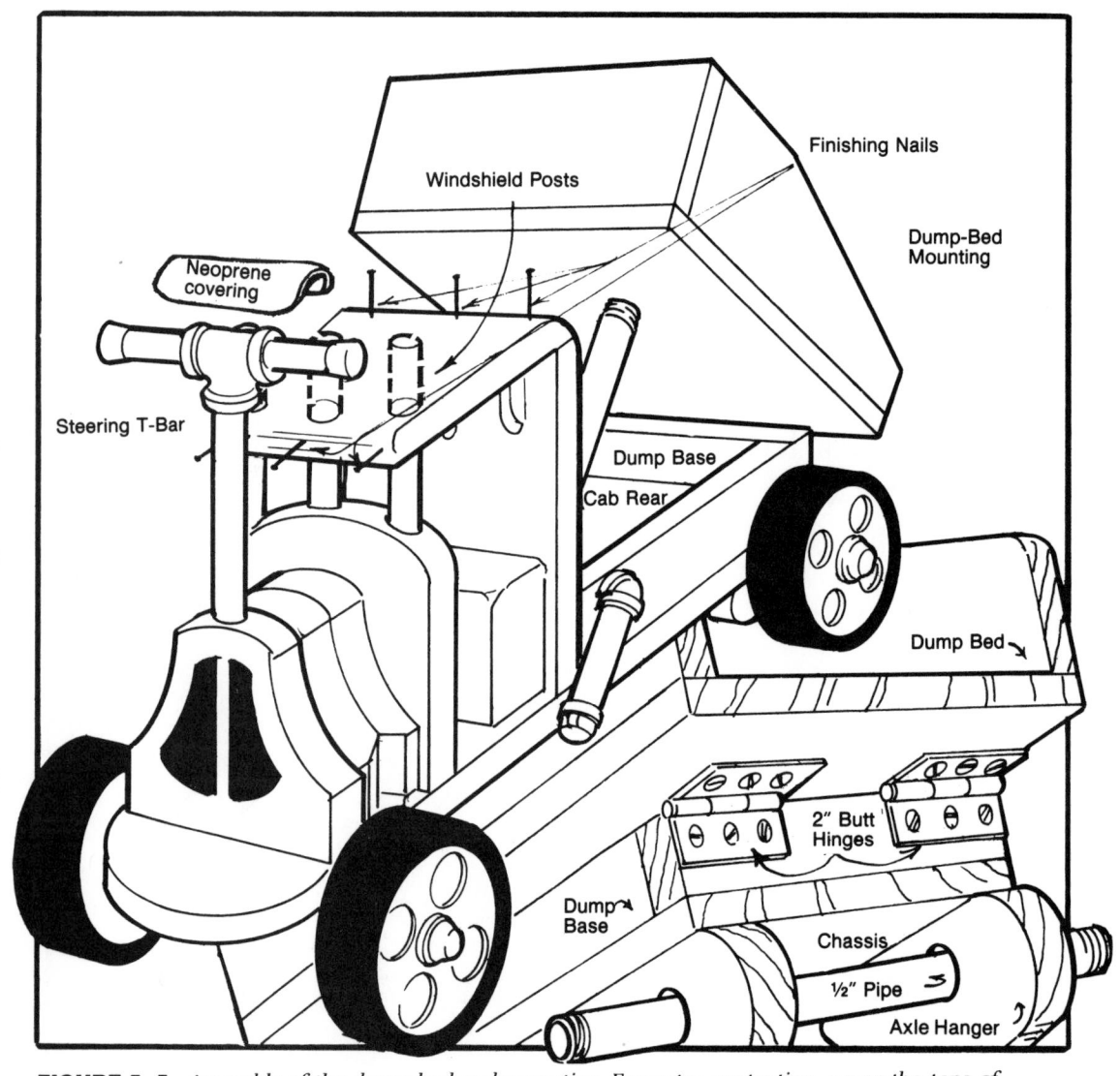

FIGURE 5–5 *Assembly of the dump bed and mounting. For extra protection, cover the tops of the steering T-bars with a pad of neoprene foam or ½"-thick foam rubber. Glue this over the top with rubber cement. Trim the windshield posts flush with the cab roof.*

Slip the hole in the other bed-base side over the 2″ length and put on an end cap. Drill two holes up through the chassis $\frac{3}{8}$″ in from the side edge. Space the screws about $\frac{3}{4}$″ and $2\frac{1}{4}$″ forward of the flat top of the axle carriers. This will allow both bed base sides to be glued and screwed onto the chassis. Attach the bed-base rear to the top of the chassis, making sure that it's flush at the rear and sides, and drive $1\frac{1}{2}$″ screws up through the chassis about $\frac{5}{8}$″ in from the axle carriers. Use a Surform shaper to round off the corners of the seat at the front-top edge, the top-end edges, and the end-front edges. Drive two screws through the rear of the cab back with the bottoms of the seat and cab back flush and the seat inset equally from the sides of the cab.

Cut three 5″ lengths of $\frac{3}{4}$″-diameter dowel. Apply glue to the holes in the top of the dashboard and tap the dowel pieces into the holes (see Fig. 5–5). Measure and mark three $\frac{3}{4}$″ holes on the cab roof; angle them back slightly from vertical when the roof is on a flat surface. Next, slip the holes in the roof over the tops of the $\frac{3}{4}$″ dowels, tapping the roof down evenly until the rear rests on top the cab rear. The bottom of the front edge of the roof should be $1\frac{1}{2}$″ above the top of the center of the dashboard. Then, using a $\frac{1}{16}$″ drill bit, drill three holes through the roof and into the center of the top of the cab rear, with the cab roof flush at the rear. Drill three more holes through the front of the cab roof and into the centers of the three dowels. Drive $1\frac{1}{2}$″ finishing nails into the holes; use a punch to set the nails down into the holes about $\frac{1}{8}$″. Before setting the rear nails, round off the rear, side, and front edges of the cab roof with the Surform shaper. Then cut off the $\frac{3}{4}$″ dowels flush with the top of the cab roof with a hand saw (or band saw), as shown in Figure 5–5.

☐ **The Dump Bed**

To assemble the dump bed, drill and drive three screws up through the bed bottom $\frac{3}{8}$″ from the front of the bed to mount the bed front onto the bottom, flush at the front, with $1\frac{1}{2}$″ screws and glue. Glue the bottom and front edges of the bed sides and drive two screws through the front and into the front edge of side. Drive three more screws up through the bottom and into the bottom of the bed side, with the side flush with the side edges of the bed bottom and front. With the bed in place, centered on top of the bed base, attach two 2″ brass butt hinges into the corner made by the bottom side of the bed bottom and the rear (see Fig. 5–5).

■ **FINISHING**

To finish the truck, round off all exposed edges of the bed, chassis, and cab. Remove the wheels and tighten a length of $\frac{7}{8}$″ pipe or dowel in a vise so that a wheel can be slipped over the top and its edges can be rounded evenly with a Surform shaper. Thread a $\frac{1}{2}$″ galvanized T-fitting onto the top of the 10″ length sticking up out of the radiator and tighten it parallel with the bottom T-fitting. Firmly thread 2″ stubs of $\frac{1}{2}$″ pipe into the end holes of the T. Slip the plastic chair-leg-bottom caps on the ends of the stubs. (Wrap the pipes with tape, if needed, for a firm fit.) Mark the grill shape forms shown full size in Figure 5–2 onto radiator with a marking pen.

Sand the truck and wheels and place the wheels over a $\frac{7}{8}$″ dowel of $\frac{1}{2}$″ galvanized pipe, tightened in a vise so the wheels can be spun slowly. With a brush or marking pen mark the edges of the black "tires" on the sides of the wheels

about $\frac{1}{2}''$ in from the outer rim. Then paint the rest of the area with satin black nonlead paint. Paint all pipes black, and apply two or three coats of satin-finish varnish to all wood surfaces. The easiest way to paint is to disassemble and remove the pipe assemblies before spray painting. After reassembling, wrap the pipe sticking out of the radiator with a few turns of black plastic tape to prevent the front wheels from falling down when the truck is picked up.

6

THE STEAM SHOVEL

■ MATERIALS LIST

4′ length of redwood 1 × 4 stock
3′ length of redwood 2 × 4 stock
2′ length of #2 pine 1 × 10 stock
5′ length of #2 pine 1 × 8 stock
4′ length of fir 2 × 2 stock
25″ length of fir 2 × 2 stock
3′ length of $\frac{7}{8}$″ dowel
8″ length of $\frac{3}{4}$″ dowel
6″ length of $\frac{1}{4}$″ dowel
Two 1″ butt hinges
4″-diameter lazy Susan bearing (optional)
$\frac{5}{16}$″ × $3\frac{1}{2}$″ bolt
$\frac{5}{16}$″ × 4″ bolt
Sixty 1″ #8 flathead wood screws
Six 1″ panhead sheet-metal screws
36″ length of $\frac{1}{4}$″ galvanized rod
Three $\frac{1}{8}$″ wire screw eyes
4″ length of $\frac{1}{4}$″ I.D. plastic tubing
5″ tin can, $3\frac{1}{2}$″ diameter (minimum)

☐ *See color insert for completed project.*

The Steam Shovel is mounted on lazy Susan bearings so that the operator can sit on the roof and still spin the bucket easily. By grabbing the boom handle, the operator can control both the reach and elevation of this bucket. A hand-grip level on the boom handle controls the drop gate on the bucket, so dirt can be dumped where it's needed. Before starting to make the Steam Shovel, read the Construction Note for the Dump Truck in Chapter 5.

■ CUTTING, DRILLING, AND ASSEMBLY

☐ The Cab Structure

Cut out the cab structure from 1″ pine stock, including the bottom, rear wall, front wall, side walls, bearing-mount disk, and chassis base. Use a saber saw or a band saw to cut the rounded tops of the end walls, a 2″ hole-saw drill attachment to cut the round windows, and a $\frac{1}{2}$″ spade bit to drill the radiused corners of the triangular front windows. Use the top from a round gallon can to draw a circle 6″ to 7″ in diameter from 1″ stock for a cab spacer.

Next, cut the front boom and the two rear booms from fir 1 × 4. Drill the $\frac{5}{16}$″ bottom pivot holes and $\frac{7}{8}$″ top pivot hole in the positions shown in Figure 6–1, then use a band saw or saber saw to cut the boom mount from the 2″ stock. Drill the pivot hole through the mount as shown.

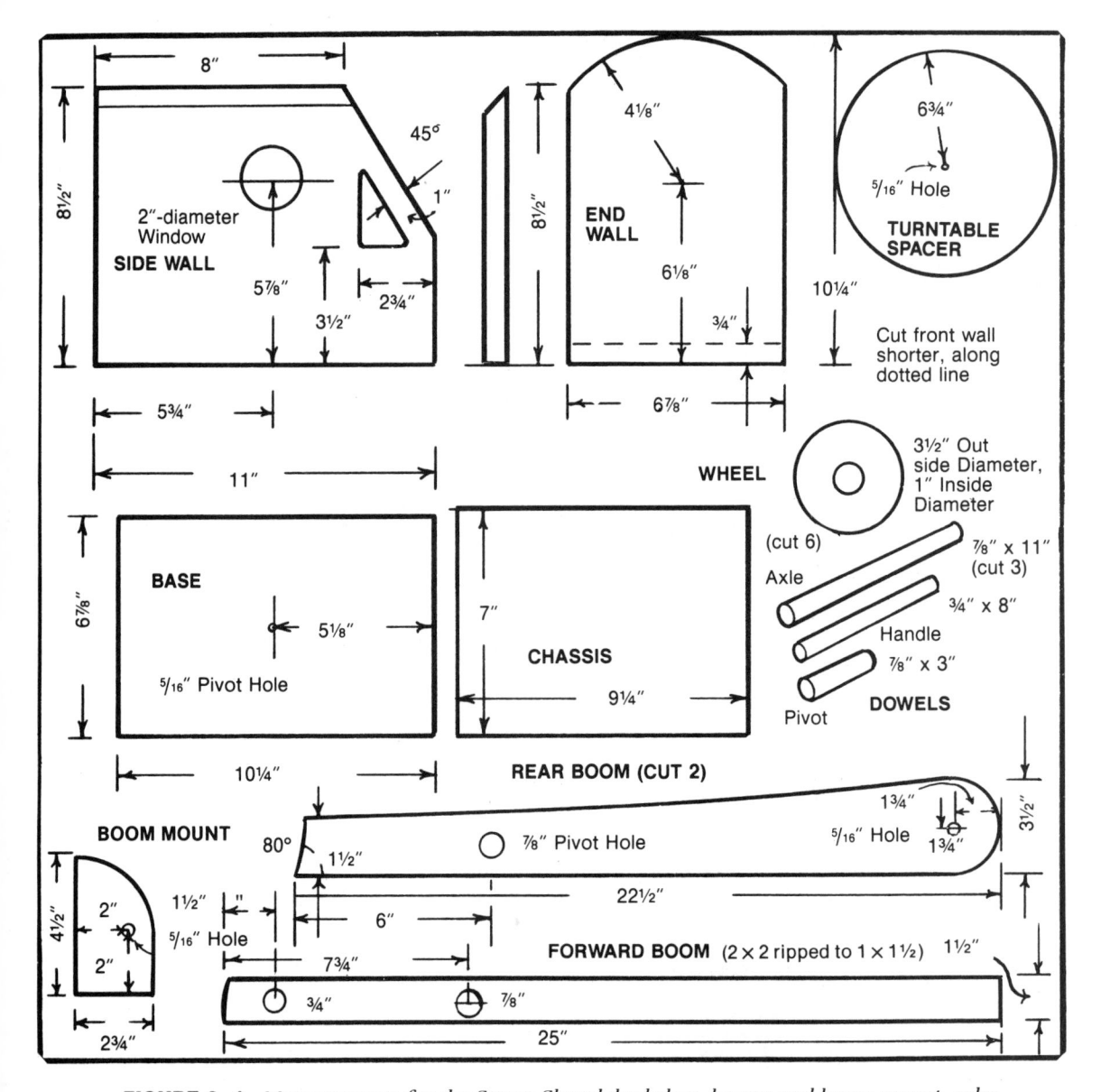

FIGURE 6—1 *Measurements for the Steam Shovel: body box, booms and boom mount, axles, and turntable spacer.*

Place in the corner of the front wall and the base, facing forward, and drill four screw holes, two coming in through the rear of the front wall and two coming up through the box bottom. Sand the boom pivot mount and the two rear booms, rounding off all sharp corners.

Next, insert a $3\frac{1}{2}'' \times \frac{5}{16}''$ hex-head pivot bolt through one boom pivot hole, through the boom mount hole, and then through the other boom pivot hole. Put on a locknut, allowing the booms to pivot on the mount without excessive play. Cut the boom top spacer (also made from 2″ redwood stock) and attach it between the booms, flush at the top, with glue. Drive a screw in through both booms, flush at the top, then a screw in through both booms and into the spacer (see Fig. 6–2, top left).

Attach the front wall to the base by driving $1\frac{1}{2}''$ screws up through the base. Set the boom mount in place with the booms bolted on. Use glue on the rear and bottom surfaces, and drive $1\frac{1}{2}''$ screws in through the back of the front wall and up through the box bottom to mount it. Now, attach the side walls to the base and front wall.

Attach the rear wall of the cab between the two side walls, flush at the rear edge and bottom, as shown in Figure 6–2, and screw it in place. Space the screws 2″ apart, $\frac{3}{8}''$ in from the rear edge, and across the bottom of the rear. Draw a line vertically up both sides at the midpoint between rows of screws for the front and rear walls (Fig. 6–3). Drive screws into this line, spaced 2″ apart to match the screws in the other rows, purely for aesthetics. Draw lines across the bottom of the cab diagonally from corner to corner; then drive a $\frac{5}{16}''$ hole through the center point where the lines cross. Follow the same steps for the cab spacer and the chassis.

Next, cut three $10\frac{1}{2}''$ lengths of $\frac{7}{8}''$-diameter dowel and drill $\frac{3}{16}''$ holes through these dowel axles. The centers of the holes should be about $\frac{5}{16}''$ in from each end.

To mount the axles, drill two screw holes through each axle 3″ in from each end, making sure that both holes are parallel. Draw three lines across the bottom of the chassis, using a square, with one line extending across the center and the other two placed $\frac{5}{8}''$ in from each end. Spread glue along one of these lines and drive $1\frac{1}{2}''$ screws through the axle dowels and into the bottom of the chassis so that the top of the axle lies along the line. Then mount the other two axles in the same way.

□ The Wheels

To cut wheels, mark six $3\frac{1}{2}''$-diameter circles on a length of 2″ stock. (We used redwood to provide color contrast; we also used it for the top boom spacer, boom pivot mount, and roof slats.) After marking the wheel-circles, use a 1″ spade bit to bore the axle hole through each, then cut out the wheels with a saber saw or band saw. Round the sharp edges with a Surform shaper, sand the wheels, and slip them onto the ends of the axles. Hold them in place with a $1\frac{1}{4}'' \times \frac{3}{16}''$ dowel pins, glued and tapped into the end holes through the axles. We nailed one mount flange of a ball-bearing lazy Susan base to the chassis centered over a $\frac{5}{16}''$ hole drilled through the center point of the chassis (see Fig. 6–2, top left).

Screw the $6\frac{3}{4}''$-round spacer to the bottom of the cab bottom so that the $\frac{5}{16}''$ center hole lines up with the center hole in the cab bottom. This spacer simply rides down on the lazy Susan. Drill a $\frac{5}{16}''$ center

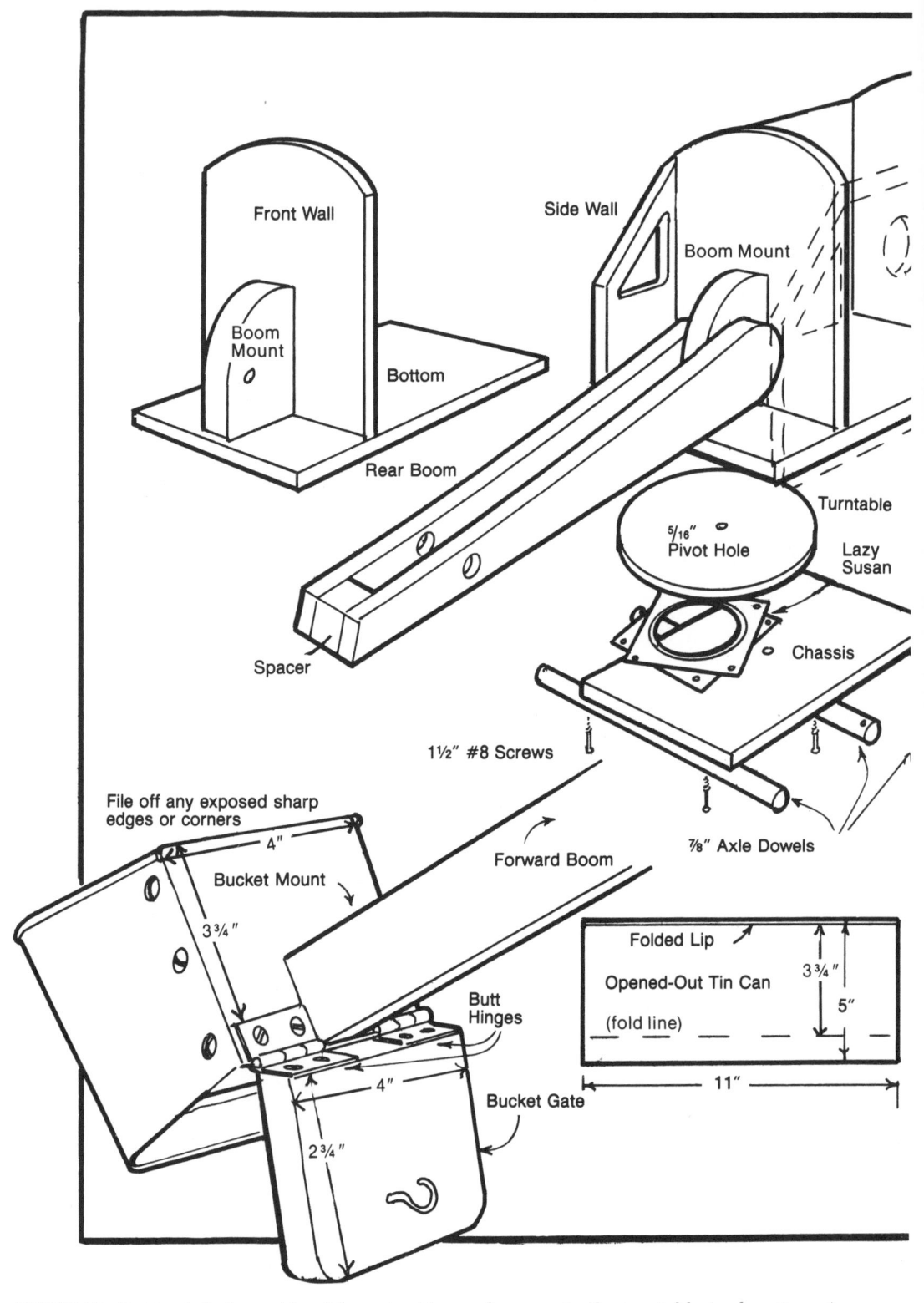

Front Wall

Side Wall

Boom Mount

Boom
Mount

Bottom

Boom Mount

Rear Boom

Turntable

5/16"
Pivot Hole

Lazy
Susan

Chassis

Spacer

1½" #8 Screws

⅞" Axle Dowels

File off any exposed sharp
edges or corners

4"

Bucket Mount

Forward Boom

3¾"

Folded Lip

Opened-Out Tin Can

(fold line)

3¾"

5"

Butt
Hinges

4"

11"

Bucket Gate

2¾"

52 **FIGURE 6–2** Top left: *Assembly of the cab with rear boom onto the turntable (or lazy Susan)
and the chassis.* Top right: *Assembly of the cab roof slats.* Bottom: *Assembly of the bucket mount
and measurements for the metal bucket liner.*

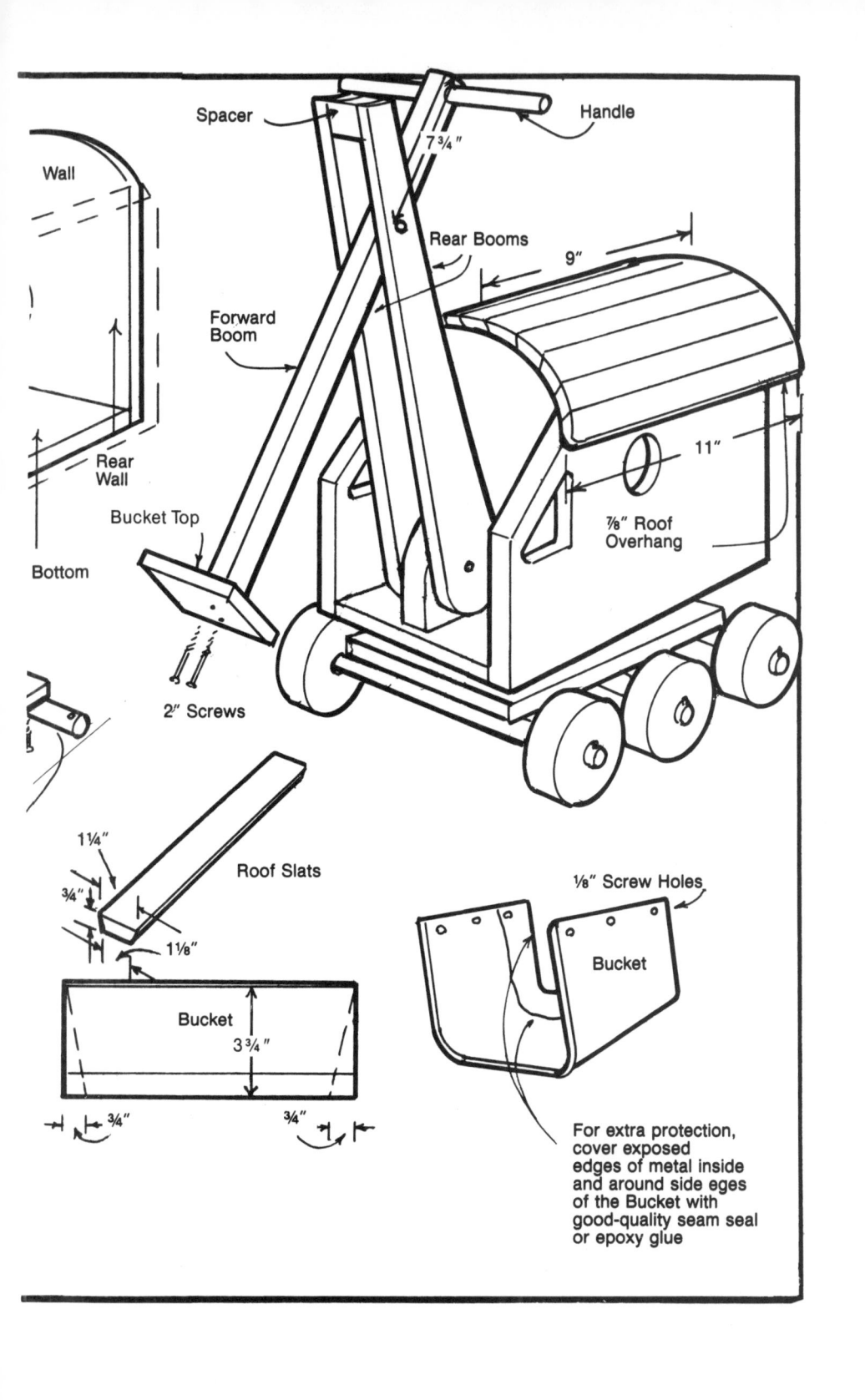

Wall

Rear
Wall

Bottom

Spacer

Handle

7¾"

Rear Booms

9"

Forward
Boom

11"

⅞" Roof
Overhang

Bucket Top

2" Screws

1¼"

¾"

Roof Slats

1⅛"

⅛" Screw Holes

Bucket

Bucket

3¾"

¾"

¾"

For extra protection,
cover exposed
edges of metal inside
and around side eges
of the Bucket with
good-quality seam seal
or epoxy glue

53

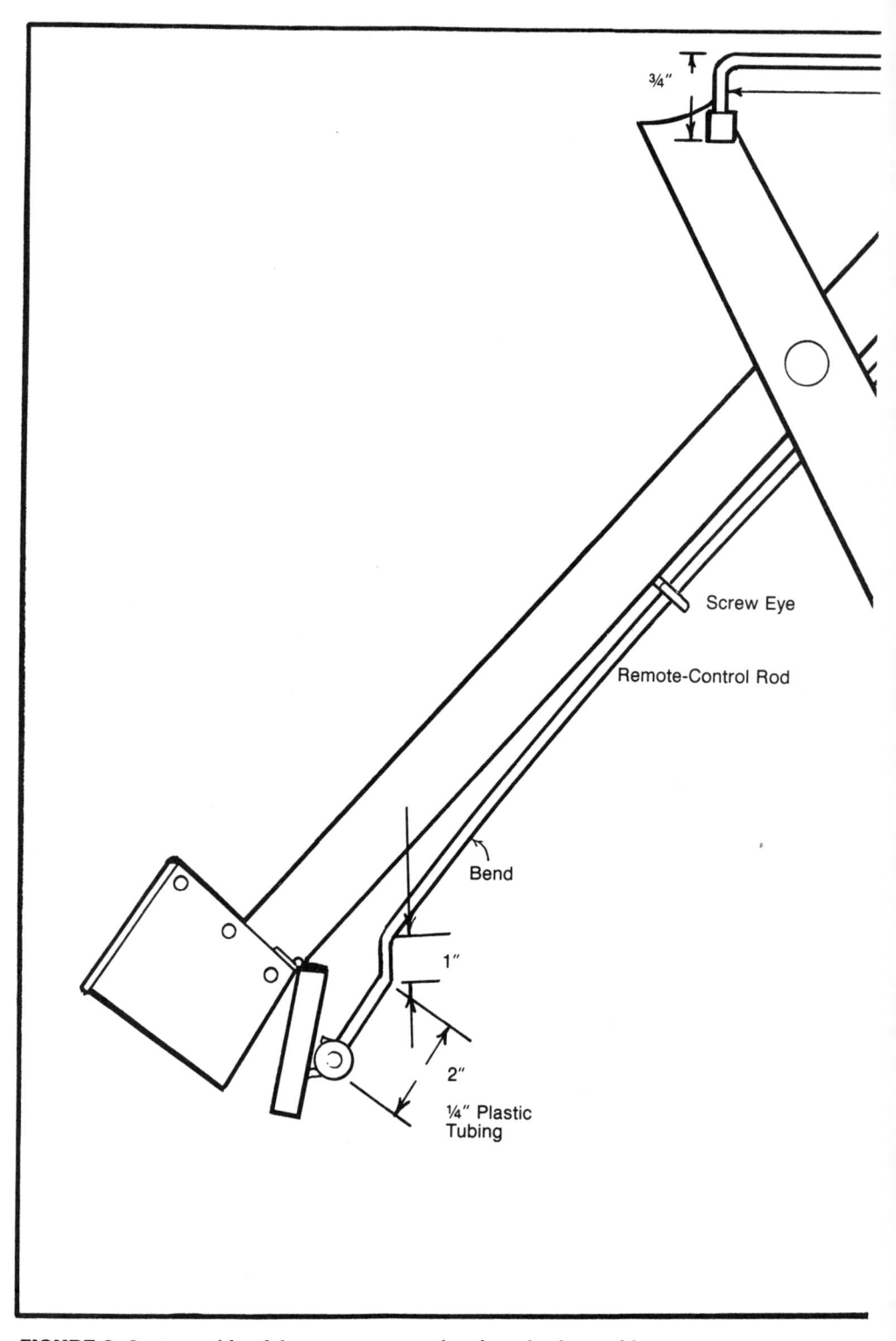

FIGURE 6—3 *Assembly of the remote-control rod on the forward boom.*

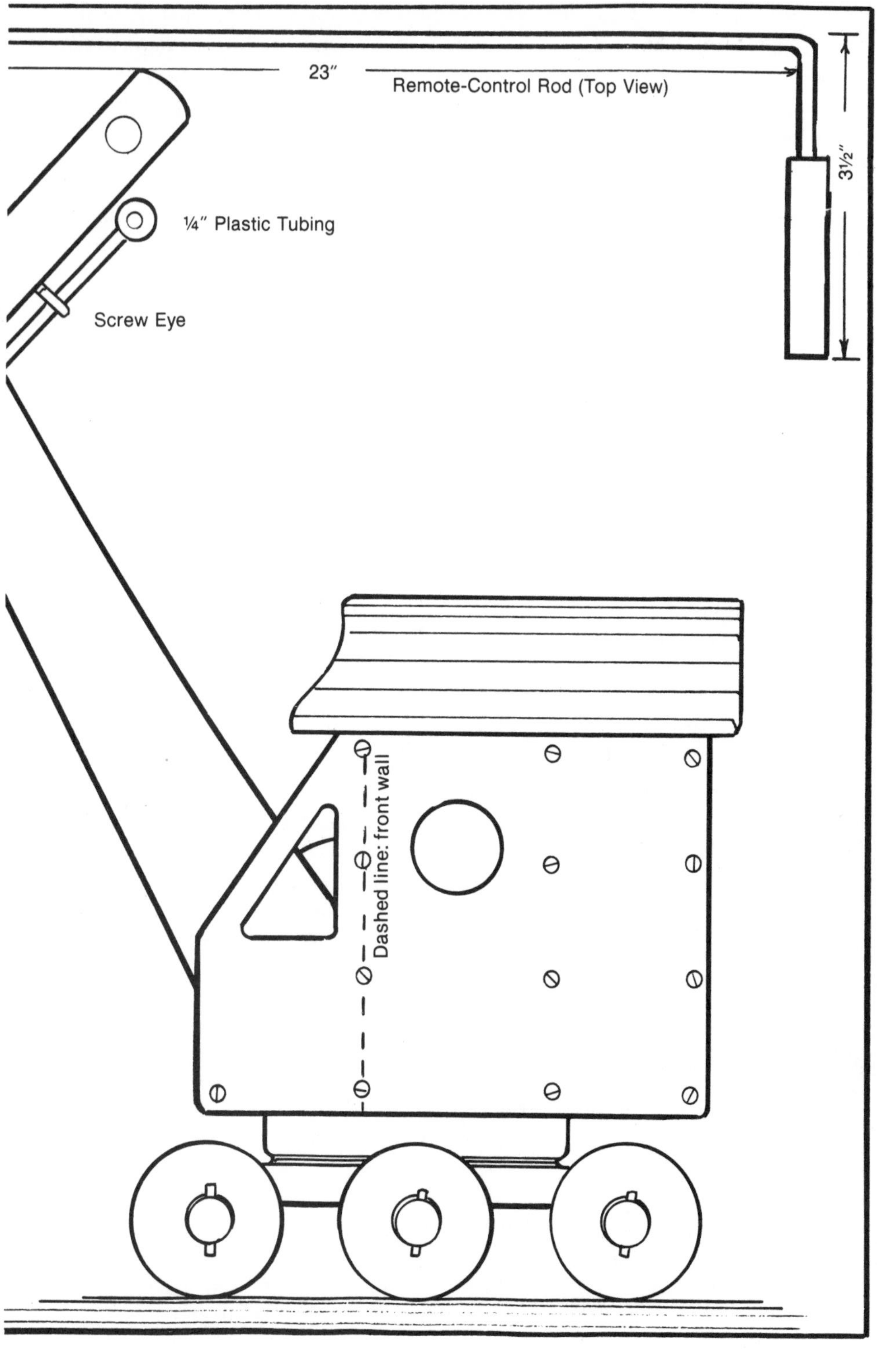

Dashed line: front wall

Screw Eye

¼" Plastic Tubing

3½"

Remote-Control Rod (Top View)

23"

hole through the chassis and on through the axle underneath. Then bolt the cab body through the center holes onto the chassis with a $4'' \times \frac{5}{16}''$ bolt, washers, and locknut. The lazy Susan bearing should not be greased. If you omit this bearing, the bottom of the round spacer can be greased or several layers of polyethylene sheet cut to $6\frac{1}{2}''$ in diameter can be laid down between the pivoting parts to act as a bearing surface.

□ The Roof (Figs. 6–2 and 6–3)

To make the roof of the cab, cut five 10" redwood slats ripped with the saw blade set at 5 degrees so that they're $1\frac{1}{4}''$ wide on top and $1\frac{1}{8}''$ wide on the bottom. Make four more slats 11" long and $1\frac{1}{4}''$ wide and cut square on the edges. Screw one of the beveled slats to the top of the front and rear walls, overhanging the rear wall $\frac{7}{8}''$ and with its center line aligned with the center line of both walls, using one screw at each wall.

Screw the rest of the beveled slats to the wall tops against the previously attached slat. The bottom two slats on each side are the squared slats, $1\frac{1}{4}''$ wide, and they are attached in the same way. Round off the bottom rear corners of the roof with a Surform shaper. Then mark the curve of the front of the roof and cut it with the saber saw; sand it smooth and round the bottom corners with the shaper.

□ The Front Boom and Bucket

To make the front boom, rip the 25" piece of fir 2×2 and drill a 1" pivot hole and $\frac{3}{4}''$ handle hole; round off the top with a Surform shaper. Round the ends of the 8" length of $\frac{3}{4}''$ dowel for a top handle.

Cut the bucket top and flap from fir or hardwood stock. Cut open a tin can and trim, fold, and drill it as shown in Figure 6–2, bottom. Bend it to shape and paint it semigloss black. Drill the bucket mount so that two 2" screws can be driven in through the bottom to attach the top (with glue) to the bottom end of the front boom, with the boom centered on the top and flush at the rear. Drive 1" panhead screws through the $\frac{1}{8}''$ holes in the bucket metal to attach the ends to the end grain of the bucket mount, flush at the top as shown.

Next, mount 1" brass butt hinges on top of the bucket mount to both sides of the front boom (see Figure 6–2, bottom left). Align their pins with the rear of the bucket mount. Screw the top edge of the bucket gate to these hinges, and insert the front boom top end up through the rear booms. Tap a length of $\frac{3}{4}''$ dowel through the pivot holes in all booms and glue into the holes of the rear booms. Tap the 8" length of $\frac{3}{4}''$ dowel for a boom handle into the top hole through the front boom. Then drill a pilot hole so that a 1" screw can be driven through the rear edge of the front boom and into the center of the handle dowel.

To open and close the bucket flap by remote control, bend a $\frac{1}{4}''$ galvanized rod as shown in Figure 6–3. Bend open three $\frac{1}{8}''$ screw eyes and screw them into the center of the rear of the front boom and $\frac{1}{4}''$ to the left of center, facing forward on the bucket flap, halfway down. Slip the rod into the opened screw eyes, and close the screw eyes over to hold the rod without binding it. Cut a $\frac{5}{8}''$ and a $2\frac{1}{2}''$ length of $\frac{1}{4}''$ black flexible plastic (or rubber) tubing; push the longer tube over the top end of the rod for a handle and the short length over the bottom end as a retainer to keep the rod from slipping out of the eye screwed into the bucket flap.

Sand the entire steam shovel, set all screws into the wood, and apply two or three coats of satin-finish varnish.

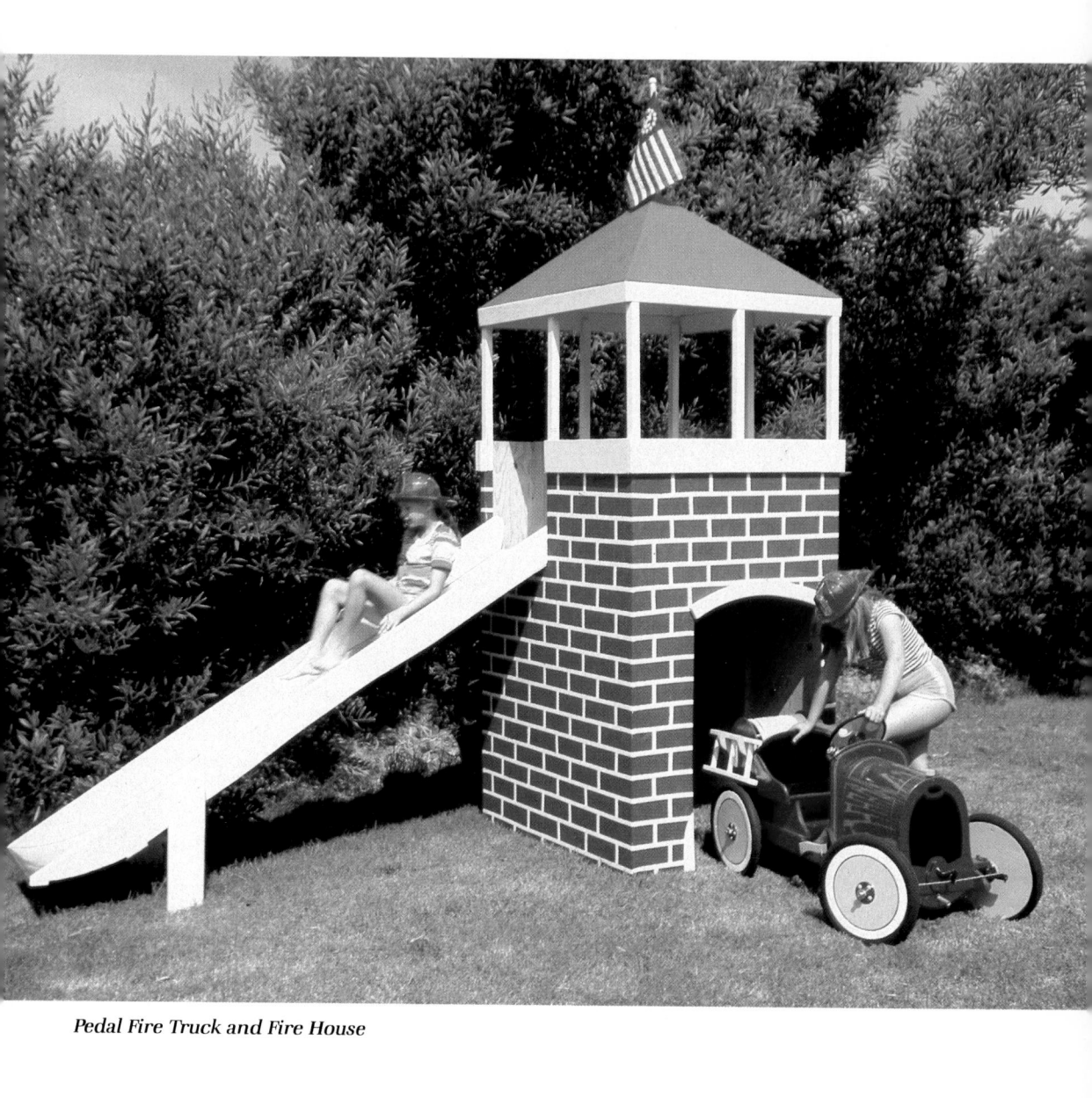

Pedal Fire Truck and Fire House

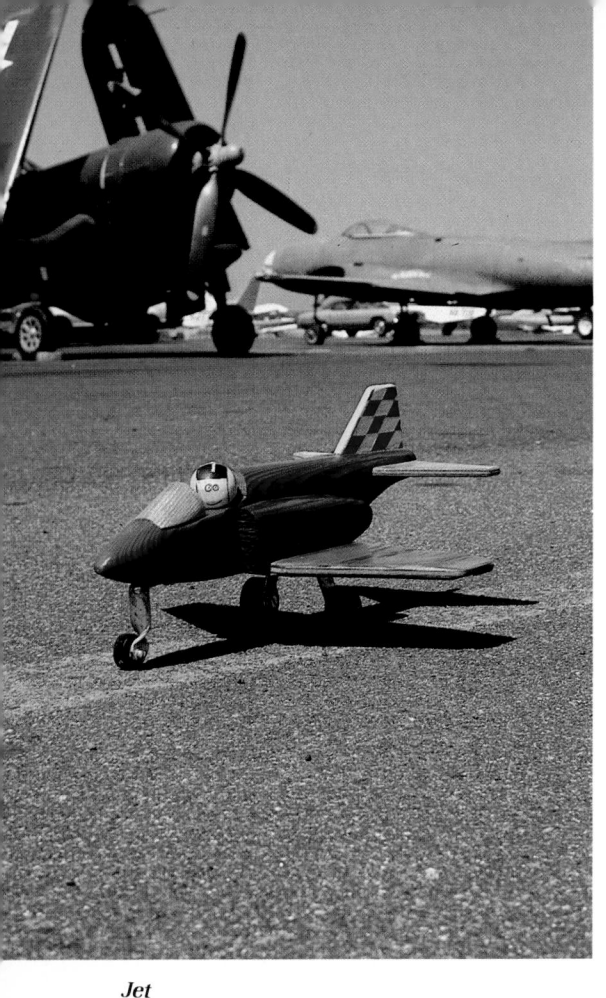

Jet

Ryan S-T

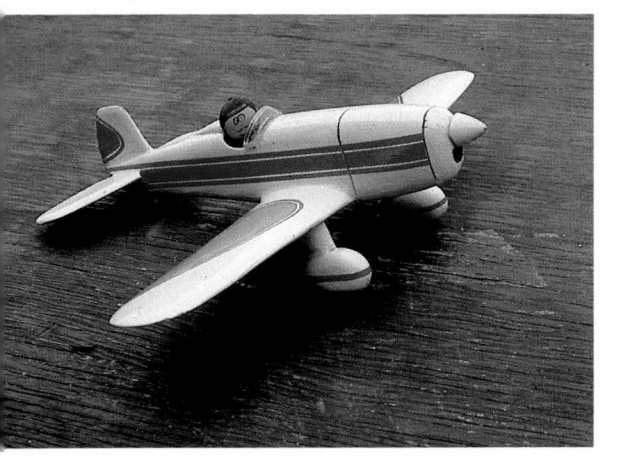

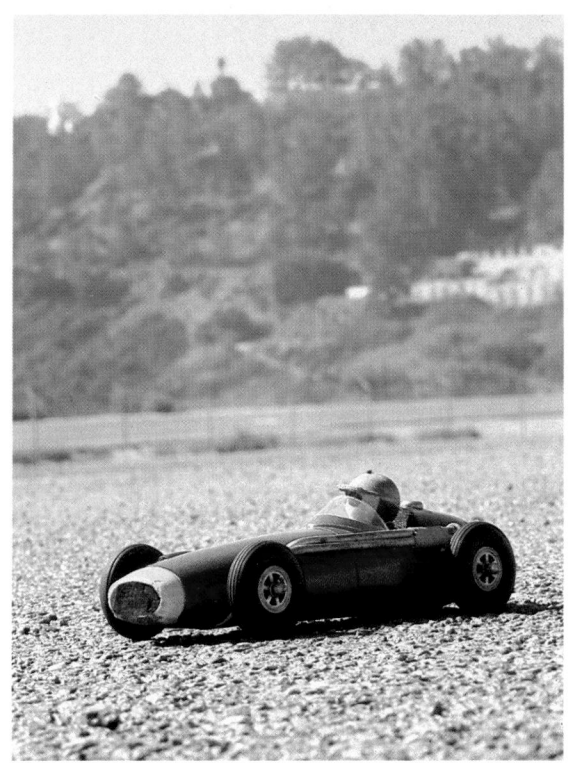

Maserati 250F

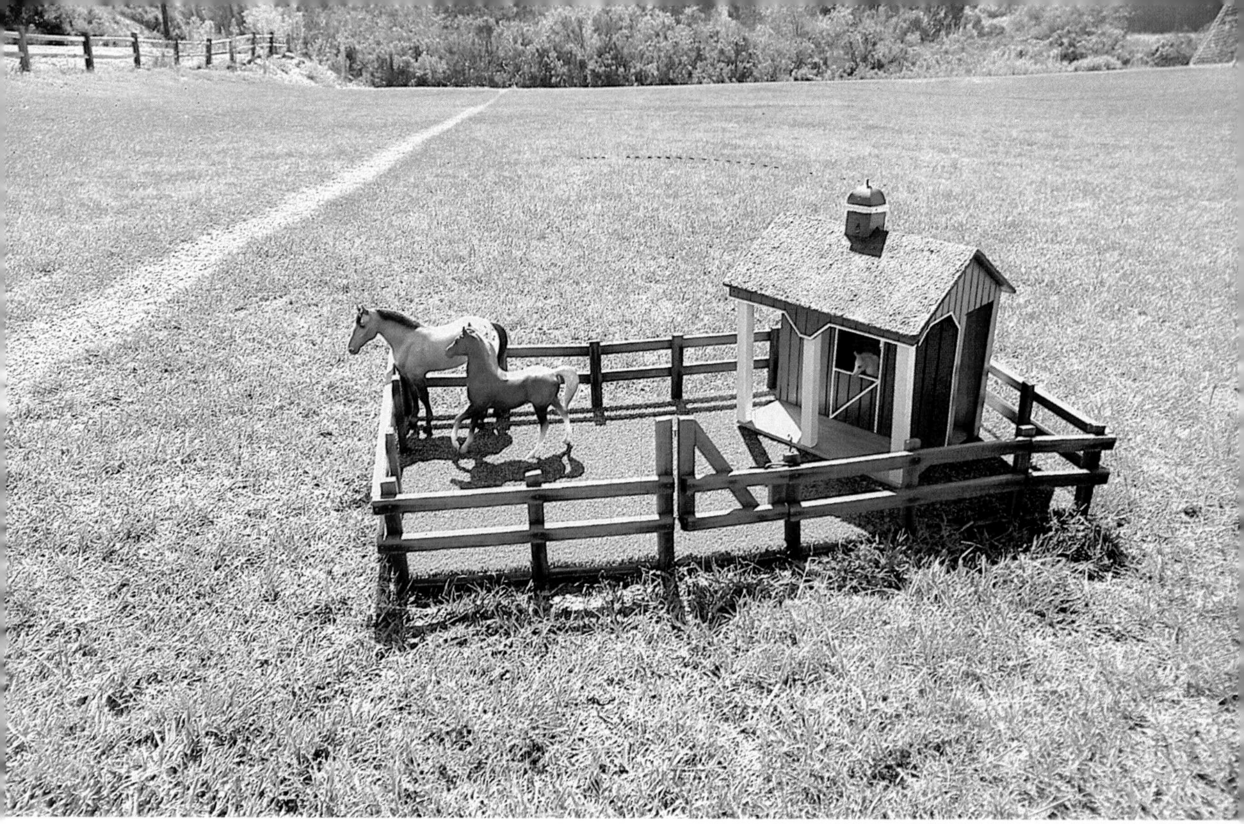

Stable Tack Room/Corral Set

Emporium

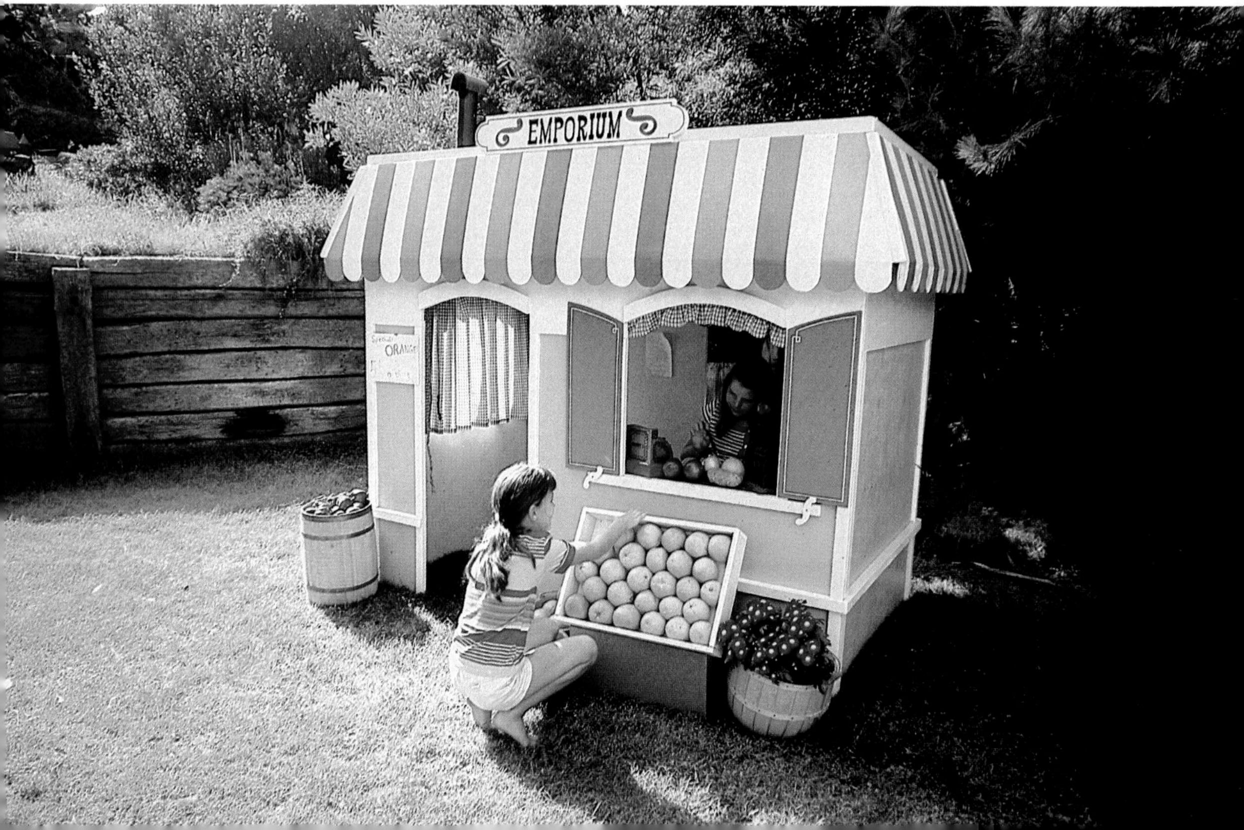

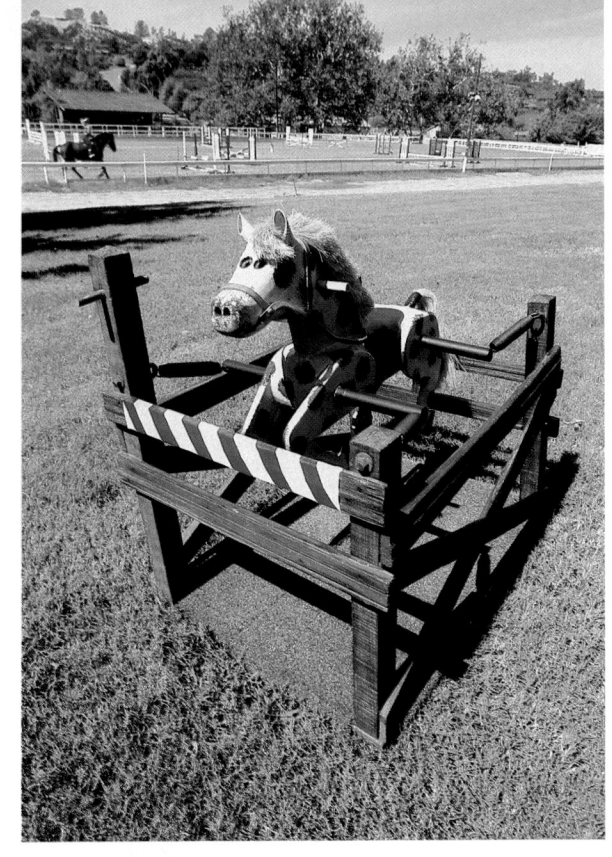

Jumping Horse

Potter's Wheel

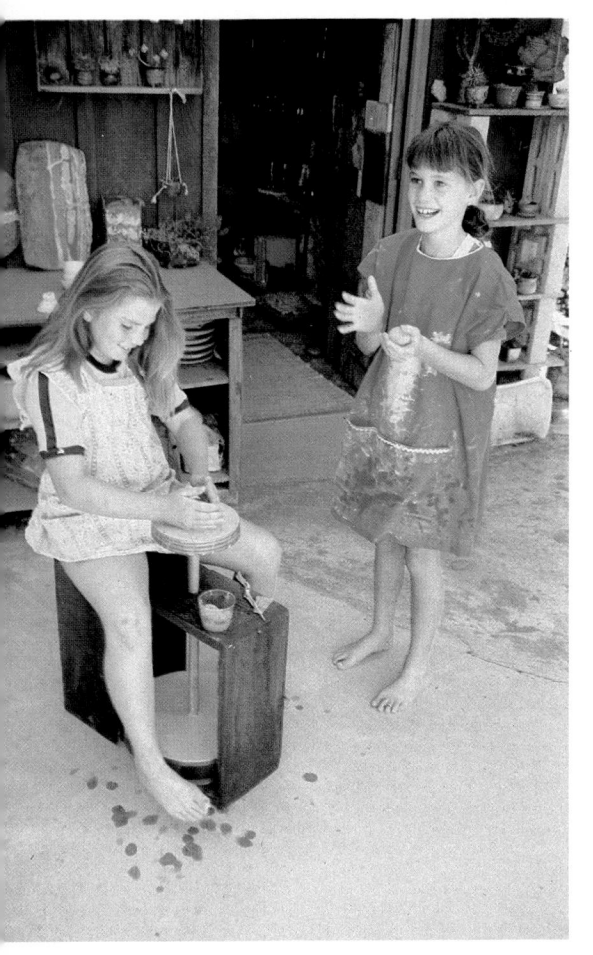

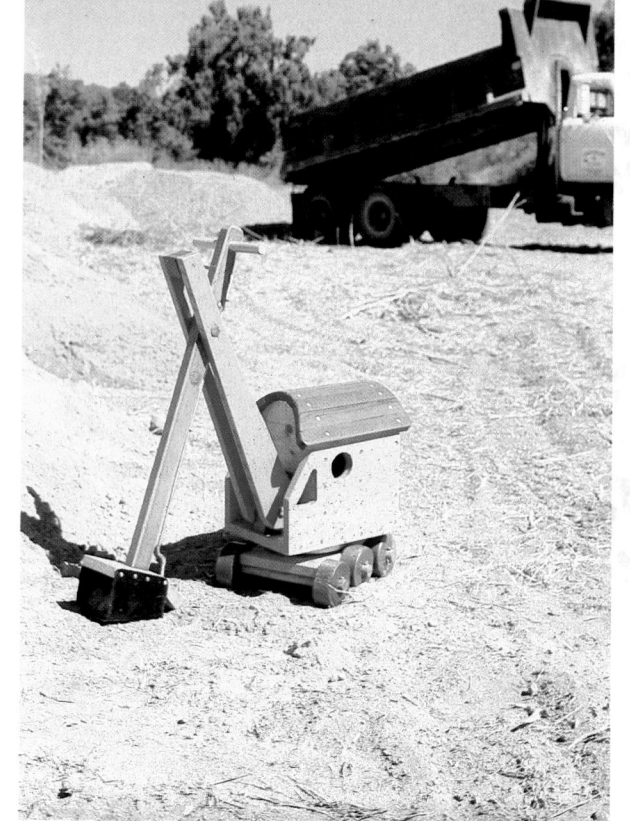

Steam Shovel

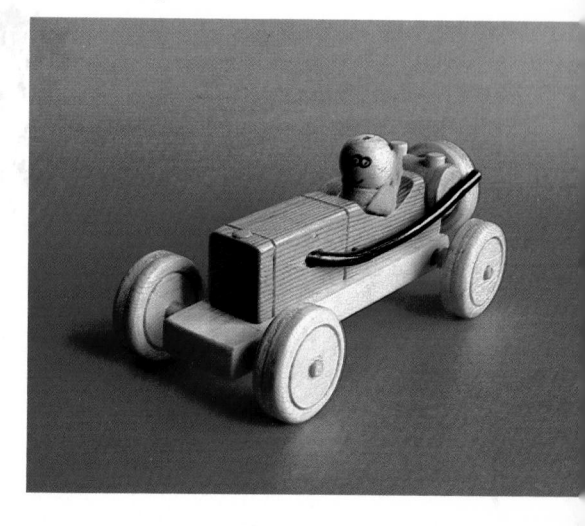

Peugeot

Dump Truck

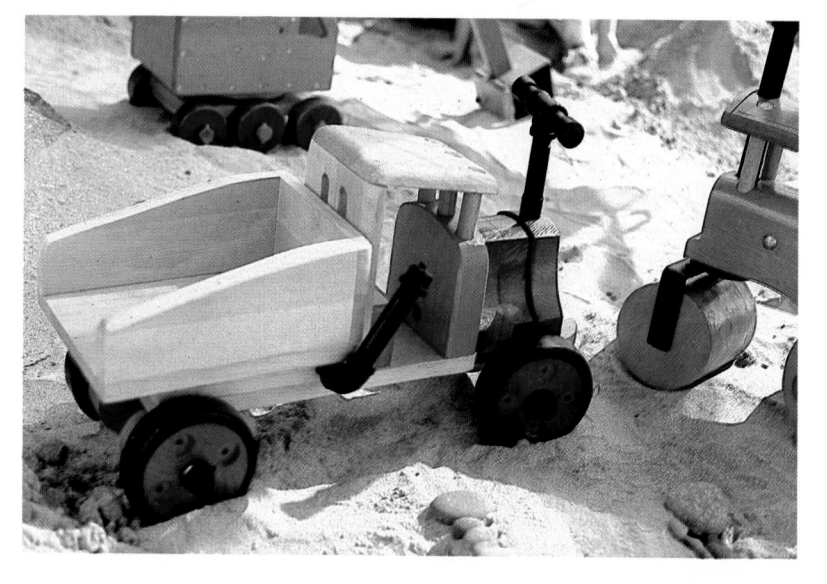

Three-Way Pedal Truck: A model of versatility, the basic Classic Car (front view shown at bottom, but with dumper attached) is also a working dump truck (center) or, with the enclosure addition, a terrific van cum traveling puppet show (top).

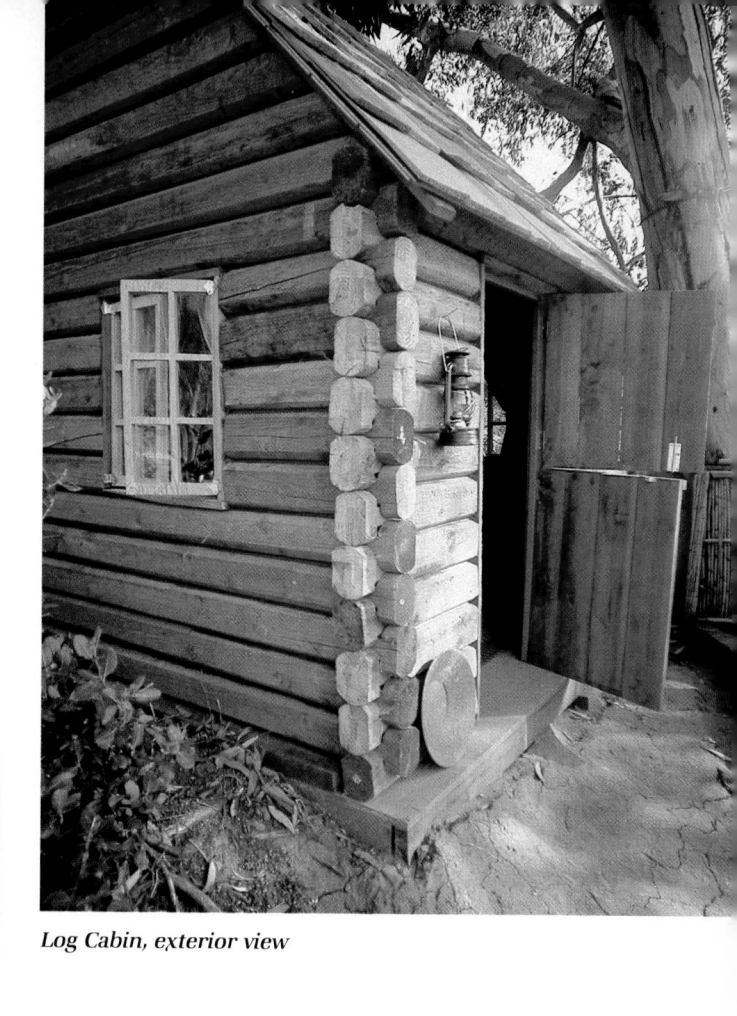

Log Cabin, exterior view

Log Cabin, interior view

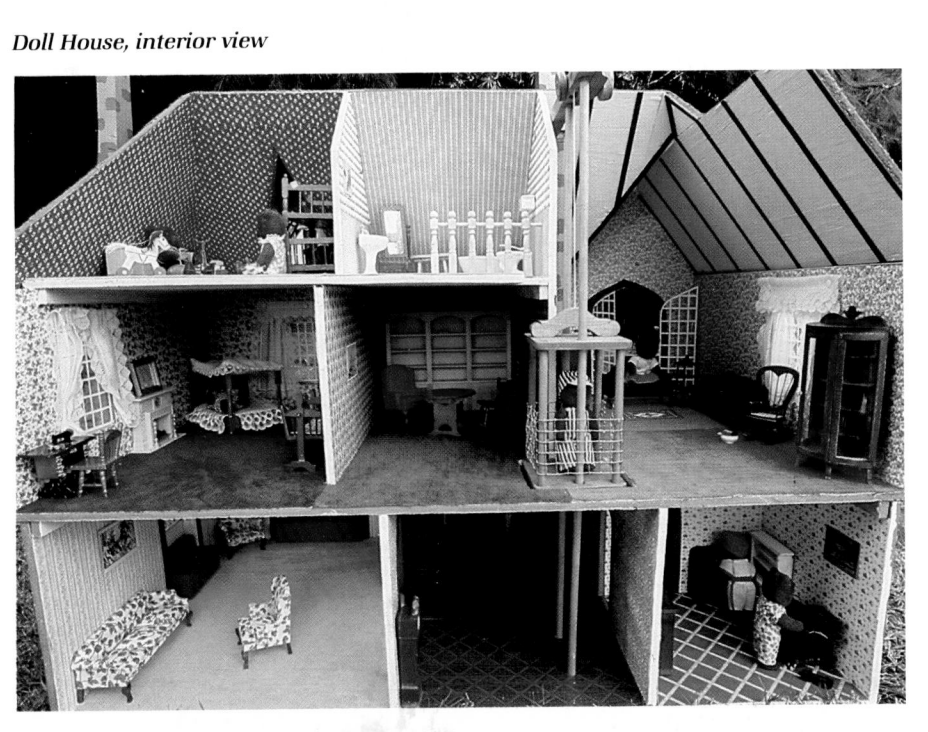

Doll House, exterior view

Doll House, interior view

THE POTTER'S WHEEL

■ MATERIALS LIST

98″ length of rough redwood 1 × 8 stock
    (or cedar or soft wood)
48″ length of 2 × 6 stock (any wood)
24″ × 24″ piece of ACX exterior-grade $\frac{3}{4}$″
    plywood
26″ length of 1″ hardwood dowel
Two dozen 3″ finishing nails
Twenty-one 1$\frac{1}{2}$″ #10 wood screws
2″ butt hinge
Plastic drinking glass
One $\frac{2}{3}$-cubic foot sack of ready-mix
    Sakrete

☐ *See color insert for completed project.*

The Potter's Wheel is a scaled-down replica of one we saw being used by a man in Tecate, Mexico, to support his whole family. He dug the clay, kicked the wheel, and made strawberry pot after strawberry pot, which he sold to nurseries in the United States. After the pots had sun-dried in the backyard, the family would gather sticks and lumber scraps to build a bonfire. The pots were placed well up on the pile, and the whole heap was covered with old corrugated iron and automobile hoods and set afire. Not surprisingly, a good percentage of pots bit the dust before the firing was half over as a result of the uneven heat. The survivors were attractive pots that could stand up to a certain amount of soaking.

Our version is made from rough redwood (or cedar) 1″ × 8″ stock. It is sanded after assembly to remove potential splinters and then sealed with one coat of satin-finish varnish, except for the plywood wheel. To keep things straight, we'll say that the rear of the wheel is the two-legged end you sit on, while the front is the end with a single leg.

■ CUTTING

The first step is to cut the three 18″ legs and the two 22″ pieces for the top and bottom from the 1 × 8 stock (Fig. 7–1). Next, make a beam compass by drilling two $\frac{1}{8}$″ holes through an 8″ or so stick about $\frac{1}{4}$″ thick, placing the holes 6$\frac{3}{4}$″ apart. Insert a nail through one hole and a pencil through the other; then, holding the nail on $\frac{3}{4}$″ plywood, swing the beam to draw two 14″-diameter circles. Mark the center point of both circles, drill a third

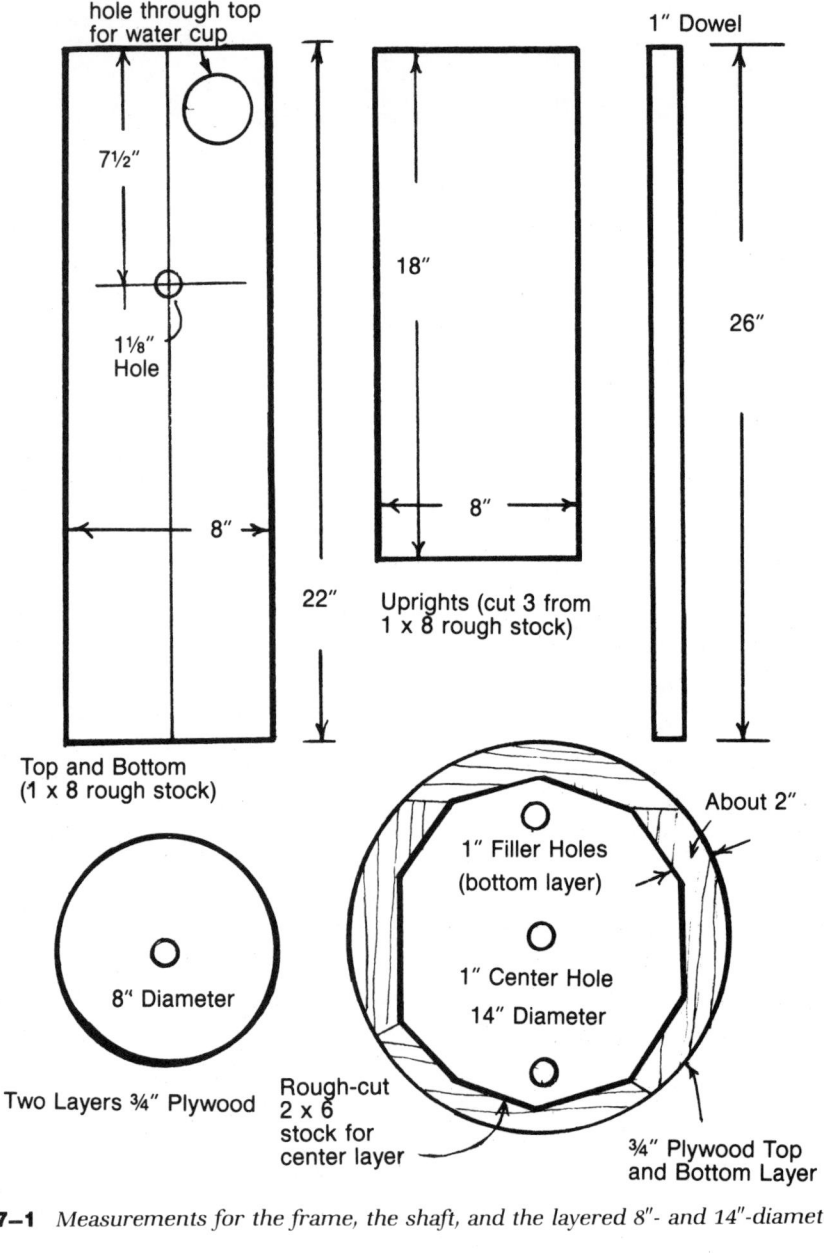

FIGURE 7–1 *Measurements for the frame, the shaft, and the layered 8"- and 14"-diameter wheels.*

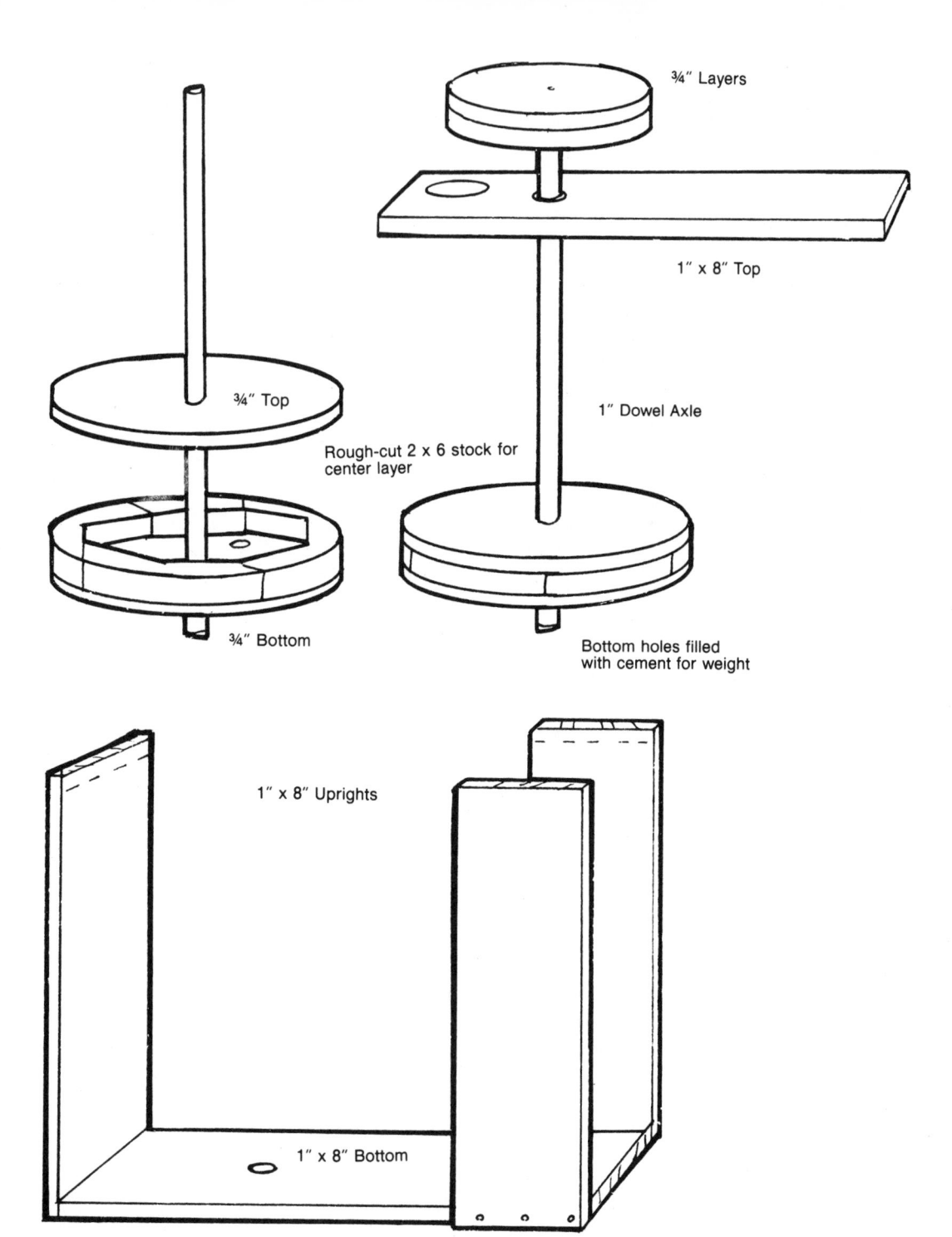

¾" Layers

1" x 8" Top

¾" Top

1" Dowel Axle

Rough-cut 2 x 6 stock for
center layer

¾" Bottom

Bottom holes filled
with cement for weight

1" x 8" Uprights

1" x 8" Bottom

FIGURE 7–2 *Assembly for the wheels on the shaft and frame.*

hole through the beam 4″ from one of the end holes, insert the nail and pencil, and draw two 8″-diameter circles, marking the center points.

■ DRILLING

Drill 1″ holes through the center points of both larger circles and one of the smaller circles. Drill the remaining small circle about two-thirds of the way through (or to about $\frac{1}{2}$″ deep), allowing the center point of the spade bit to poke through a little. Drill these center holes with a 1″ wood spade bit using a square, a drill press, or an alignment-jig attachment to make sure the drill is held perpendicular to the plywood surface. Cut out the outlines of all four circles with a saber saw, then cut a 24″ length of hardwood 1″ dowel (Fig. 7–2).

There are two ways to make bearings for the potter's wheel—a simple way and an even simpler way. Potter's wheels usually make a mess, so they're usually run in service areas like garages, or on back patios. One simple way to make a bottom bearing for the shaft (which *will* support a fairly heavy weight and take a bit of side thrust from the kicking) is to mark the placement of the bearing holes in the top and bottom pieces as shown in Figure 7–1, then drill through the top piece with a $1\frac{1}{8}$″ spade bit.

Cut the $2\frac{1}{4}$″ hole for the water glass with a saber saw or a hole-saw drill attachment. For the simplest kind of bearing, just cut the bottom end of the shaft to a shallow point (see Fig. 7–3), and drill a $1\frac{1}{8}$″ hole through the bottom piece at the shaft point so that the shaft can rest on the cement floor, using this hole as a locator.

For a high-tech bottom bearing, a small metal plate, such as half of a butt hinge, can be screwed onto the top of the bottom piece so that a $\frac{1}{8}$″ hole can be drilled through the plate and the bottom at the shaft pivot point, as shown in Figure 7–3. Then a 3″ finishing nail can be held in a vise and its tip head cut off just below the flared end. Next, drill a $\frac{1}{16}$″ pilot hole squarely into the center of the bottom end of the shaft. Tap the nail gently up into the shaft, then run the tip of the nail into the hole in the plate (filing the nail and enlarging the hole as needed for a smoothly turning bearing).

The final step in cutting is to rough-cut the wheel spacers from the redwood stock.

■ ASSEMBLY

Glue and nail one of the larger $\frac{3}{4}$″ plywood circles to the 2″ redwood stock. Then insert the shaft through the other large circle and on through the circle with the 2″ stock attached. Spin the shaft to make sure that the two circles align squarely on the shaft. Then nail the second circle to the 2″ stock, spacing the nails about 4″ apart.

Drill two 1″ holes through the bottom circle (or bottom surface of the wheel), spaced about 4″ from the center. Tap the shaft until $1\frac{1}{2}$″ of it sticks out below the bottom of the wheel (or $\frac{3}{4}$″ if using the nail bearing). Next, drive two $1\frac{1}{2}$″ screws into $\frac{1}{8}$″ pilot holes, angling into the surface of the wheel (about $\frac{3}{4}$″ out from the shaft) so that the screws can be driven through the plywood and into the shaft.

Place the wheel and shaft solidly upside down and mix a batch of Sakrete (a ready-mix mortar) in a bucket to a fairly sloppy consistency. Pour the cement through the holes in the bottom of the

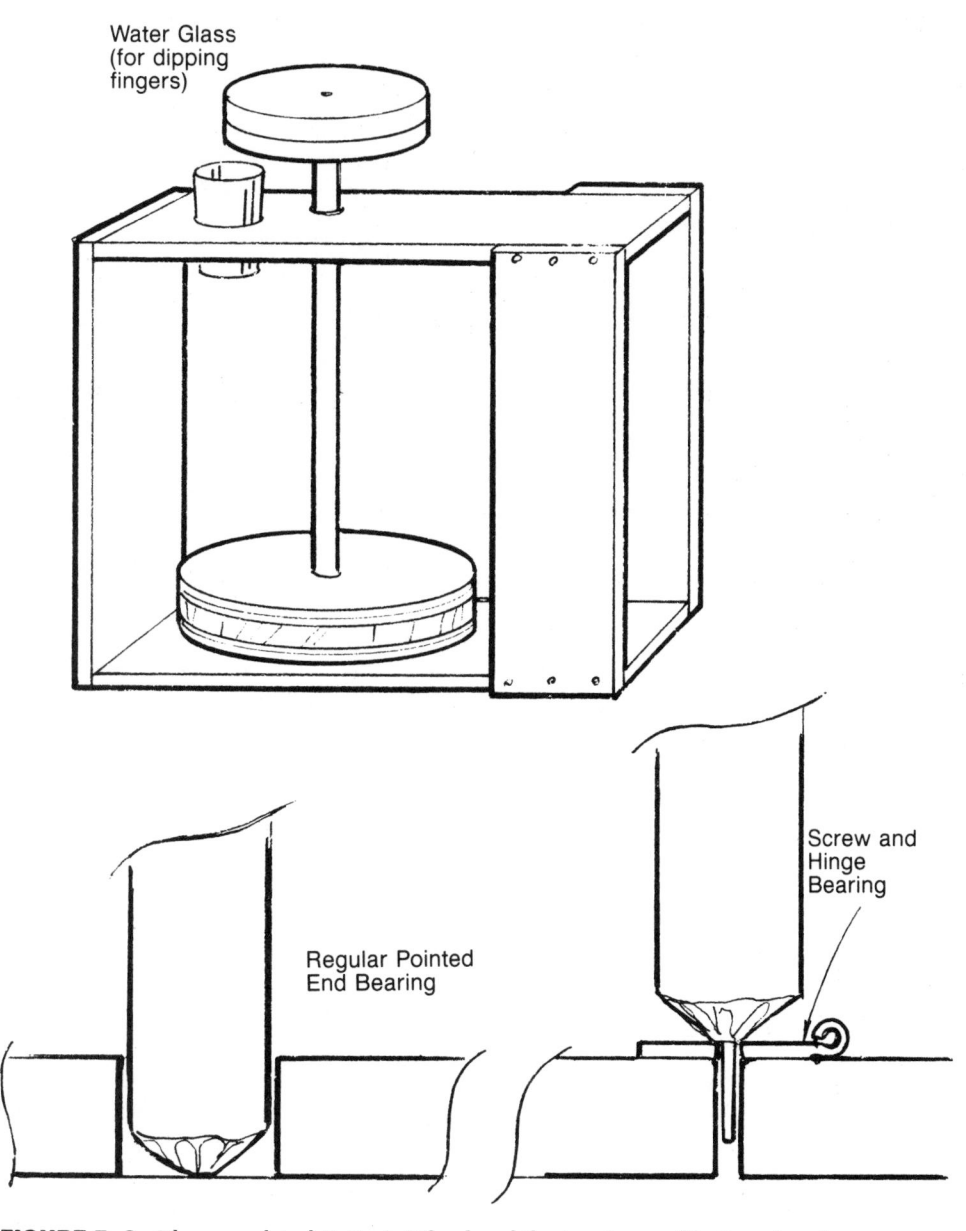

Water Glass
(for dipping
fingers)

Screw and
Hinge
Bearing

Regular Pointed
End Bearing

FIGURE 7–3 *The completed Potter's Wheel and the two types of bottom bearings.*

wheel (see Fig. 7–1). Bounce and jostle the wheel to remove air bubbles. When the cement appears to be level in both holes, allow the shaft assembly to cure.

Screw the smaller circle with the 1″ center-hole all the way through to the side of the other circle with the 1″ center-hole using four 1½″ screws spaced evenly and about 1″ in from the edge.

Insert the wheel shaft through the hole in the top piece, then glue the top wheel assembly of the two 8″ circles in the center hole and tap it down over the end of the shaft, spinning it to make sure that it's squared on the shaft. Drive a 1½″ screw through the small center hole of the top wheel and into the top end of the shaft and allow the glue to dry.

To assemble the frame (see Fig. 7–2) use three 3″ nails to fasten one of the rear legs to the side of the bottom piece. Nail the other rear leg to the other side edge of the bottom piece. Then nail the front leg to the other end of the bottom piece.

Make sure that all the pieces are flush at the bottom and sides.

Next, insert the shaft bottom into the bottom bearing and position the top piece in between the two rear legs and the front leg. Lay the frame on a firm surface and drive nails through the legs and into the side edges of the top piece (to attach the rear legs) and into the end edge of the top (to attach the front legs), being careful to miss the hole for the water glass.

Soak the wood around the two bearings with light oil so that some oil will feed the bearing areas through the grain. Place a plastic water glass in the hole for dipping fingers in to smooth the clay. Give the frame a light sanding to remove splinters and seal it with a coat of satin-finish varnish. Paint the tops of the wheels with enamel for further splinter protection and color appeal.

Now, center the clay, kick the wheel, and throw your first strawberry pot.

THE PEDAL FIRE TRUCK

■ MATERIALS LIST

4' × 8' ACX exterior-grade plywood
  panel, $\frac{3}{8}''$ thick
8' length of #2 pine 1 × 12 stock
8' length of clear fir (or medium
  hardwood) 1 × 3 stock
6' length of clear fir (or medium
  hardwood) 1 × 3 stock
Two dozen $\frac{5}{8}'' \times 5''$ corrugated fasteners
One hundred $1\frac{1}{2}''$ #8 plated flathead wood
  screws
Two hundred 1'' #8 plated flathead wood
  screws
Three dozen 1'' #6 roundhead wood
  screws
One dozen $\frac{3}{4}''$ #8 flathead wood screws
Two 36'' × $\frac{1}{2}''$ galvanized iron rods
Three dozen $\frac{7}{8}''$ #6 roundhead wood
  screws
$\frac{5}{8}'' \times 2\frac{1}{2}''$ iron corner bracket
$\frac{1}{2}''$ stainless hose clamp
18'' × 36'' sheet of aluminum flashing
  (.035'' to .065'' thickness)
Roll of pinstriping tape
One tube DAP tub-and-tile sealer
One quart oil-base gloss enamel paint
Four $\frac{3}{8}'' \times 1\frac{1}{2}''$ roundhead bolts with wing
  nuts

Six $\frac{1}{4}'' \times 1\frac{1}{4}''$ roundhead bolts, nut, and
  washers
One $\frac{1}{4}'' \times 2''$ hex-head bolt with three
  nuts
Sixteen $\frac{1}{4}'' \times 2\frac{1}{2}''$ round head bolts, nuts,
  and washers
Eight $\frac{1}{4}'' \times 1\frac{1}{2}''$ roundhead bolts, nuts, and
  washers
Two $\frac{3}{8}'' \times 6''$ hex-head bolts (threaded full-
  length)
Eleven $\frac{1}{4}'' \times 1''$ roundhead bolts, nuts, and
  washers
Ten $\frac{1}{2}''$ washers
Seven $\frac{5}{16}''$ nuts
One $\frac{5}{16}''$ cable clamp U-bolt
One $\frac{5}{16}'' \times 24''$ threaded rod

$\frac{1}{2}''$ *Galvanized Pipe Fittings:*
Ten four-hole floor-flange fittings
Five two-hole flange fittings
Eleven bushings ($\frac{1}{2}''$ male to $\frac{1}{4}''$ female)
Two T fittings
Four $1\frac{1}{4}''$ nipples
One $1\frac{1}{2}''$ nipple
Two 2'' nipples
One 6'' nipple
One coupler
One 24'' length of $\frac{1}{2}''$ pipe (threaded on
  one or both ends)

One 12″ length of $\frac{1}{2}$″ O.D. copper tubing

Bicycle Parts:
Four 16″ × 1$\frac{3}{4}$″ Schwinn bike tires (for
    S–7 tubular rims)
Two 36-tooth front chain-wheel sprockets
    (preferably Peugeot)
One 77″ bike chain to fit sprockets

For Removable Fire-Engine Back:
14″ × $\frac{5}{16}$″ threaded rod with 4 nuts and 4
    washers
Two 36″ × $\frac{5}{16}$″ dowels
36″ × $\frac{7}{8}$″ dowel
18″ × $\frac{7}{8}$″ dowel
4′ length of pine or fir 1 × 6 stock
4′ length of pine or fir 1 × 8 stock
6′ length of fir 1 × 2 stock
15′ length of garden hose

☐ *See color insert for completed project.*

If you happen to remember a favorite pedal car somewhere back in your early automotive past, then you know what an important piece of machinery it can be to the young "motorist." After all, a lot of long afternoons have been spent learning to back and fill around a crowded driveway, without scraping too much paint off Daddy's car. So we thought we'd make a classic pedal car with a movable seat, so the driver can get in many years behind the wheel without outgrowing the machine. In fact, the seat is so adjustable that even a six-footer can drive it (which he may, if gas prices keep rising).

The key parts to a classic old-style pedal car are the wheels, and unfortunately the traditional spoke wheel is getting hard to find. The kind we used several years ago is no longer in ready supply coast to coast, and the type used on garden carts are too expensive for a project such as this.

Figure 8–1 shows the general construc-tion layout of the car. The frame is made of clear fir 1 × 3s at the front to hold the front-wheel pivots (or kingpins). The body is made mostly of $\frac{1}{8}$″ plywood. Pedal power is transmitted from the bent $\frac{1}{2}$″ rod crank to one rear wheel via bicycle sprockets and a chain.

■ CUTTING, DRILLING, AND ASSEMBLY

☐ The Wheels

Building the wheels is a major part of the building time and cost, so if you can find 16″-diameter wheels that can be adapted to $\frac{3}{8}$″ and $\frac{1}{2}$″ axles for around $15 apiece, you might as well buy your wheels rather than making them. We've found that having fancy ball bearings doesn't make that much difference on a relatively low-efficiency machine like this that is used on flat surfaces at low speeds. Note that be-cause the Fire Truck has the tall look of an old car, it also has a fairly high center of gravity and should be used on flat ground with adult supervision. If you live in hilly terrain, fit a hand brake to scrub on the tire or ground for extra safety. Pedal cars should never be used where there is direct access to traffic, of course, to prevent any chance of tangling with adult drivers (we all know what they're like).

If you find wheels to buy, bear in mind that you'll need to bolt a bike sprocket to one rear wheel (or, if the wheel already has a sprocket, you'll need a matching one to bolt to the crank). We used a one-to-one ratio, which gives good power while keeping speeds from getting out of hand.

Figure 8–2 shows how to cut and as-semble the wheels. The first step is to draw the disks, as shown, on to a 4′ × 8′

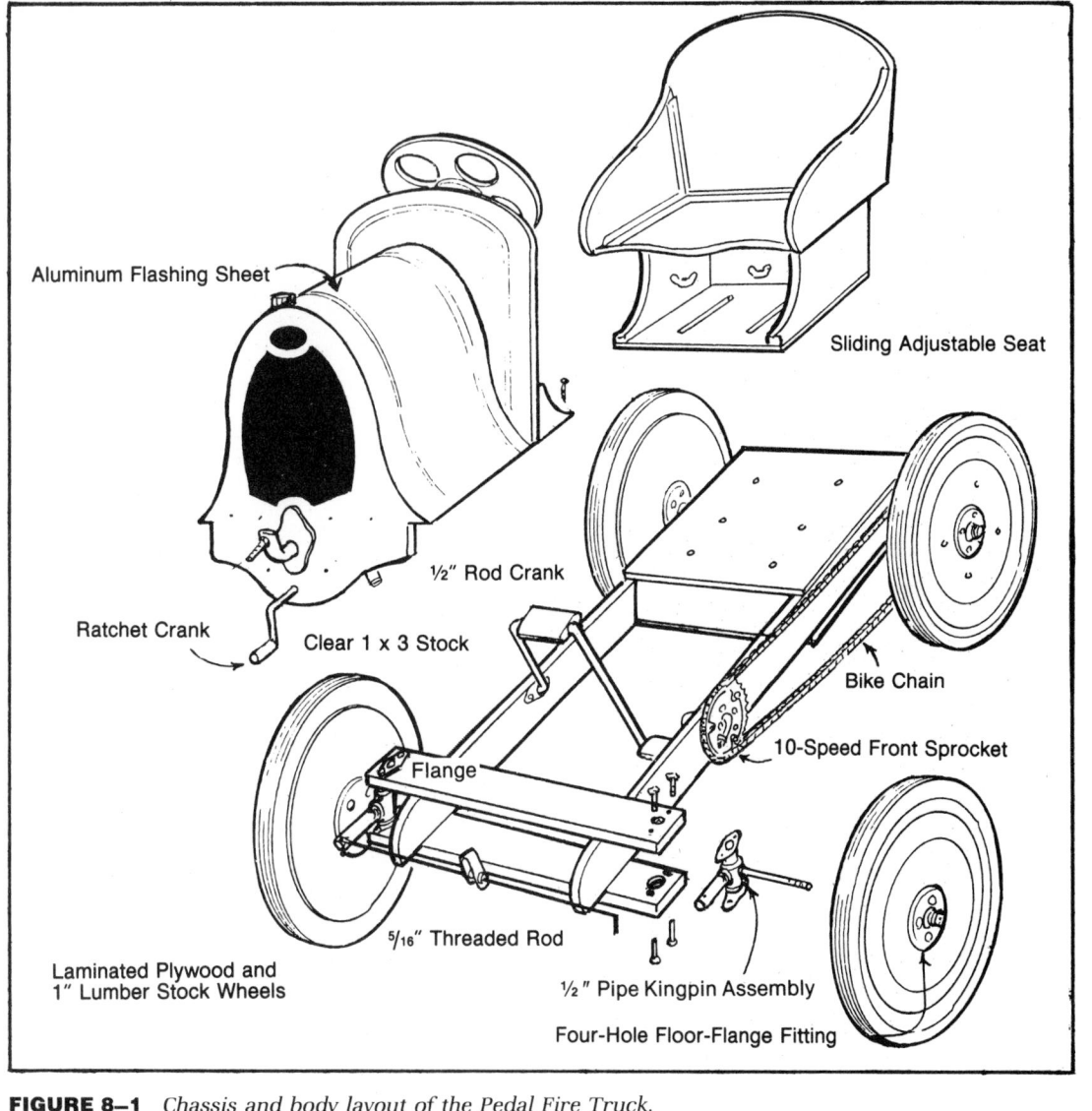

Aluminum Flashing Sheet

Sliding Adjustable Seat

½" Rod Crank

Ratchet Crank

Clear 1 x 3 Stock

Bike Chain

10-Speed Front Sprocket

Flange

Laminated Plywood and
1" Lumber Stock Wheels

⁵⁄₁₆" Threaded Rod

½" Pipe Kingpin Assembly

Four-Hole Floor-Flange Fitting

FIGURE 8—1 *Chassis and body layout of the Pedal Fire Truck.*

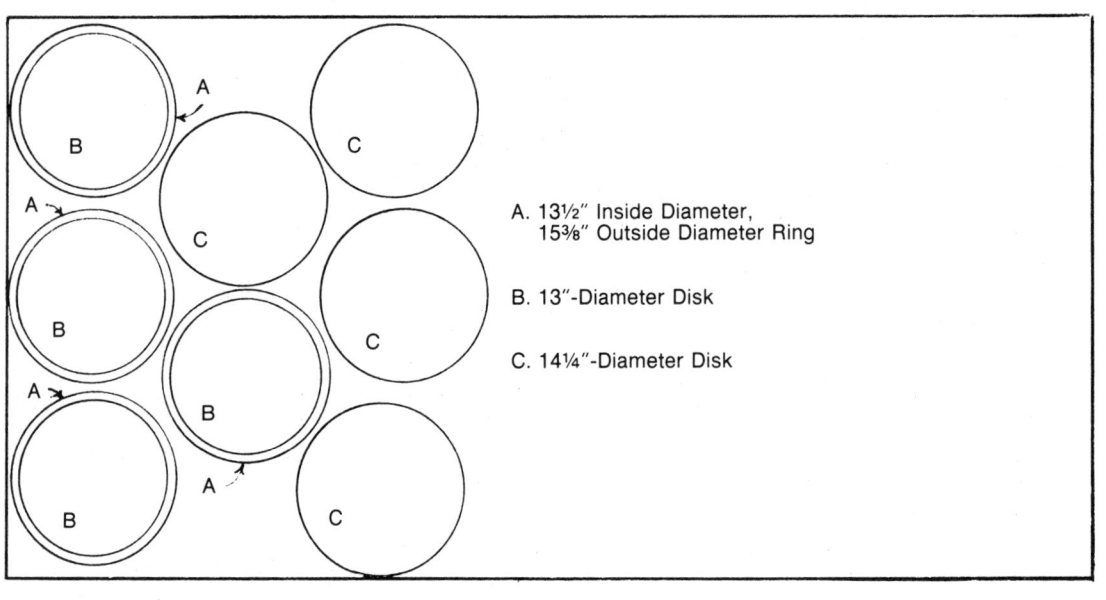

FIGURE 8–2 *Wheel layout for the 4′ × 8′ plywood panel.*

panel of $\frac{3}{8}''$ ACX plywood. We used two plywood disks, one plywood ring, and one disk made from #2 pine for each wheel.

To save plywood, draw the plywood rings outside each of the smaller plywood disks. To draw the circles, use a simple beam compass made from a $\frac{1}{4}'' \times \frac{3}{4}'' \times 12''$ stick. Drill a $\frac{1}{8}''$ hole through the stick about 1″ in from the end, then measure along the stick the distance of the radius of the circle to be drawn. Then drill another $\frac{1}{8}''$ hole. Stick a nail through one of the holes and hold it on the plywood as a center pivot. Insert the tip of a pencil through the other in order to draw an arc (see Fig. 8–3, top). Draw the outside of the four rings first. The diameter is $15\frac{3}{8}''$, so drill the holes in the beam compass $7\frac{11}{16}''$ apart and draw the circles as shown. (Keep an outward pressure on the pencil at all times when drawing the circles in order to keep the radius constant.)

The inside diameter of the rings is $13\frac{1}{2}''$, so drill holes in the beam compass $6\frac{3}{4}''$ apart; draw the insides of the rings using the same center pivot points as before. Next, draw the outside of the smaller plywood disk using the same center pivot points again with a $6\frac{1}{2}''$ radius. Draw the four larger disks close to the rings using a $7\frac{1}{8}''$-radius beam compass.

With a saber saw, cut out the disks and rings, starting with the smaller disks. Since there's a $\frac{1}{4}''$ difference between the disk and the inside of the ring, drill a few $\frac{1}{4}''$ holes in this gap, angling the drill to connect the adjacent holes to create a slot between the disk and the ring about $\frac{3}{8}''$ long. This will enable you to insert the saber saw and cut the disk. After cutting the four smaller disks, cut the rings, then the four larger disks.

The next step is to cut the four disks from the 1″ #2 pine. Since the widest stock we could find was 1″ × 12″ (about $11\frac{1}{4}''$ wide), we made the disks from two pieces of the 1 × 12, shown in Figure 8–3, right. Use one of the rings (the outside diameter) to draw the $15\frac{3}{8}''$-diameter arcs onto the 1 × 12. After marking around the ring, mark on the underside the side edge of the 1 × 12 where the ring overhangs. Next, align these edge marks on the underside of the ring with the opposite side edge of the 1 × 12; then draw the remaining portion of the disk onto the 1 × 12. Repeat these steps to draw both parts of all four disks onto the 1 × 12. Then cut out the disk parts with a saber saw and join the pairs with white glue and corrugated fasteners (see Fig. 8–3, top).

The cross section drawing in Figure 8–3 (bottom) shows how the bike tire wraps around the pine disk with ring attached and how it is clamped in place by the smaller plywood disk (next to the ring) and the larger disk on the other side of the wheel. To allow a smooth fit of the tire, round off the edges of the disks and rings where they touch the tire, as shown.

Round off the inner and the outer edges of the disks evenly with a Surform wood shaper. Then glue the rings on their unrounded surfaces and place them onto the pine disks, aligning the outer perimeters (with the grain of the plywood aligned at right angles to the grain of the pine disk), and screw the rings onto the disks. Space 1″ #8 plated flathead wood screws about 3″ to 4″ apart. Whenever attaching plywood to lumber stock, first drill a pilot hole for each screw using a combination pilot-hole bit/countersink tool, that can save a lot of time and frustration.

After attaching the rings to the pine disks, round off the opposite edges of the disks as shown in the cross-section view

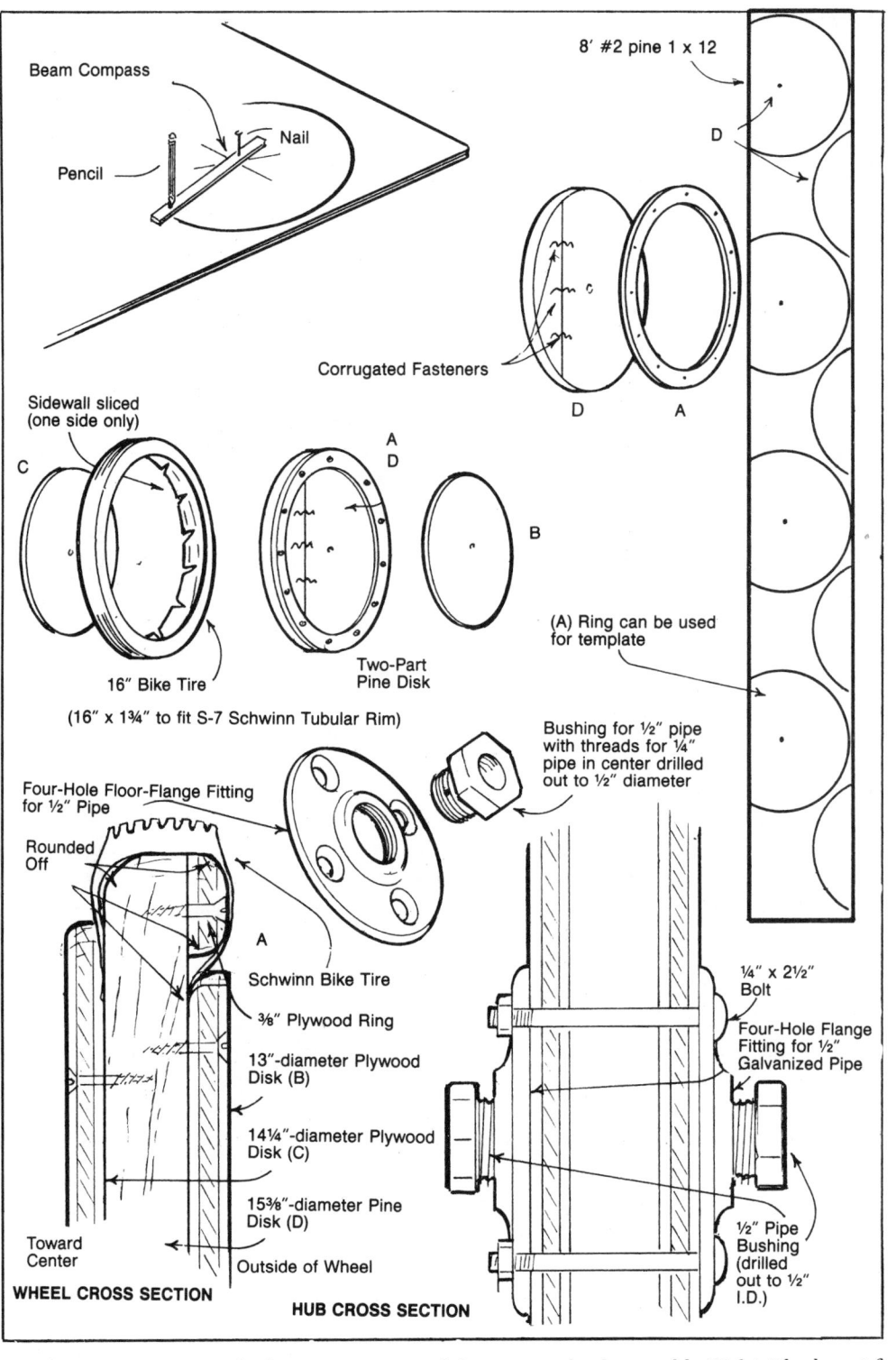

Beam Compass

Nail

Pencil

8' #2 pine 1 x 12

D

Corrugated Fasteners

D   A

Sidewall sliced
(one side only)

C

A
D

B

16" Bike Tire

(16" x 1¾" to fit S-7 Schwinn Tubular Rim)

Two-Part
Pine Disk

(A) Ring can be used
for template

Four-Hole Floor-Flange Fitting
for ½" Pipe

Rounded
Off

A

Schwinn Bike Tire

Bushing for ½" pipe
with threads for ¼"
pipe in center drilled
out to ½" diameter

⅜" Plywood Ring

13"-diameter Plywood
Disk (B)

14¼"-diameter Plywood
Disk (C)

15⅜"-diameter Pine
Disk (D)

Toward
Center

Outside of Wheel

WHEEL CROSS SECTION

¼" x 2½"
Bolt

Four-Hole Flange
Fitting for ½"
Galvanized Pipe

½" Pipe
Bushing
(drilled
out to ½"
I.D.)

HUB CROSS SECTION

FIGURE 8–3 Top left: *The beam compass and three-part wheel assembly.* Right: *The layout for the pine disks.* Bottom: *Cross section of the wheel and hub.*

in Figure 8–3 (bottom). Next, carefully measure and mark the centers of all four disks; drill through the center points of all the disks with a $\frac{1}{8}''$ bit. If you have a drill press or an alignment attachment for your drill, use these to get a good, straight-in hole. Otherwise, use a square to align the drill perpendicular to the wood before drilling.

The next step is to place the smaller disk against the pine disk inside the ring, then place the larger disk against the other side of the pine disk and insert a $\frac{1}{8}''$ drill through all three center holes to align the disks.

With the three aligned disks lying on a flat surface with the rings facing up, mark 8 screw placements 1″ in from the edge of the smaller disk and about $4\frac{1}{2}''$ apart. Center the smaller disk on the pine disk and drill pilot holes, then drive in the screws. Flip the joined disks over, centering the larger disk on the pine disk, and drive 8 screws to attach the larger disk on the other side of the pine disk. Space screws 1″ in from the perimeter of the disk and about 5″ apart. Next, mark a line across each disk and onto the pine disk/ring assembly to show how the disks are mounted. Then remove all screws and plywood disks, numbering the sets for easy reassembly.

To fit the tires onto the wheel disks, use 16″ × $1\frac{3}{4}''$ bike tires to fit on Schwinn S-7 tubular rims. Cut the inner bead on one side of each tire with a hacksaw, making cuts about $\frac{7}{8}''$ up one side wall of the tires and spacing the cuts about 3″ apart, as shown in Figure 8–3 (top left). Next, set the pine disk/ring assembly in the tire and pry the cut sidewall of the tire over the disk so that the side of the disk with the ring attached is *not* on the same side of the wheel as the cut sidewall.

Next, using the rings molded into the sidewalls as a guide to help center the tire on the disks, push the smaller disk down on the uncut sidewall. This forces it down over the inside of the plywood ring and clamps it to the pine disk. Re-align the smaller disk and drive screws in to mount the disk. Finally, align the larger disk with the screw holes and screw firmly in place to clamp the cut beading of the tire to the other side of the pine disk.

☐ The Hubs

Use $\frac{3}{8}''$ bolts for front axle stubs and $\frac{1}{2}''$ rod for a rear axle. Use four-hole galvanized iron pipe floor-flange fittings (for $\frac{1}{2}''$ pipe) for hubs, with one flange on the side of each wheel, through-bolt to sandwich the disks between the flanges.

To mount the hubs, draw a straight line through the center hole of a wheel, then draw another line through the center hole at right angles to the first line. Next, place one of the flanges over the center of the wheel so that the four bolt holes are directly over the lines. Then mark the positions of the four bolt holes on the wheel and drill straight through with a $\frac{1}{4}''$ bit. Drill all bolt holes in the flanges to make sure a $\frac{1}{4}''$ bolt will fit through. Then drill the center hole of the wooden wheel with a 1″ spade wood bit, following the direction of the $\frac{1}{8}''$ center hole through the disks.

Insert four $\frac{1}{4}''$ × $2\frac{1}{2}''$ roundhead bolts through the holes in one flange, through the holes in the wheel (on the side with the plywood ring), then through the holes in another flange mounted with its flat side against the other side of the wheel disk. Finger-tighten the nuts. Next, drill the $\frac{1}{2}''$ pipe bushings, leaving a $\frac{1}{2}''$ hole. Thread them firmly into the two attached flanges. Then insert a $\frac{1}{2}''$ rod or bolt

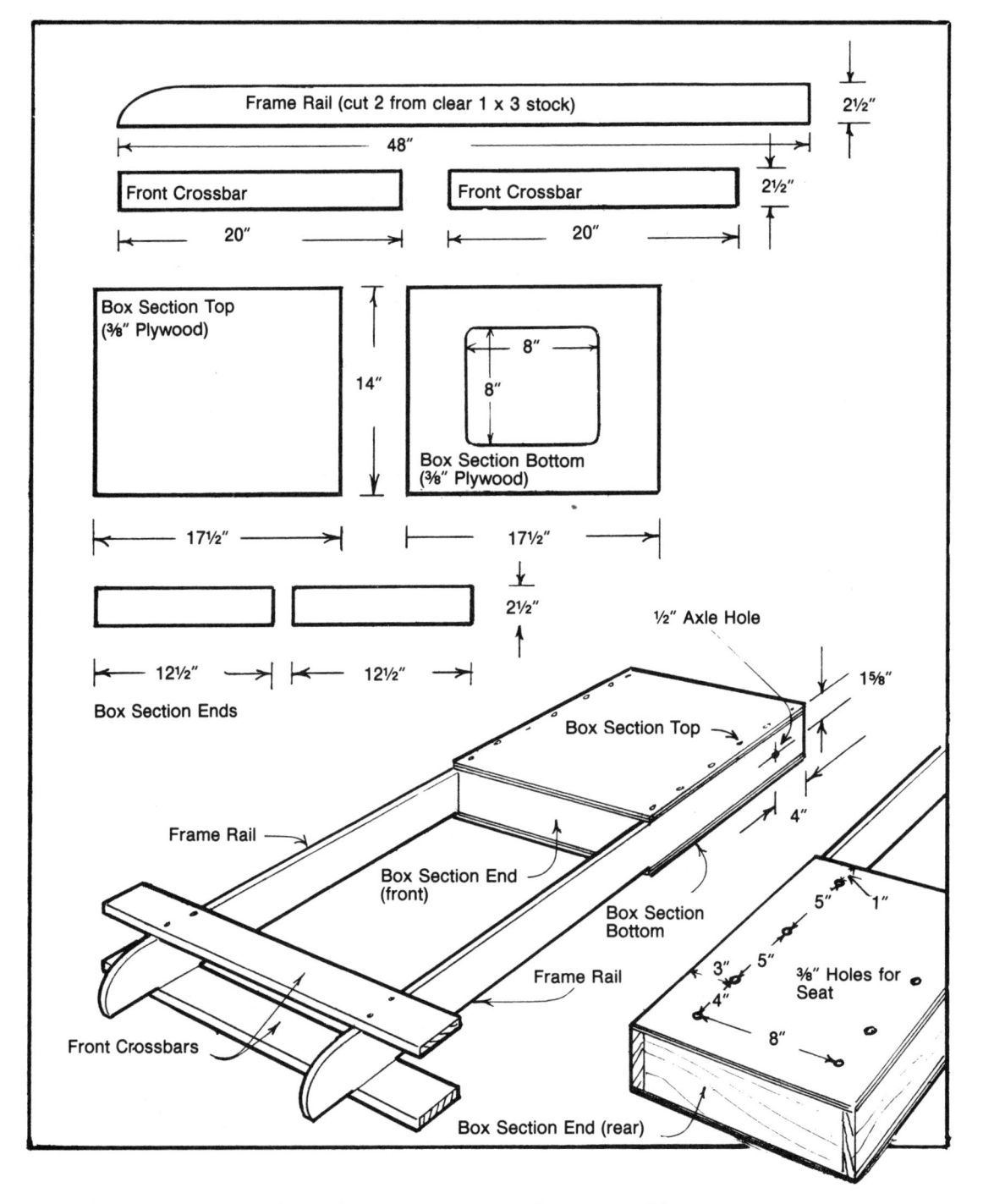

Frame Rail (cut 2 from clear 1 x 3 stock)

2½"

48"

2½"

Front Crossbar

Front Crossbar

2½"

20"

20"

Box Section Top
(⅜" Plywood)

14"

8"

8"

Box Section Bottom
(⅜" Plywood)

17½"

17½"

2½"

Box Section Ends

12½"

12½"

½" Axle Hole

1⅝"

Box Section Top

Frame Rail

Box Section End
(front)

Box Section
Bottom

4"

5"

1"

Frame Rail

3"

5"

⅜" Holes for
Seat

4"

Front Crossbars

8"

Box Section End (rear)

FIGURE 8–4 Top: *Chassis frame parts.* Bottom: *Chassis assembly.*

70 THE PEDAL FIRE TRUCK

through the two bushings to align them and run on the nuts on the four flange mounting bolts tight after spinning the wheel to check for wobble. Remove the $\frac{1}{2}''$ rod and drill the wheel hub through the center with the $\frac{1}{2}''$ bit for final alignment.

After repeating these steps to complete all four wheels, insert a short length of $\frac{1}{2}''$ (O.D.) soft copper tubing into the center holes of two of the wheels and cut the tubes off flush with the bushings (reaming the cut-off ends to remove burrs). The copper tubing serves as plain bearings in the front, while the rear wheels run on the bushings.

□ The Chassis and Steering Column

Figure 8–4 shows how the chassis frame is assembled and the steering kingpins attached. Cut two frame rails, as shown, from clear fir 1×3; also cut the two front crossbars and two box-section ends. Next, cut the box-section top and bottom panels from the $\frac{3}{8}''$ plywood, as shown.

Drive $1''$ screws through the box section top and into the center of the top of the frame rails, spacing the screws $4''$ apart and using glue to attach the box section top to the tops of the rails flush with the outside and rear ends of the rails. Flip this assembly over and mount the box-section bottom to the bottom of the rails in the same way. Drill $\frac{3}{8}''$ seat-mount holes through the top panel, as shown in Figure 8–4, along with $\frac{1}{2}''$ axle holes through each rail in the position shown.

Next, glue all four edges of the box-section ends, insert them in between the top and bottom box-section panels (at both the front and rear), then drive $1''$ screws about $4''$ apart through the top and bottom panels and into the top and bottom edges of the box-section ends.

Use a square to mark lines across the two front crossbars $3''$ in from both ends. Then align the rails and crossbars so that the front edge of each crossbar is $3''$ from the front tips of the rails; the outer sides of the rails should be $3''$ in from each end of the crossbars. Spread glue onto all joining surfaces and drill pilot holes, driving two $1\frac{1}{2}''$ #8 flathead plated wood screws through the crossbars and into the edges of the rails.

To make the kingpin assemblies (Fig. 8–5), first drill each $\frac{1}{8}''$ hole squarely through the center of the side of each galvanized $\frac{1}{2}''$ pipe T-fitting, checking with a square to keep the drill at right angles to the end holes in the T. Then drill the hole to $\frac{3}{8}''$ diameter. Cut a $6''$ length of threaded $\frac{1}{2}''$ pipe in half with a hacksaw (or a pipe cutter, if you have one), and drill a $\frac{5}{16}''$ hole through each half, with its center $\frac{3}{8}''$ in from the cut end. Thread these pipes into the side hole of each T and tighten firmly with $\frac{5}{16}''$ holes aligned with the through-holes of the T.

To attach the kingpin assemblies to the crossbars, drill $1''$ holes through the ends of each crossbar, with the centers of the holes on the center lines of the crossbars and $1''$ in from the ends. Next, cut away the top edges of the holes in the top crossbar and the bottom edges of the holes in the bottom crossbars so that two-hole $\frac{1}{2}''$ pipe flanges (or "waste nuts") can be positioned as shown in Figure 8–5, with their raised centers extending into the rounded-out $1''$ holes and their mounting plates flat against the crossbars. Then, using the flanges as positioning guides, drill through the bolt holes in the flanges and on through the crossbars with a $\frac{1}{4}''$ bit, aligning the holes $1''$ in from the ends of the crossbars.

Next, thread $1\frac{1}{4}''$-long nipples of $\frac{1}{2}''$ pipe lightly into each of the four two-hole

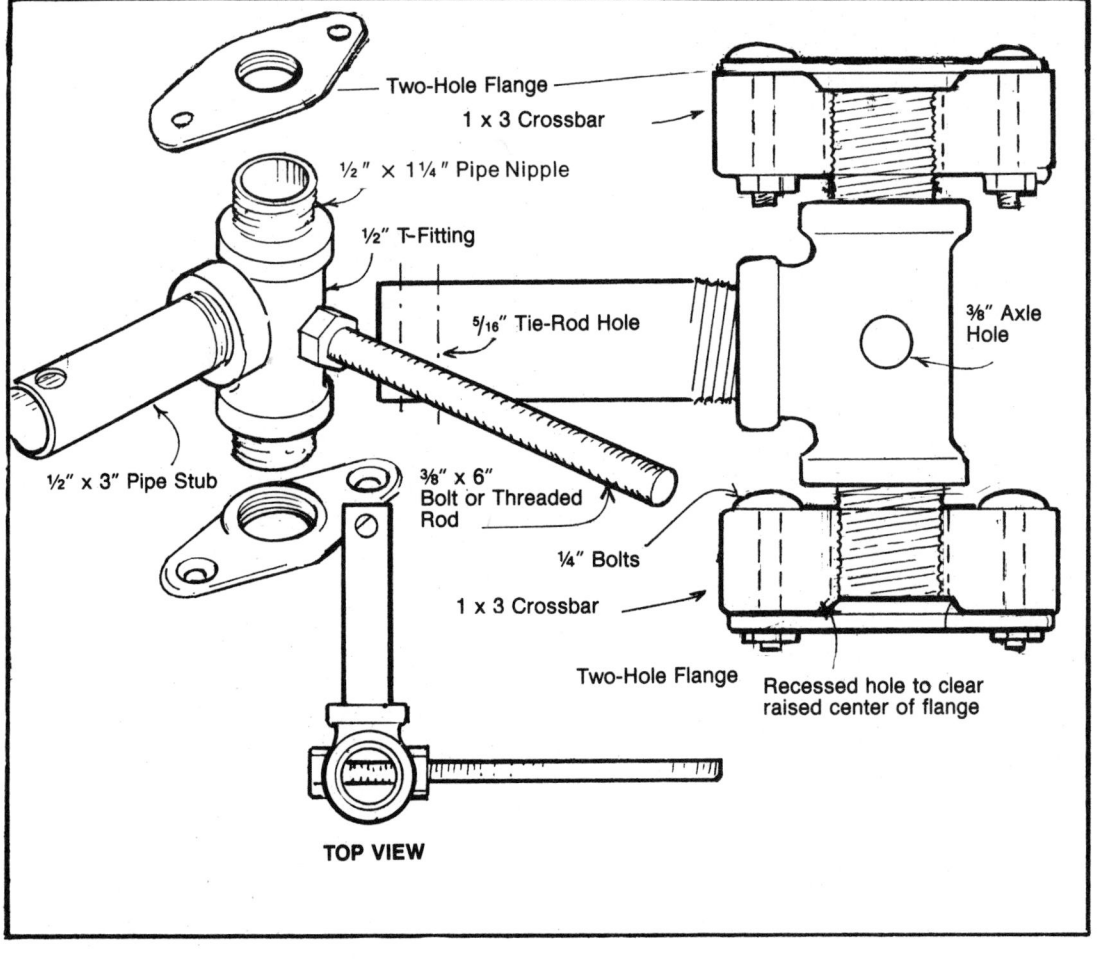

Two-Hole Flange

1 x 3 Crossbar

½" × 1¼" Pipe Nipple

½" T-Fitting

⁵⁄₁₆" Tie-Rod Hole

³⁄₈" Axle Hole

½" x 3" Pipe Stub

³⁄₈" x 6" Bolt or Threaded Rod

¼" Bolts

1 x 3 Crossbar

Two-Hole Flange

Recessed hole to clear raised center of flange

TOP VIEW

FIGURE 8–5 *Kingpin assembly.*

flanges (after applying grease to all threads). Insert the other end of each nipple through the 1″ holes in the crossbars. With the T-fittings positioned between the crossbars (Fig. 8–5), thread the nipples into the T-fittings top and bottom, then insert the $\frac{1}{4}″ \times 1\frac{1}{2}″$ roundhead bolts down through the top flanges and crossbars. Insert the remaining bolts through the bottom crossbar with flanges underneath; tighten the nuts securely, but not so tight as to prevent the free pivoting of the kingpin. If a nipple refuses to turn easily in a flange, remove the parts and thread the nipple extra hard into the flange so that it will turn more easily when backed out.

To mount the front axle nipples, thread a $\frac{3}{8}″ \times 6″$ hex-head bolt full-length out through the hole in each T-fitting, then run a nut all the way up to the side of the fitting. (If you can't find hex-head bolts, use a $\frac{3}{8}″$ threaded rod with nuts on both sides of the T-fitting.) With a hefty wrench, tighten this nut on either side of the fitting as hard as you can against the T. To attach the front wheels, grease the $\frac{3}{8}″$ bolt, run on a wide washer, slip on the wheel, run on another wide washer then thread on a nut. Tighten the nut, back it off one-quarter turn, and drill a $\frac{3}{8}″$ hole through the nut and the axle bolt. Secure the wheel with a cotter pin.

After oiling the rear axle hole thoroughly, cut a 26″ length of $\frac{1}{2}″$ galvanized iron rod, drill $\frac{1}{8}″$ cotter-pin holes $\frac{3}{16}″$ in from each end, and insert the rod through the axle holes in the frame rails. Then slip on wide washers, the 2″ galvanized pipe nipples, another wide washer, the rear wheels (greased), and another wide washer. Secure with cotter pins as shown in Figure 8–7, bottom.

For a tie-rod, use a 22″ length of $\frac{5}{16}″$ threaded rod. To make a slip joint connecting the steering column with the tie-rod, bend over a $\frac{5}{8}″ \times \frac{1}{8}″ \times 2\frac{1}{2}″$ (on a side) predrilled iron corner bracket (a $\frac{5}{8}″ \times \frac{1}{8}″ \times 5″$ strap could be substituted), as shown in Figure 8–6. Bend the strap bracket into a U shape with about $\frac{5}{16}″$ between the arms of the strap. Drill $\frac{5}{16}″$ hole through both arms of the strap, with the centers of the holes about $\frac{1}{2}″$ from the ends of the straps.

Insert a $\frac{5}{16}″$ nut between the holes in the strap, then thread on the rod until the nut is positioned in the center of the threaded rod. Next, thread a nut onto each end of the rod and tighten them against the outsides of the strap on both sides.

To align the front wheels, carefully measure the distance between the centers of the kingpin flanges. Mark this distance, minus $\frac{5}{16}″$ on the threaded rod, and bend the rod over 90 degrees, using a vise and hammer to pound the rod into a squared bend. After inserting the ends through the $\frac{5}{16}″$ holes in the $\frac{1}{2}″$ pipe stubs sticking forward from the T-fittings, check the wheel alignment with a measuring tape at the front and rear wheels. Make any adjustments by altering the bends of the rod and cut the bent portions off about $1\frac{1}{2}″$ long. Thread a nut and locknut onto the tie-rod ends and tighten against each other to allow free pivoting when steering.

To make a steering wheel/steering column assembly, draw the shape of the steering wheel onto $\frac{3}{8}″$ plywood, using a beam compass to draw the outer circle. Mark straight lines at right angles across the center point, then mark the centers of the four $2\frac{1}{4}″$-hole cutouts. Drill these holes with a $2\frac{1}{4}″$-diameter hole-saw attachment for the power drill, then cut out the wheel with a saber saw, as shown in Figure 8–6.

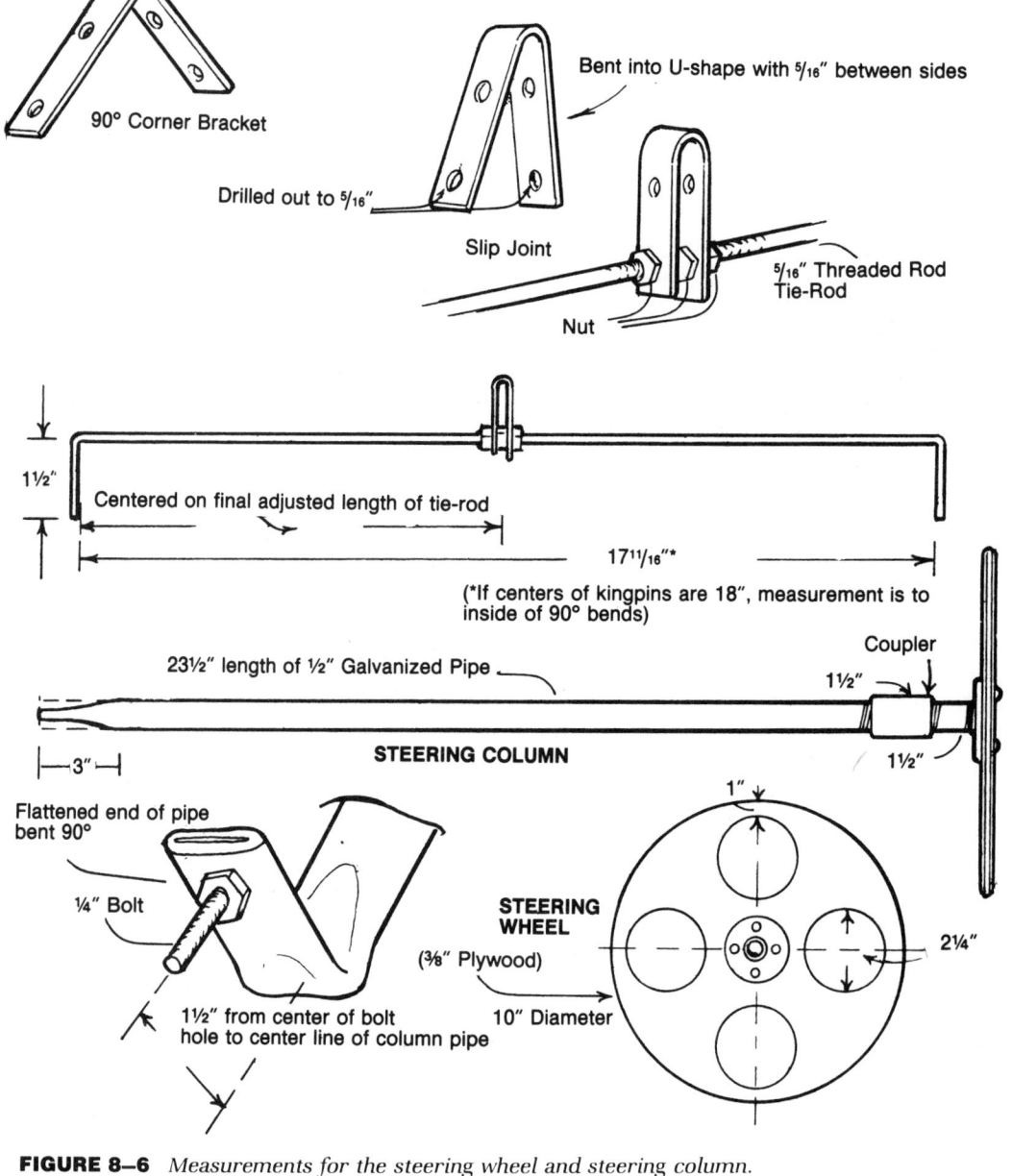

90° Corner Bracket

Drilled out to 5/16"

Bent into U-shape with 5/16" between sides

Slip Joint

Nut

5/16" Threaded Rod
Tie-Rod

1½"

Centered on final adjusted length of tie-rod

17¹¹/₁₆"*

(*If centers of kingpins are 18", measurement is to
inside of 90° bends)

Coupler

1½"

23½" length of ½" Galvanized Pipe

STEERING COLUMN

1½"

|—3"—|

Flattened end of pipe
bent 90°

¼" Bolt

1½" from center of bolt
hole to center line of column pipe

STEERING
WHEEL

(3/8" Plywood)

10" Diameter

1"

2¼"

FIGURE 8–6 *Measurements for the steering wheel and steering column.*

Place a four-hole $\frac{1}{2}''$ floor-flange pipe fitting over the center of the wheel; mark the positions of the four bolt holes, drill them with a $\frac{1}{4}''$ bit, and bolt the flange onto the bottom side of the steering wheel using a $\frac{1}{4}'' \times 1\frac{1}{4}''$ roundhead bolt inserted from the top.

Thread a $1\frac{1}{2}'' \times \frac{1}{2}''$ nipple into the flange, then thread a $1\frac{1}{2}''$-long coupler onto this. Tighten both with a large pipe wrench. We tightened all joints in the steering column as tightly as we could with a pipe wrench and haven't had any problems with the column unscrewing while steering. However, drilling into each joint and securing with a cotter pin would add an extra safety margin.

To make the bottom part of the steering column, cut a $\frac{1}{2}''$ pipe threaded on one (or both) ends to $23\frac{1}{2}''$. Next, place the cut-off end on a firm base and pound it flat along the last $3''$ with a hammer (see Fig. 8–6). After flattening the end, bend the pipe $2''$ from the end to 90 degrees, then drill a $\frac{1}{4}''$ hole through the flattened end $1\frac{1}{2}''$ from the center of the column. Insert a $\frac{1}{4}'' \times 2''$ hex-head bolt out through the hole, run on a nut, and tighten securely.

The steering column is held in place by the $\frac{3}{8}''$ plywood doublers (A and B in Fig. 8–7) when attached to the $\frac{3}{8}''$ plywood grill and dashboard. Cut out all parts (to be assembled in a later step) with a saber saw, being extra careful when cutting out the line between the grill and dashboard (see Fig. 8–7).

☐ The Pedals

Use a single $\frac{1}{2}''$ galvanized iron rod for the crankshaft of the car, marking the bends shown at left in Figure 8–8. We've made a number of these cranks, and they're not quite as hard to cope with as they look, although bending a crank *will* work up a good sweat. The trick is to use a vise and an old 3'- or 4'-length of $\frac{1}{2}''$ galvanized pipe for a bending handle.

Mark the spot on the rod to show the beginning of the inside of each bend, placing the $\frac{1}{2}''$ pipe over the rod with its end about $\frac{1}{16}''$ above the mark. Place the rod in the vise about $\frac{1}{16}''$ below the mark. Start the bend, then remeasure and complete after marking any last-minute adjustments. After each bend, sight the crank across its plane (like looking across a plate edgewise), and make adjustments to remove any side bend, with the pipe-bending handle, the vise, or a hammer.

After bending both throws of the crank (F in Figure 8–8) start making provisions for mounting the sprocket (without having to weld) by drilling out a male $\frac{1}{2}''$ pipe bushing to $\frac{1}{2}''$ diameter on the inside. Slip this bushing onto the end of the crank with its threads facing the end of the crank (Fig. 8–8 center) and make the final 90-degree bend, starting $3\frac{3}{4}''$ from the previous bend. Cut the last length of crank to $1\frac{3}{4}''$ long.

Use a 36-tooth sprocket from a Peugeot ten-speed (this is the smaller chain wheel from the two at the crank of the bicycle). The exact size of the sprockets used isn't as important as the fact that they're exactly (or approximately) the same size (and use the same type of chain, of course).

To mount the sprocket to the crank, cut a disk of scrap $\frac{1}{2}''$ ACX plywood to a diameter of about $1''$ less than the overall diameter (including teeth) of the sprocket (Fig. 8–9). Next, drill a $\frac{1}{2}''$ hole through the center point. Then slip a four-hole $\frac{1}{2}''$ floor-flange pipe fitting onto the end of the crank, around the last corner; thread it tightly onto the bushing. Slip the plywood disk onto the crank end and force it around the last bend. With the disk sit-

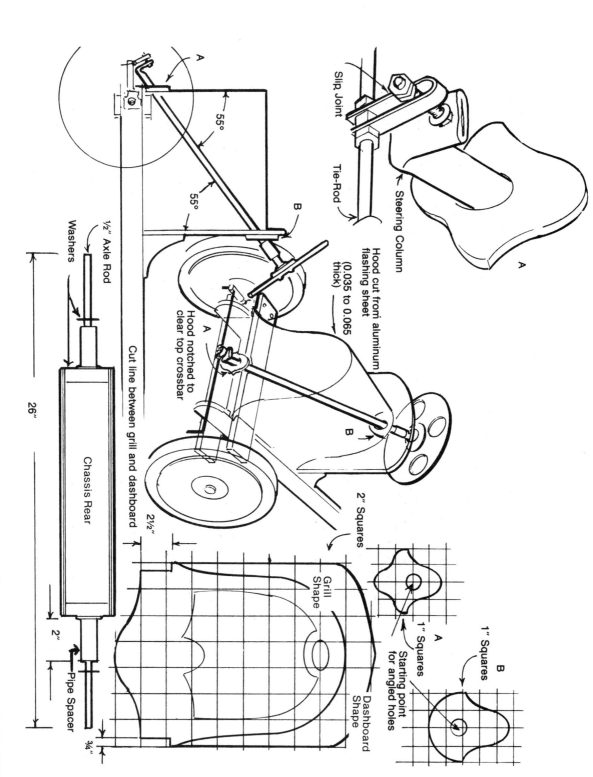

FIGURE 8–7 Assembly of the steering wheel/steering column and the pattern for the radiator and grill.

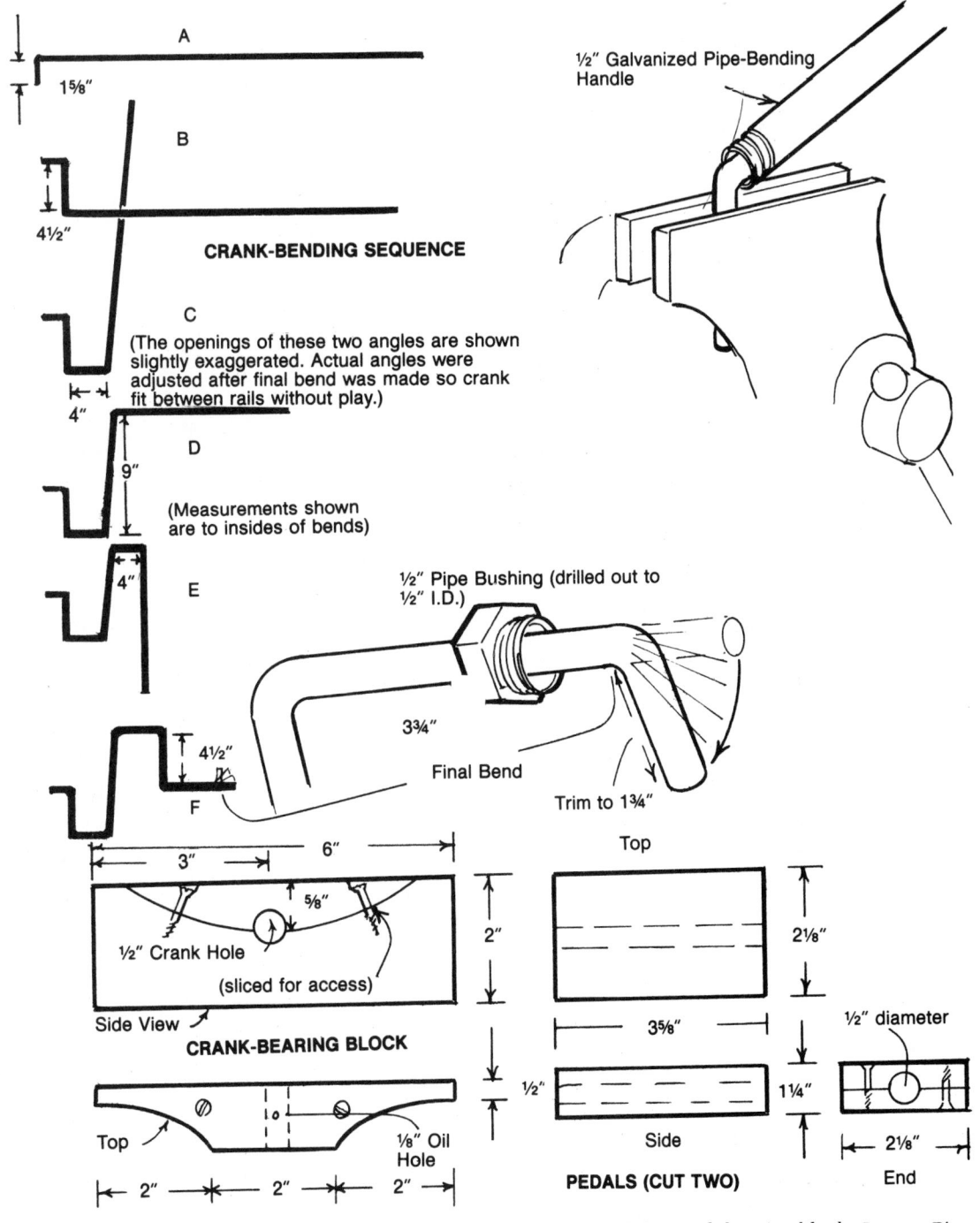

A

1⅝"

B

4½"

CRANK-BENDING SEQUENCE

C

(The openings of these two angles are shown slightly exaggerated. Actual angles were adjusted after final bend was made so crank fit between rails without play.)

4"

D

9"

(Measurements shown are to insides of bends)

4"

E

4½"

F

½" Galvanized Pipe-Bending Handle

½" Pipe Bushing (drilled out to ½" I.D.)

3¾"

Final Bend

Trim to 1¾"

6"

3"

5/8"

2"

½" Crank Hole

(sliced for access)

Side View

CRANK-BEARING BLOCK

Top

⅛" Oil Hole

2"   2"   2"

Top

2⅛"

3⅝"

½"

Side

1¼"

½" diameter

2⅛"

End

PEDALS (CUT TWO)

FIGURE 8–8 Top left: *Crank-bending sequence.* Bottom left: *Crank-bearing block.* Center: *Pipe bushing.* Top right: *Pipe-bending handle.* Bottom right: *Pedals.*

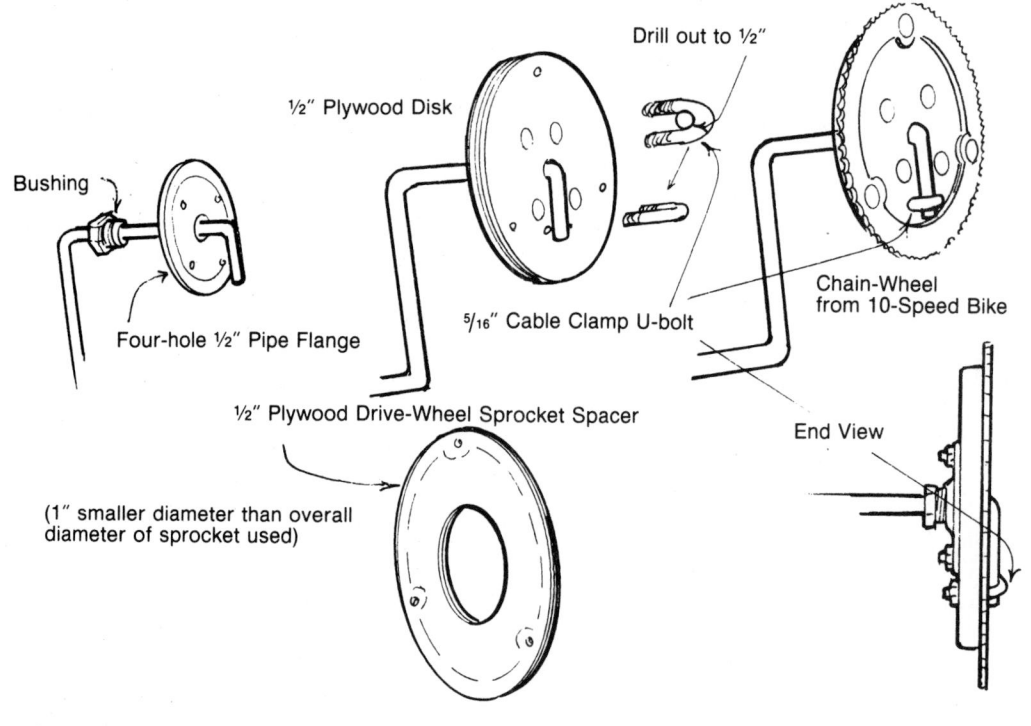

Bushing

½" Plywood Disk

Drill out to ½"

Four-hole ½" Pipe Flange

⁵⁄₁₆" Cable Clamp U-bolt

Chain-Wheel
from 10-Speed Bike

½" Plywood Drive-Wheel Sprocket Spacer

End View

(1" smaller diameter than overall
diameter of sprocket used)

FIGURE 8–9 *Assembly of the bicycle sprocket and chain on the crankshaft.*

ting up against the flange, drill $\frac{1}{4}''$ holes through the bolt holes in the flange and on through the disk. Bolt the flange firmly to the disk with $1'' \times \frac{1}{4}''$ roundhead bolts, using wide washers between the nuts and the plywood.

Next, drill out a $\frac{5}{16}''$ U-bolt from a cable clamp to an inside diameter of $\frac{1}{2}''$ (at the bend) and slip it onto the end of the crank so that the ends of the U-bolt sit against the plywood disk. Mark the position of the ends of the U-bolt on the disk, then drill $\frac{5}{16}''$ holes through (to miss the flange on the other side). Attach the U-bolt to the crank and bolt tight with wide washers against the plywood. Center the sprocket on the disk and drill $\frac{1}{4}''$ holes through the mounting-bolt holes of the sprocket and on through the disk. Bolt the sprocket to the disk with wide washers against the plywood, as shown in Figure 8–9, lower right.

To provide a wide bearing for the crank as it passes through the frame rail, cut a wooden block bearing, as shown in Figure 8–8, lower left, from clear fir (although mahogany or hardwood might even be better). Cut the block to shape (the curves are just for looks and could be left out) as shown, then drill a $\frac{1}{2}''$ hole squarely through the side and a $\frac{1}{8}''$ oil hole down from the top. With the saber saw, cut the curved slice through the block. (Its shape isn't important so long as it cuts through the center of the hole and allows easy positioning.) Replace the cut-off top, then drill $1\frac{1}{2}''$ screw holes down from the top and screw the top and bottom together. Next, redrill the $\frac{1}{2}''$ hole to restore its original diameter (after the slice has been cut).

Before mounting the crank, cut and drill, then slice and redrill (in the same way), to make two pedals from blocks of medium to hardwood as shown in Figure

8–8 at bottom. Mount these to the crank and oil the wood bearings (Fig. 8–10).

The sprocket end of the crank can be mounted facing either left or right, according to any body-finish details you may have in mind. To mount the crank, drill $\frac{1}{2}''$ holes through both frame rails, with the centers of the holes $\frac{5}{8}''$ down from the top and $27\frac{1}{2}''$ forward of the centers of the rear axle holes (see Fig. 8–10). Next, cut out the wood above the crank hole through the frame side near the sprocket end so that the crank can be dropped down into what is now a notch with a rounded bottom.

To form a pivot bearing for the other end of the crank (near the first 90-degree corner bend), drill out another $\frac{1}{2}''$ male pipe-fitting bushing and thread it firmly into a two-hole flange. Insert the end of the crank through the bushing and then into the $\frac{1}{2}''$ crank hole in the rail opposite the sprocket end of the crank. Drill $\frac{1}{4}''$ holes through the bolt holes of this flange and on through the rail, then bolt the flange to the frame rail with $\frac{1}{4}'' \times 1\frac{1}{2}''$ bolts. With the crank resting in its pivots, spin it to see if any warping has crept into the original bending, then rebend the crank as needed, especially at the sprocket end, to remove any whip or wobble.

Next, place the bottom crank bearing block between the frame and the sprocket, attaching it to the frame under the crank with screws and glue. Attach the top of the block bearing onto the bottom. Before attaching the crank, however, check for end play by slipping a washer on from the end of the crank and running it all the way up to the inside of the rail at the sprocket end. Position this end-play washer bearing with a stainless-steel hose clamp and tighten it onto the crank to prevent the crank from sliding toward

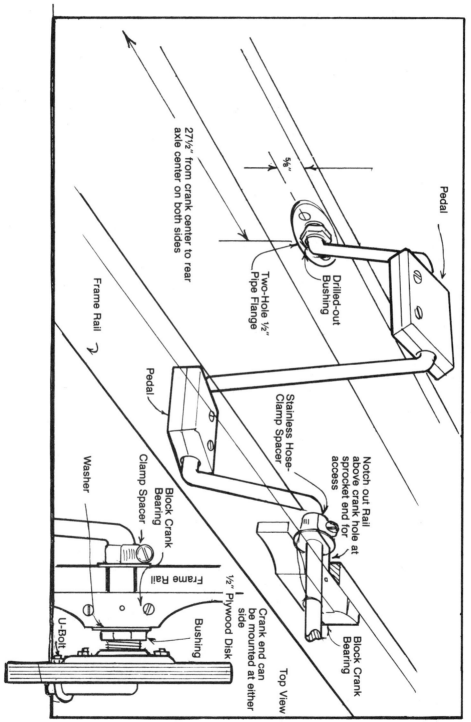

FIGURE 8—10 *Assembly of the pedals and crankshaft on the frame rails.*

Pedal

⁵⁄₈"

Drilled-out
Bushing

Two-Hole ½"
Pipe Flange

27½" from crank center to rear
axle center on both sides

Frame Rail

Pedal

Stainless Hose-
Clamp Spacer

Notch out Rail
above crank hole at
sprocket end for
access

Block Crank
Bearing

Washer

Clamp Spacer

Block Crank
Bearing

Frame Rail

½" Plywood Disk

Bushing

Crank end can
be mounted at either
side

Top View

U-Bolt

the sprocket end. Finally, insert the end of the crank into the bushing on the rail, screw the bearing-block top down, and oil all bearings.

Attach a complete two-sprocket bicycle chain-wheel to the rear wheel with a $\frac{3}{8}''$ disk of plywood sandwiched between the larger sprocket and the wheel, making sure that the alignment of the chain is straight and parallel to the frame rail. Use the double-sprocket chain wheel to set the smaller sprocket out from the spacer disk so that the side of the chain clears the disk. Cut the $\frac{3}{8}''$ plywood disk with the same radius as the outside of the larger sprocket. Then draw a circle exactly the same radius as the four-hole flange on the drive wheel. Cut out this inner circle with a saber saw using a $\frac{1}{2}''$ hole for a starting point. Place the cut-out disk onto the inside suface of the drive wheel, then center the sprockets carefully on the disk. Drill $\frac{1}{4}''$ holes through the sprocket-mount holes, through the disk, and on through the wheel. Mount the sprockets with three $\frac{1}{4}'' \times 2\frac{1}{2}''$ bolts. Tighten all nuts on the chassis and running gear using Loctite to secure the nuts to the threads, then trim all exposed ends of bolts with a hacksaw and file them smooth.

Use an inexpensive chain-breaker tool (a center punch can be substituted) to cut the chain to length and rejoin the ends ($\frac{1}{2}''$ to $\frac{3}{4}''$ play in the middle is about right). Run the chain onto the sprockets to connect the drive wheel and crank.

As with a lot of newborn rolling stock, there's usually a bit of fine tuning needed at first to get rid of minor bugs and teething problems. Bearings usually need to be loosened up by running with no load for a while; sprockets may need to be aligned with shims or washers to prevent derailing. A chain that slackens and then tightens means an off-center sprocket (or

a little whip or sidebend in the crank). Make sure that the space between the sprocket on the drive wheel and the frame is equal to the space between the crank sprocket and the frame. (Adjust the rear-wheel spacers on the axles to align.) Any joining of metal and wooden parts in a working machine requires some readjustment at first as the metal parts seat themselves on the wood. And some nuts may need to be tightened.

☐ The Body

Cut out the remaining body parts from the 4′ × 8′ × $\frac{3}{8}''$ plywood panel, as shown in Figure 8–11. To make the hood assembly, cut a 17″ × 34$\frac{3}{8}''$ rectangle of aluminum flashing and draw a line across its center (or top point when mounted). Wrap it over the top of the grill shape and, starting at the top center, drill $\frac{1}{16}''$ holes through the aluminum and into the center lamination of the plywood. Since small variations in curves will alter the size of the aluminum panel needed, we measured the actual length of the grill curve to be covered, using a measuring tape, before trimming and fitting on the aluminum. Space the holes $\frac{3}{16}''$ back from the front edge of the aluminum and 2″ apart.

After drilling each hole, work from the center down both sides, drive in a 1″ #6 roundhead screw to secure the aluminum to the edge of the plywood. After screwing the front edge to the edge of the grill, repeat the steps to screw the back edge to the inside curve of the dashboard flush at the rear. Next, drive two screws in through the front of the dashboard and into the triangular corner braces cut from 1″ stock and mounted on the back side of the dashboard on both sides, flush at the bottom, as shown in Figure 8–12,

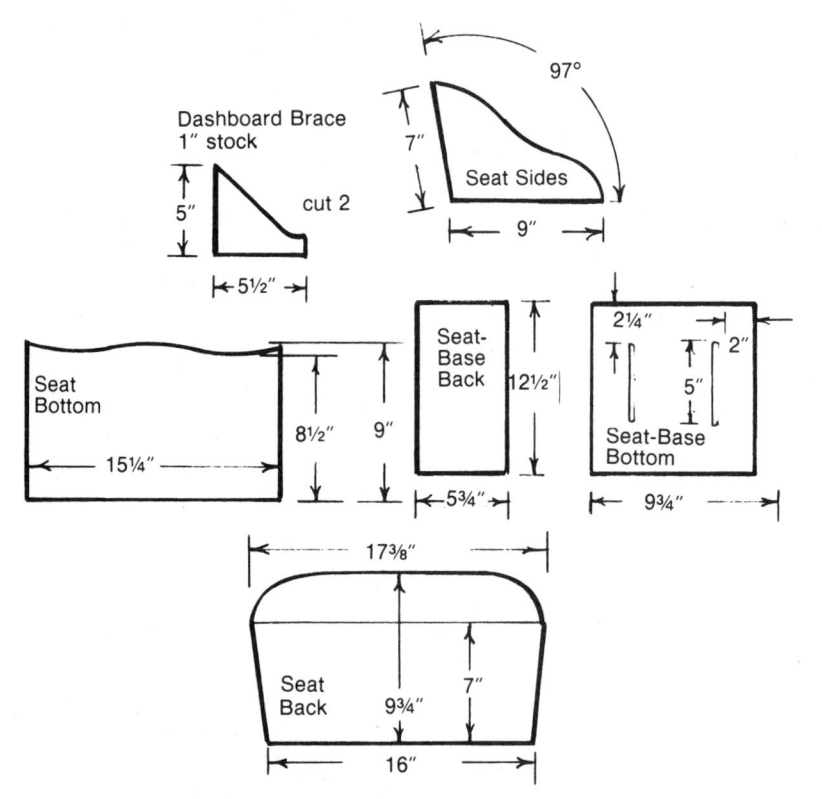

FIGURE 8–11 *Seat components for the Pedal Fire Truck. Note $\frac{3}{8}'' \times 5''$ slots for seat bolts, allowing positioning adjustments.*

top left. Trim a $1'' \times 2\frac{1}{2}''$ rectangular notch in the bottom edges of the aluminum just behind the grill on both sides so that the hood metal will clear the top cross bar, using tin snips.

■ ASSEMBLY

To mount the hood to the chassis frame, place the hood assembly on the frame tops, then drive screws (about six) in through the front of the grill and into the front edges of the frame crosspieces. Next, drive $1\frac{1}{2}''$ screws down through each triangular brace behind the dashboard and into the top edges of the frame rails, about $1''$ forward of the rear of the brace. To align the front of the braces with the frame rails, drill $\frac{1}{4}''$ holes through the rails $1''$ back of the dashboard and $\frac{1}{2}''$ down from the frame tops. Then bolt them through from the inside with $\frac{1}{4}'' \times 1\frac{1}{4}''$ roundhead bolts (with wide washers on both sides to clamp the brace parallel to the frame-rail top).

To mount the steering column, use a $\frac{7}{8}''$ spade bit to drill the steering-column holes through the column mounts cut from $\frac{3}{8}''$ plywood (shown as A and B in Figure 8–7), approximating the 55-degree angle shown in the side view at the bottom left in Figure 8–7. Next, screw the rear mount (B) and glue it to the rear of the dashboard, with the top of the pivot hole flush with the bottom of the aluminum hood; center it and attach with three $\frac{3}{4}''$ #8 wood screws. Draw a line across the front of the grill with a straight edge, level with the tops of the frame rails. At the center, drill a $\frac{7}{8}''$ hole in through the front of the grill, angling up to the rear steering-column hole. (This hole will cut a slight groove through the

front top edge of the top frame crossbar.) Align the bearing doubler (A in Figure 8–7) with this hole and attach it with $\frac{3}{4}''$ screws. Then rebore the hole on the same angle to align the hole in (A) with the hole in the grill.

Insert the steering column up through the column holes from the front. Then thread and tighten the steering wheel, spacer, and coupler onto the rear top end of the column. Drill holes for cotter pins if you want to be even safer. Finally, loosen the strap slip-joint nuts on the tie-rod, slip the strap over the $\frac{1}{4}''$ bolt at the bottom of the steering column, tighten locknuts on both sides of the tie-rod firmly against the strap, locking it in position at right angles to the steering column, as shown in Figure 8–7 left. Trim the tops of the frame rails a little with a chisel to clear the tie-rod when the steering is at full lock left or right.

Assemble the seat, as shown in Figure 8–12 at top, first attaching $\frac{3}{4}'' \times \frac{3}{4}''$ gussets around the bottom of the seat bottom with screws and glue. Attach the seat sides and rear to the gussets, flush at the bottom. Push out the tops of the sides and rear at a slight angle, aligning the corner edges; screw the gussets (with rounded-off tops) in the corners between the sides and the rear pieces, using glue at all joints.

Screw the plywood bottom panel of the seat base on the bottom edges of the seat-base sides. Then screw the plywood rear panel to the rear edges of the seat-base sides flush at the top and sides. Center the seat bottom on the seat base and drive screws down through the bottom and into the top edges of the seat-base sides. Push $\frac{3}{8}'' \times 1\frac{1}{2}''$ roundhead bolts up through one set of seat-bolt holes and set the slots in the seat base

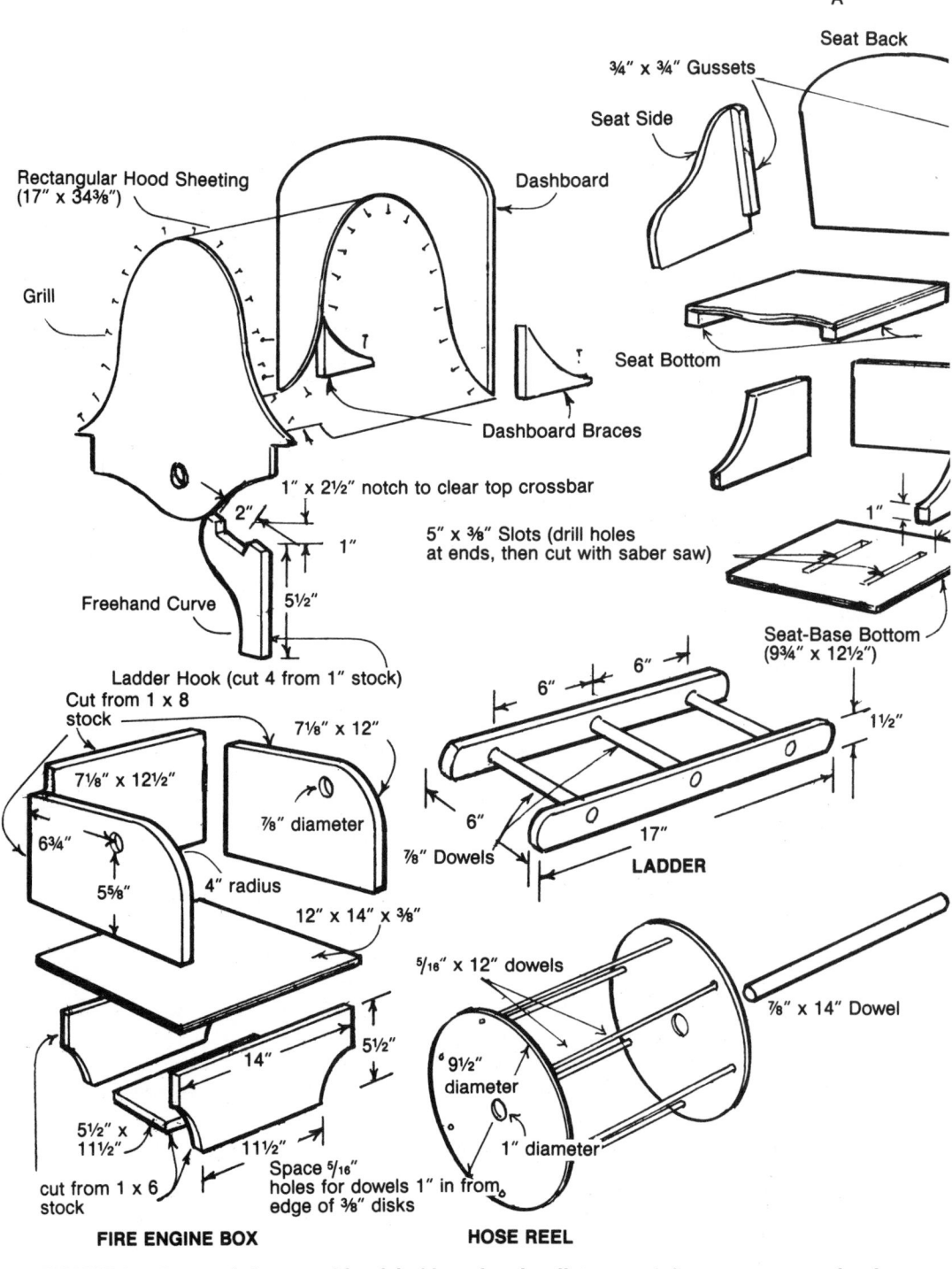

A

SEAT

Seat Back

¾" x ¾" Gussets

Seat Side

Rectangular Hood Sheeting
(17" x 34⅜")

Dashboard

Grill

Seat Bottom

Dashboard Braces

Seat-Base Bottom
(9¾" x 12½")

1" x 2½" notch to clear top crossbar

2"

1"

5" x ⅜" Slots (drill holes
at ends, then cut with saber saw)

1"

Freehand Curve

5½"

Ladder Hook (cut 4 from 1" stock)
Cut from 1 x 8
stock

7⅛" x 12"

6"

6"

7⅛" x 12½"

1½"

⅞" diameter

6¾"

5⅝"

4" radius

6"

17"

12" x 14" x ⅜"

⅞" Dowels

LADDER

5/16" x 12" dowels

⅞" x 14" Dowel

5½"

14"

9½"
diameter

5½" x
11½"

11½"

1" diameter

cut from 1 x 6
stock

Space 5/16"
holes for dowels 1" in from
edge of ⅜" disks

FIRE ENGINE BOX

HOSE REEL

FIGURE 8–12 Top left: *Assembly of dashboard and grill.* Bottom left: *Measurements for the ladder and hose reel, as well as the fire-engine box.* Top right: *Seat assembly.* Bottom right: *Side view of truck showing placement of the ladder hooks.*

84

ASSEMBLY

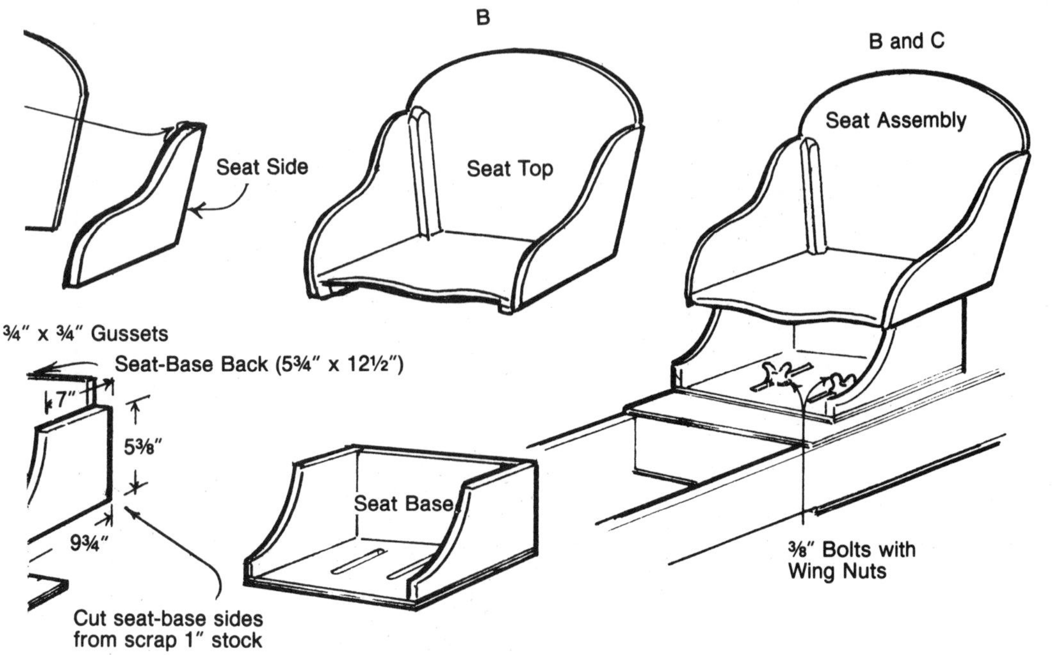

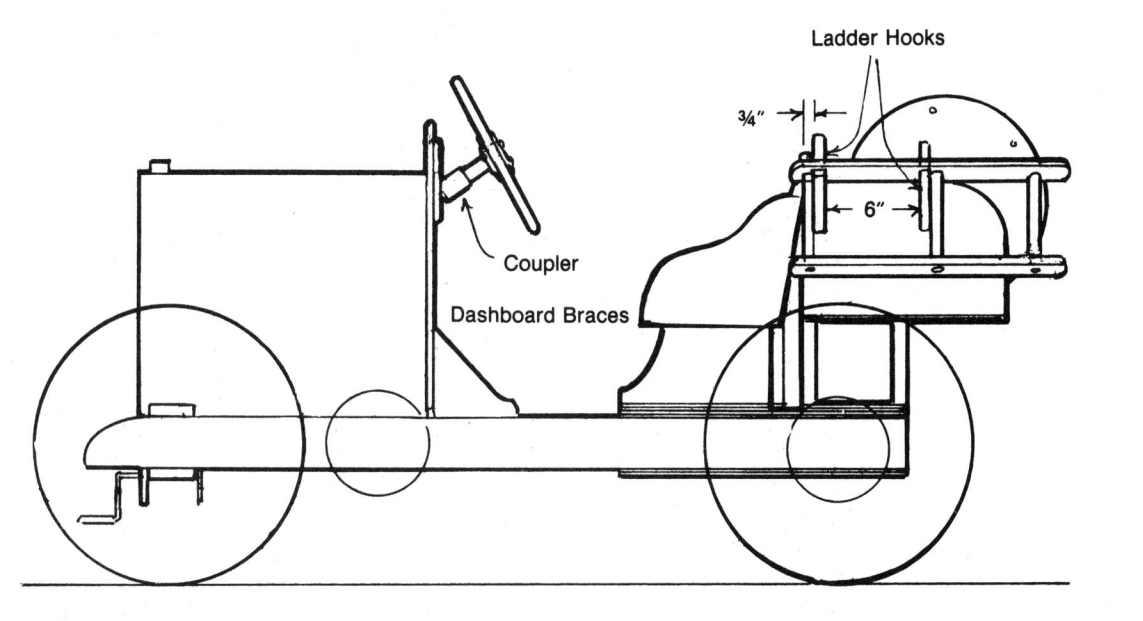

B

Seat Side

Seat Top

B and C

Seat Assembly

¾" x ¾" Gussets

Seat-Base Back (5¾" x 12½")

7"

5⅜"

9¾"

Seat Base

Cut seat-base sides from scrap 1" stock

⅜" Bolts with Wing Nuts

Ladder Hooks

¾"

6"

Coupler

Dashboard Braces

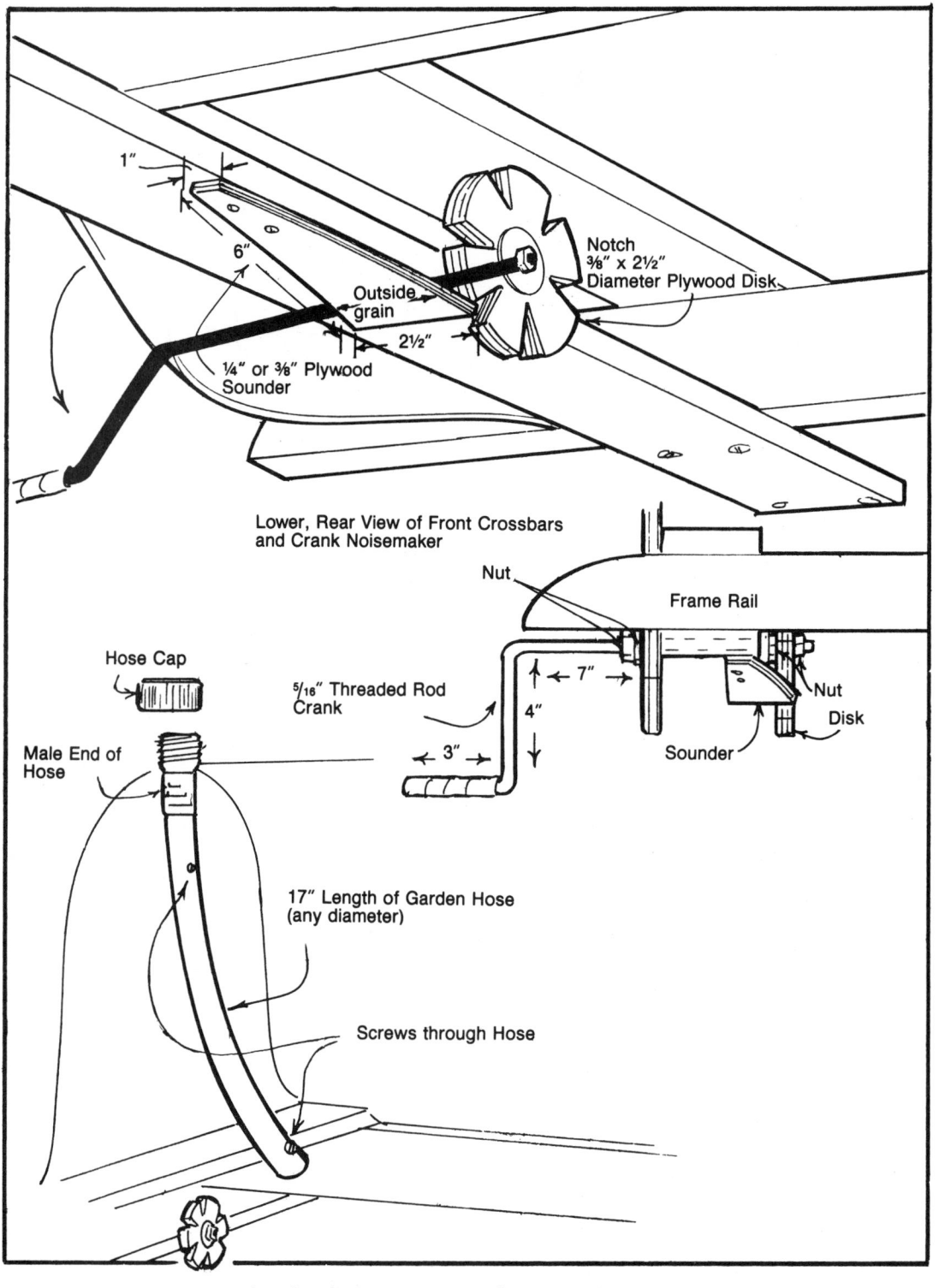

1"

6"

Outside
grain

Notch
⅜" x 2½"
Diameter Plywood Disk

2½"

¼" or ⅜" Plywood
Sounder

Lower, Rear View of Front Crossbars
and Crank Noisemaker

Nut

Frame Rail

Hose Cap

⁵⁄₁₆" Threaded Rod
Crank

7"

Nut

Disk

4"

Male End of
Hose

3"

Sounder

17" Length of Garden Hose
(any diameter)

Screws through Hose

FIGURE 8–13 *Crank and radiator cap accessories.*

down over the ends of the bolt. Run on wide washers and wing nuts to fasten the seat in the position desired.

We made up a Fire Engine rear assembly just for looks that can be bolted on to the top of the frame box section panel (like the seat base) when the seat is in a forward position. If you want to include this, put together the box assembly, as shown in Figure 8–12, lower left, using glue and $1\frac{1}{2}''$ galvanized box nails. Cut the ladder from a piece of $\frac{7}{8}''$ dowel (or a broom handle) as shown. Cut the ladder hooks (just under the hood in Figure 8–12) from 1'' scrap stock. Screw them to the outsides of the Fire Engine box, flush at the top on both sides in the positions shown in the side view.

Cut a reel to hold the hose as shown, cutting two plywood disks and drilling as indicated. Drill holes for the $\frac{7}{8}''$ axle dowel and tap the dowel in from one side to be glued in both side holes of the engine box.

Figure 8–13 shows the optional crank and radiator-cap accessories that drivers seem to get a kick out of fiddling with. The radiator cap is simply a short length of garden hose with a male end sticking out of a $\frac{7}{8}''$ to 1'' hole cut through the aluminum hood just behind the radiator panel (we used a hole-saw drill attachment). Attach the hose to the back of the radiator and the top crossbar on the frame. Use brass or plastic hose cap for a radiator cap.

The starter crank was designed to make a satisfying racket when the handle is given a twist. Figure 8–13 shows the rear of the frame crossbars from a rear, low-angle view. The noise is made by a notched wheel cut from plywood that clacks against a plywood sounder. Cut a $\frac{5}{16}''$ threaded rod to 14'' and bend it at right angles in a vise. Drill a $\frac{5}{16}''$ hole in through the center of the grill panel so that it passes through the center of the lower crossbar. Run the nuts onto the rear end of the crank rod, up to about 4'' from the end, and tighten them against each other to provide a stop. Next, run a washer onto the rod, insert the rod back into the hole through the hole in the grill and crossbar, run on another washer, then a nut and another washer, the notched wheel, another washer, and a nut. Tighten the nuts on either side of the wheel securely.

Next, cut the plywood sounder (see Fig. 8–13) with the grain showing running across the length of the piece. Screw the sounder to the bottom of the lower cross-piece so that it lies against the wheel with a slight bend to it. Wrap the exposed length of the crank rod with several layers of black tape, making the layers thicker at the handle to provide a grip.

Round off all edges with a Surform wood shaper, then sand smooth. Run a bead of DAP tub-and-tile sealer along the back edge of the aluminum hood sheet to prevent scraped knees. Give the car three coats of an oil-base gloss enamel and trim it with plastic pinstriping tape available at auto-parts stores.

9

THE JUMPING HORSE

■ MATERIALS LIST

4′ × 4′ ACX exterior-grade plywood
    panel, $\frac{3}{4}$″ thick
1′ length of rough redwood 4 × 4 stock
8′ length of rough redwood 2 × 2 stock
6″ length of fir, cedar, or redwood 2 × 6
    stock
Two 10′ lengths of fir, cedar, or redwood
    1 × 3 stock
8′ length of fir, cedar, or redwood 1 × 3
    stock
6″ length of $\frac{1}{2}$″ dowel
9″ length of $\frac{5}{8}$″ dowel
6″ length of $\frac{7}{8}$″ dowel
3′ length of $\frac{3}{4}$″ I.D. galvanized pipe
Four 6″ heavy-duty tension springs
Four 4″ × $\frac{5}{16}$″ eyebolts, nuts, and double
    washers
One hundred $1\frac{1}{2}$″ #8 flathead wood
    screws
30″ × 36″ rectangle of plastic grass
    carpet
4′ length of $\frac{3}{4}$″-diameter hemp rope
One pound of 3″ galvanized box nails
Roll of $\frac{3}{4}$″ plastic tape
Dog leash
12″ × 12″ square of dark-colored
    Naugahyde

12″ × 12″ square of red felt
$\frac{5}{8}$″ staples

☐ *See color insert for completed project.*

The jumping horse, suspended on tension springs attached to the surrounding
corral fence, provides lively jumping action for young children in a wide range of
ages. However, because it *is* high-spirited,
it should be used with adult supervision.

The body of the horse is made of three
layers of 2″ × 6″ redwood, cedar, or pine
(or any other medium soft-wood stock),
with $\frac{3}{4}$″ plywood legs. The head is cut
from a redwood 4 × 4.

■ CUTTING AND DRILLING

☐ The Corral

The first step in building the jumping
horse is to cut the corral posts from
rough redwood or cedar 2 × 2s. These can
be sanded to prevent splintering, but use
rough-cut stock to get the extra-large size
of lumber. (Finished 2 × 2s will measure
$1\frac{1}{2}$″ × $1\frac{1}{2}$″ and are too small.) The rails
and crosspieces can be cut from finished

or rough 1″ × 3″ stock (or split grape stakes with a cross-section size close to this size).

Cut the 30″ × 23″ plywood base (we used ACX for better weather protection). Then cut three $20\frac{1}{2}$″ posts and one $28\frac{1}{2}$″ post from the 2 × 2, trimming the top ends to a blunt bevel with a cross-cut saw. Drill $\frac{1}{8}$″ pilot holes through the base at the corners so that the bottoms of all four posts can be attached to the base $\frac{3}{4}$″ in from the long side edges and flush with the end edges. Drive $3\frac{1}{2}$″ nails up through the bottom of the base and into the end grain of the posts.

Drill pilot holes for the wood screws through the rails and crosspieces and screw them to the posts (Fig. 9–1). Notch the crosspieces at the midpoint and bend them slightly so they can cross without being notched. Screw the two crosspieces together at the corner to add stability to the corral frame.

Next, drill through the four posts in the positions shown with a $\frac{5}{16}$″ bit, then insert a $\frac{5}{16}$″ eyebolt in each hole from the inside of the corral. Bolt them tight with a washer and locknut, and trim the bolt flush with the nut (filing the ends to round off). Drill a $\frac{1}{2}$″ hole through the "hitching post" as shown; then cut and insert a 6″ length of $\frac{1}{2}$″ dowel. Sand all sharp corners and potential splinters at the edges with 80-grit, then 150-grit sandpaper. Apply two coats of satin-finish, exterior-grade varnish.

After varnishing, cut a 30″ × 36″ rectangle of plastic grass carpet, notching to clear the posts (Fig. 9–2). Wrap the edges of the grass carpet under the base and staple it in place with $\frac{5}{8}$″ staples. The top rail at the front of the corral (the hitching-post end) can be wrapped with alternating spirals of red and white plastic tape to provide the look of a competition jump. Hook the heavy-duty tension springs onto the eyebolts at the corner posts, using a pair of pliers to open the spring eyes. Use the pliers to crimp the spring and eyes after mounting to prevent the springs from becoming detached during a ride.

☐ **The Horse** (Fig. 9–3)

To build the horse, start by making the patterns for the front and hind legs and transfer them to the $\frac{3}{4}$″ plywood. Drill holes for the 1″ pipe-hanger poles as shown in Figures 9–4 and 9–5.

Make the pattern for the body, following the dimensions in Figure 9–6. Transfer the pattern to the 2 × 6 and cut three of these pieces for the body. Mark the positions of the 1″ holes for the pipe hangers and drill through all three layers with a 1″-diameter spade bit for the power drill. Select one piece to form the center layer. Next, mark the dotted cut-off lines on the center layer shown in Figure 9–6 and cut along them to provide a mounting slot for the next piece of 2 × 6.

Make the pattern for the neck piece and transfer it onto the remaining 2 × 6 stock (Fig. 9–7). Cut out the neck piece. Then place the legs in position on the two outside body layers and mark the outlines onto the body parts. Nail and glue (driving pilot holes through the other layers, if needed, to prevent splitting) each side layer to the center body layer and to the neck piece. Align all parts flush at the top surface of the body (the jumper's back), positioning the nails within the outlines of the legs so that the heads will be hidden when the legs are attached.

(Text continues on page 97)

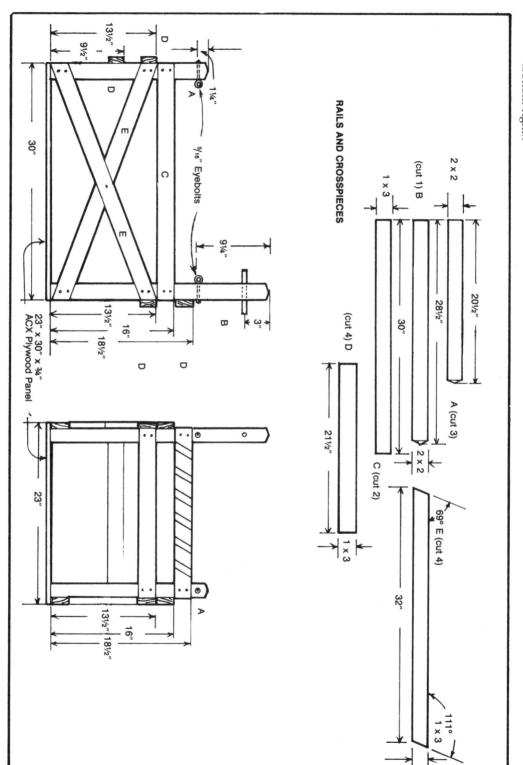

FIGURE 9–1 *Measurements for the Corral's rails and crosspieces and the corral assembly; side view (bottom left) and end view (bottom right).*

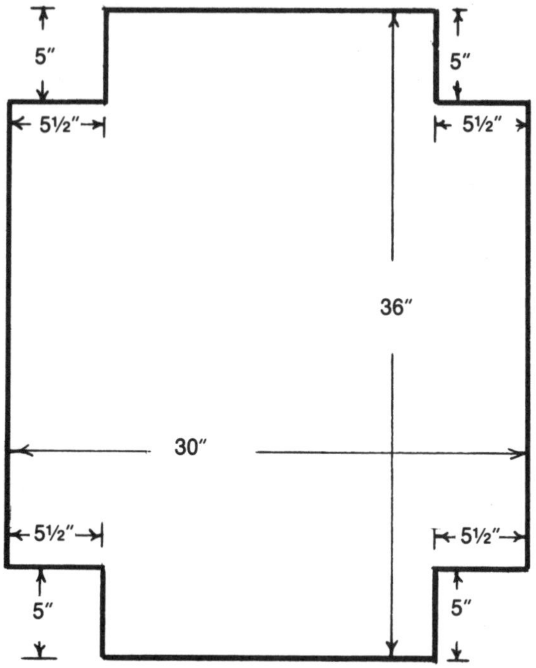

FIGURE 9–2 *Pattern for the plastic grass carpet.*

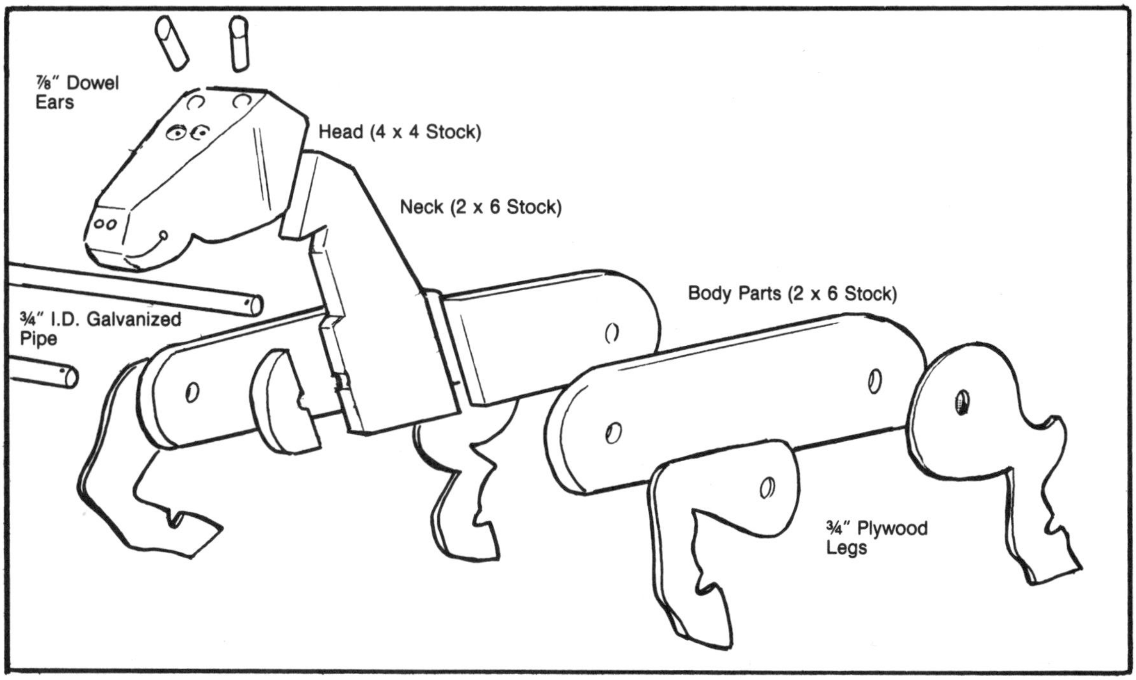

5"

5"

5½"

5½"

36"

30"

5½"

5½"

5"

5"

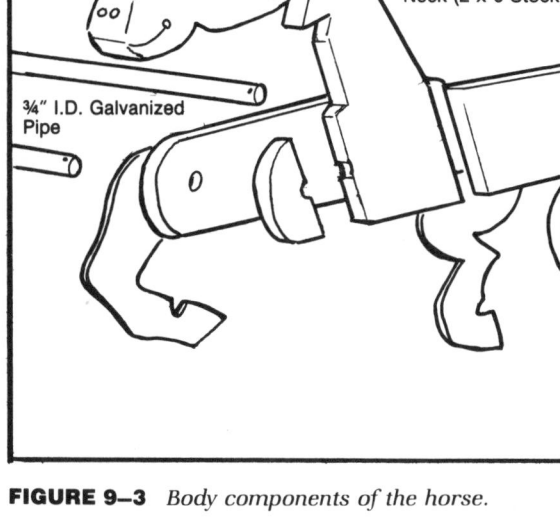

⅞" Dowel
Ears

Head (4 x 4 Stock)

Neck (2 x 6 Stock)

Body Parts (2 x 6 Stock)

¾" I.D. Galvanized
Pipe

¾" Plywood
Legs

FIGURE 9–3 *Body components of the horse.*

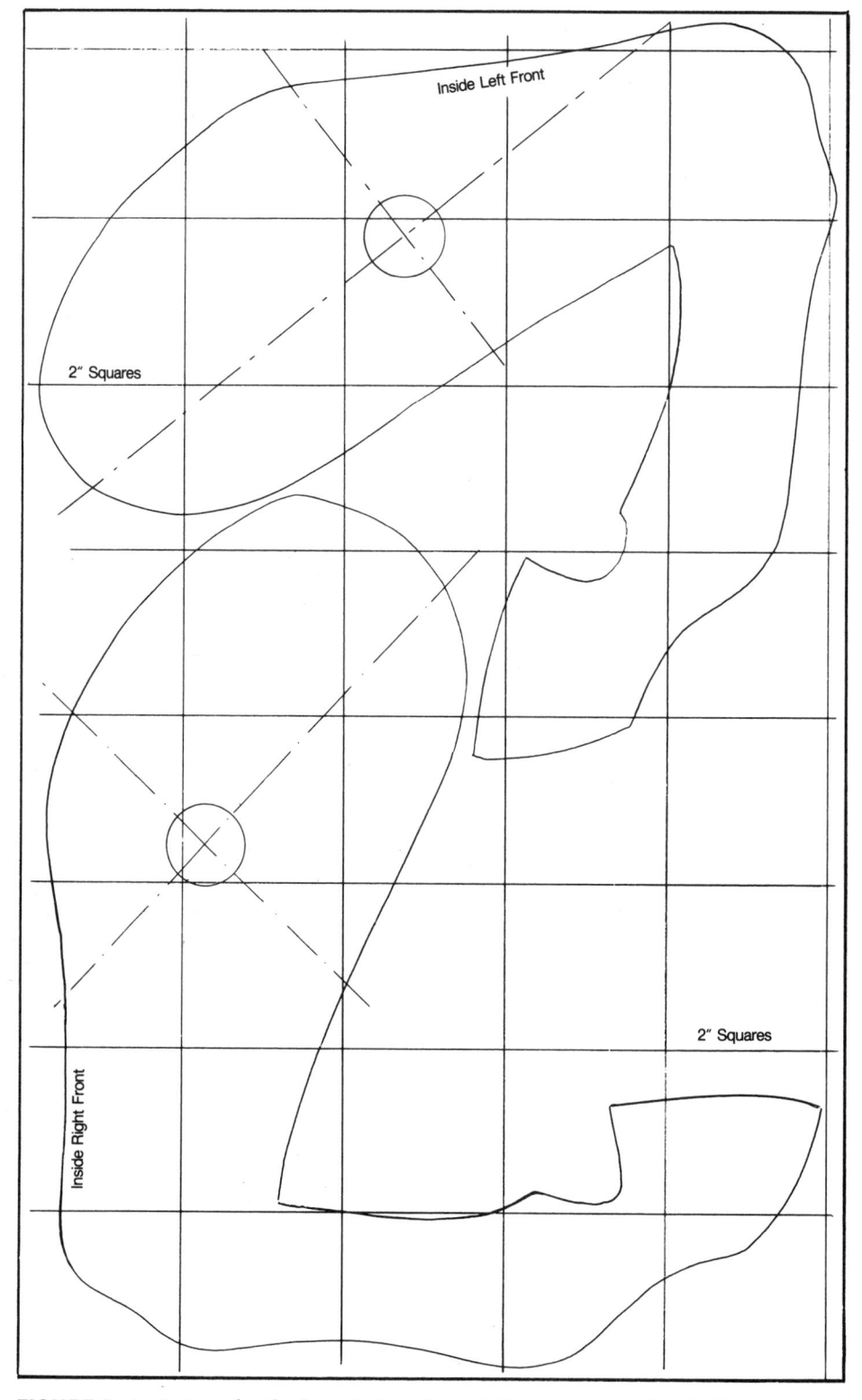

Inside Left Front

2" Squares

Inside Right Front

2" Squares

FIGURE 9–4 *Pattern for the horse's front legs. Enlarge onto a grid with 2" squares.*

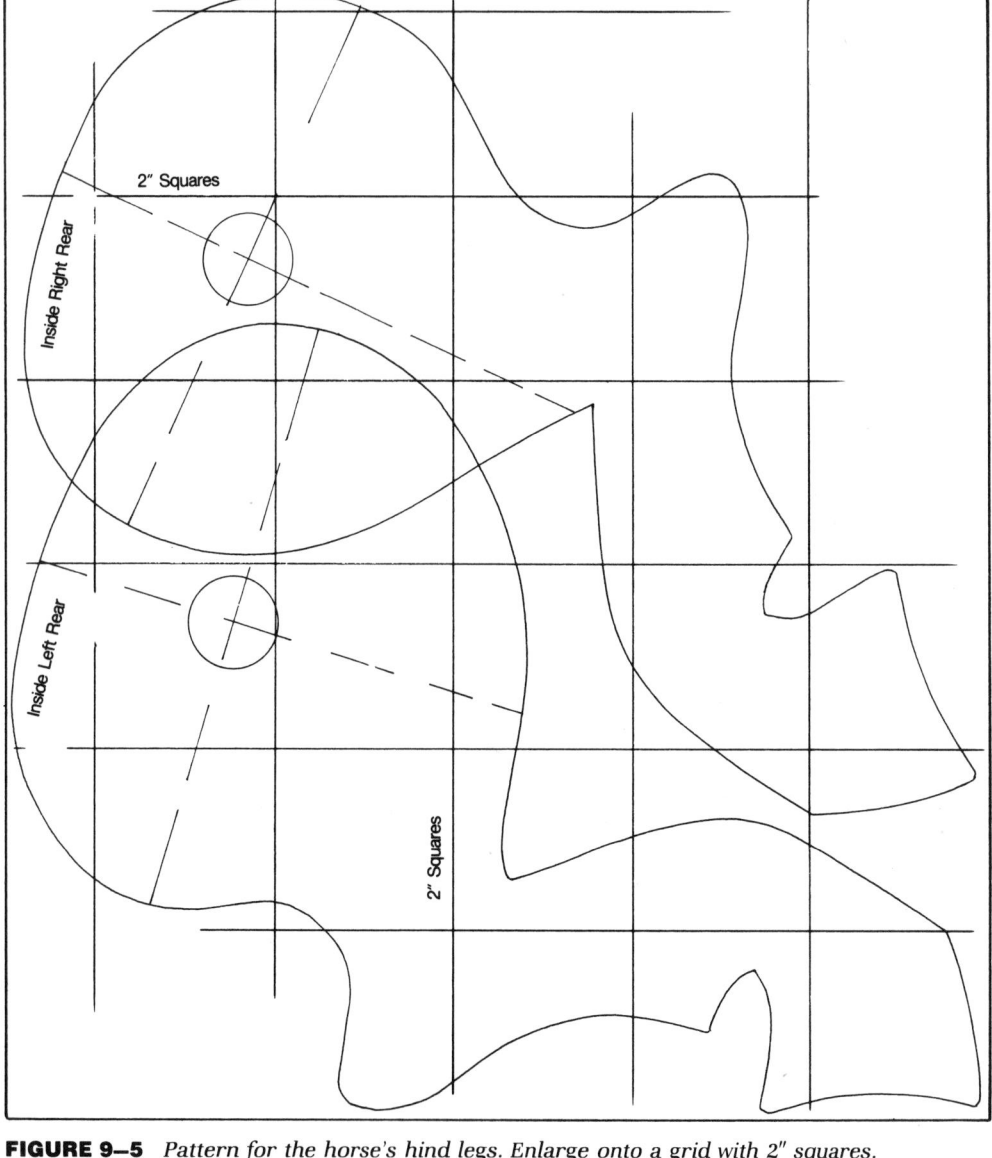

FIGURE 9–5 *Pattern for the horse's hind legs. Enlarge onto a grid with 2″ squares.*

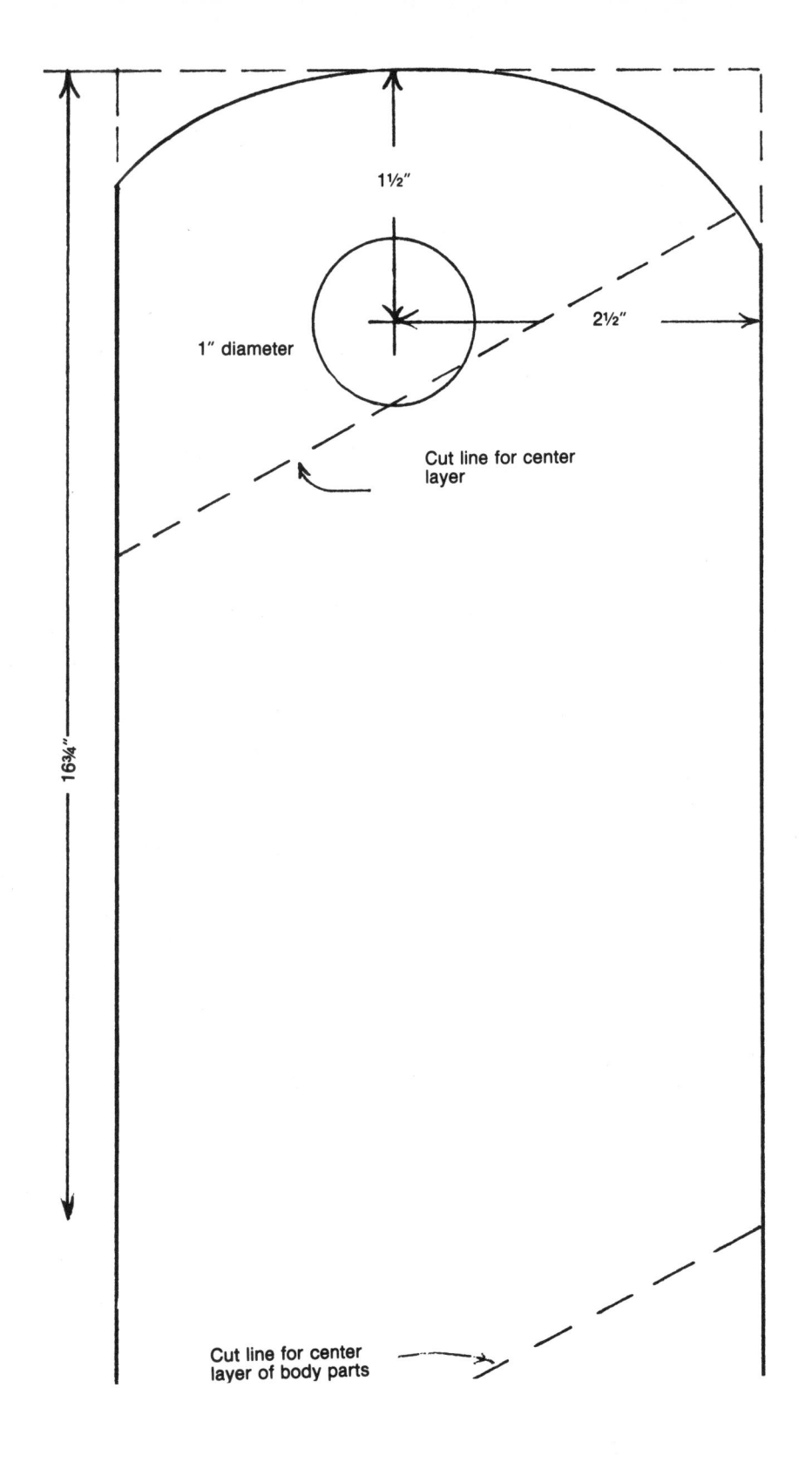

1½"

1" diameter

2½"

Cut line for center
layer

16¾"

Cut line for center
layer of body parts

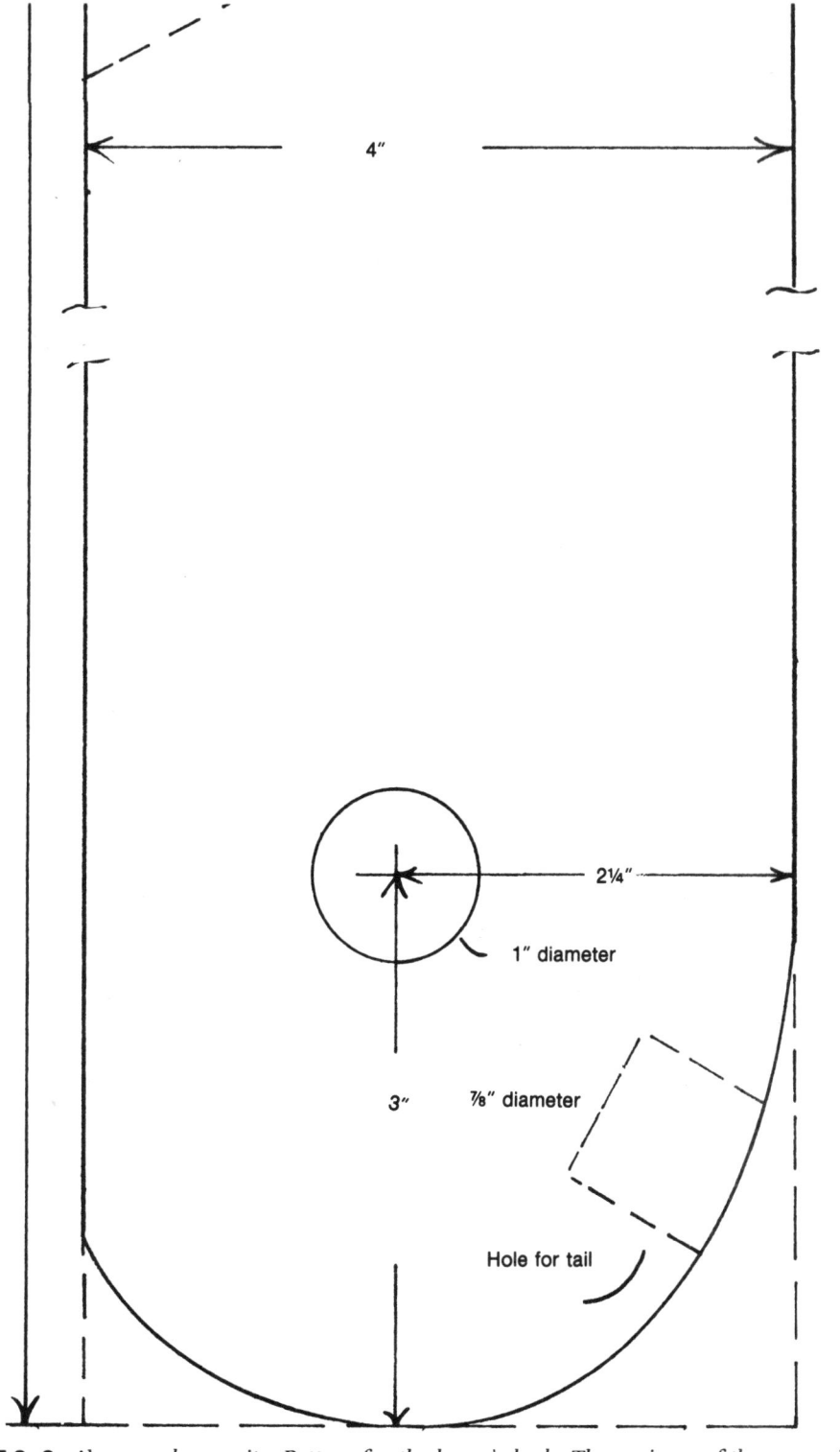

FIGURE 9–6 Above and opposite. *Pattern for the horse's body. Three pieces of the same size are cut from the fir, cedar, or redwood 2 × 6 stock and glued together. The end curves are shown full scale.*

95

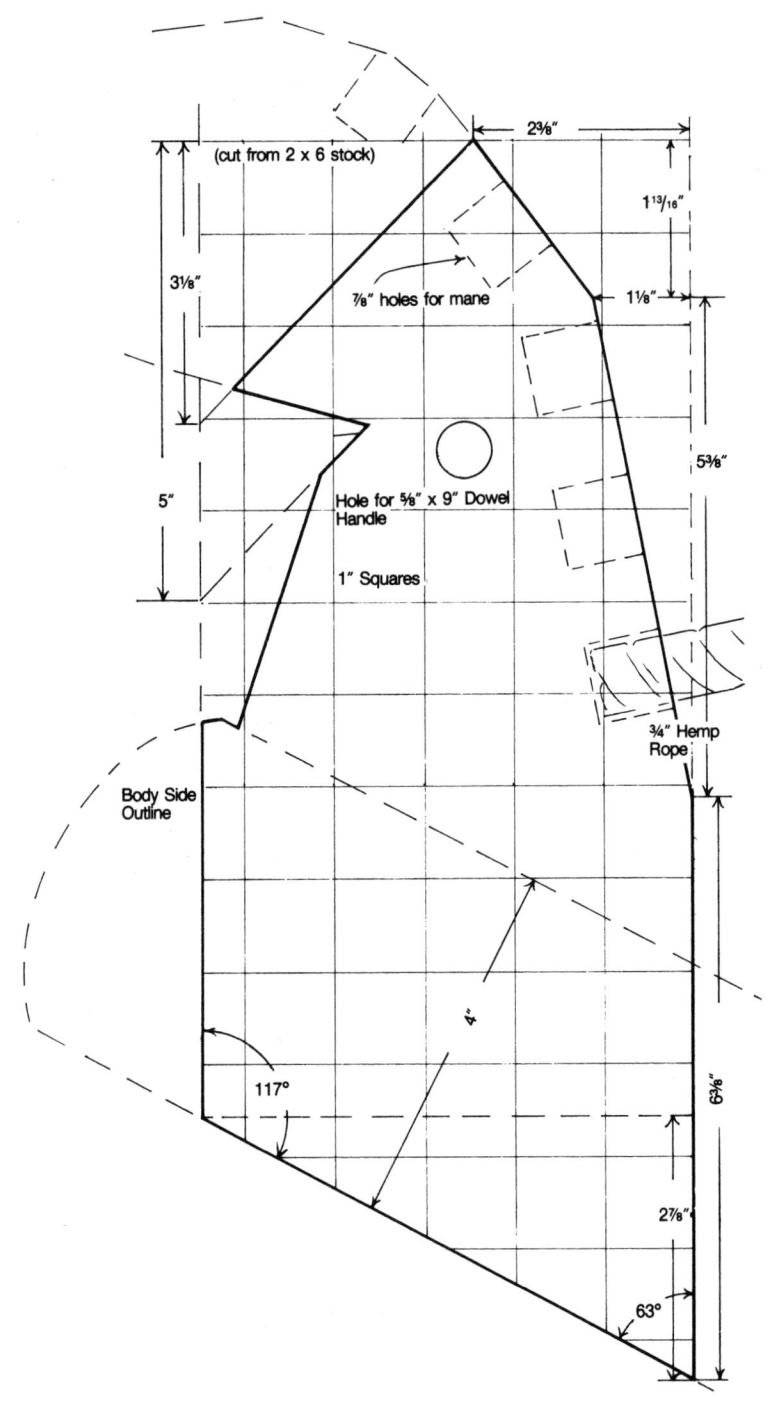

2⅜"

1¹³/₁₆"

3⅛"

(cut from 2 x 6 stock)

⅞" holes for mane

1⅛"

5⅜"

5"

Hole for ⅝" x 9" Dowel
Handle

1" Squares

¾" Hemp
Rope

Body Side
Outline

4"

117°

6¾"

2⅞"

63°

FIGURE 9–7 *Pattern for the horse's neck.*

The next step is to cut the 18″ × $\frac{3}{4}$″ inside-diameter pipe hangers. Then drill $\frac{5}{16}$″-diameter holes through one side of the pipe with the center of the holes spaced $\frac{1}{2}$″ in from each end of each pipe. Insert the pipes through the holes in the body, then slip the legs over the ends of the pipe and slide them up to the sides of the body. Screw or nail them in place with glue. Wrap the hanger pipes with $\frac{3}{4}$″ black plastic tape next to the sides of the jumper to a thickness of about $\frac{1}{8}$″ to prevent side slip.

Cut the head from a short length of rough redwood 4″ × 4″ (Fig. 9–8). (Cedar or pine can be substituted and the head laminated from six layers of 1″ × 6″ stock cut in profile, glued together, then trimmed to size from the top view.) The profile and top views can be cut with a hand saw and rounded with a Surform wood shaper or cut with a band saw. Cut the profile first, then the top outline. Finally, drill the ear, eye, and nostril holes with wood spade bits to the diameters shown. The exact angle of the ear holes isn't crucial, so long as they point out and forward a little to show that the jumper's in a good mood. Drill the eye and nostril holes about $\frac{1}{4}$″ deep.

The notch for the neck can be cut out, as shown, with a band saw or hand saw, using a chisel to cut down the front to remove the wood in the notch. Cut the $\frac{7}{8}$″-diameter dowel ears and glue and screw them to the earholes. Glue and slip down the slot at the back of the head onto the neck and drive screws in through pilot holes, as shown in Figure 9–8, to mount the head solidly on the neck. With the jumper body complete, use a Surform wood shaper to round off all sharp edges and remove splinters. Sand the body

smooth with #80-grit then 150-grit sandpaper and either paint or varnish the horse and frame.

Make a bridle and reins from an inexpensive dog leash, as shown in Figure 9–9. To make a saddle, cut the shape shown in the grid pattern from Naugahyde; then cut another layer $\frac{1}{4}$″ larger all the way around from the red felt. Glue both layers in place with contact cement. Paint the crossbars and hooves, as well as the top spangled surface of the ears, the hanger springs, and eyebolts, semigloss black.

Drill $\frac{7}{8}$″-diameter holes in the neck, rump, and top of the head as shown in the patterns to provide anchor points for the mane and tail. Cut five 6″ sections of rope for the mane. Wrap one end of each with black plastic tape and insert into holes on head and neck. Use remainder of rope for tail and treat similarly. To hold the rope in place, angle and drive small finishing nails through it. After anchoring the rope, unravel and fluff it into a continuous mane; trim to the appropriate length with scissors. Wrap the base of the tail with more tape to help it stand up, then unravel the end and comb it out.

■ ASSEMBLY

To mount the jumper on the hangers, bend the end eyes of the springs open with pliers enough to slip into the holes on the top sides of the hanger pipes. Close the eyes with pliers to make sure nothing will come loose. Round all sharp corners of the metal parts with a file and tape the corners where possible.

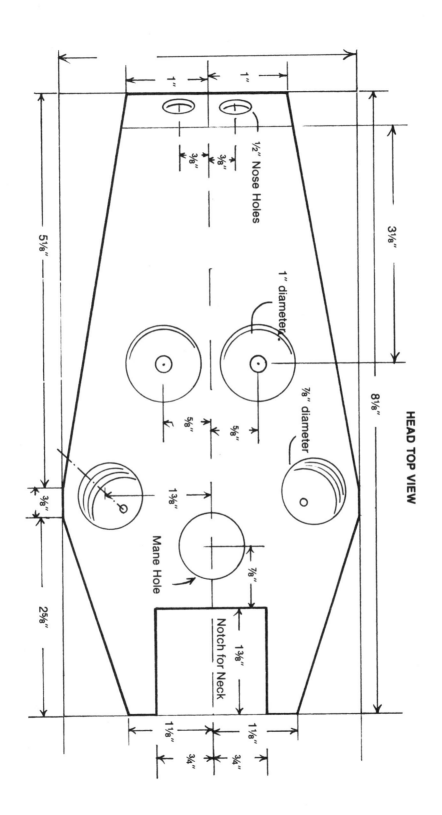

½" Nose Holes

3/8"
3/8"

1"
1"

5⅛"

3⅛"

1" diameter

8⅛"

⅞" diameter

5/8"
5/8"

3/8"

1⅜"

⅞"

Mane Hole

25/8"

1⅜"

Notch for Neck

1⅛"

1⅛"

3/4"
3/4"

1⅛"

HEAD TOP VIEW

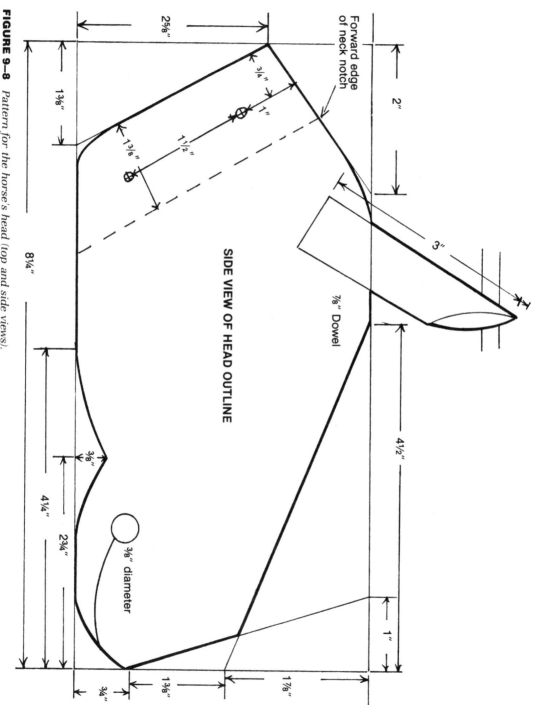

SIDE VIEW OF HEAD OUTLINE

Forward edge
of neck notch

2⁵⁄₈″

1³⁄₈″

³⁄₄″

1″

1¹⁄₂″

1³⁄₈″

8¹⁄₄″

2″

3″

⁷⁄₈″ Dowel

4¹⁄₂″

³⁄₈″

4¹⁄₄″

2³⁄₄″

³⁄₈″ diameter

1″

¹⁄₈″

1³⁄₈″

³⁄₄″

FIGURE 9-8   *Pattern for the horse's head (top and side views).*

Tack Strap

11"

11"

FIGURE 9–9 *Make a pattern for the saddle by wrapping a piece of tracing paper around the back of the horse. Round off the shape as shown, fold it for symmetrical side pieces, and cut.*

THE DOLLHOUSE

■ MATERIALS LIST

Two 4′ × 8′ ACX plywood panels, $\frac{3}{8}$″ thick
Two 36″ lengths of $\frac{3}{8}$″ dowel
4′ length of redwood 2 × 6 stock
4′ length of pine 1 × 6 stock
4″ of $\frac{3}{4}$″ quarter-round molding
12″ × 12″ square of $\frac{1}{2}$″ hardware cloth
    mesh screening
100 1$\frac{1}{2}$″ #7 flathead screws
Six $\frac{3}{4}$″ brass hinges
36″ length of braided nylon string
Small bag of paint texturing material
One quart of catalyzed auto-body putty
2′ × 2′ square of clear Plexiglas, $\frac{1}{8}$″ thick
Scrap of redwood 2 × 3 or 2 × 4

☐ *See color insert for completed project.*

If the Dollhouse looks like something
from an old English movie, there's a good
reason. After looking around for some
time for a Tudor country-house design
that would lend itself to a dollhouse, we
happened to be watching Alec Guiness's
Man in the White Suit, when the perfect
house came on the screen. A few thumb-
nail sketches later and we were on our
way to a finished design.

The house was built one-inch-to-the-
foot scale in two sections, with the top
two stories fitting down on the ground-
level rooms for two reasons. First, since
the basic material costs were low, we decided to build big. The Dollhouse has lots
of room in three levels, but it's too bulky
to carry from room to room. Second, decorators can have better access to the
lower rooms with the top section removed, and if you happen to have two
decorators and one house, they can work
in two separate sections with plenty of
room.

■ LAYOUT

Each new owner who takes possession of
the house will have a different idea of
how the rooms ought to be used. But for
the purposes of keeping things reasonably straight during construction, we'll list
the positions of the rooms and divider
walls according to the layout we finally
settled on.

Looking at the lower level from the
front, the attached garage is on the left
with the kitchen/pantry directly behind
this with a connecting doorway. The entry is in the middle of the front wall, leading back into a kind of entry parlor with

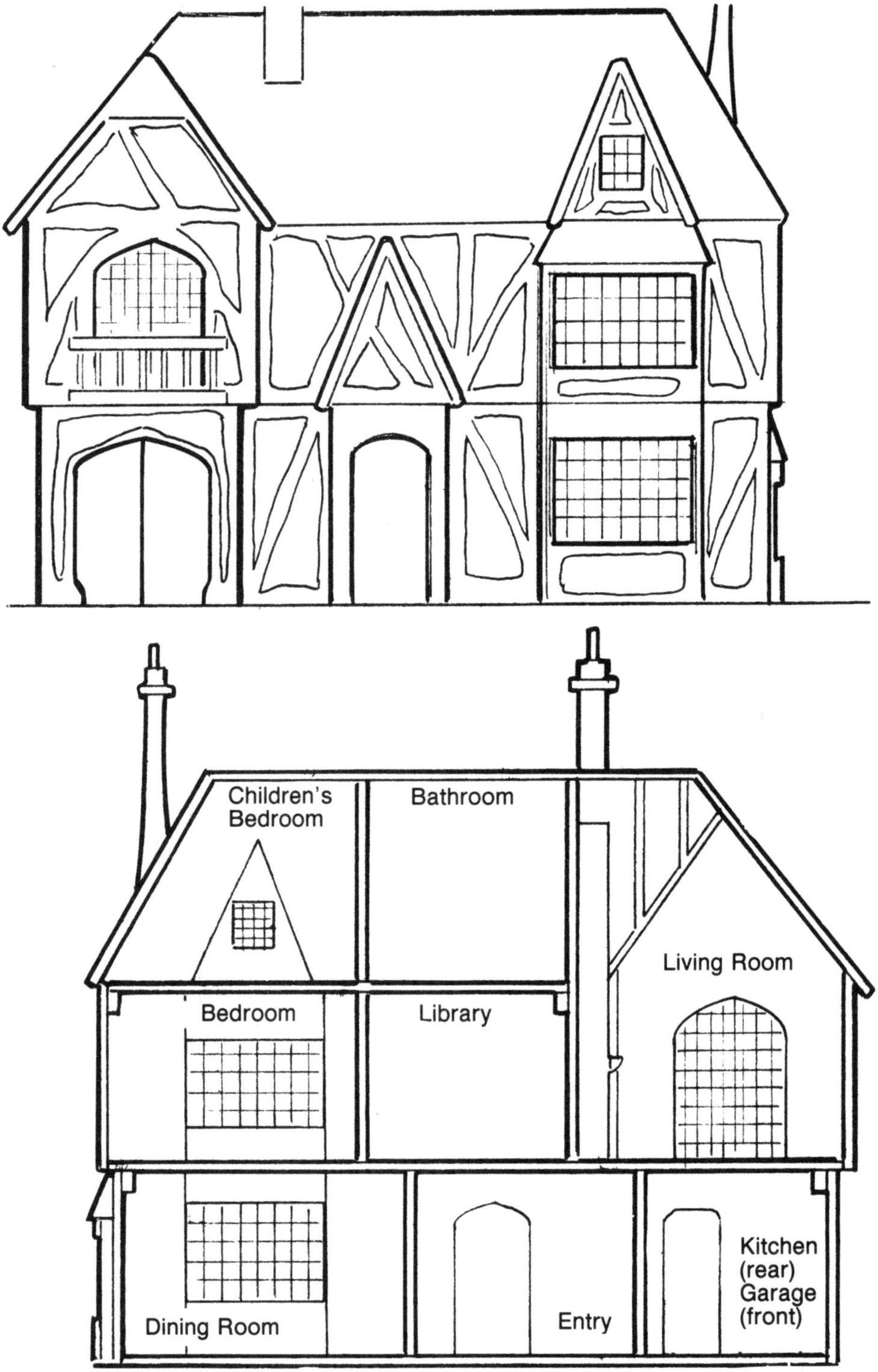

FIGURE 10–1 *Front and back views of the Dollhouse (elevator omitted).*

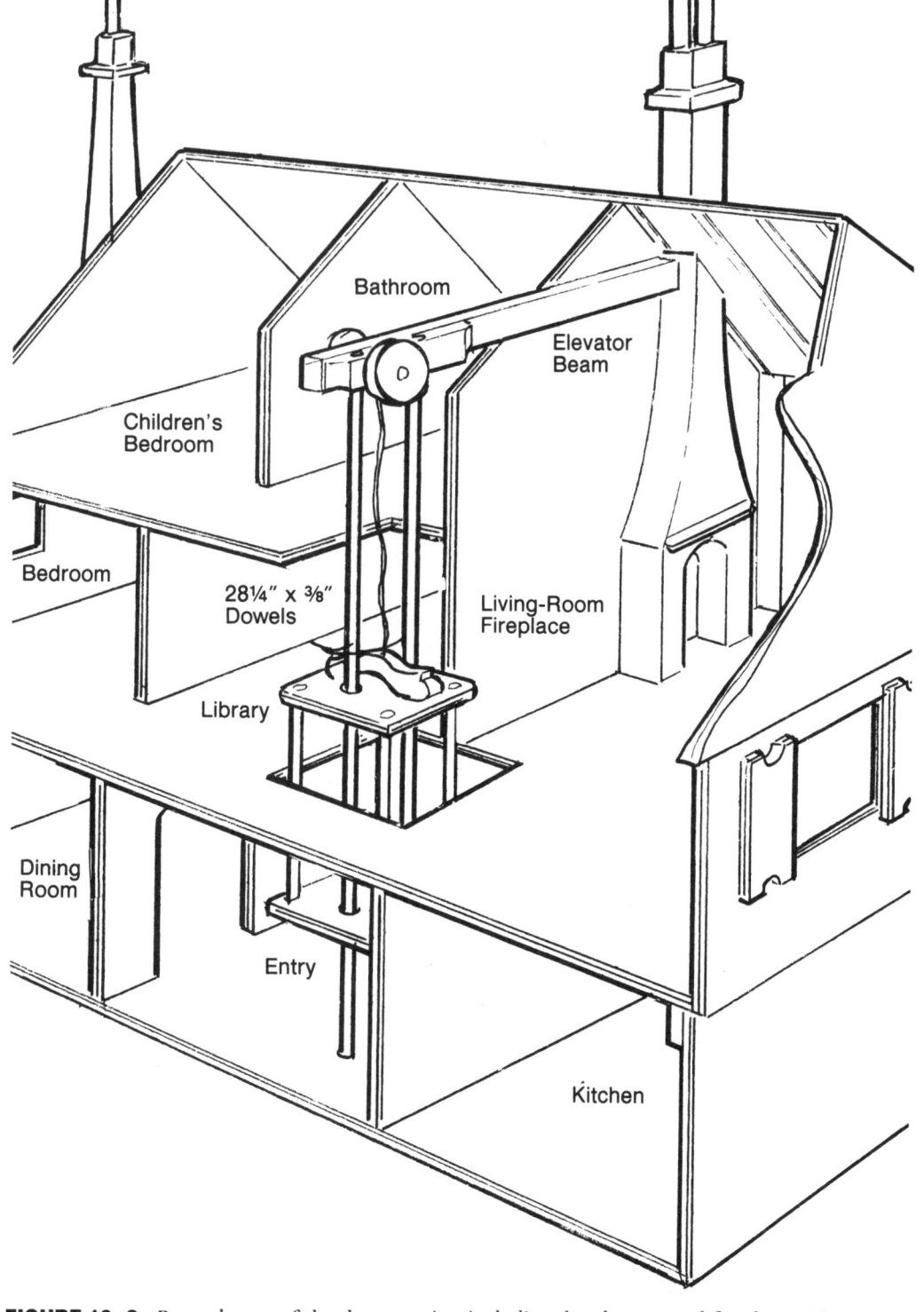

FIGURE 10–2 *Room layout of the three stories, including the elevator and fireplace with chimney.*

Bathroom

Elevator Beam

Children's Bedroom

Bedroom

28¼" x ⅜" Dowels

Living-Room Fireplace

Library

Dining Room

Entry

Kitchen

access to the kitchen to the left and dining room to the right.

To get upstairs, we use something not found in all dollhouses: an elevator. This is the old-style, cage-type exposed elevator, the kind you might find in old European hotels. The elevator was also the result of several design considerations. Stairs are awkward and space-consuming, blocking open access to the rooms. Also, we completely forgot to plan for them until we'd already planned out the rooms. With no easy remedy for the stair problem, we decided on the elevator, and it has proved to be the most popular feature of the house.

Looking at the second level from the front, there is a clerestory main living room with balcony and fireplace to the left. In the center is a library-study and on the right is the master bedroom. On the top, attic level is a bathroom in the center and a children's bedroom/playroom to the right with a dormer and window facing front.

The elevator, off from the entry parlor in the center of the ground-level rooms, gives access from either side of the cage to the study, living room, and bathroom.

■ CONSTRUCTION NOTE

The house is constructed of $\frac{3}{8}''$ ACX plywood, with simple butt joints at each corner of the walls. It would be possible to drill $\frac{1}{16}''$ pilot holes for nails through one side of the butt joints to sink into the center of the edge grain of the butted piece, but this method has a few drawbacks. Nails don't grab the edge grain very securely, and the hammering process tends to loosen the first joints by the time you get to the last joints. Screws make a tight joint that you can reposition

perfectly without tearing down the whole structure in the process.

To make the butt joints, we placed the parts in position, drilled pilot holes with a combination countersink/drill bit in through the side of one piece, about $\frac{3}{16}''$ to $\frac{1}{4}''$ in from the edge and angling into the center of the edge of the butted piece. We used yellow squeeze-bottle glue on the surfaces to be joined, then drove in $1\frac{1}{4}''$ #7 plated flathead wood screws.

Whenever joining the edge of one panel to the side of another (but in from the edge so that you can't tell where to drill holes), we used the "blind" method for drilling pilot holes. With this, you position the part in place (such as a divider wall onto a floor) and square it up. Then draw around the part onto the adjoining part to mark its placement. Next, drill pilot holes (without countersinking) within these marks and place the parts back into position. We drilled the pilot holes from the other side, so the drill bit enters the edge grain of the butted part, drilling in all the way so that the side of the joined part is countersunk at each hole from the other side. Then the joining surfaces of the parts could be glued and screws driven through the larger panel and into the edge of the butted panel. We spaced the screws three or four inches apart along each butt joint. We used a saber saw to cut the doorways.

■ CUTTING AND ASSEMBLY
□ The First Floor

Cut and assemble the parts one story at a time. First, cut the floor, front walls, end walls, and divider walls for the first floor (Figs. 10–3 and 10–4).

To assemble the first-floor rooms (Fig. 10–5), drill, glue and screw the garage

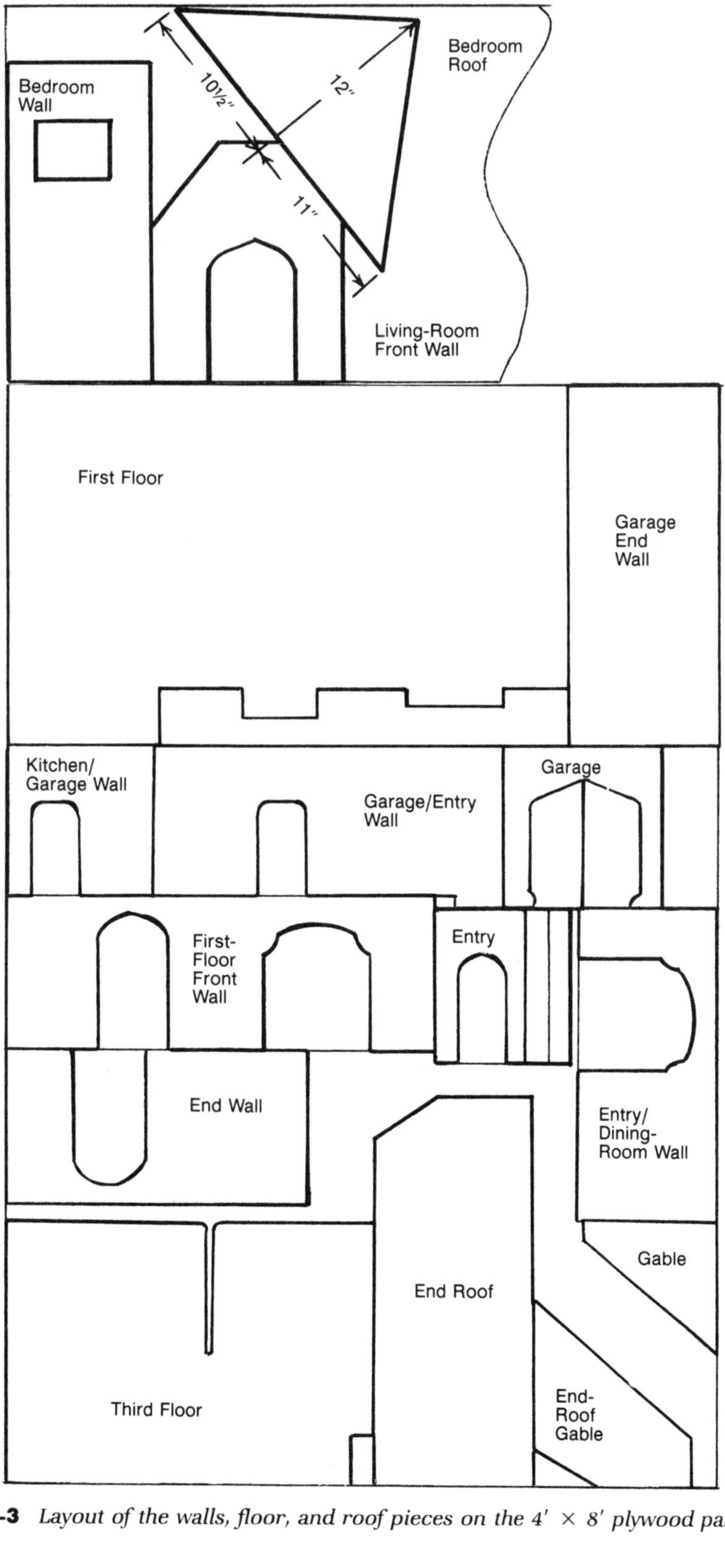

FIGURE 10-3 *Layout of the walls, floor, and roof pieces on the 4' × 8' plywood panel.*

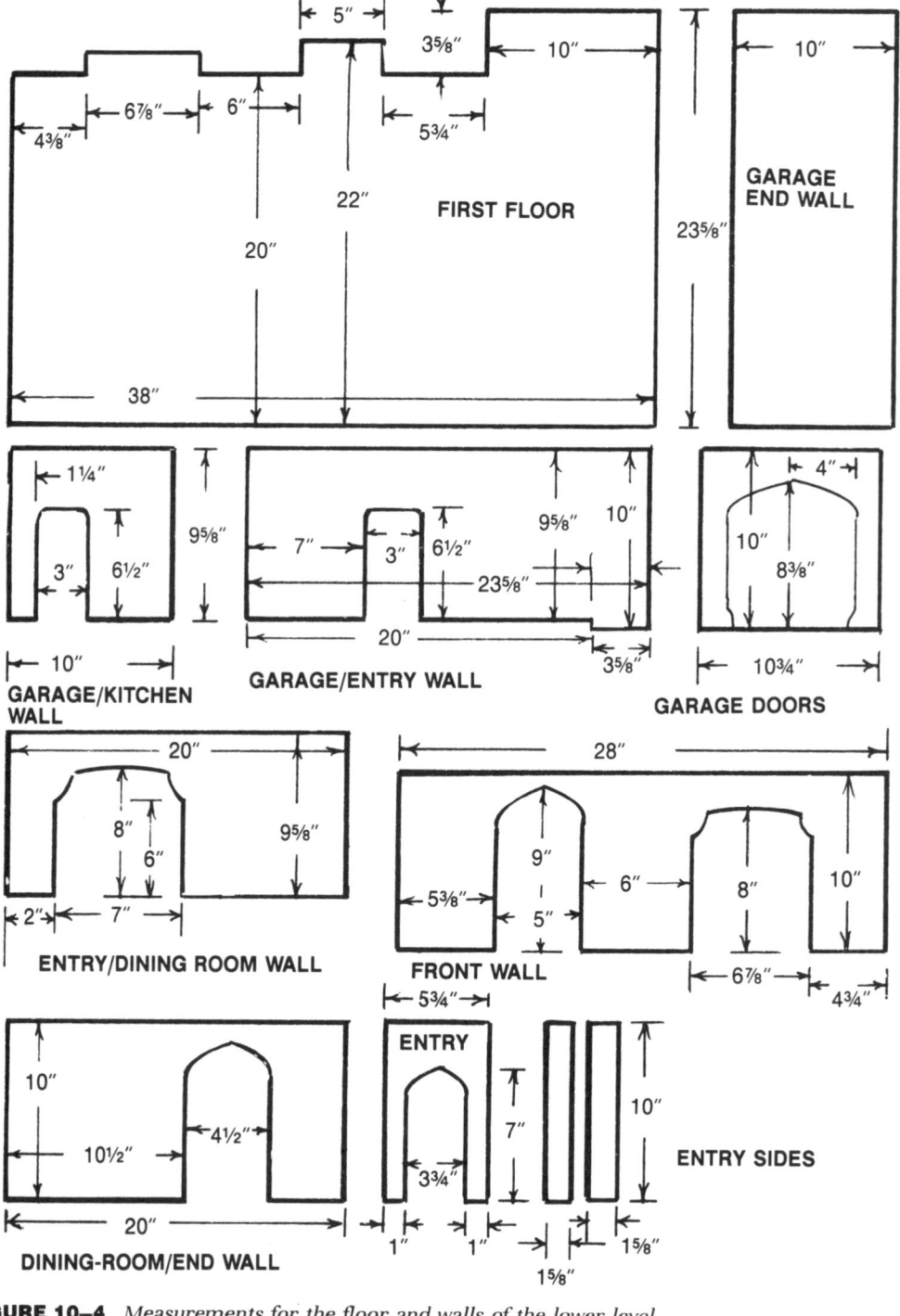

FIGURE 10–4 *Measurements for the floor and walls of the lower level.*

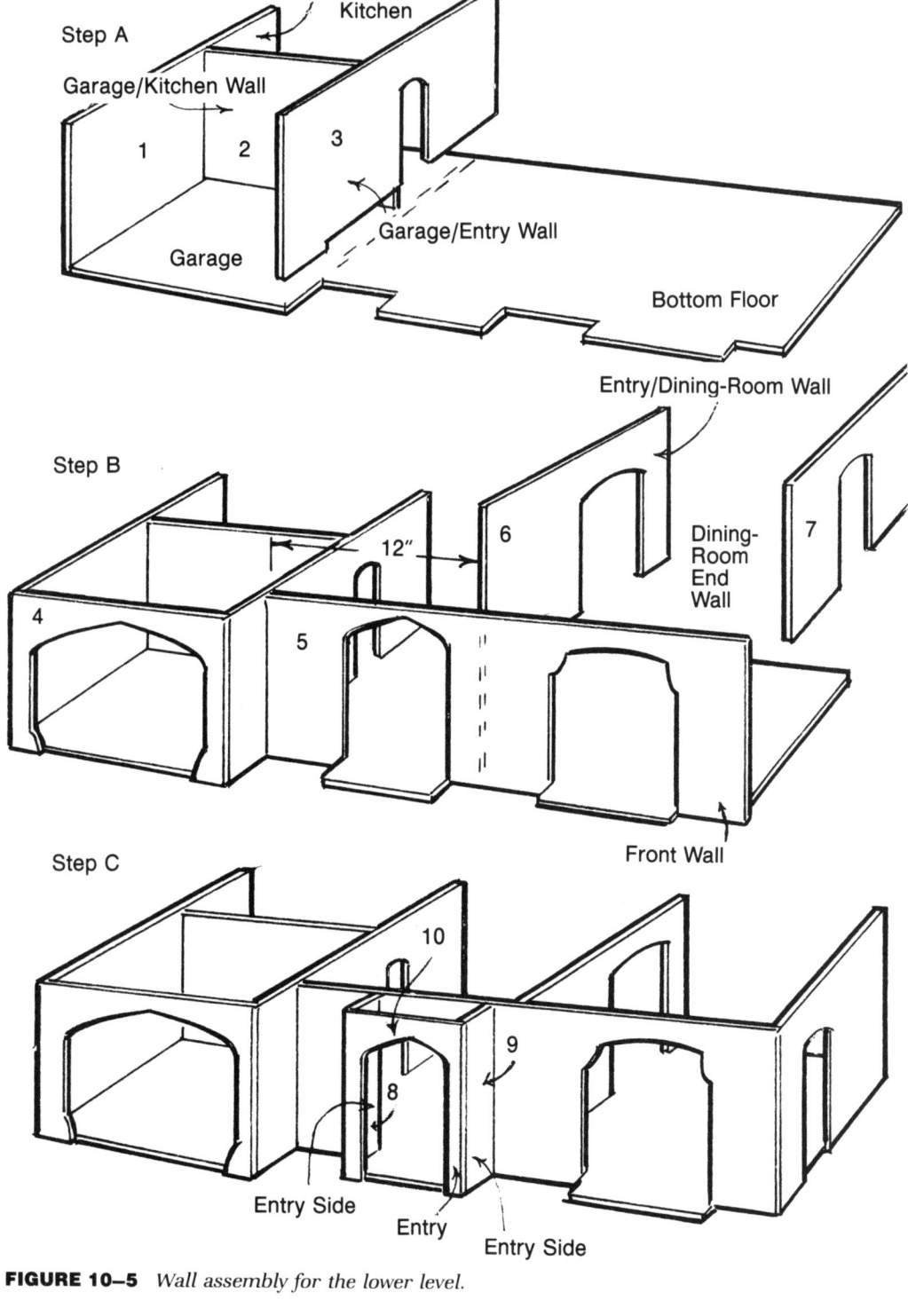

FIGURE 10–5 *Wall assembly for the lower level.*

107

end wall (1) to the left end of the floor panel using the joining method just described. Next, attach the inner wall between the garage and the kitchen (2) to the end wall and floor, squaring it up in position and marking its placement for the blind mounting method. Then attach the opposite garage wall (3) to the floor and the end of the divider wall that you've just attached, squaring up the placement. Attach the garage front wall (4) to the front edges of the two garage walls and front edge of the floor panel.

The next step is to attach the front wall (5) to the front of the floor panel. Square up the end of the front wall against the garage wall and drive in one screw through the garage wall about 1″ down from the top and into the edge grain of the front wall. Attach the dining-room end wall (7) to the end of the floor panel, then attach the front wall to the edge grain of the end wall at the corner. Mark and attach the divider wall (6) between the entry parlor and the dining room to the floor panel and rear of the front wall, squared in position and attached using the blind method.

Trim the redwood 2 × 6 to the shape shown for the roof of the end window seat (A), as shown in Figure 10–6. Then cut the two side pieces (B) and one front wall (C) of the window seat and screw the two side pieces to the rear of the front piece, making sure that they're flush at the sides and bottom. Attach the assembly to the outside of the end wall as shown in (7) in Figure 10–5, flush at the bottom, by driving screws through the end wall. Make sure that the sides are flush with the sides of the window opening. Attach the window-seat roof by driving screws out through the wall, centered over the window seat.

Cut and attach the sides and front for the front-wall window seat (X through Z) in the same way, centered on the window seat opening (see Fig. 10–6). Cut the sides of the window seat from the pine 1 × 6 with the saw blade set at a 15-degree angle on the outer surfaces. Cut the sides and front of the entry doorway (see Fig. 10–4) from plywood, then assemble and attach them in the same way as the window seats.

Attach the front door and garage stable doors (cut out from the door openings—see Fig. 10–4), hinged on $\frac{3}{4}$″ brass butt hinges, with small brass screws. Cut $\frac{1}{8}$″ × $\frac{3}{4}$″ indentations in the hinged edges of the doors to provide hinge clearance, then screw the hinges to the door edges and door openings to mount the garage and front doors.

□ **The Second and Third Floors**

Cut the second and third floor panels, end walls, front walls, inner walls, and roof panels from plywood (Fig. 10–7 through 10–9).

Attach the bedroom end wall (number 1 in Fig. 10–10) to the second floor, flush at the bottom. Then attach the upper front wall (2) to the front edge of the floor panel, flush at the bottom, and to the front edge of the end wall. Attach the short side wall that comes forward from the front wall to the front of the living-room balcony wall (3) to floor panel and to the front of the front wall. Attach the living-room end wall (4) to the end edge of the floor panel. Then attach the front balcony wall (5) to the floor panel and to the front edge of the end wall and the short living-room wall.

Cut the upper-front window seat on

(Text continues on page 114)

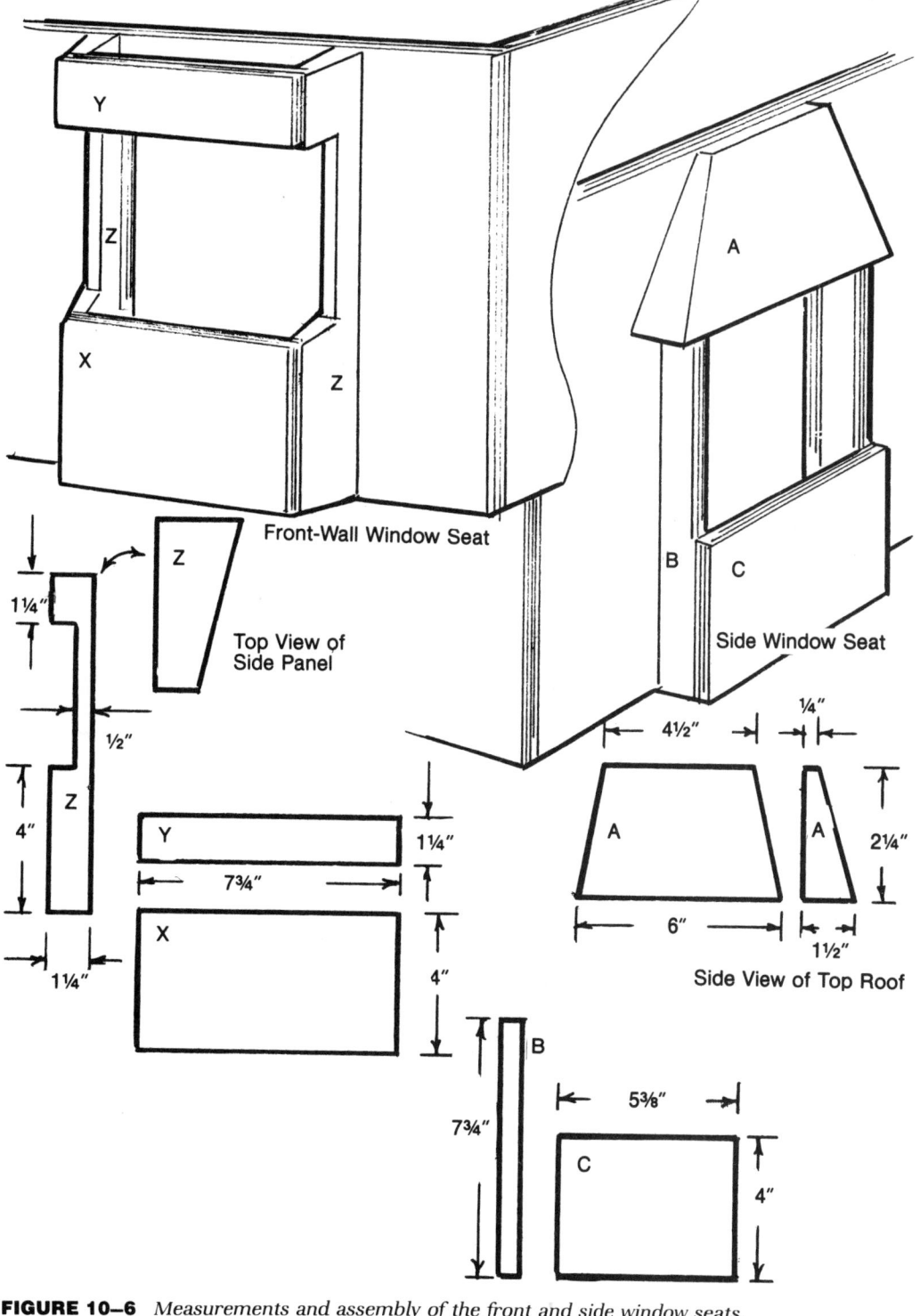

Y

Z

X

Z

Front-Wall Window Seat

A

B   C

Side Window Seat

Z

Top View of
Side Panel

1¼"

½"

4"

Z

1¼"

Y

7¾"

1¼"

X

4"

4½"

¼"

A

6"

A

1½"

2¼"

Side View of Top Roof

B

7¾"

5⅜"

C

4"

FIGURE 10–6 *Measurements and assembly of the front and side window seats.*

109

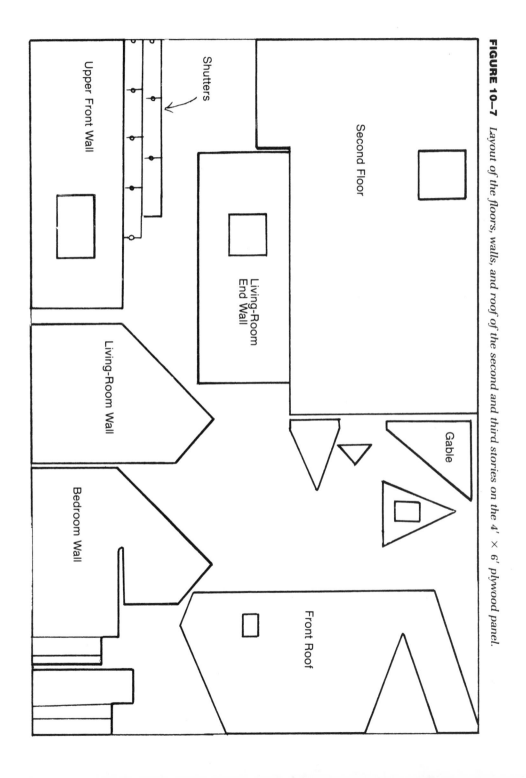

FIGURE 10-7 *Layout of the floors, walls, and roof of the second and third stories on the 4' × 6' plywood panel.*

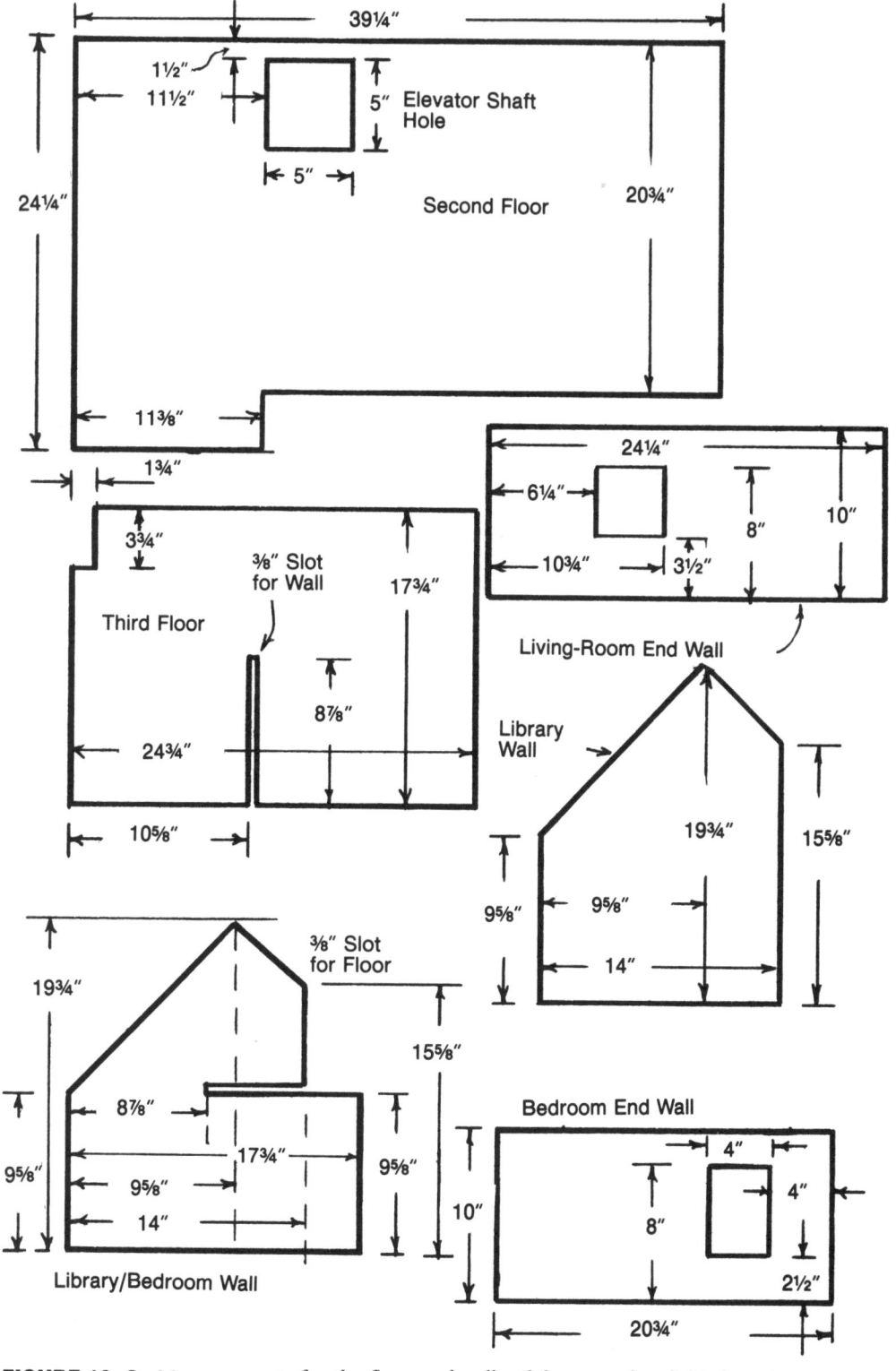

FIGURE 10–8 *Measurements for the floor and walls of the second and third stories.*

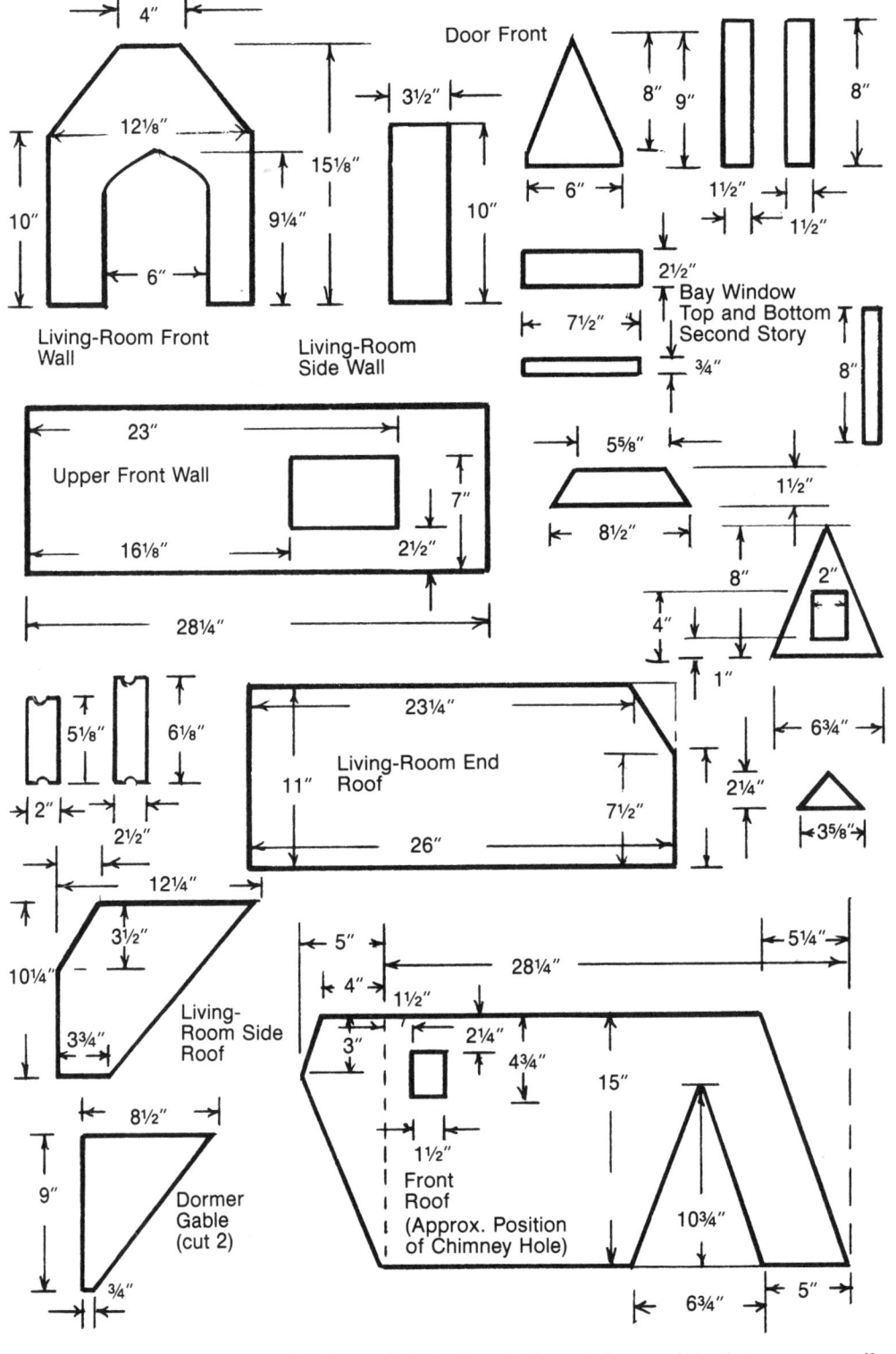

FIGURE 10–9 *Measurements for the roof, including the bay window, and the living-room walls.*

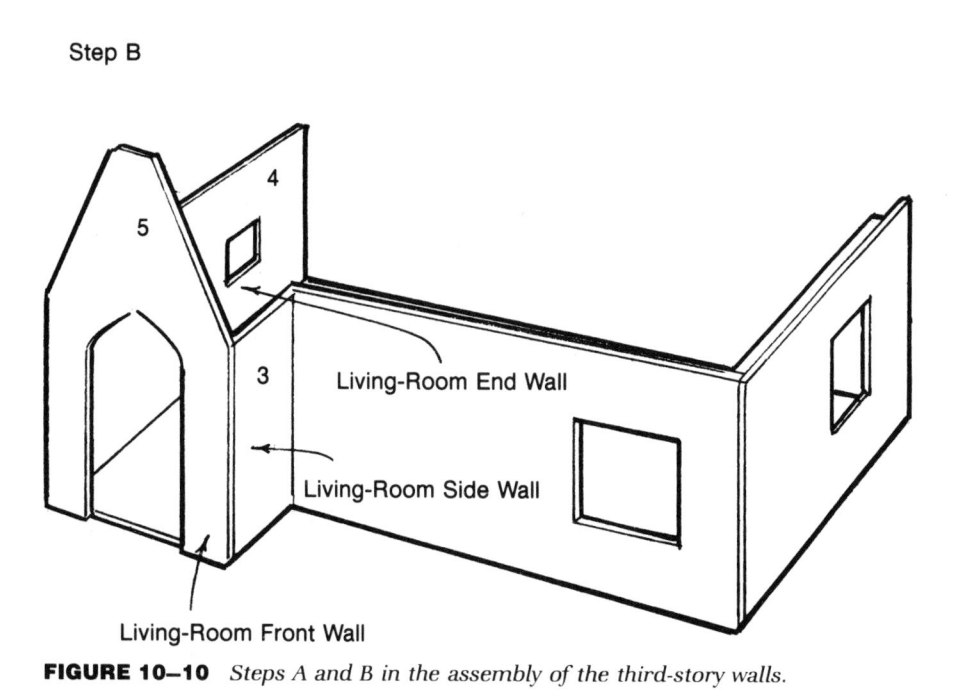

Step A

2

Second Floor

Upper Front Wall

1

Bedroom End Wall

Step B

4

5

Living-Room End Wall

3

Living-Room Side Wall

Living-Room Front Wall

FIGURE 10–10 *Steps A and B in the assembly of the third-story walls.*

the angle shown in Figure 10–6 and attach like the lower window-seat casements.

Cut the balcony from 1″ stock and drill holes for the dowels, as shown in Figure 10–12. Then cut seven 4″ lengths of $\frac{1}{2}$″ dowel and glue them in the holes in the balcony base and railing. Attach the balcony base and the ends of the railing to the front of the balcony wall with screws, driving them out through the front of the balcony wall on either side of the french-door opening.

Cut both sides of the gable roof that goes over the entry door, trimming them at the top joint (Fig. 10–11). Cut the gable front and attach it to the extended part of the floor panel. Attach the roof panels on top of the gable front, then drive a screw out through the front wall and into the rear of each gable roof side to pull them back onto the front wall.

The next step is to cut and attach the third-story floor and the two upstairs divider walls (see Fig. 10–11). Cut and attach $\frac{3}{4}$″ × $\frac{3}{8}$″ or $\frac{1}{2}$″ cleat to the library/living-room divider on the study side of the level of the tops of the upper front and end walls. Attach another cleat to the bedroom end wall on the inside, flush at the top. Using the two notches, slide the bedroom/library divider wall and the third-story floor panel together. Now set the floor panel down on the bedroom end wall and front wall, flush at the outsides, and screw it in place.

Square up the bedroom/library divider wall and mark its placement. Then measure and mark the positioning of screw holes through the bottom of the second-story floor panel and front wall to attach this divider wall. Next, position the library/living-room divider wall against the end edge of the third-story floor panel (resting down on the wall cleat). Square

up the wall and drive screws in through the front wall and up through the second-floor panel to attach the divider wall. Drive screws through the third-story floor panel and into the wall cleat.

☐ The Roof

The first step in roofing the house is to cut all roof panels from $\frac{3}{8}$″ plywood (see Figs. 10–3, 10–7, and 10–12). There would be all sorts of exotic angles to be cut if we were doing finish carpentry. But since the outside of the roof is to be covered with a thick layer of textured paint (which effectively fills in all gaps and cracks in the joinery), and the interior ceilings are to be covered with either wallpaper or cardboard "beams," you can cut all roof panels off straight with the saw blade left at the usual 90-degree position to the wood. After cutting out the panels, follow the roofing sequence in Figure 10–13.

Position the main front panel of the roof in place with two screws, overlapping the upper front wall by about $\frac{1}{2}$″ with its lower, front edge parallel to the upper edge of the wall (See Fig. 10–11). Then mark the hole for the living-room chimney or the living-room side of the divider wall. Cut this hole and the window hole by drilling a $\frac{1}{4}$″ or larger starter hole within the window outline; then cut out all sides with a saber saw.

Attach the main front roof panel to the top edges of the two divider walls, flush at the top angle, and onto the top of the front wall with screws angling down into the top edge grain of all three walls (see Fig. 10–11). Next, attach the triangular end roof panel (number 10 in Figure 10–11) to the underside of the main roof panel, flush along its angled end and to the bedroom end wall, overlapping it about $\frac{1}{2}$″ to $\frac{5}{8}$″. Angle the pilot holes down

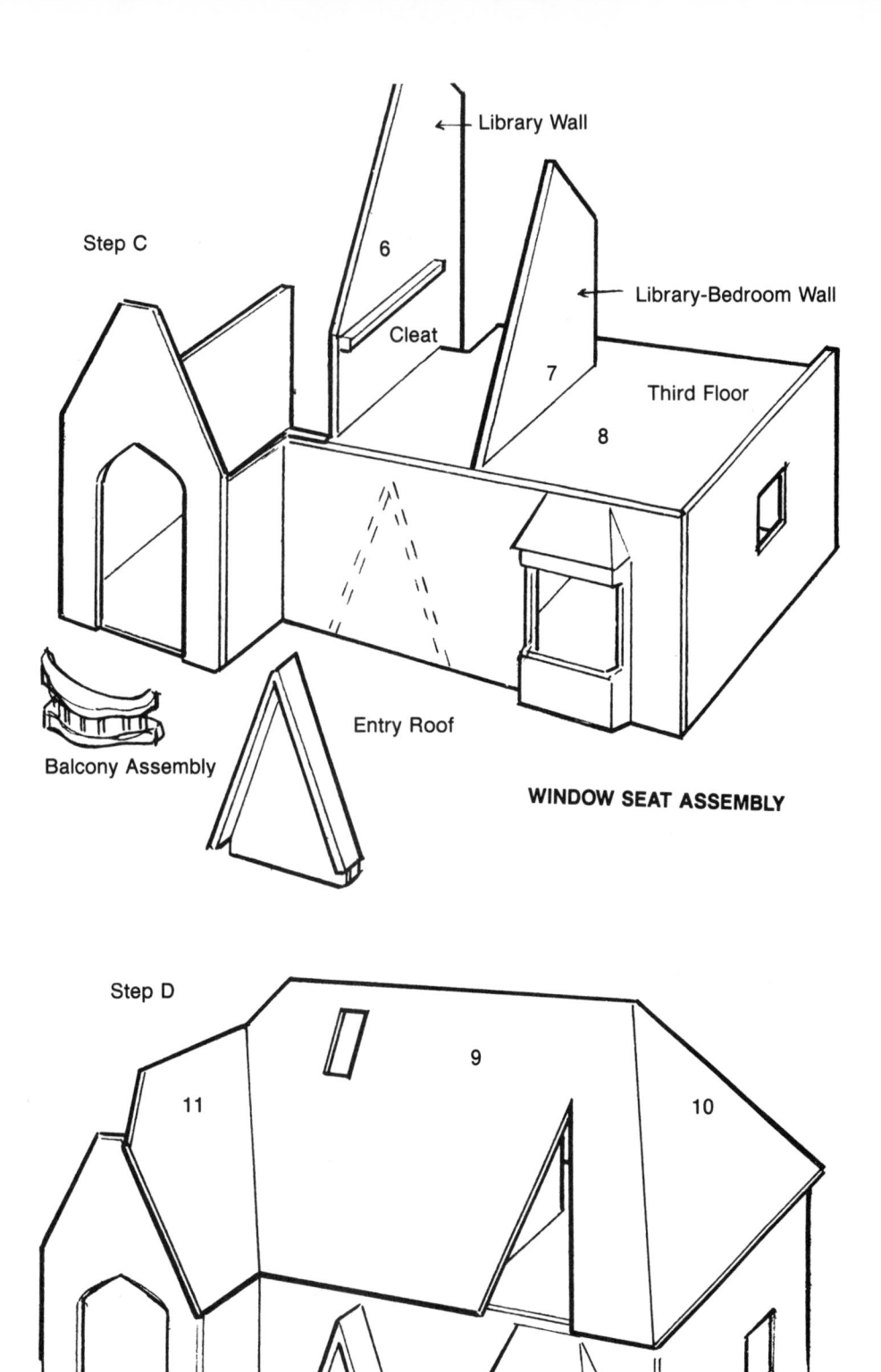

Step C

Library Wall

6

Cleat

Library-Bedroom Wall

7

Third Floor

8

Balcony Assembly

Entry Roof

WINDOW SEAT ASSEMBLY

Step D

9

11

10

FIGURE 10–11 *Steps C and D in the assembly of the third-story walls and roof.*

115

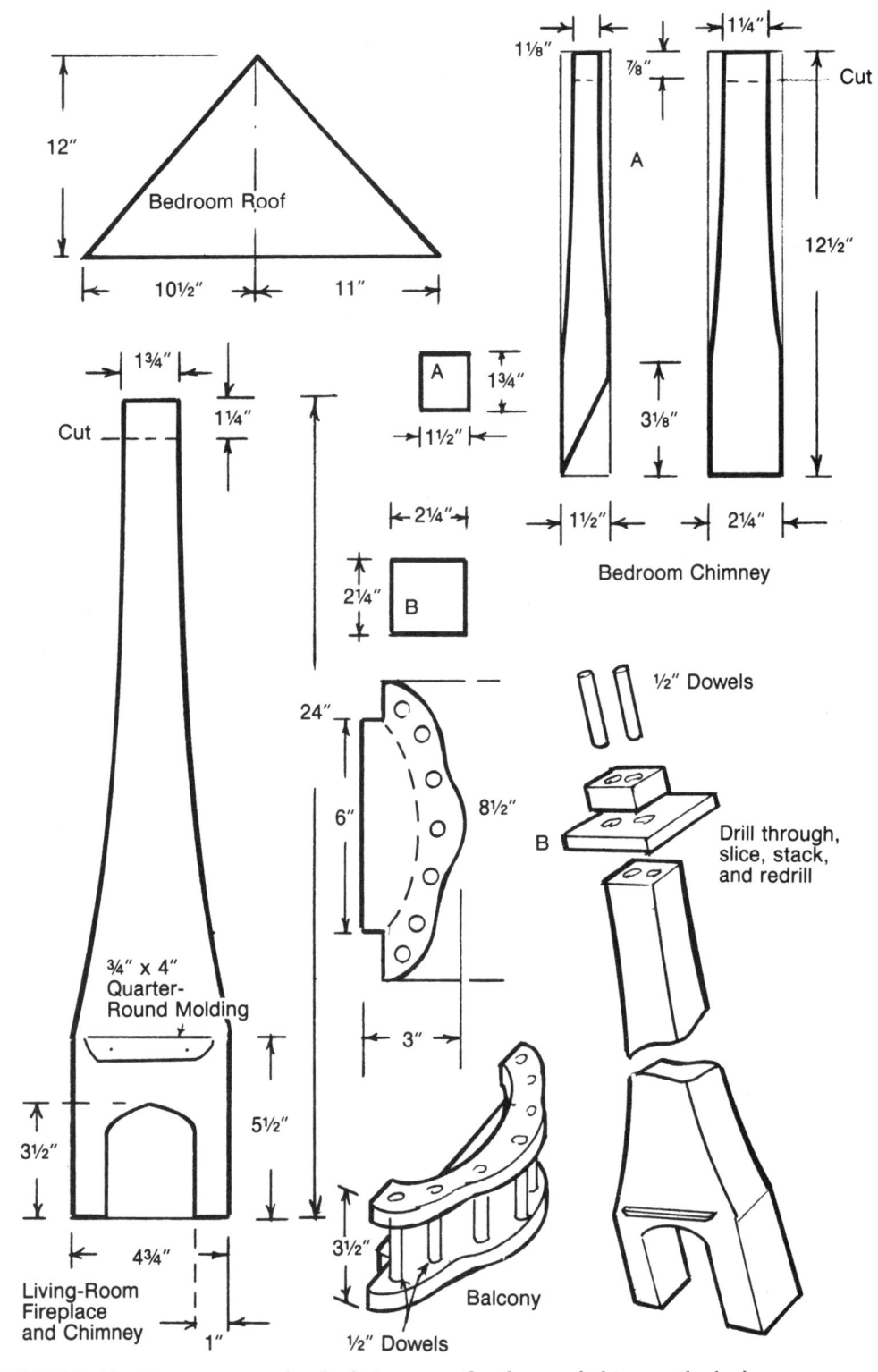

FIGURE 10–12 *Measurements for the living-room fireplace and chimney, the bedroom chimney, and the balcony and bedroom roof.*

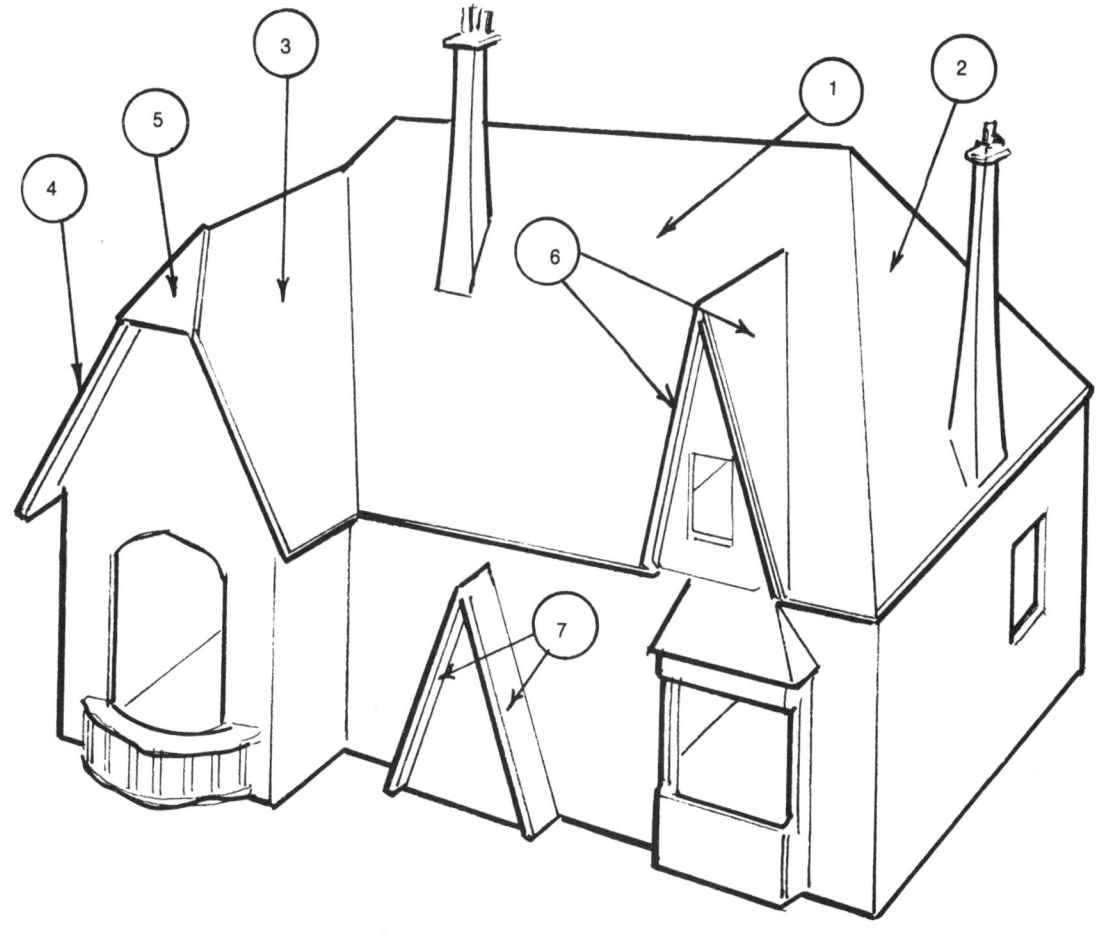

FIGURE 10–13 *Roofing sequence: (1) front roof; (2) bedroom roof; (3) living-room inboard roof; (4) living-room end roof; (5) living-room roof wedge; (6) dormer gables; and (7) entry gables.*

through the main roof panel, to sink into the edge grain of the end roof panel, and angle additional holes down through the end roof panel and into the top edge of the bedroom end wall.

The next step is to attach the small side of the gable roof over the living room that faces toward the center of the house (number 11 in Fig. 10–11). Drive screws forward through the main roof panel along its angled end edge and into the edge grain of the gable roof panel facing the rear of the house. Also drive screws through this panel and into the top edge grain of the balcony front wall and the short side wall facing the entry gable. Next, attach the end roof panel (number 4 in Fig. 10–13) by driving screws through it and into the top edge of the balcony front wall. Continue down into the top edge of the end wall with the roof eave overlapping the top of the wall about $\frac{3}{4}''$ to $\frac{7}{8}''$ then through the panel along its top edge and into the underside of the top edge of the gable panel just attached. Glue and nail the small triangle over the front of the balcony wall with 1" finishing nails.

Assemble the dormer roof panels (number 6 in Fig. 10–13) by placing the dormer window front on top of the lower front wall, aligned parallel to its front. Then place the right-side gable roof panel on it and drive screws in through the roof and into the top edge of the dormer. Drive more screws forward through the main roof panel along the right side of the dormer cutout so that the roof gable can be mounted flush with the inside of the cutout. Screw the opposite side of the gable to the other side of the top edge of the dormer front, and drive more screws out through the main roof panel and into the rear edge of the dormer roof gable. Drive screws in through one of the roof gables near the parallel top edges of the gables

to hold the halves together along this top line.

The next step is to cut the two chimneys from the redwood 2 × 4 stock (see Fig. 10–12). To create a chimney-tile effect, drill two $\frac{1}{2}''$-diameter holes into the top of the larger chimney and one hole into the shorter one. Cut off both chimneys about $1\frac{1}{4}''$ down from the top. Then cut the small squares of plywood, center the chimney tops over them, and mark the placement of the $\frac{1}{2}''$ holes of the chimney tops onto these squares. Drill the $\frac{1}{2}''$ holes through the squares, then tap a 3" length of $\frac{1}{2}''$ dowel down through the top of only the short chimney, through the square, and into the hole in the chimney itself. Make sure that both the chimney top and the square are facing the right way up before inserting the dowel. To hold the assembly together, glue all joining surfaces. The top of the dowel can be cut off on an angle from 1" to $1\frac{1}{2}''$ above the chimney top.

Place the shorter chimney vertically against the bedroom end-roof panel, then drive two screws through the roof panel and into the angled base of the chimney.

Nail the 1" × 4" quarter-round molding horizontally over the fireplace of the longer chimney to serve as a mantelpiece. Insert the top of this chimney through the hole in the roof. Then attach the fireplace with screws driven in through the library/bathroom side of the divider wall. Now glue and tap the $\frac{1}{2}''$ dowels through the holes in the chimney top, the square, and into the chimney itself. Trim about 1" $1\frac{1}{2}''$ above the chimney top.

☐ The Elevator

The elevator (Fig. 10–14) is made from a plywood top and bottom, with $\frac{3}{8}''$-dowel

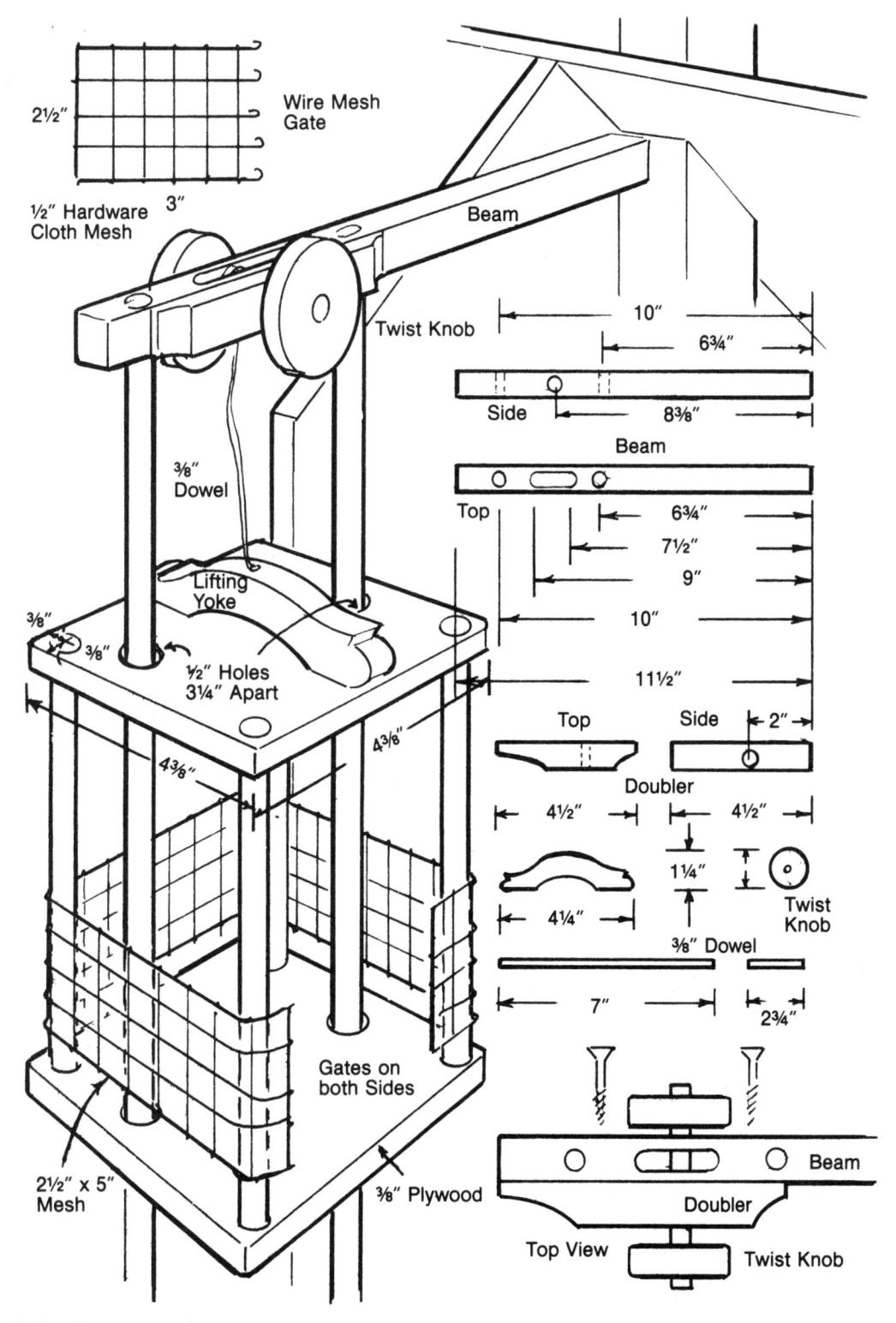

FIGURE 10–14 *Elevator measurements and assembly.*

corner posts and hardware-cloth mesh screening to provide the cage railing. The cage slides up and down along $\frac{3}{8}''$ dowels, which slip through $\frac{1}{2}''$ holes in the cage roof and floor, and a small twist knob at the top frame attached to the house winds the string that pulls the cage up and lets it down. Pretty complex.

To make the cage, cut the two squares of $\frac{3}{8}''$ plywood for the top and bottom panels. Then drill the $\frac{3}{8}''$ holes for the corner posts and the $\frac{1}{2}''$ holes for the guide dowels. For easy movement, all holes for the guide dowels must be aligned and the dowels must be straight. Cut the lifting yoke from the pine 1 × 6 as shown, drill a $\frac{1}{8}''$ hole into its raised center, then drive 1" screws through the bottom of the cage top to attach the yoke. Next, cut the four $\frac{3}{8}''$-dowel corner posts and glue and tap them firmly into the corner holes of the cage top and bottom (with the $\frac{1}{2}''$ dowel holes aligned).

Cut the beam, as shown, from the pine 1 × 6. Then drill $\frac{3}{8}''$ holes for the dowel slides, aligning them with the $\frac{1}{2}''$ holes in the cage on center. Drill two more holes so that you can use the saber saw to cut out the slot for the wound-up string on the twist shaft. Cut the doubler from the pine scrap and screw it to the lift beam.

Drill $\frac{3}{8}''$ hole through the side of the beam and doubler at the center of the slot. Next, cut a 1"-diameter disk of plywood and a $1\frac{1}{2}''$ disk from the pine scrap (using a hole-saw attachment for the power drill). Enlarge the center holes of the two disks to $\frac{5}{16}''$. Then tap a $2\frac{3}{4}''$ long piece of $\frac{3}{8}''$ dowel down into the glued center hole of the plywood disk. Next insert the other end of the dowel through the beam and the doubler and tap the end of the dowel into the $1\frac{1}{2}''$ disk. This shaft should turn (but not spin) in the hole through the beam. Drill a $\frac{1}{8}''$ hole

through the $\frac{3}{8}''$ dowel shaft inside the cut-out slot in the beam to accept the string.

Cut a $2\frac{1}{2}''$ to 3" band of $\frac{1}{2}''$ hardware-cloth mesh screening to fit around the four posts of the cage, leaving an opening about 2" wide on one side. Cut the hardware-cloth door as shown, and wrap the leftover ends around the adjacent mesh to form a hinge.

Next, cut the two $\frac{3}{8}''$ dowel guides to length and tap them into the bottom of the holes in the beam. Insert the bottoms of these dowels through the slide holes in the cage and hold the beam against the living-room side of the library/living-room divider wall, with the dowels extending down so that the elevator cage can be slid up and down the guide dowels without running into anything. Mark the position of the lift beam on the divider wall and the placement of the lower ends of the guide dowels on the bottom floor panel. Drill $\frac{3}{8}''$ holes at these points, insert the bottom ends of the dowels into the holes without glue, and screw the lift beam to the divider wall. Tie a length of string through the hole in the twist shaft; secure the other end through the yoke. After staining and painting, the guide dowels of the cage can be oiled to help sliding.

■ FINISHING

To prepare the walls, inside and out, and the roof panels for finishing, round off all sharp corners and edges, especially around the roof panels, with a Surform wood shaper. Any large knotholes or cracks on the interior of the rooms can also be filled with putty, flush with the surface, for easier painting or wallpapering.

To hold the upper stories in position,

place the upper unit over the lower one, with the front window seats and entry walls aligned and the overhang centered at the other walls. Place $\frac{3}{4}'' \times \frac{3}{4}''$ cleats up under the second-story floor and against the insides of the end walls. Mark the placement, then remove the upper unit, drive screws through the cleats and into the floor to attach them to keep the upper unit centered over the lower during play.

To fill in all the screw holes or cracks and gaps in the exterior finish of the walls, mix a batch of catalyzed polyester auto-body putty (or "Bondo") and spread it over the exterior surfaces of the walls with a 2" putty knife, using quick, short strokes to create a stuccolike texture. Skim the putty on, only $\frac{1}{16}''$ to $\frac{1}{8}''$ thick, and leave it slightly rough for a rustic effect. The same process can be used to texture the chimneys. After treating the walls, mix enough granular texturizer for a quart into rust-red enamel for the roof paint. This textured goo should be painted on $\frac{1}{8}''$ to about $\frac{3}{16}''$ thick over the whole roof surface. After applying the texture, brush the last strokes vertically to provide a thatchlike look. Paint the exterior of the house semigloss antique ivory, then paint on the brown half-timbering.

All glazing in the house is made from $\frac{1}{8}''$ Plexiglas. After cutting to shape, set the windows in place with a hot-glue gun (DAP tub-and-tile caulk also works well).

To give the effect of small-pane windows characteristic of Tudor houses, you can use $\frac{1}{8}''$-wide white tape, which is available either as pin striping tape at auto-supply stores or as border tape at art and graphic-supply stores. The cross-hatching should be $\frac{3}{4}''$ between vertical stripes and 1" between horizontal stripes. Then run a border around each window.

Cut the shutters from scrap plywood, as shown in Figure 10–7, sand and paint them a flat green, and nail them in place.

Give the french doors at the front of the upstairs living room the same tape treatment as the windows to create the illusion of small-paned windows. Make a hinge for each door by running about $\frac{1}{4}''$ of 2" gray duct tape up the sides of the two doors; smooth the rest of the tape onto the adjacent wall on either side of the french-door opening. The tape on the wall will be covered by the wallpaper.

Paint the garage and vaulted ceiling of the living room with off-white semigloss latex. We've used both commercial dollhouse wallpaper available at hobby stores and Contact paper to cover the walls. Smooth the paper into place, then run a fingernail around the edges of the wall to mark the dimensions directly onto the paper. Do the forward walls first, allowing them to overlap onto the adjacent side walls. Then cut the side walls to size, providing an overlapped corner at each joint.

THE STABLE TACK ROOM/CORRAL SET

■ MATERIALS LIST

One 4′ × 4′ plywood panel, $\frac{3}{8}''$ thick
One 5″ length of clear-grained fir, 2 × 2
    stock, or any substitute
One 12″ length of clear-grained redwood,
    1 × 6 stock
50 1″ galvanized finishing nails
Scrap of a redwood 2 × 2
2 doz. $1\frac{1}{2}''$ #7 flathead screws
2′ × 3′ plywood, $\frac{3}{8}''$ thick
6′ clear-grained 1″, redwood stock
$\frac{3}{4}''$ paneling nails
$\frac{3}{4}''$ brass butt hinges

☐ *See color insert for completed project.*

The Stable Tack Room/Corral Set was created to provide a storage place for the
popular Brier plastic horses that are so
important to many preteens. The scale
that we used was picked to fit both popular sizes of these collector horses and to
fit loosely into the scale of the Dollhouse.

Like the Dollhouse, the Stable was built
of $\frac{3}{8}''$ plywood, using butt joints at the corners with $1\frac{1}{2}''$, #7 plated flathead wood
screws and squeeze-bottle glue to make
the joints secure. To provide a good grip
without splitting, we used an adjustable

drill/countersink bit to fit in the power
drill. We drilled through the side of one
panel about $\frac{3}{16}''$ to $\frac{1}{4}''$ in from the edge and
angled into the center lamination of the
edge grain of the butted plywood panel.

Screws were used instead of nails to
prevent the first joints from being
pounded loose before completion of the
last joints. Screws also permit easy repo-
sitioning of parts if adjustments are
needed.

■ CUTTING

To start construction of the Stable Tack
Room, cut out all the plywood panels as
shown in Figure 11–1. Cut the windows
by marking the outlines, drilling a $\frac{1}{4}''$ or
larger starter hole within them, and then
cutting out the shapes with a saber saw.
There are several ways of giving a rough
board-and-batten appearance to the
walls. Thin strips of spruce, about $\frac{1}{8}'' \times$
$\frac{1}{16}''$ (available at airplane-model supply
stores) can be glued on approximately $\frac{3}{4}''$
apart after the structure has been assembled but before it has been painted. Alter-
natively, you can score the walls with a
hand-held circular saw by setting the

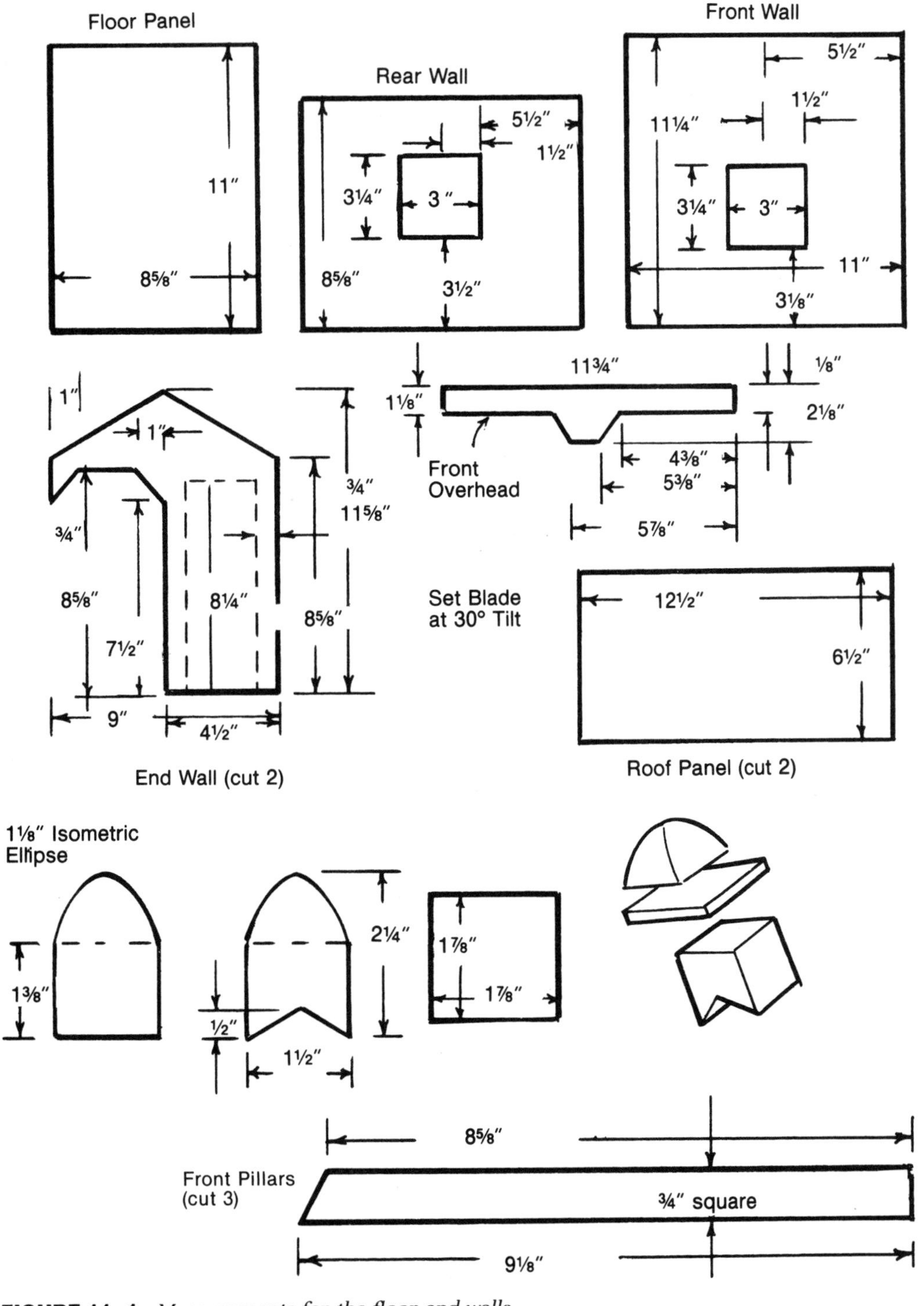

Floor Panel

Front Wall

Rear Wall

11"

8⅝"

5½"

1½"

3¼"

3"

8⅝"

3½"

5½"

1½"

11¼"

3¼"

3"

11"

3⅛"

1"

1"

¾"

11⅝"

¾"

8⅝"

8¼"

7½"

8⅝"

9"

4½"

End Wall (cut 2)

1⅛"

11¾"

⅛"

2⅛"

Front
Overhead

4⅜"

5⅜"

5⅞"

Set Blade
at 30° Tilt

12½"

6½"

Roof Panel (cut 2)

1⅛" Isometric
Ellipse

1⅜"

2¼"

½"

1½"

1⅞"

1⅞"

8⅝"

¾" square

Front Pillars
(cut 3)

9⅛"

FIGURE 11–1 *Measurements for the floor and walls.*

blade depth to about $\frac{1}{8}$", marking vertical lines up the walls about $\frac{3}{4}$" apart, and then cutting along these lines to make a scored face representing individual boards. We ripped the three posts supporting one side of the roof (about $\frac{3}{4}$" square) from the 1×6 stock.

Cut the dovecote on the ridge of the roof from a scrap of a redwood 2×2. Slice it so that the square of plywood can be sandwiched between the top and the bottom as shown (in a manner similar to that for the chimneys on the Dollhouse). Drill a $\frac{1}{16}$" hole down through the top at the center, penetrating all three layers. Then glue all joining surfaces and drive a $2\frac{1}{2}$" finishing nail down through the layers, leaving about $\frac{1}{2}$" of nail sticking out the top as a sort of topknot.

■ ASSEMBLY

To assemble the building, follow Figures 11–2 and 11–3. Drive in screws about $2\frac{1}{2}$" apart through the rear side wall near the bottom and into one of the longer edges of the floor panel. Next, attach the end panels to the end edges of the floor panel and the back wall panel with screws and glue. This is a good time to decide which interior fixtures should be included, (such as dowels coming out of the walls about 3" to 4" up from the floor to store saddles, and hooks on the walls to hang up bridles and reins. After doing the necessary drilling and gluing to fix up the interior, attach the center walls by drilling and driving screws in through the end walls and up through the floor. Mount the walls flush with the front edges of the side walls.

Attach the end posts to the insides of the end walls (flush at the front edges) and to the floor panel (flush with the corners). Attach the front overhead to the fronts of these two posts, with the top edge either beveled to match the roof angle or mounted down from the tops of the end walls about $\frac{1}{8}$" to clear the bottom of the roof panel. Then attach the center post to the back of the overhead and to the floor.

Next, attach the rear roof panel to the tops of the rear and end walls. Center this panel with the beveled edge lying along the top of the center ridge over the front wall. Attach the dovecote to the center of the front roof panel, with its midpoint over the beveled edge of the panel, by driving a screw up through the bottom of the panel and into the lower edge of the dovecote base.

Round the corner edges of the roof panels with a Surform serrated wood shaper. Then give the structure a light sanding before painting the walls with semigloss latex enamel green (including the sides of the dovecote). Paint the roof panels with the same textured paint mix that was used on the roof of the Dollhouse. Then cut a $1\frac{1}{4}$"-diameter disk from a scrap of $\frac{1}{4}$" plywood. Glue it to the midpoint of the end wall (the one without a door opening), with its center about 2" down from the top of the wall; then paint on a clock face.

We painted the clock, the posts, and the plywood square on the dovecote a glossy white. We used $\frac{1}{8}$" wide auto-body trim pinstripe tape around the door and the window to outline openings.

To build the corral, cut a base from $\frac{3}{8}$" plywood as shown in Figure 11–4, using a circular saw for the outer dimensions and a saber saw for the notches. Rip the fence posts and rails from clear-grained 1" redwood stock ($\frac{3}{8}$" $\times$ $\frac{3}{4}$") and nail them together with ribbed $\frac{3}{4}$" paneling nails. Nail together the sides, the gate, and the ends,

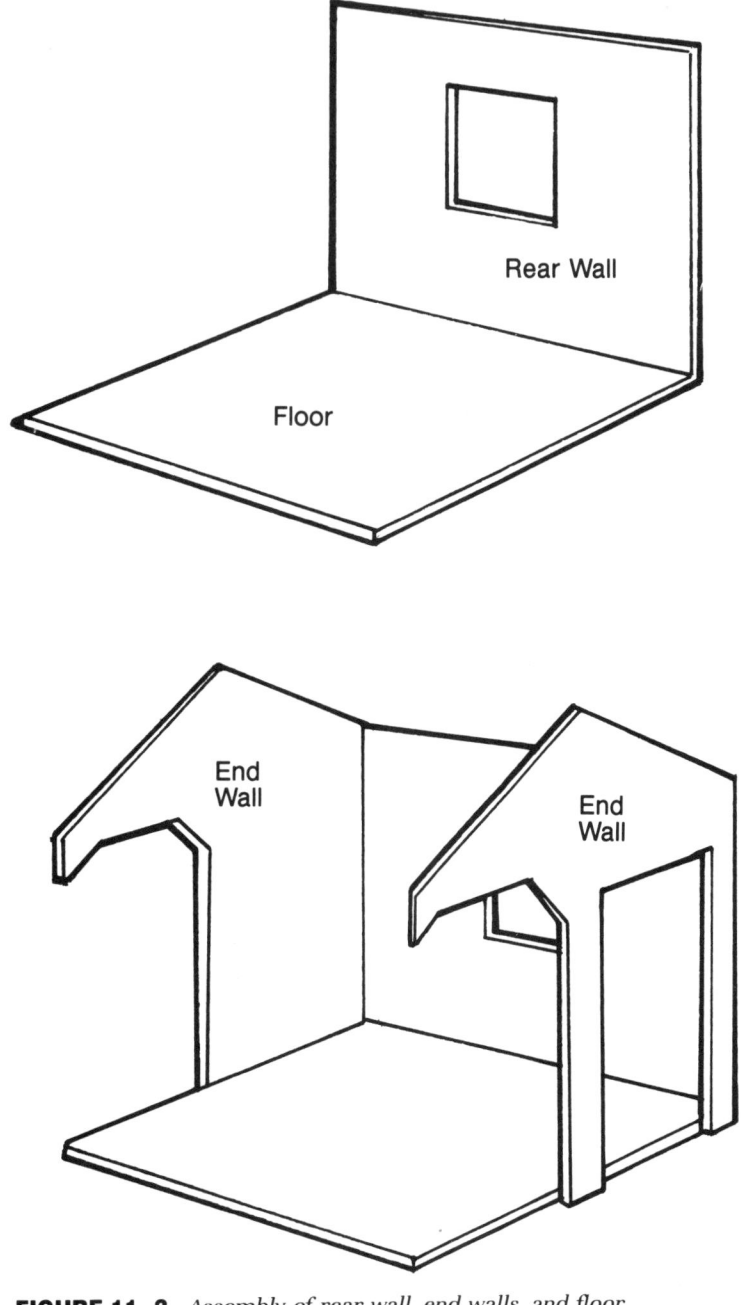

FIGURE 11–2 *Assembly of rear wall, end walls, and floor.*

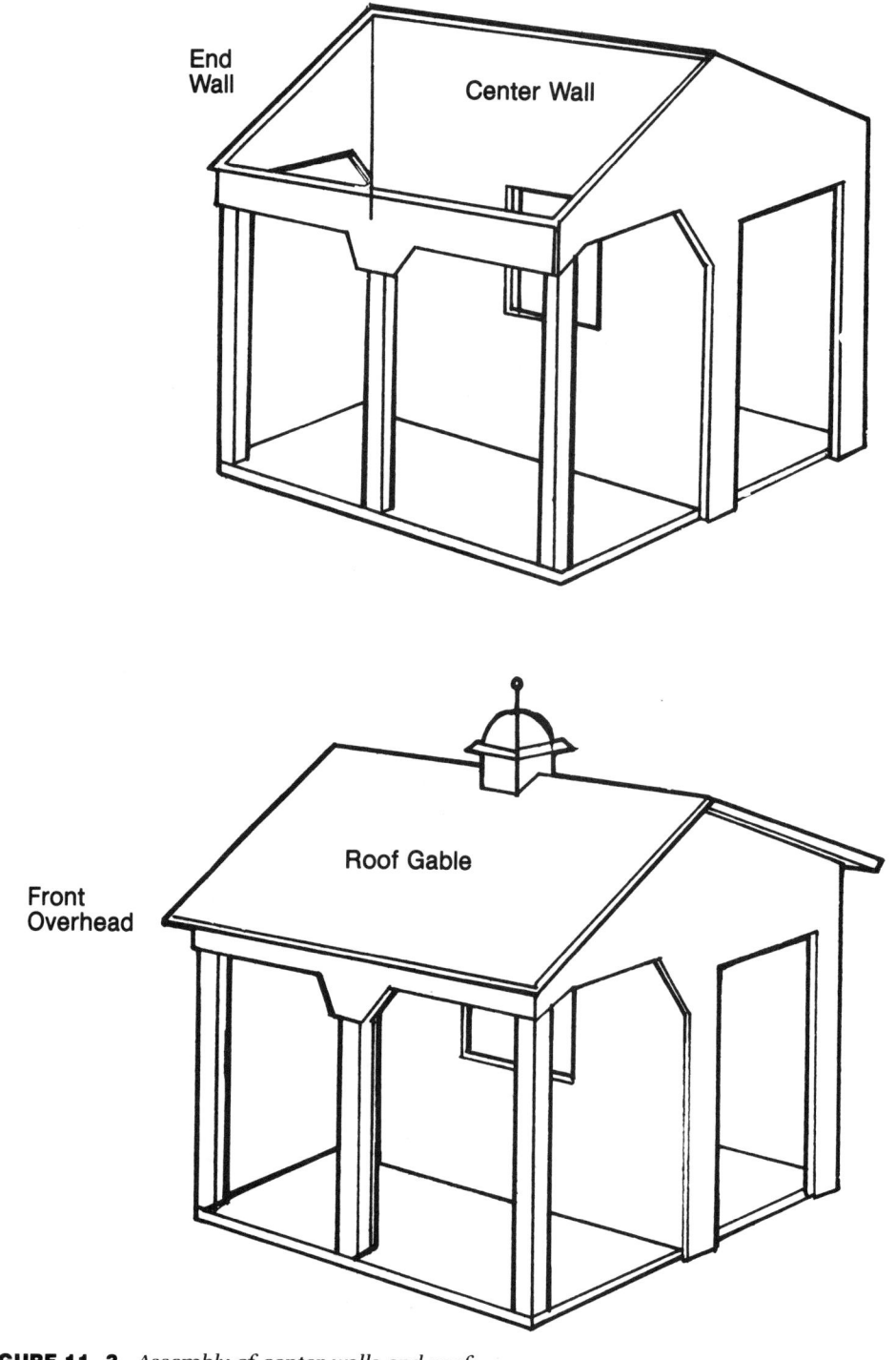

FIGURE 11—3 *Assembly of center walls and roof.*

THE STABLE TACK ROOM/CORRAL SET

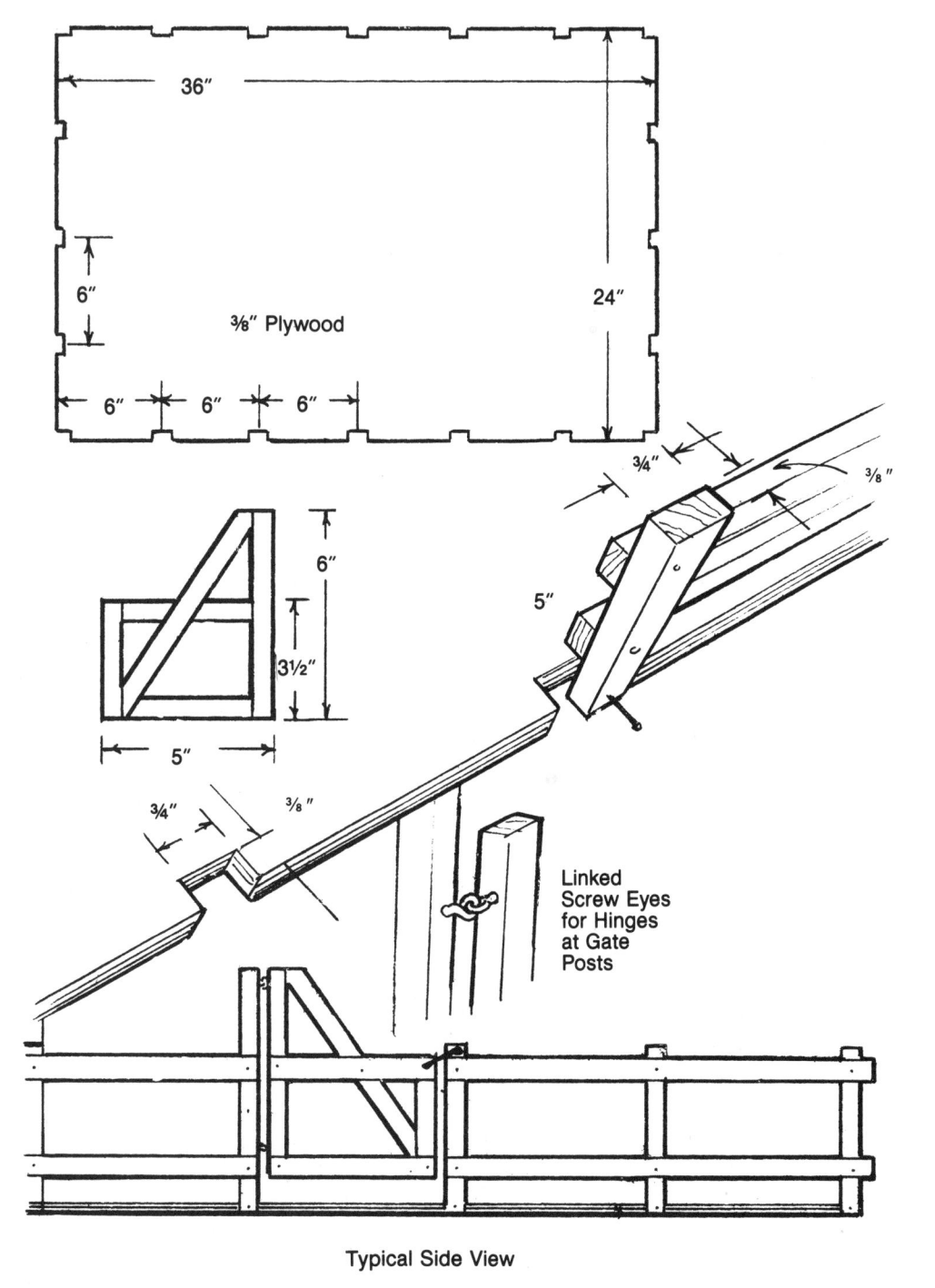

36″

6″

24″

⅜″ Plywood

6″   6″   6″

6″

3½″

5″

¾″   ⅜″

5″

¾″   ⅜″

Linked
Screw Eyes
for Hinges
at Gate
Posts

Typical Side View

FIGURE 11–4 *Corral assembly.*

and put glue at each overlapped joint. To attach the sides and ends to the base, drill $\frac{1}{16}''$ pilot holes through the bottom of posts fitted into the notches of the base. Nail the posts to the base with 1″ nails.

Use $\frac{3}{4}''$ brass butt hinges and a bent nail latch, as shown, to hang the gate. Cut the pasture from green plastic indoor/outdoor "grass" carpeting.

THE THREE-WAY PEDAL TRUCK

■ MATERIALS LIST

8' length of #2 pine 1 × 12 stock
Two 10' lengths of clear fir 1 × 3 stock
Four 6' lengths of $\frac{3}{4}'' \times \frac{3}{4}''$ pine or fir
    molding
8' length of $\frac{1}{2}''$ quarter-round molding
4' × 8' ACX exterior-grade plywood, $\frac{1}{2}''$
    thick
4' × 4' ACX exterior-grade plywood, $\frac{3}{8}''$
    thick
4' × 4' ACX exterior-grade plywood, $\frac{1}{4}''$
    thick

Bolts:
Twelve $\frac{1}{4}'' \times 3''$
One $\frac{1}{4}'' \times 2''$
Eight $\frac{1}{4}'' \times 1''$
Sixteen $2\frac{1}{2}'' \times \frac{1}{4}''$
Two $\frac{3}{8}'' \times 6''$ (or $\frac{3}{8}'' \times 6''$ threaded rod
    with nuts)

Washers:
Five $\frac{1}{4}''$
Two $\frac{5}{16}''$
Four $\frac{3}{8}''$
Four $\frac{1}{2}''$

Nuts:
Thirty-eight $\frac{1}{4}''$
Five $\frac{5}{16}''$

Four $\frac{3}{8}''$
Four $\frac{1}{2}''$

Cotter Pins:
Two $\frac{1}{8}''$

U-Bolts:
Three $\frac{1}{4}'' \times 3''$

Threaded Rods:
$\frac{5}{16}'' \times 21''$
$\frac{1}{2}'' \times 24''$

Unthreaded Rods:
Two $\frac{3}{8}'' \times 36''$
Two $\frac{1}{2}'' \times 36''$

Pipe Fittings:
Two $\frac{1}{2}''$ galvanized T-fitting
Eleven $\frac{1}{2}''$ galvanized four-hole floor
    flanges
Two 3" lengths of $\frac{1}{2}''$ galvanized pipe
$23\frac{1}{2}''$ length of $\frac{1}{2}''$ galvanized pipe
Two 3" lengths of $\frac{3}{8}''$ galvanized pipe
Two $38\frac{1}{2}''$ lengths of $\frac{3}{8}''$ galvanized pipe
Two $\frac{3}{8}''$ brass 90-degree ell fitting
$\frac{1}{2}''$ galvanized coupler
8" length of $\frac{1}{2}$ O.D. copper pipe
Five $\frac{1}{2}'' \times 1''$ long galvanized nipples
Two $\frac{1}{2}'' \times 1''$ long brass nipples
Four $\frac{3}{4}''$ galvanized pipe caps
Four $\frac{3}{4}''$ male, $\frac{1}{2}''$ female reducer bushings
Eight $\frac{1}{2}''$ male, $\frac{1}{4}''$ female reducer bushings

Other Hardware and Accessories:
$\frac{5}{8}'' \times 2\frac{1}{2}''$ iron 90-degree angle bracket
Four $\frac{5}{8}'' \times 3''$ iron straps
Two 2" butt hinges
Two 3" butt hinges
Window twist latch
$1\frac{1}{4}'' \times 3''$ galvanized conduit hanger strap
15' length of underground feeder cable
　　($\frac{1}{4}'' \times \frac{1}{2}''$ 2-wire electric line)
11" × 11" square of expanded aluminum
　　or iron
$16\frac{1}{4}'' \times 16\frac{1}{4}''$ aluminum or galvanized
　　flashing sheeting
Four 16" × $1\frac{3}{4}''$ Schwinn bike tires (to fit
　　S–7 rims)
Two 4" diameter battery ceiling lights
Two bike reflectors (red)
21" length of garden hose (male end)
Garden-hose end cap
Two plastic garden-hose-replacement end
　　clamps
One roll of chrome tape
One quart polyester auto-body putty
One tube DAP tub and tile sealer
Three hundred 1" #8 plated flathead
　　wood screws
One hundred $1\frac{1}{2}''$ #8 plated flathead wood
　　screws
One hundred 1" ribbed paneling nails
One hundred 1" × $\frac{5}{8}''$ corrugated
　　fasteners
One gallon oil-base gloss enamel paint
One pint satin black enamel

For Van Back:
4' × 8' ACX exterior-grade plywood, $\frac{1}{4}''$
　　thick
4' length of fir or pine 1 × 4 stock
Two 8' lengths of $\frac{3}{4}'' \times \frac{3}{4}''$ fir or pine
　　molding
10' length of fir 1 × 2 stock
Window twist latch
Four ornamental hinges
Barrel bolt latch

12' length of underground feeder cable
$2\frac{1}{2}'$ × 4' piece of vinyl

☐ *See color insert for completed project.*

Since the handmade wheels for The Pedal Fire Truck in Chapter 8 worked out well, with the right proportions for a vintage machine, we decided to be even more ambitious and try lever drive and full fenders, features we'd drawn up in countless designs but never used. As it turned out, assembling the bent plywood fenders wasn't the test of will we were prepared for, and looking back, we wished we'd tried making them years ago.

The result is a three-way pedal truck based loosely on Model A Ford lines, with a few Hispaño-Suiza lines thrown in around the fenders. The truck, with all the detailing that's so much fun to add, is heavy. And although it can be driven by relatively young drivers, thanks to a low-geared drive system, it should be kept away from steeper hills when there's no adult supervision. The lever drive can also be back-pedaled for an effective brake, and even though there are no crank-mounted pedals to flail around at speed, a lot of momentum can be built up on a long hill. In spite of the truck's weight, we're continually amazed at how some pretty small drivers have skidded to a downhill stop and taken off on some steep grades.

The truck can be used in three different modes. Switching from one to another takes only a few minutes and a screwdriver. The van back is held to the rear-deck box with two wing nuts, and the windshield posts are fastened to the cowl with two removable screws. The van back has double rear doors and side and front window openings for a not-too-en-

closed feel in the cab. With the van back removed, half-hinges mounted to the bottom of the dump/pick-up back can be locked down onto the deck with removable hinge pins.

A door was cut into the left side of the cab and latched with a window clasp. Body-trim lines were made from double-wire underground feeder cable bent and nailed in place. The hood louvers were cut from $\frac{1}{2}''$ quarter-round moldings. With kingpins made from greased $\frac{1}{2}''$ galvanized pipe fittings, steering is quick and precise.

■ CONSTRUCTION NOTE

To join all quarter-inch or half-inch plywood panels to frame parts, we used 1" #8 flathead plated wood screws, after first drilling a corresponding pilot hole with a combination drill/countersink bit. When joining two 1" lumber parts together, we used $1\frac{1}{2}''$ #8 plated flathead wood screw.

Screws are better than nails for creating a strong structure without pounding it to pieces before you've even finished building it. But setting screws can wreck your wrist, so we used either a Yankee push-type screwdriver or the screwdriver bit from the Yankee mounted in a variable-speed $\frac{3}{8}''$ drill.

We used yellow squeeze-bottle aliphatic glue on all joints, except at the fender mounts (to allow easy removal) and the outboard wheel disks (to permit eventual tire replacement).

Figure 12–1 shows the general construction layout. The truck has a chassis and front-suspension cross-members cut from 1" × 3" clear fir (or other medium to hard wood, like spruce). The engine box was made from $\frac{1}{4}''$ ACX exterior-grade plywood, whereas the cab, rear deck, and

dump bed were cut from $\frac{1}{2}''$ ACX plywood. The van back was made of $\frac{1}{4}''$ plywood with 1" × 2" fir windshield posts. Fenders were assembled from $\frac{1}{2}''$ plywood backs with $\frac{1}{4}''$ plywood screwed down to the edge grains of the backs.

The most important components of a vintage car project like this are the wheels, which have to be reasonably accurate in proportions of diameter to thickness to maintain that 1920's look. Unfortunately, there aren't many wheels left on the market with the right look (and they're expensive if you do find them). To solve this supply problem with the Pedal Fire Truck, we developed a sandwiched, three-layer wheel out of 1" pine stock and $\frac{3}{8}''$ plywood, with a four-hole galvanized-pipe floor flange holding copper bearings. This provides extremely sturdy wheels that clamp over the side-walls of standard Schwinn 16" × $1\frac{3}{4}''$ bike tires. These wheels have gone many miles now without any trouble (or a flat!), so we used them on the Model A pedal truck, too.

■ CUTTING, SHAPING, AND ASSEMBLY

□ The Wheels

Building the wheels is a major part of the construction steps as well as the cost. So if you do happen to find a set of four 16" diameter wheels that can be adapted to $\frac{3}{8}''$ to $\frac{1}{2}''$ axles for around $15, go ahead and buy them. Ball or roller bearings aren't essential for a light, low-speed machine like this, so if you can find some wheels with hubs that can be drilled to take $\frac{1}{2}''$ O.D. copper tubing in front and $\frac{1}{2}''$ I.D. copper pipe at rear, you can use the copper as a plain bearing. Since the rear axle is bent into a crank and the standard length of

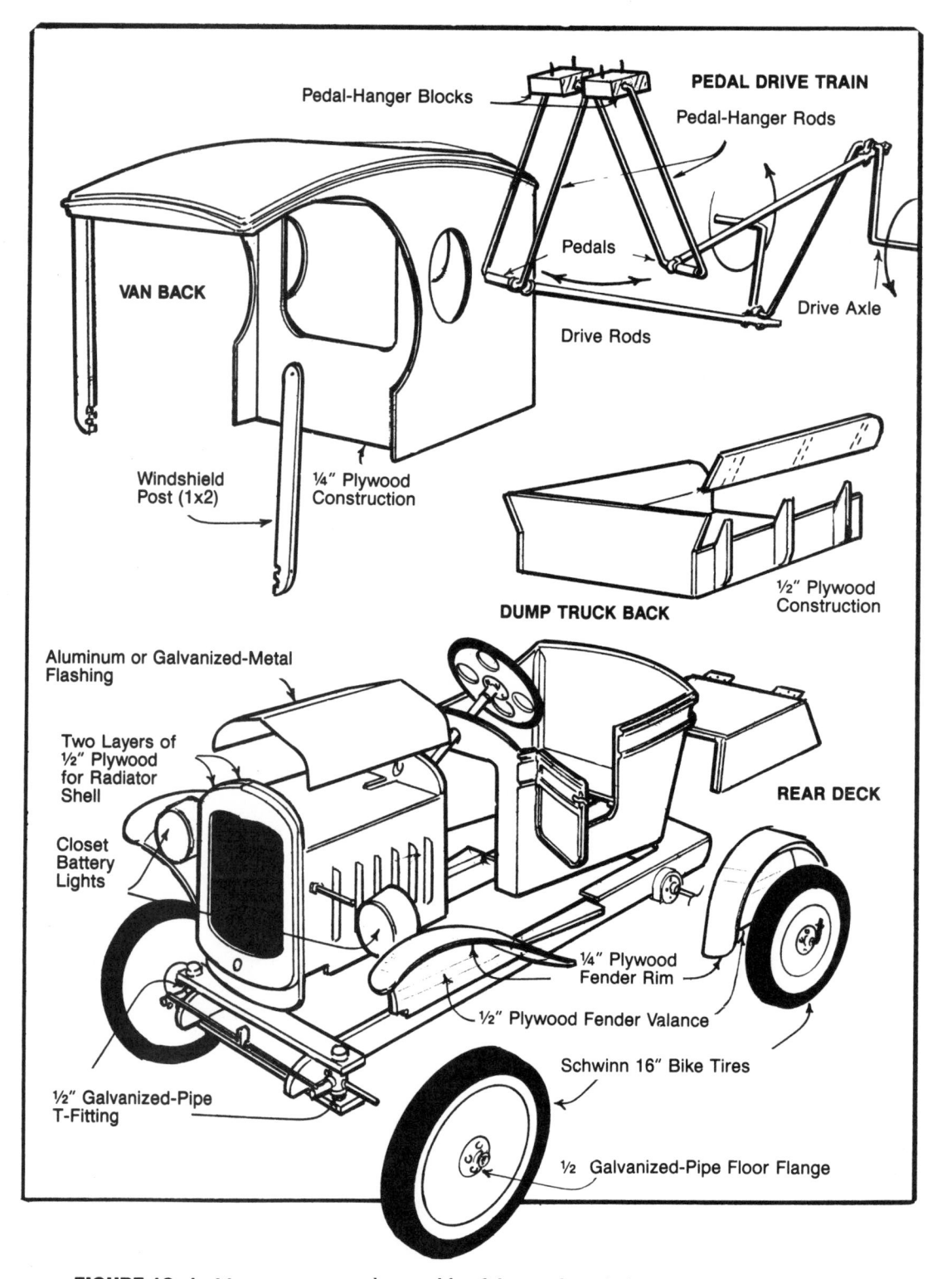

FIGURE 12–1 *Measurements and assembly of the truck, including* (top right) *the pedal drive train and dump-truck base and* (top left) *the van back.*

common soft-iron rods is 36″, we use two axles to mount the rear wheels—one to spin as a crank driving one of the wheels and a second, stationary axle to carry a free wheel.

If you find a set of wheels, remember that one will have to be fastened securely to the drive axle. (Figure 12–7, top left, shows how to bend the axle over so that it can be U-bolted to the wood wheel.) The joint between the axle and the drive wheel takes a lot of torque, so if you're bolting to a spoke wheel, clamp the axle to a ring that in turn you have clamped or fastened to all the spokes on one side of the wheel. This will spread the force to the entire wheel. The neater way, of course, is to weld the axle tightly to the wheel at the hub.

Figures 12–9 (top) and 12–2 show how the wheels are cut and assembled from a half-sheet of $\frac{3}{8}$″ plywood and an 8′ length of 1″ × 12″ #2 pine. Each wheel is made up of a $15\frac{3}{8}$″-diameter pine disk in the center, with a $14\frac{1}{4}$″-diameter disk mounted to the inboard side. The $15\frac{3}{8}$″-diameter plywood ring and 13″-diameter disk are mounted on the outboard side.

The basic construction goes like this: The two-part pine disk is assembled edge to edge. Then the $15\frac{3}{8}$″ O.D./$13\frac{1}{2}$″ I.D. ring is screwed to the outboard side of the wheel. The tire is slipped on and the 13″ disk screwed to the outboard side of the wheel and the $14\frac{1}{4}$″ disk to the inboard, as shown in Figure 12–2, bottom left. This clamps the tire to the pine disk, whereas the ring inside the tire gives a little natural bulge on the outer sidewall.

To build the wheels, use a beam compass to draw the rings and disks onto the plywood as shown in Figure 12–9, with the small disk (B) drawn inside the rings to save wood. Make a compass from a 16″ length of batten or a stick about the width and thickness of a yardstick. Drill a $\frac{1}{8}$″ hole through the stick about 1″ in from one end. Then measure from the center of this hole to the length of the radius of the circle to be drawn and drill a second $\frac{1}{8}$″ hole. Insert a nail through one hole and a pencil point through the second, then swing the stick with a nail holding the center and the pencil drawing the arc (Fig. 12–2, top).

Draw the outside of the four rings first. Drill the holes in the compass $7\frac{11}{16}$″ apart on center and draw the circles (A), keeping an outward pressure on the pencil throughout the swing. Next, draw the inboard disks (C) with the holes on the compass $7\frac{1}{8}$″ apart, the inside circle of the rings with the holes $6\frac{3}{4}$″ apart, and finally the outboard disks with the compass holes $6\frac{1}{2}$″ apart (B).

Use a saber saw, cutting slowly to avoid lifting the grain at the cuts, starting with the disks inside the rings. Since there's a $\frac{1}{4}$″ difference between the disks and the inside circle of the rings, drill a $\frac{1}{4}$″ starter hole between the circles and insert the saber-saw blade to get the cut underway. Cut the 13″-diameter disks, then the inside and outside of the rings. Finally, cut the $14\frac{1}{4}$″-diameter disks.

The next step is to cut the inner disks from pine. Since the widest boards we could find were 1 × 12s (about $\frac{3}{4}$″ × $11\frac{1}{4}$″), we made the disks in two parts as shown in Figure 12–2 (top). We used the outer edge of one plywood ring to mark $15\frac{3}{8}$″-diameter arcs onto the 1 × 12, marking where its edge lies against the bottom of the ring. Then we aligned these edge marks on the ring with the edge of the 1 × 12 to draw the smaller portion of the circle onto the board (Fig. 12–2, right). We repeated these steps to draw both parts of all four disks onto the 1 × 12. Then we cut out the parts with the saber saw and

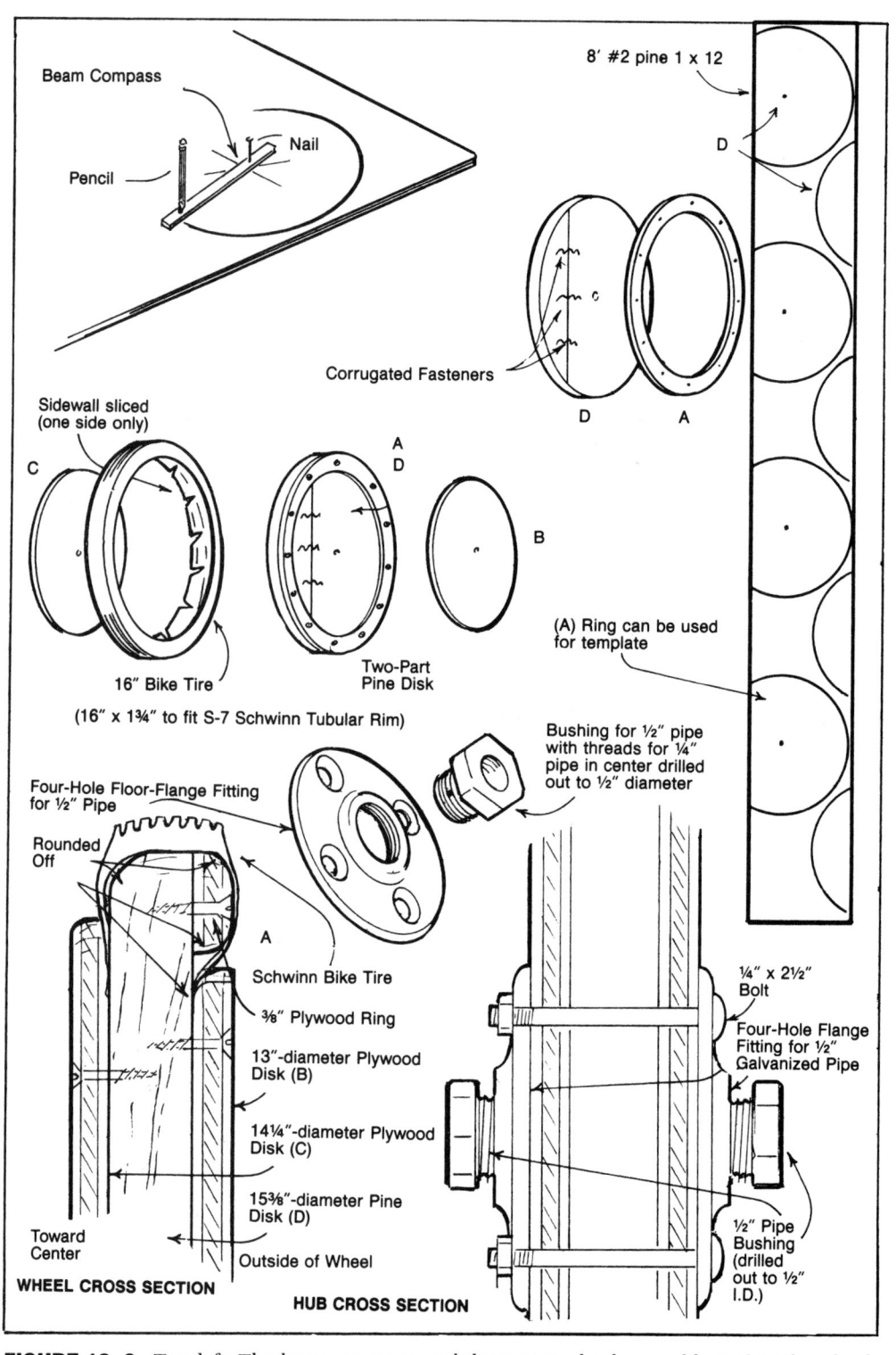

Beam Compass

Pencil

Nail

8' #2 pine 1 x 12

D

Corrugated Fasteners

D   A

Sidewall sliced
(one side only)

C

A
D

B

16" Bike Tire

Two-Part
Pine Disk

(16" x 1¾" to fit S-7 Schwinn Tubular Rim)

(A) Ring can be used
for template

Bushing for ½" pipe
with threads for ¼"
pipe in center drilled
out to ½" diameter

Four-Hole Floor-Flange Fitting
for ½" Pipe

Rounded
Off

A

Schwinn Bike Tire

⅜" Plywood Ring

13"-diameter Plywood
Disk (B)

14¼"-diameter Plywood
Disk (C)

15⅜"-diameter Pine
Disk (D)

Toward
Center

Outside of Wheel

WHEEL CROSS SECTION

¼" x 2½"
Bolt

Four-Hole Flange
Fitting for ½"
Galvanized Pipe

½" Pipe
Bushing
(drilled
out to ½"
I.D.)

HUB CROSS SECTION

FIGURE 12–2 Top left: *The beam compass and three-part wheel assembly.* Right: *The wheel layout for the 1 × 12 pine disks.* Bottom: *Cross section of the wheel and hub.*

joined their edges with corrugated fasteners, as shown, after gluing the joining parts.

The cross section in Figure 12–2 (bottom) shows how the bike tire wraps around the pine disk with the plywood ring attached. It is clamped in place by the smaller disk (inside the ring) and the larger disk on the opposite side of the wheel.

Use a Surform wood shaper to round off the inside edge of the rings. Then align the outer edge of the rings with the pine disks and join them with glue and 1″ #8 plated flathead wood screws spaced about 5″ apart around the ring. The outer grain of the plywood should be at right angles to the grain of the pine and the rounded edge of each ring should face out. Use the Surform to round off the outer edges of the wheel-disk assemblies. Now round the edge of the smaller disks (B) on the unfinished side of the plywood; round the edges of the larger disks (C) on their finished side.

Next, carefully drill $\frac{1}{8}$″ holes through the center points of the pine and plywood disks, making sure that you hold the drill perpendicular to the surface. (A drill press or an alignment jig for a power drill comes in handy here; otherwise, use a square to help align the bit.) Stack the disks as shown and push the drill through the center holes to check alignment. Next, drive in 1″ screws about 1″ in from the edges of the plywood disks and about 5″ apart; hold the center holes in alignment with a drill or nail. Align the outer grain of the plywood disks at 90 degrees to the grain of the pine disk. Remove the screws and mark the plywood disks to show where the parts will be attached. Also number the joining surfaces of the disks so that you can reassemble the wheels.

Use Schwinn 16″ × 1$\frac{3}{4}$″ bike tires for Schwinn S–7 tubular rims. To fit the tires onto the wooden wheels, choose a side of the tire to face out, then use a hacksaw to make cuts up from the bead edge of the tire on the inboard side, cutting about $\frac{7}{8}$″ up the sidewall and spacing the cuts about 3″ apart.

To mount the tires, set the wheel disk into the tire with the ring side of the disk facing the same direction as the uncut side of the tire. Then pry the cut sidewall over the disk. With the wheel placed on its backside with the cut sidewall facing down, push the smaller plywood disk firmly and evenly down over the uncut sidewall, pushing down inside the ring with the tire sidewall evenly centered. Mount the disk with screws. Rejoin the larger disk on the back side of the wheel, driving in screws to clamp the cut sidewall to the disk. To align all disks while mounting, insert a $\frac{1}{8}$″ drill through the pilot holes and check that it's square to the wheel side.

☐ The Hubs

Use $\frac{3}{8}$″ bolts for the front axle stubs and $\frac{1}{2}$″ galvanized iron rod for the rear axles. Use four-hole galvanized floor-flange fittings for $\frac{1}{2}$″ pipe as hub carriers on both sides of the wheels. (See Figure 12–2, which shows the wheel sandwiched between the flanges and through-bolted with $\frac{1}{4}$″ × 2$\frac{1}{2}$″ bolts.)

To mount these flanges, first draw a line through the center of the $\frac{1}{8}$″ center pilot hole. Then with a square, draw a line at right angles to the first line, but also through the center of the pilot hole. Next, measure the greatest distance between the holes in the floor flange. Now measure from the center of the pilot hole half of that distance to mark the $\frac{1}{4}$″ bolt

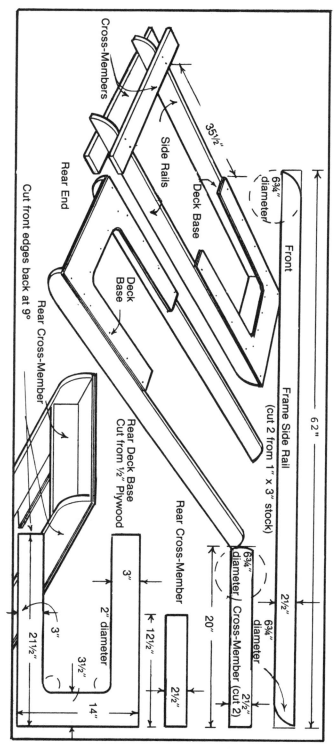

FIGURE 12–3   Measurements and assembly of the chassis frame.

holes, so the wheel for the floor flange will be centered to prevent wheel wobble. Drill through with a $\frac{1}{4}''$ bit and drill the holes through the flanges, if needed, to $\frac{1}{4}''$. After securely mounting all floor flanges, thread in $\frac{1}{2}''$ pipe male-thread/$\frac{1}{4}''$ pipe female-thread reducer bushings into the floor flanges, as shown, and tighten securely with a pipe wrench. Then drill out the center holes of these bushings to $\frac{1}{2}''$ in diameter, drilling through to align the holes in each pair of bushings for each wheel. For the front wheels, tap in a length of $\frac{1}{2}''$ O.D. copper tubing and cut it off flush with the outsides of the bushings for plain bearings. One of the rear wheels doesn't rotate on the drive axle; the other rotates on a stub axle if you can't find $\frac{1}{2}''$ rod 48" long. In this case, substituting brass bushings for iron will provide better, softer bearings.

☐ The Chassis

Cut the frame rails as shown in Figure 12–3 from clear fir 1" × 3" stock. Cut two frame rails, two 20" front cross-members, and one $12\frac{1}{2}''$ rear cross-member. Mark the downward curve at the front of the rails and the upward curve at the rear, using a round gallon can as a guide. When cutting the ends of the front cross-members, use the can to draw an arc at both ends to be cut, as shown, just for looks. Cut the $\frac{1}{2}''$-rear deck base from one corner of the 4' × 8' sheet of $\frac{1}{2}''$ plywood, using the panel layout guide in Figure 12–9.

Mount the rear deck base to the top edges of the frame rails; its squared-off end should be flush with the upcurved ends of the frame rails and flush at the sides of the rails. Use glue and drive in 1" screws every 4". Next, mount the rear cross-member between the rails under

the plywood with its front edge flush with the cutout of the plywood, using glue and 1" screws driven into the top edge of the cross-member and two $1\frac{1}{2}''$ screws driven in through the sides of the rails and into the ends of the cross-member (Fig. 12–3, bottom right).

Mark lines across the top edges of both side rails $35\frac{1}{2}''$ in front of the forward edge of the plywood deck base. Mount one front cross-member to the top edges of the rails, with its rear edge on the line marked $35\frac{1}{2}''$ in front of the plywood base. Both ends should overlap the rails by 3". Use two $1\frac{1}{2}''$ screws at each rail, but no glue. Next, with a square, mark a line down the outsides of both rails at the rear of the top cross-member. Mount the bottom cross-member to the bottom of the rail the same way as the top cross-member (also without glue), aligning its rear with this mark on both sides.

☐ The Suspension and Steering

The sequence shown in Figure 12–4A illustrates the kingpin arrangement using a $\frac{1}{2}''$ galvanized-iron pipe T-fitting, with male stubs threaded on firmly and allowed to rotate in the female threads of $\frac{1}{2}''$ to $\frac{3}{4}''$ female-male reducer bushings tightened down in holes drilled through the cross-members.

The sequence for drilling the reduced holes to anchor the reducers to the cross-members is shown at left in Figure 12–4A. Remove both cross-members and mark $\frac{1}{4}''$ holes to be drilled 1" in from the ends of the members and centered $1\frac{1}{4}''$ in from each side. Then use an inexpensive hole-saw attachment for a power drill (the kind with a circular blade that can cut out a plug) to make a $1\frac{1}{2}''$-diameter hole. On the bottom side of the top member and on the top side of the bottom, insert

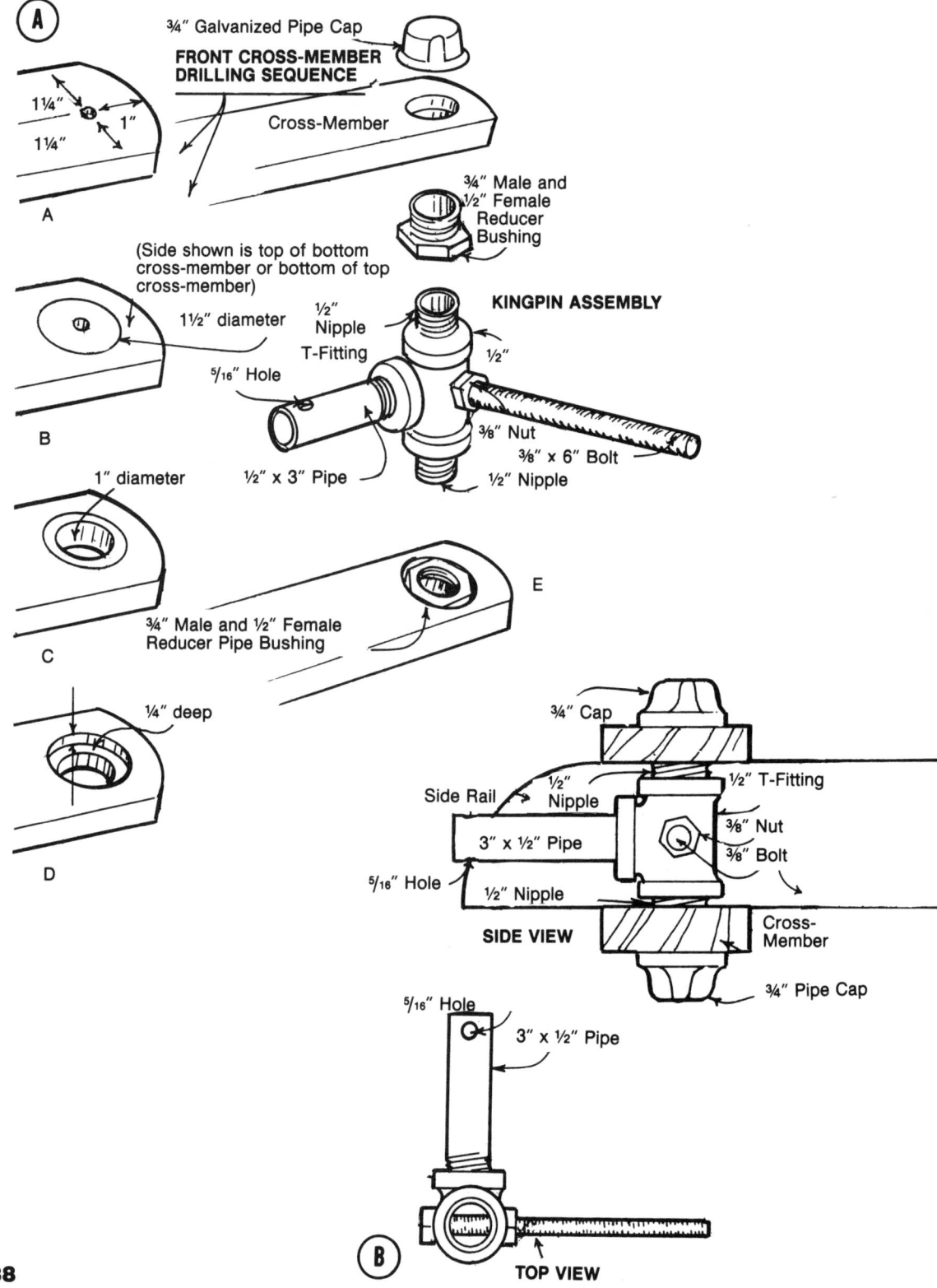

(A) **FRONT CROSS-MEMBER DRILLING SEQUENCE**

¾" Galvanized Pipe Cap

Cross-Member

1¼"
1"
1¼"

A

¾" Male and ½" Female Reducer Bushing

(Side shown is top of bottom cross-member or bottom of top cross-member)

1½" diameter

5/16" Hole

B

KINGPIN ASSEMBLY

½" Nipple

T-Fitting

½"

3/8" Nut

3/8" x 6" Bolt

½" x 3" Pipe

½" Nipple

1" diameter

E

¾" Male and ½" Female Reducer Pipe Bushing

C

¼" deep

D

¾" Cap

Side Rail

½" Nipple

½" T-Fitting

3" x ½" Pipe

3/8" Nut
3/8" Bolt

5/16" Hole

½" Nipple

Cross-Member

SIDE VIEW

¾" Pipe Cap

5/16" Hole

3" x ½" Pipe

(B)

TOP VIEW

138

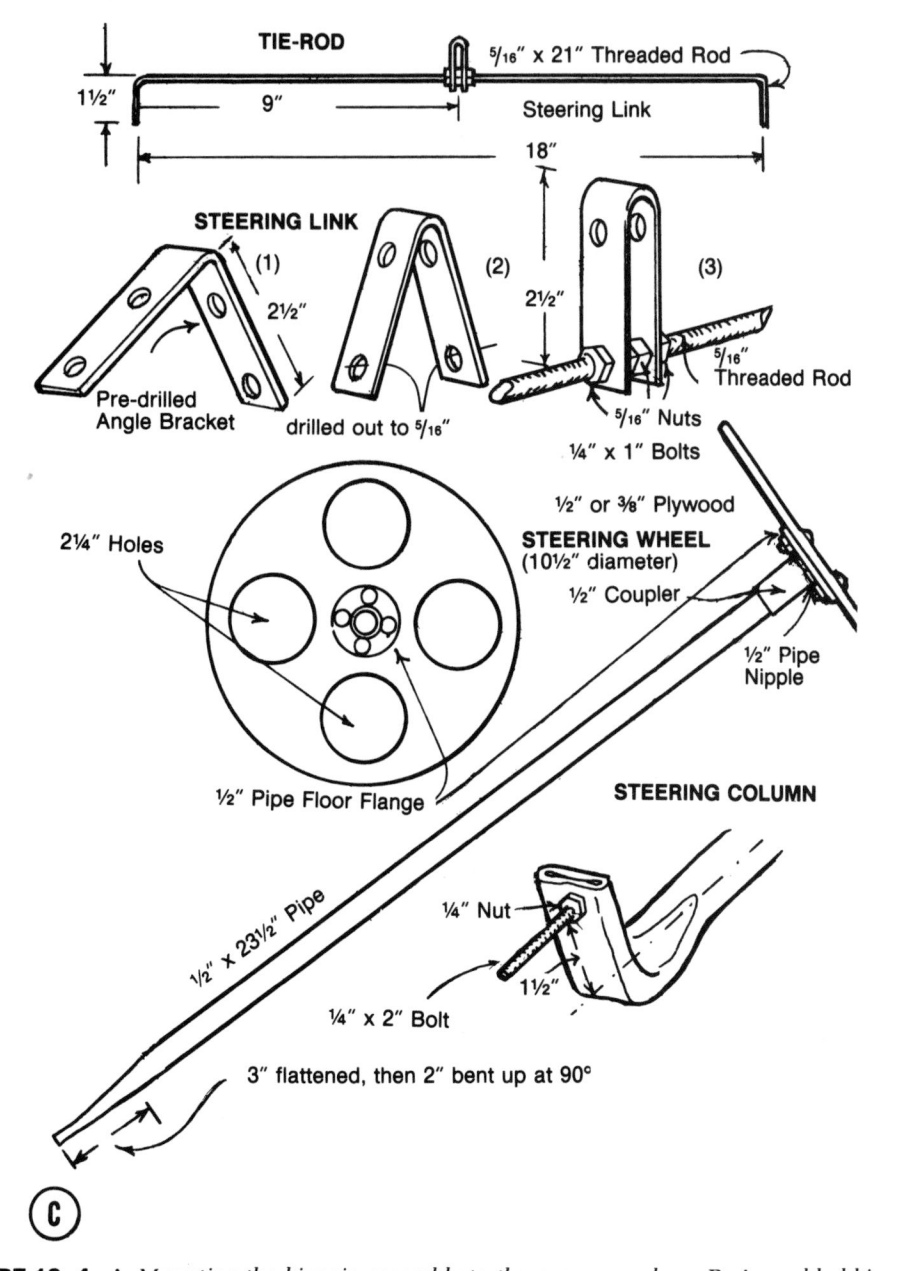

TIE-ROD

5/16" x 21" Threaded Rod

1½"

9"

Steering Link

18"

STEERING LINK

(1)

2½"

Pre-drilled
Angle Bracket

drilled out to 5/16"

(2)

(3)

2½"

5/16"
Threaded Rod

5/16" Nuts

¼" x 1" Bolts

2¼" Holes

½" or ⅜" Plywood

STEERING WHEEL
(10½" diameter)

½" Coupler

½" Pipe
Nipple

½" Pipe Floor Flange

STEERING COLUMN

½" x 23½" Pipe

¼" Nut

¼" x 2" Bolt

1½"

3" flattened, then 2" bent up at 90°

Ⓒ

FIGURE 12–4 A. *Mounting the kingpin assembly to the cross-members.* B. *Assembled kingpin (shown mounted to cross-members at top).* C. *Steering linkage.*

the center bit of the hole saw into the $\frac{1}{4}''$ holes near the ends, and cut the wood with the hole saw about $\frac{1}{4}''$ deep (B in Fig. 12–4A). Next, use the 1" hole saw to cut all the way through, cutting from both sides where needed, (C in Fig. 12–4A). With a wood chisel, cut away the wood inside the $1\frac{1}{2}''$ circle to about $\frac{1}{4}''$ deep, leaving a recessed hole like the one shown in D.

To make one of the two kingpin assemblies, drill a $\frac{5}{16}''$ hole straight through a 3" length of $\frac{1}{2}''$ galvanized pipe, with the center of the hole $\frac{5}{16}''$ in from one end (with good threads at the other end), using a center punch to locate the hole for the drill bit. Then mark and punch a hole placement at the center point of a $\frac{1}{2}''$ T-fitting (as shown in Fig. 12–4B) for the axle bolt; align it square to the center lines of the two opposing holes in the T.

Watching the drill to check that it is square with the center line, drill straight through the T from the side with a sharp $\frac{1}{8}''$ bit, then redrill. Recheck the squareness, then redrill with a $\frac{1}{4}''$ bit and finally with a $\frac{3}{8}''$ bit. Insert $\frac{3}{8}'' \times 6''$ fully threaded bolts (the harder the better) and bolt tight through the T. Next, thread $\frac{1}{2}''$ galvanized pipe nipples 1" long into the top and bottom holes of the T and carefully and firmly tighten them, being careful not to damage the exposed end threads. Thread the 3"-long drilled length of pipe into the remaining hole in the T and tighten with its $\frac{5}{16}''$ hole facing parallel to the length of the T. The assembled kingpin should look like the one pictured in Figure 12–4B.

Next, firmly thread the $\frac{3}{4}''$ male/$\frac{1}{2}''$ female reducers onto the threads of a spare length of $\frac{1}{2}''$ pipe to expand the $\frac{1}{2}''$ female threads slightly. Then remove the reducers and grease the insides; also grease the end threads of the kingpins. Thread the reducers lightly onto the top and bot-

tom threads of the kingpins, then slip the 1" holes in the cross-members over the $\frac{3}{4}''$ threads of the reducers. Thread and hand-tighten $\frac{3}{4}''$ galvanized-pipe end caps on to the threads after slipping both cross-members over both ends of the two kingpins. Run on the end caps finger-tight and slip this assembly over the front ends of the frame rails to check the alignment of the kingpins. If the cross-members are too close together to fit snugly over the rails, back the kingpins off the threads. If they are too loose, tighten them. The object is to glue and screw the cross-members to the rails without placing pull or push on the kingpin threads. The threads must easily make a one-quarter turn without binding.

Cut the tie-rod from a 21" length of $\frac{5}{16}''$ galvanized threaded rod (Fig. 12–4C). Before bending the ends, run on a nut, then drill and bend the galvanized-iron corner bracket used as a control link (with a nut run on the rod between the arms of the U-shaped link and a third nut). Thread these onto the center point of the rod and finger-tighten against each other. Insert bent ends into the holes in the stubs sticking forward from the kingpins and run washers and $\frac{5}{16}''$ locknuts onto the bottom of each end.

For final alignment, spin the wheels on the axle bolts to check for wobble. Then measure the distance between the wheels at the back and front. Use a length of pipe over the axle-stub bolts to make any bends needed to produce some positive camber; the wheels should lean out a little at the top.

To make the steering column, cut a length of $\frac{1}{2}''$ pipe to $23\frac{1}{2}''$, keeping the threads on one end. Place the cut end in a vise and flatten with a hammer about 3" from the end (Fig. 12–4C). Drill a $\frac{1}{4}''$ hole through the flattened part of the pipe

about $\frac{1}{2}''$ from the end, then bend the last 2″ of this to right angles with the lengths of pipe. Insert a 2″ × $\frac{1}{4}''$ bolt through this hole and run a nut on tight against the flattened pipe.

Thread a $\frac{1}{2}''$ coupler loosely onto the steering-column pipe, a 1″ nipple of $\frac{1}{2}''$ pipe, then a four-hole floor flange (as used on the wheel hubs). For a steering wheel, use a beam compass with holes $5\frac{1}{4}''$ apart to draw a $10\frac{1}{2}''$ circle on either $\frac{3}{8}''$ or $\frac{1}{2}''$ plywood. Next, draw two lines at right angles through the center and mark them $3\frac{1}{4}''$ out from the center which will allow for a $2\frac{1}{4}''$-diameter hole saw to make the cutouts shown in Figure 12–4C. Center the floor flange of the steering column on the wheel, mark the hole positions on the wheel, and drill through and attach the wheel with $\frac{1}{4}''$ × 1″ roundhead bolts. The flange, nipple, and coupler on the column will be securely tightened, using two pipe wrenches, in the final body assembly later on.

☐ The Pedals

One hurdle we had to cross in making the rear-drive axle was that $\frac{1}{2}''$ galvanized soft iron rods weren't readily available at lumberyards in lengths over 36″ long. Figure 12–6 shows how we got around this by running two rear axles: one from the drive wheel through the frame rail to the opposite rail, taking the push from the pedal rods, and another stationary axle stub coming out about 1″ behind the drive axle on the other side. If you can find a rod longer than 36″, you can simply add 5″ to the end opposite the drive wheel and attach a freewheel to this with a cotter pin to locate it and a U-bolt hook up to provide drive torque.

To bend the soft $\frac{1}{2}''$ iron rod see Figure

12–5. Use about a 3′ length of scrap $\frac{1}{2}''$ galvanized pipe as a handle to slip over the free end of the rod. Mark the placements of the bend and put the pipe in a vise about $\frac{1}{8}''$ above the vise jaws. Check with a protractor to make sure the angle of the bend is adjusted correctly. Always sight down the rod from the end (after the first bend) to make sure all bends are lined up on the same plane. Adjust the side bend if needed (although the crank can be placed on a flat, hard surface and pounded straight or, actually, flat) with a hammer.

At Step B in the bending sequence in Figure 12–5, measure from the center of the rod to the starting point of the next bend, which is $4\frac{3}{8}''$. When you get to Step F in the sequence, you can stop and sight down the ends of the rod to make sure they are aligned straight. The next step is to slip a drive wheel onto the end and bend up the drive tab as shown in Step G. Place a $\frac{1}{4}''$ × 3″ U-bolt with ends about 1″ apart over the drive-tab end; angle the U-bolt over the rod so that both arms sit against it. Mark the U-bolt holes onto the wheel side by tapping it with a hammer, then drill through the wheel at these marks with a $\frac{1}{4}''$ bit. Tighten the U-bolt nuts on the wheel and check for wheel wobble by spinning the axle resting on the vise, opened about $\frac{3}{8}''$, and adjust the bend of the end tab. Then bolt it tight.

To mount the rear axles, mark the outside of both frame rails $46\frac{3}{4}''$ back from the lower-front cross-member and $\frac{3}{4}''$ up from the bottom edges of the rails. Drill holes through, then cut the hole through the left rail into a rounded notch, cutting with a hand saw from the hole sides straight out to the edge of the rail.

Next, cut the rail braces (see Fig. 12–5, upper right) from scrap 1″ stock, drill through their curved edges, and counter-

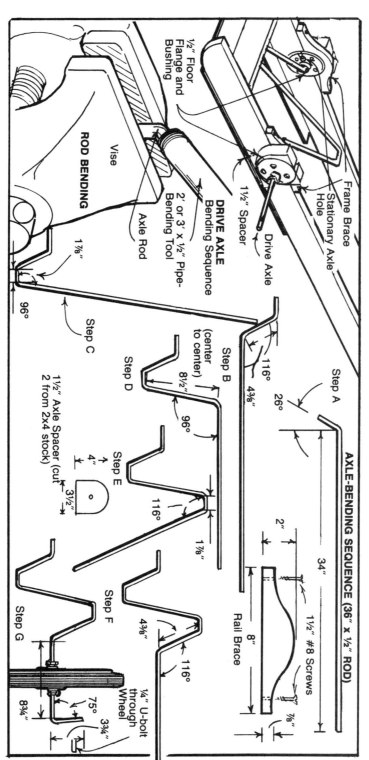

FIGURE 12–5 The drive-axle bending sequence.

sink so that $1\frac{1}{2}''$ screws can be driven through the edges and into the bottom edges of the frame rails with the centers of the braces directly under the axle holes.

Drill a $\frac{1}{2}''$ hole through a floor flange between the $\frac{1}{4}''$ mounting holes and the same distance from the center of the flange as the $\frac{1}{4}''$ holes, as shown in Figure 12–6 at right. Tighten a $\frac{1}{2}''$ brass nipple onto this flange, then cut off about $\frac{1}{8}''$. Thread the other end of the nipple onto the remaining floor flange and cut off the same way. Then drill $\frac{1}{4}''$ holes through the right-hand frame rail (with the plywood rear facing up) so that the flange with the extra $\frac{1}{2}''$ hole can be mounted to the inside of the rail; its center should be aligned with the axle hole and the extra hole positioned to the rear on the same level with the axle hole (as shown in Fig. 12–7). Drill $\frac{1}{4}''$ holes through the left frame rail so that the other flange to the outside of a $1\frac{1}{2}''$-thick wood spacer mounted to the side of the frame rail, shown in Figure 12–7 at top, has its center aligned with the axle hole.

Mount the right-hand axle-bearing flange with $3'' \times \frac{1}{4}''$ flathead bolts run through the other $1\frac{1}{2}''$ spacer and on through to the frame, with nuts run up against the flange and the bolts cut off flush. Mark a hole placement about $\frac{1}{8}''$ in from the straight end of the axle crank with a center punch, then drill a $\frac{1}{8}''$ hole through the crank for a cotter pin. Next, slip the axle-bearing flange (without the extra hole from the stationary axle) onto the end of the axle crank, nipple-side first, and run all the way on through the bends of the crank.

Attach the other flange to the inside of the right frame in the position already described, with bolts pushed in through the frame holes but without the wood spacer.

Insert the end of the axle crank through the center of this flange bearing, bolt the other flange bearing in position, and slip a washer over the end of the axle crank on the outside of the right rail. Insert a cotter pin through the axle end hole and bend it over (recessing the frame rail or adding extra washers to take out end play and allow free movement). Recess the inboard side of the spacer to clear the axle end with a drill, then bolt the flange, rail, and spacer together. Shoot grease into all bearing parts and check the crank alignment and bearing mounting to make sure the crank spins freely.

Next, bend the stationary axle, as shown in Figure 12–6, from the remaining $\frac{1}{2}''$ soft iron rod. Drill the $\frac{1}{2}''$ hole in the flange and on through the rail and spacer, then insert the end of the rod through this hole and mark placements for two $\frac{1}{4}''$ U-bolts. Drill holes through the rear cross-member and left frame rail and bolt the stationary axle tight to them. (The axle doesn't have to be aligned exactly.) Firmly mount the axle and bend with the 3' scrap of $\frac{1}{2}''$ pipe. Use a carpenter's square to align the axle stub squarely with the side of the frame.

Slip on enough $\frac{1}{2}''$ washers to extend the wheel hub, slip on the free wheel and another washer, and mark the placement for the cotter pin. Remove the wheel, place the axle end on a firm surface, mark the hole placement with a punch, drill an $\frac{1}{8}''$ hole, and cut off the axle about $\frac{1}{8}''$ from the hole; then replace everything (after greasing) and insert a cotter pin.

We did not install the pedal drive at this point, but so long as we were bending iron and all warmed up, we made the parts, as shown in Figure 12–7.

Make the drive rods from $38\frac{1}{2}''$ lengths of $\frac{3}{8}''$ galvanized iron pipe, threaded at least on one end. Use a vise and hammer

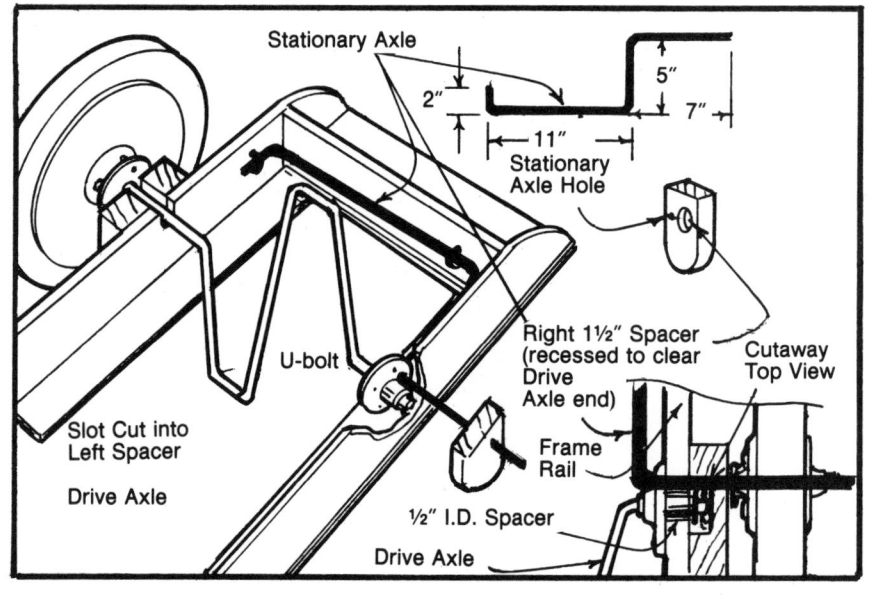

FIGURE 12–6 *Assembly of the drive axle and stationary axle.*

to flatten the rear ends of the pipes for about $2\frac{1}{2}''$. Mark hole placements with a punch through the center of the flat end; one hole should be $\frac{1}{2}''$ from the end and the other $2\frac{1}{2}''$ from the end. Drill through with a $\frac{1}{4}''$ bit. Next, cut $1\frac{1}{2}''$ lengths of $\frac{1}{2}''$ PVC plastic pipe and slice them lengthwise into two halves (see Fig. 12–7). Place them over the flat parts of the crank throws and wrap them with tape (any kind) to hold them in place. To attach the drive rods to the crank (actually done after body work is in place), we slipped 3″-long, $1\frac{1}{4}''$-wide galvanized conduit pipe straps over the taped PVC pipe and bolted them to the drive rods with 1″ × $\frac{1}{4}''$ hex-head bolts.

Use $\frac{3}{8}''$ brass-pipe 90-degree ells and 3″ lengths of galvanized pipe for pedals (Fig. 12–7, center). First, thread a short $\frac{3}{8}''$ nipple into the ells as a guide, then drill out through the nipple and the ell with a $\frac{3}{8}''$ bit, continuing in the direction of the nipple. Thread on the 3″ lengths of pipe firmly and redrill to recheck alignment and enlarge the hole a little.

To hang the pedals, use $\frac{3}{8}''$ soft galvanized iron rod. Bend the end of a 36″ rod in a vise, make the second 90-degree bend, slip on the pedal, make the third and fourth bends, and align the ends. Cut two $3\frac{3}{4}''$ lengths from a fir 2 × 4. Then drill $\frac{3}{8}''$ holes into the center points of both ends of both blocks; also drill $\frac{1}{4}''$ holes through the sides of the blocks in the middle and $\frac{3}{4}''$ in from the edges, as shown in Figure 12–7. These blocks will be bolted to the bottom of the hood box later on.

☐ The Body

Figure 12–8 shows the dimensions and assembly steps for the hood box. (See Figure 12–9 for the layout of the body parts on the 4′ × 8′ plywood panel.) The box is made up of a $\frac{1}{4}''$ plywood top, $\frac{1}{4}''$ sides, and two layers of $\frac{1}{2}''$ for the grill shell. Cut the grill front, grill back, hood top-rear curve, and dashboard cowl from $\frac{1}{2}''$ plywood to the shapes in the patterns in Figure 12–15.

Then cut an opposing pair of hood sides from $\frac{1}{4}''$ plywood, mount $\frac{3}{4}'' \times \frac{3}{4}''$ gussets on their inboard, unfinished sides, flush at the top edge and front edge, as shown. Mark lines for the placement of the $\frac{1}{2}''$ quarter-round pine moldings used as louvers (Fig. 12–8). Cut twelve 7″ lengths of the quarter-round molding, then round off the curved portions with the Surform shaper. Attach these to the outsides of the hood sides with nails, staples, or $\frac{3}{4}''$ #7 flathead screws driven out through the sides.

After attaching the louvers, glue and attach the hood sides to the insides of the chassis rails, with the notches at the front of the sides up against the front crossmembers and the bottom of the sides $\frac{3}{4}''$ below the tops of the rails, using 1″ screws driven out through the sides about 5″ apart. Next, screw the grill back to the fronts of both cross-members, flush with the bottom member; apply glue, then drive three $1\frac{1}{2}''$ screws into the bottom member and two into the top member.

Apply glue and drive 1″ screws in through the grill back and into the centers of the gussets mounted to the front edges of the hood sides, spacing the screws about 4″ apart and aligning the sides flush with the grill back. Slant the sides of the hood and dashboard inward and the seat back out a little (these small angles add a professional touch and keep the truck from looking too squared off).

Next, cut the hood top as shown, screw a 10″ gusset to the bottom (centered and

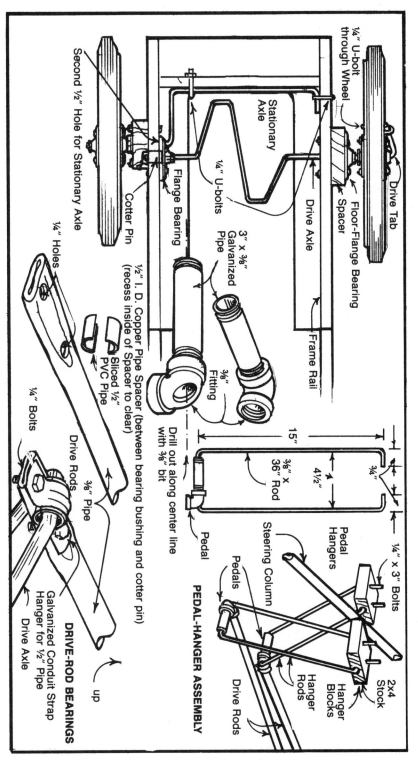

FIGURE 12–7 *Left: The axle assembly. Top right: The pedal-hanger assembly. Bottom right: The drive rods and bearings.*

¼" U-bolt through Wheel

Stationary Axle

Floor-Flange Bearing Spacer

Drive Tab

Drive Axle

¼" U-bolts

Frame Rail

3" x ⅜" Galvanized Pipe

Second ½" Hole for Stationary Axle

Cotter Pin

Flange Bearing

⅜" Fitting

½" I. D. Copper Pipe Spacer (between bearing bushing and cotter pin) (recess inside of Spacer to clear)

Sliced ½" PVC Pipe

Drill out along center line with ⅜" bit

Pedal

15"

4½"

⅜" x 36" Rod

¾"

¼" x 3" Bolts

PEDAL-HANGER ASSEMBLY

Pedal Hangers

Steering Column

Pedals

2x4 Stock

Hanger Blocks

Hanger Rods

Drive Rods

¼" Holes

¼" Bolts

Drive Rods

⅜" Pipe

Galvanized Conduit Strap Hanger for ½" Pipe

Drive Axle

up

DRIVE-ROD BEARINGS

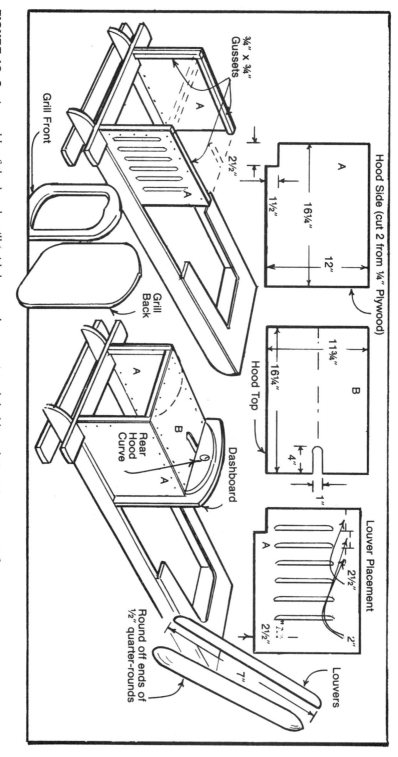

FIGURE 12–8 Assembly of the hood, grill (with louver placement), and dashboard. See Figure 12–15 for patterns.

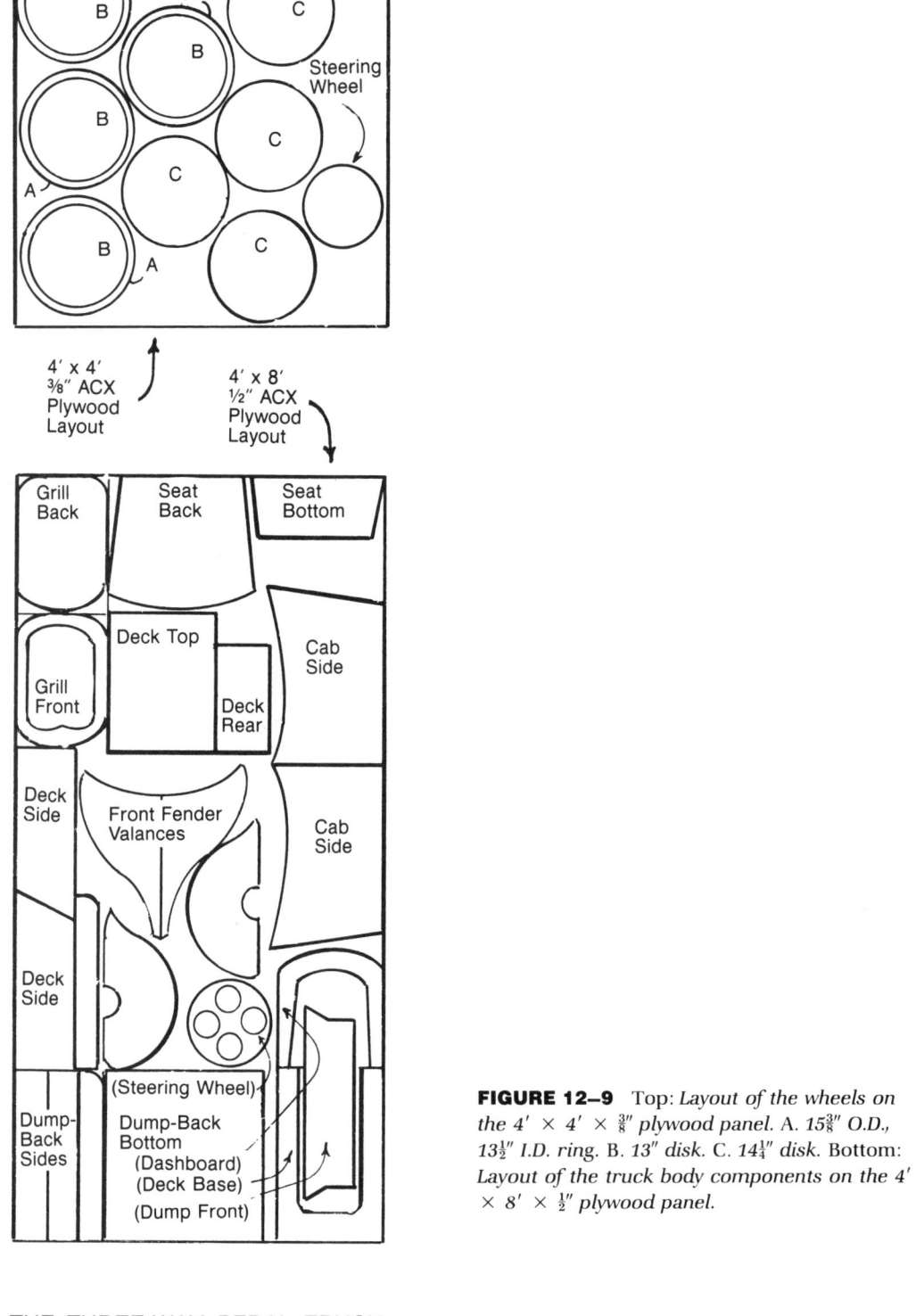

4' x 4'
3/8" ACX
Plywood
Layout

4' x 8'
1/2" ACX
Plywood
Layout

Grill Back

Seat Back

Seat Bottom

Grill Front

Deck Top

Deck Rear

Cab Side

Deck Side

Front Fender Valances

Cab Side

Deck Side

(Steering Wheel)

Dump-Back Sides

Dump-Back Bottom
(Dashboard)
(Deck Base)
(Dump Front)

FIGURE 12–9 Top: *Layout of the wheels on the 4′ × 4′ × $\frac{3}{8}$″ plywood panel. A. 15$\frac{3}{8}$″ O.D., 13$\frac{1}{2}$″ I.D. ring. B. 13″ disk. C. 14$\frac{1}{4}$″ disk. Bottom: Layout of the truck body components on the 4′ × 8′ × $\frac{1}{2}$″ plywood panel.*

flush at the front), glue and screw the hood top onto the top gussets of the sides (flush at the outsides), and drive screws in through the front of the grill back and into the top front gusset.

Glue the top-rear hood curve on its bottom and drive 1½" screws up through the hood top and into the bottom of the curve, making sure that it's centered and flush at the rear. Glue the rear of the curve and place the dashboard against it, with its bottom legs flush with the outside of the chassis rails. Drive four 1" screws in through the dashboard and into the rear of the hood curve (with no screw at the center of the dashboard).

☐ The Cab

To assemble the cab, first cut two mounting wedges (Fig. 12–10, center top) from 1" stock. Attach these to the tops of the frame rails, flush at the inside and up against the rear of the dashboard legs, with 1½" screws and glue (Fig. 12–10, bottom left).

Draw the seat back and bottom (Fig. 12–10, top left) and two sides on the ½" plywood (marking one side, cutting it, flipping it, and using it as a pattern for the opposite side). The smaller sketch of the side, at right in Figure 12–10, shows the placement of the door cut, seat gussets, and trim moldings. Although none of the corners is actually square (they're about 2 degrees out-of-square), use ¾" × ¾" square molding for gussets. If ripping your own, set the blade at 2 degrees for a perfect fit.

After cutting the door opening with a saber saw, mark the positions of the seat-bottom gussets on the inboard surfaces of the side pieces and mount them with glue and 1" screws. Next, place a ¾"-square molding against the back of one of

the legs of the dashboard. Drive screws in through the front of the dashboard to mount the gusset flush with the outside edge with glue. Repeat these steps to mount a gusset to the other side of the dashboard and to the front of the seat back, flush at the sides.

Attach the cab sides by driving screws in through the sides and into the bottom wedges and dashboard gussets, using glue and spacing the screws 4" to 5" apart; the side pieces should be positioned flush with the front of the dashboard and with the bottoms of the wedges. Insert the seat back between the cab sides, flush with the bottoms of the wedges, and drive screws in through the sides and into the centers of the seat-back gussets. Make sure that the seat is flush against the sides. This will push the sides out at the top, and the door (which doesn't twist) will seem to fit poorly when first mounted. After you attach the body molding, however, this discrepancy won't show. The twist is necessary to keep the truck from looking like square-cut boxes placed end to end.

When the sides are on, mount a gusset for the seat bottom across the back of the seat. Make it level with the rear ends of the seat gussets on the cab sides. Then glue the seat bottom and screw it into the tops of these gussets.

Next, mark drill, and cut the steering-column spacer (Fig. 12–10, top right), using a 1" spade bit in the drill. Place the spacer in position and draw it through the steering-column hole and onto the back of the dashboard. Now drill through the dashboard and mount the spacer in position with two screws driven through the front of the dashboard and glued. Re-drill the hole to ensure alignment. Drill the front steering-column hole through the base of the grill by marking a point at

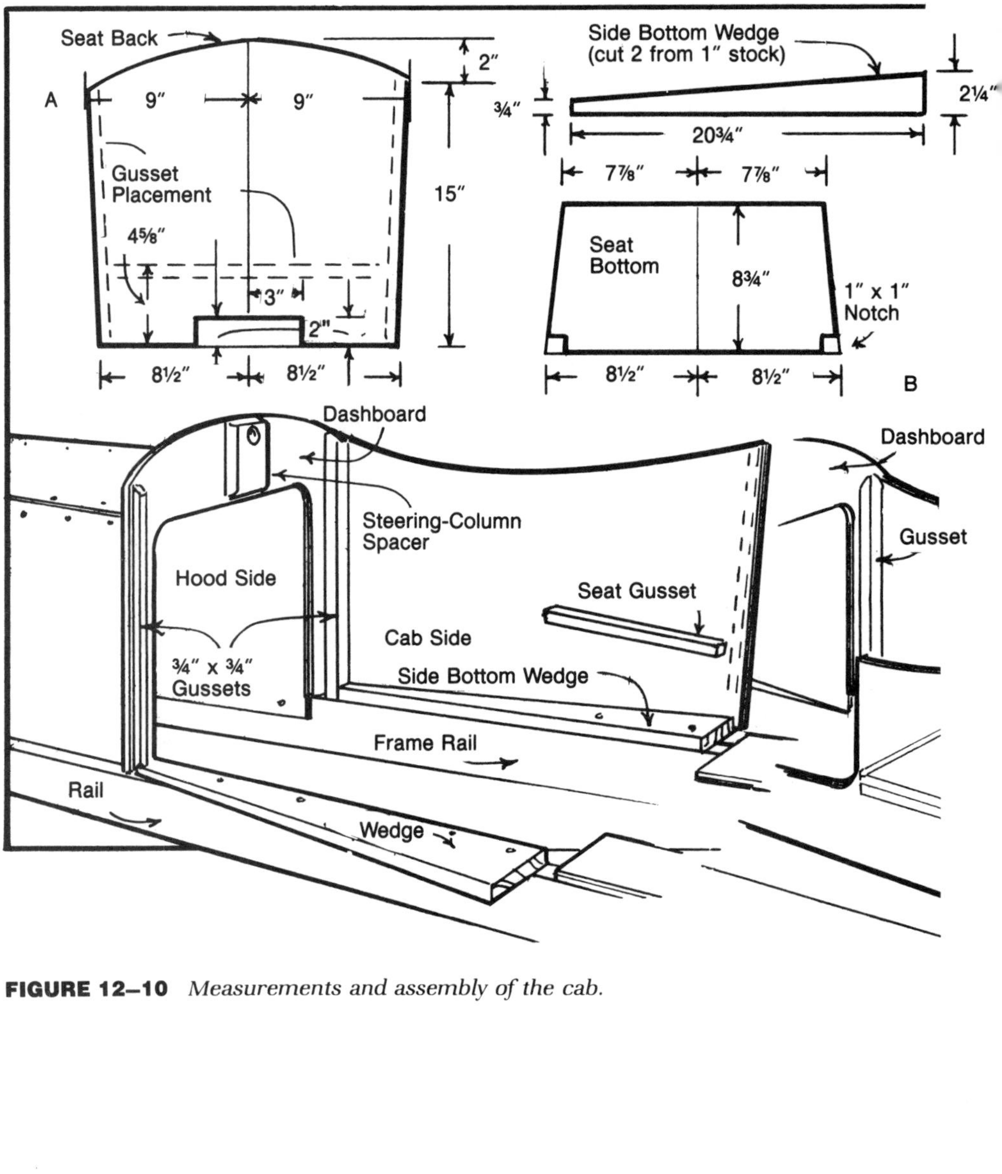

FIGURE 12–10 *Measurements and assembly of the cab.*

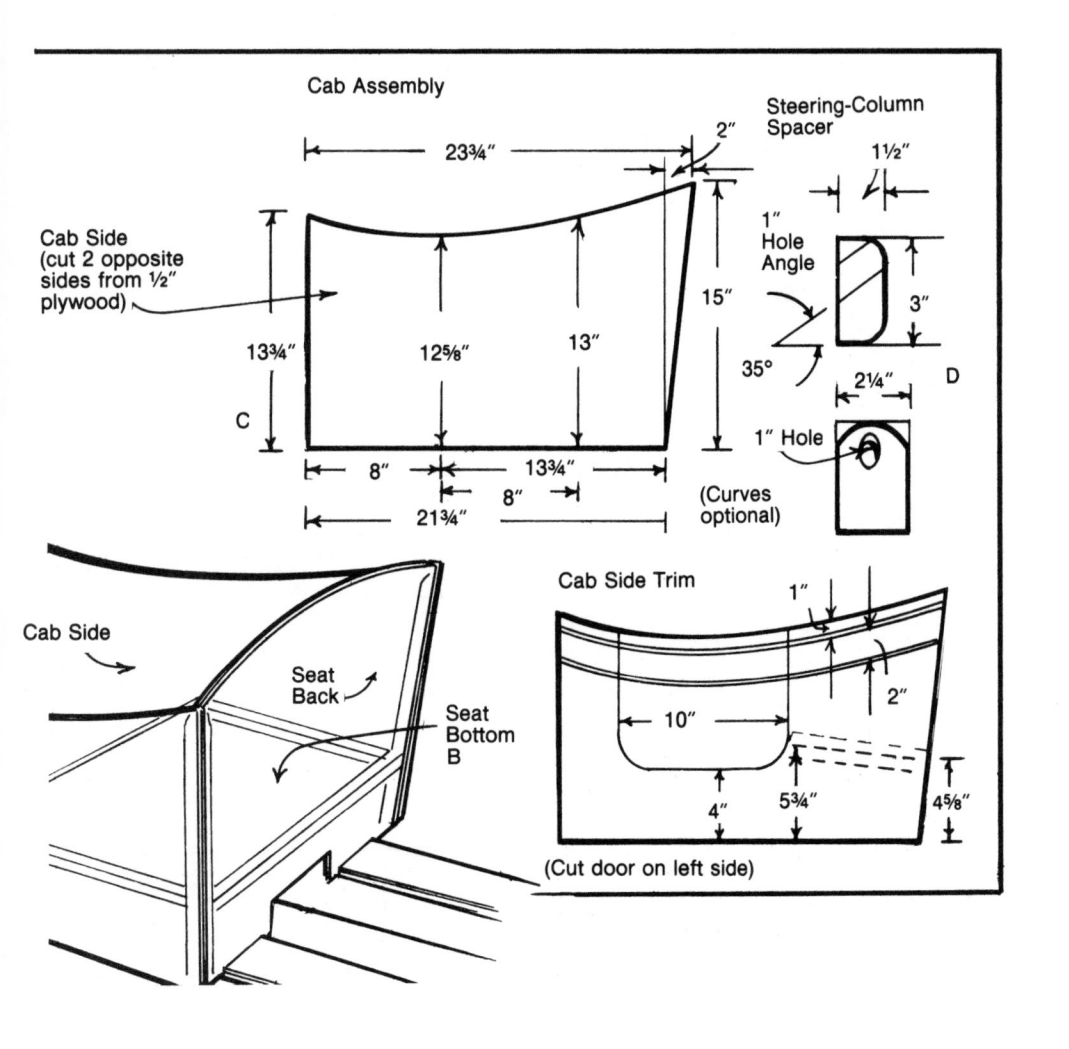

Cab Assembly

Steering-Column Spacer

Cab Side (cut 2 opposite sides from ½" plywood)

23¾"

2"

1½"

13¾"

12⅝"

13"

15"

1" Hole Angle

3"

35°

C

8"

13¾"

8"

21¾"

2¼"

D

1" Hole

(Curves optional)

Cab Side

Seat Back

Seat Bottom B

Cab Side Trim

1"

10"

4"

5¾"

2"

4⅝"

(Cut door on left side)

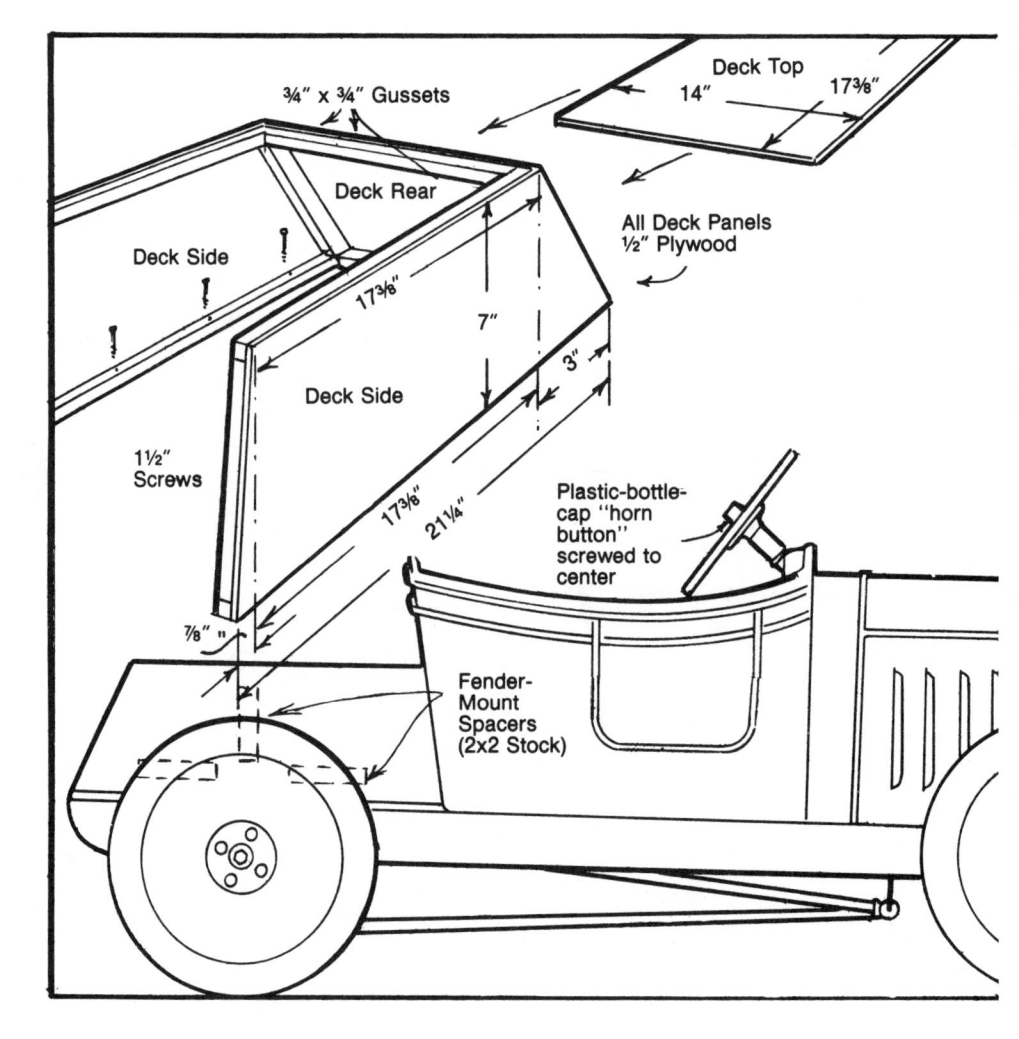

FIGURE 12–11 *Side views of truck showing assembly of the door and accessories.* Left: *Assembly of the deck.*

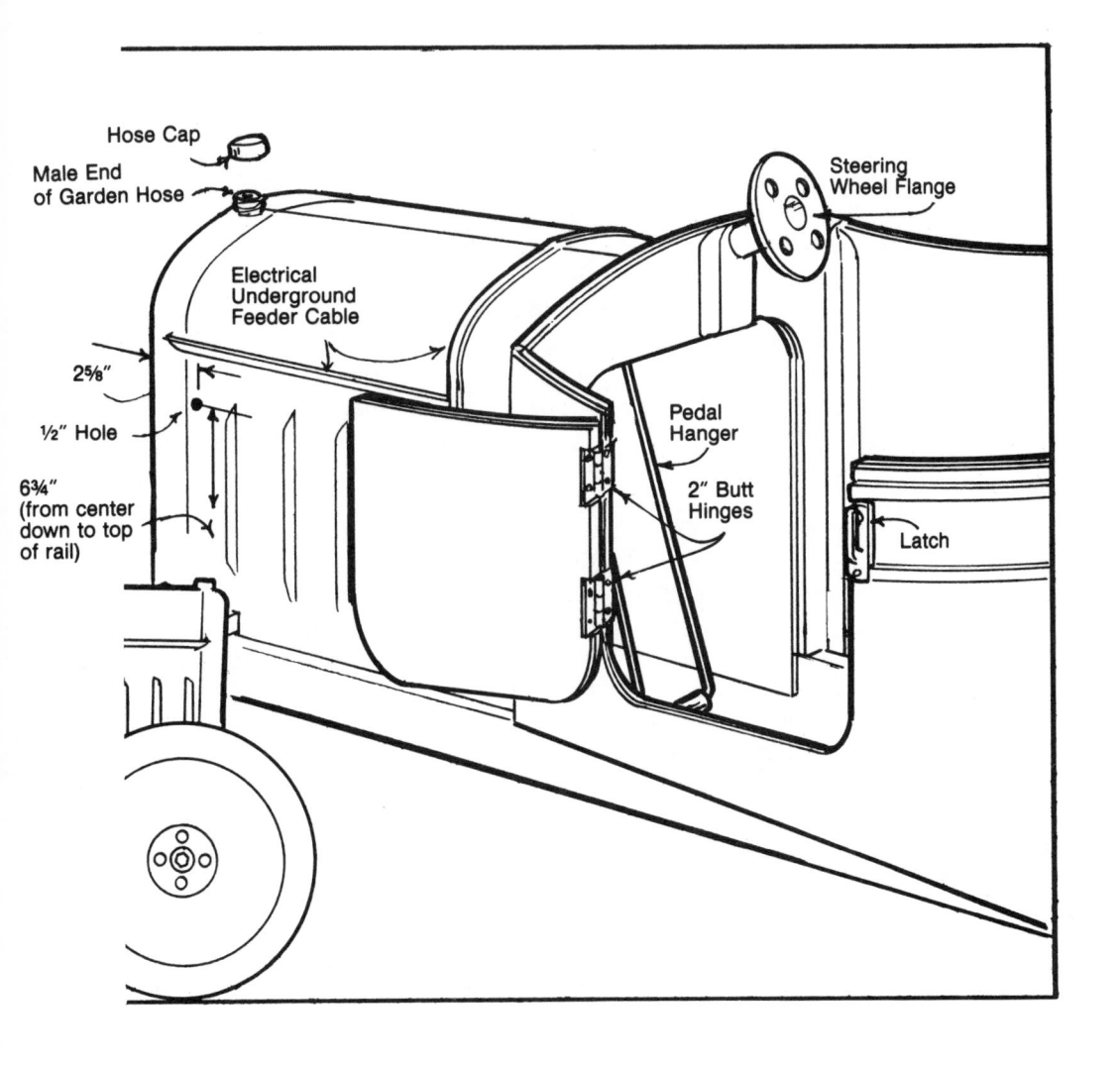

Hose Cap

Male End
of Garden Hose

Electrical
Underground
Feeder Cable

Steering
Wheel Flange

2⅝"

½" Hole

6¾"
(from center
down to top
of rail)

Pedal
Hanger

2" Butt
Hinges

Latch

the center of the rear of the grill back $\frac{3}{8}''$ above the upper cross-member. Drill down through, approximating the angle needed to align it with the top steering-column hole. Sight through this hole from the front and redrill as needed to align the holes.

To hook up the steering, remove the $\frac{5}{16}''$ threaded tie-rod from the kingpins, insert the steering column up through the holes (after oiling the holes), and run the coupler, nipple, and steering wheel onto the top end of the column. Hold the column under the hood with a pipe wrench and tighten the steering wheel as firmly as possible. To be doubly safe, drill through the coupler and wheel at each threaded joint and insert a locking cotter pin. If you can find a 1"-wide washer, insert it between the coupler and the wooden spacer to prevent wear, which may let the steering column slip down a little in time (not a serious condition).

Next, fit the tie-rod center link over the $\frac{1}{4}''$ bolt on the bent end of the steering column; then fit the ends through the holes in the kingpin drag links. If this is difficult, loosen the nuts holding the center link and attach them to the kingpins first. Put a washer on the end of the steering-column bolt and secure it with a locknut, as at the ends of the tie-rod.

To mount the pedal hangers, first cut a $9\frac{1}{4}''$ length of 1" × 4" scrap stock. Then, with the truck on its back, place the 1×4 on the ceiling of the hood box squarely across and $5\frac{1}{4}''$ forward of the rear of the dashboard. Oil the $\frac{3}{8}''$ holes with the pedal-hanger rods inserted, then position the 2×4 blocks onto the 1×4 so that they sit on squarely. Both the $\frac{3}{8}''$ L-fittings of the pedals should face toward the center, and the bottoms of the hanger rods should clear the sides of the hood box by about $\frac{3}{8}''$. Drill through the $\frac{1}{4}''$ holes in the

hanger blocks, through the 1×4, and through the $\frac{1}{4}''$ hood top, and bolt tight with four $\frac{1}{4}''$ × 3" bolts. Then thread the $\frac{3}{8}''$ drive rods into the ell fittings at the pedals and bolt the drive rods to the drive crank.

☐ The Rear Deck

Cut the sides, top, and back of the rear deck from $\frac{1}{2}''$ plywood, as shown in Figure 12–11, top left. Cut two 13" gussets on a 20-degree angle for the top and bottom of the deck back. Mount gussets to the inboard sides of the side pieces at bottom, top, and front as shown. Attach these sides to the deck base on the chassis and to the rear of the seat with glue and $1\frac{1}{2}''$ screws. Use a square and measure to make sure the 14"-wide top will fit flush at the sides.

Next, fit the top onto the sides and drive screws into the center of the top gussets $\frac{7}{8}''$ in from edge. Then attach the angled gussets top and bottom at the rear opening, screw the side gussets to the front of the rear piece (cut to clear the top and bottom gussets), and screw on the deck back.

At this point, the truck can be road-tested to make sure all systems are working freely. But first, grease all pivot or bearing points.

☐ The Hood and Grill

To complete the hood, drill a 1" hole down through the hood top just touching the rear of the grill back. Then cut a $16\frac{1}{4}''$ × $16\frac{1}{2}''$ rectangle of aluminum or galvanized-steel flashing material. Mark a center line down the center of the long way, $16\frac{1}{2}''$ long. Place this line over a sharp, straight edge, such as the edge of a table saw or a length of angle iron, with its cor-

ner facing up. Push down on the metal and pound it with your fists to create a uniform crease down the center. Then place the metal over the top edges of the grill back and the top curve just in front of the dashboard.

With the metal pulled down tightly over the top curves, staple or tack the four corners, driving into the top gusset of the hood side. Then tack or staple the full length of the hood firmly to the hood sides.

With a 1″-diameter hole saw, cut a hole through the hood material with its front just touching the rear of the grill back. Insert 21″ length of scrap garden hose with a male end fitting through the hole and tack it to the rear of the grill front at top and to the rear of the bottom cross-member, nailing right through the hose. An end cap on top (preferably brass) makes a good radiator cap.

Cut notches for folded 2″ butt hinges in the front edge of the door. The top hinge should be placed 1″ down from the edge of the door top and the lower hinge 2″ down from that. Carefully drill pilot holes with a $\frac{1}{8}$″ bit and mount the hinges into the edge grain of the $\frac{1}{2}$″ plywood body side and door edge with $1\frac{1}{2}$″ screws. Use a pivoting window latch at the rear, about 1″ down from the top, to secure the door. Mount the twist handle on the door and the catch on the body side. (Before mounting the door, use it as a pattern for the outline of a second door on the other side in the same position for mounting body molding.)

Round off the front, outside corner edges of the grill front with a Surform shaper. Fill any gaps between the grill and the hood with catalyzed polyester auto-body putty.

Make the body molding from lengths of electrical underground feeder cable. (We did this because we found it was easy to bend on edge and still lie flat for the desired look.) Nail through the flat side between the copper wires and into the body with 1″ ribbed paneling nails. Cut off the nails with wire cutters on the inside of the body and grind off the protruding ends with a grinding-wheel attachment in a power drill. This sounds like a lengthy process, but it doesn't take long, and it adds instantly to the looks of the truck. After tacking on the molding wire, run a bead of DAP tub-and-tile caulk into the corner between the molding and the hood to make it an authentic match for the best machines of 1920s.

For the molding, follow this sequence: run a strip straight up one side of the hood, over the top, and down the other side, cutting it to length with a hacksaw $2\frac{1}{2}$″ in front of the dashboard. Then tack a straight piece to each hood side horizontally to cover the staples on the edges of the hood metal. Cut the forward ends of this line at an angle. Run a line of molding around the outside of the cab about $\frac{5}{8}$″ down from the top edge; then run a second line about $1\frac{1}{2}$″ below the first. Run a line around the outline of the door shape on the right side of the body. Bend and tack a line to the door, following its outline. Finally, attach the top and bottom cab molding lines to the door, following the other cab lines. Nip and grind the ends of the nails and run a bead of DAP along the moldings.

☐ The Fenders

Mark and cut two opposing fender valance shapes onto the $\frac{1}{2}$″ plywood. Use the pattern in Figure 12–16. Cut the curved edge so that the cut will angle out at the bottom when you cut 38 degrees with a hand saw or a saber saw. To cut the

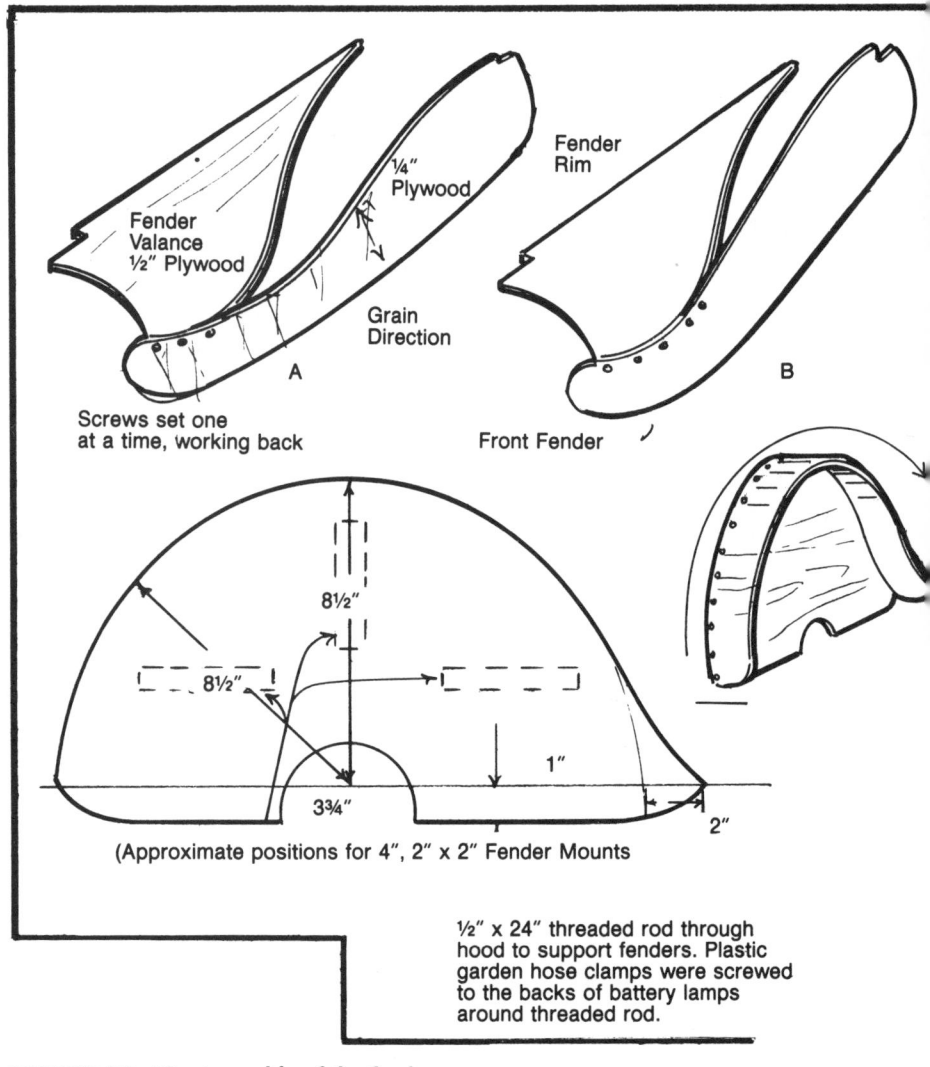

Fender Valance ½" Plywood

¼" Plywood

Fender Rim

Grain Direction

A

B

Screws set one at a time, working back

Front Fender

8½"

8½"

3¾"

1"

2"

(Approximate positions for 4", 2" x 2" Fender Mounts)

½" x 24" threaded rod through hood to support fenders. Plastic garden hose clamps were screwed to the backs of battery lamps around threaded rod.

FIGURE 12–12 *Assembly of the fenders.*

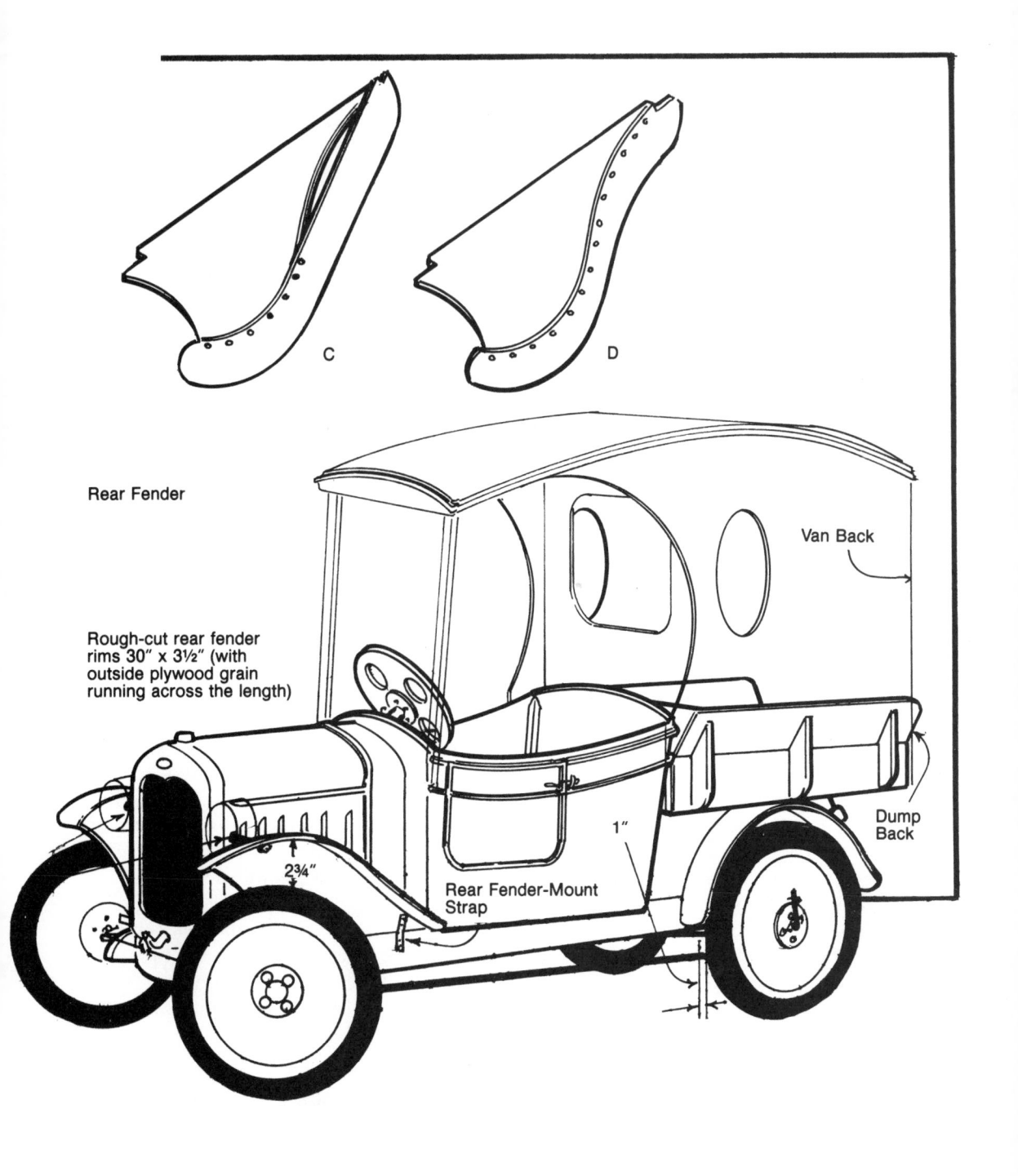

C

D

Rear Fender

Van Back

Rough-cut rear fender rims 30" x 3½" (with outside plywood grain running across the length)

Dump Back

2¾"

1"

Rear Fender-Mount Strap

straight edge, set the saw so that the cut will angle in at the bottom at 30 degrees. Cut the curves of the rear fender valances at 0 degrees (square) throughout. Cut the fender rims from $\frac{1}{4}''$ plywood to the shapes shown, avoiding all knots on both sides of the plywood and cutting so the outer grain lies across the length of the rims. Make all cuts at 0 degrees and angle the edges after mounting.

Joining the rims to the curved edges of the valances seems to take about twelve hands at first, but once you drive in the first few screws, the going gets easier. (See Fig. 12–12, top left, for the fender assembly.)

The method we used to fabricate the front fenders goes like this: Place the valance on any firm chair with the top edge angling out at the bottom. Place the front of the rim on the edge of the valance, its forward point flush with the forward point of the valance. Then drill a pilot hole for a 1" screw about $\frac{3}{8}''$ in from the edge of the rim (and $\frac{3}{4}''$ from the tip), angled so that it sinks straight into the center grain of the $\frac{1}{2}''$ valance. Spread glue along and bend the rim inward; drive a second screw in the same way about 2" back down the edge.

With a foot on the valance to hold it on the chair, using one hand to pull the rim back in and another to drill, drive one screw at a time (take a little time to allow the wood to get used to bending) to pull the plywood into a tight bend. You could never get away with this simply by bending the part in your hands, which lets the weakest point take all the force.

The procedure is the same at the back fenders. Starting at the front, drive in one screw at a time back to the rear. Make sure that you sink a screw in the hollow of the recurve at the rear.

To mount the fenders, draw a line up from the base of the valance of the front fenders. Follow the vertical cut of the front notch at right angles to the base cut $7\frac{1}{2}''$ up from the notch cut. Then place a mark $\frac{7}{8}''$ in front of this point and drill a $\frac{1}{2}''$ hole at 30 degrees, parallel to the angled bottom cut. Drill $\frac{1}{2}''$ holes through the sides of the hood, $2\frac{5}{8}''$ back from the grill front and $6\frac{3}{4}''$ up from the top of the upper cross-member. Poke a 24" × $\frac{1}{2}''$ threaded rod through these holes, center it, and run nuts on to clamp it firmly to the hood sides. Next, slip the holes in the fenders over the ends of this rod and set the fenders in place on top of the frame rails. Bend 3" × $\frac{1}{2}''$ drilled straps in the middle to match the angle between the outsides of the frame rails and the valances (about 150 degrees). Screw these straps to the frame rails and valances, mounting them vertically about 1" back of the front notch and 4" in front of the rear, as shown in Figure 12–12.

Cut lengths of 2" × 2" stock as shown in Figure 12–11, and screw them in place to the sides of the rear deck within the outline of the rear wheel with $1\frac{1}{2}''$ screws. Mount the rear fenders to these spacers with screws driven through the valances and into the spacers. Then mount the fenders with their tops about $\frac{1}{4}''$ below the top of the rear deck and the front bottom about 1" in front of the tire. Place a mark near the bottom of the frame rail 1" in front of the tire before removing the free wheel, or remove the bearing bolts on the drive-wheel side to drop it down to mount the fenders. The front bottom of the fender rim should be about level with the bottom of the frame rail.

☐ The Dump Bed

Cut the dump bed from $\frac{1}{2}''$ plywood; also cut three side braces on both sides from

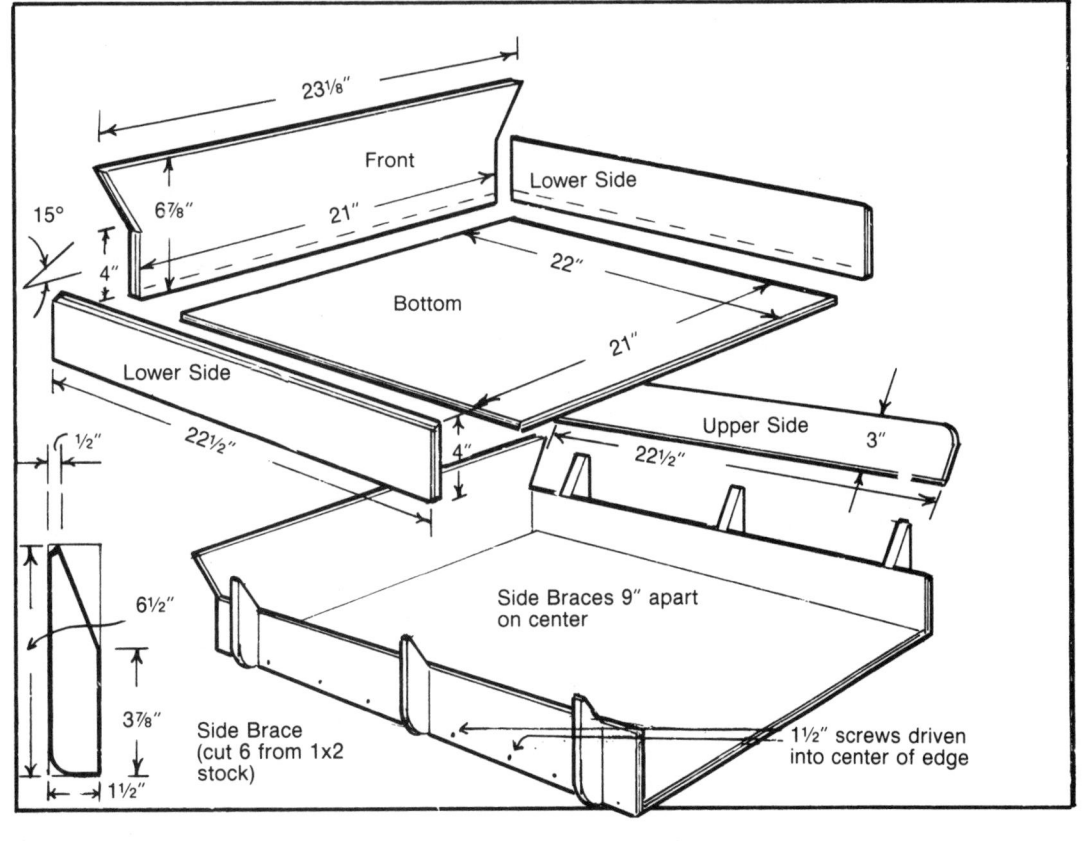

FIGURE 12–13 *Measurements and assembly of the dump bed.*

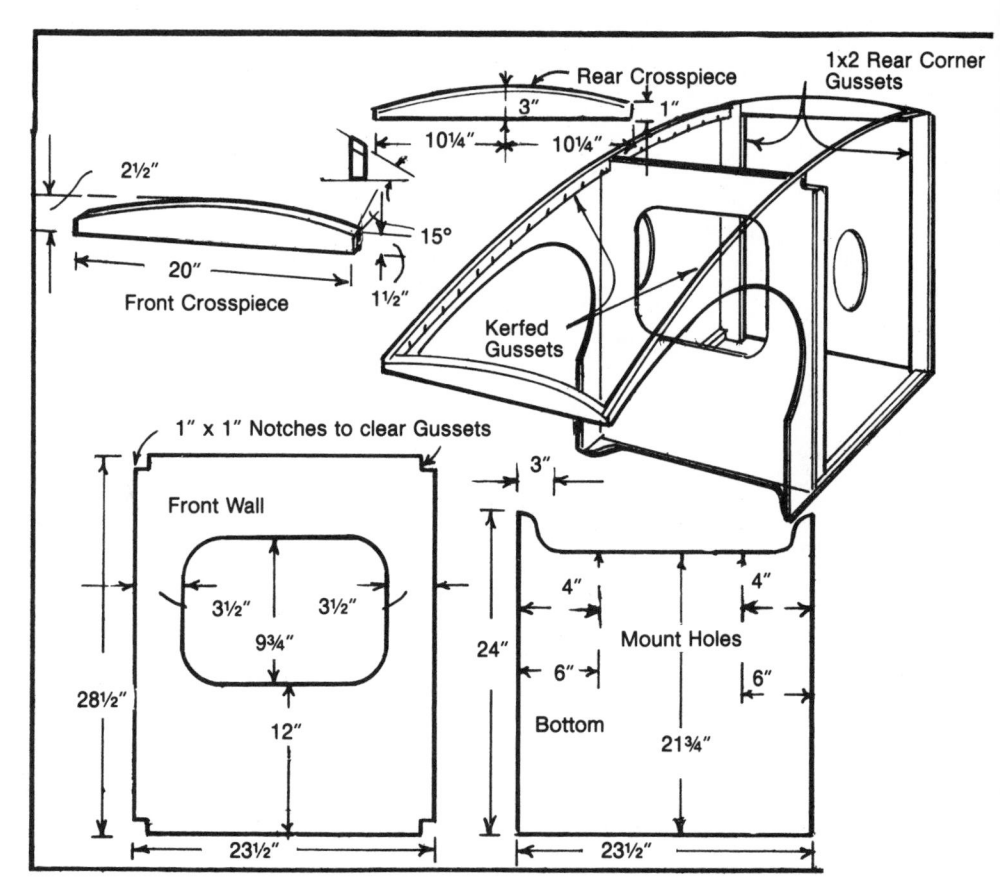

FIGURE 12–14 *Measurements and assembly of the van back. The procedure for curve marking is as follows:* a. *Draw parallel lines vertically, 6″ apart.* b. *Mark dimensions up from base.* c. *Drive nails into marks.* d. *Push batten up to nails on inside of curve and mark curve on outside of batten.*

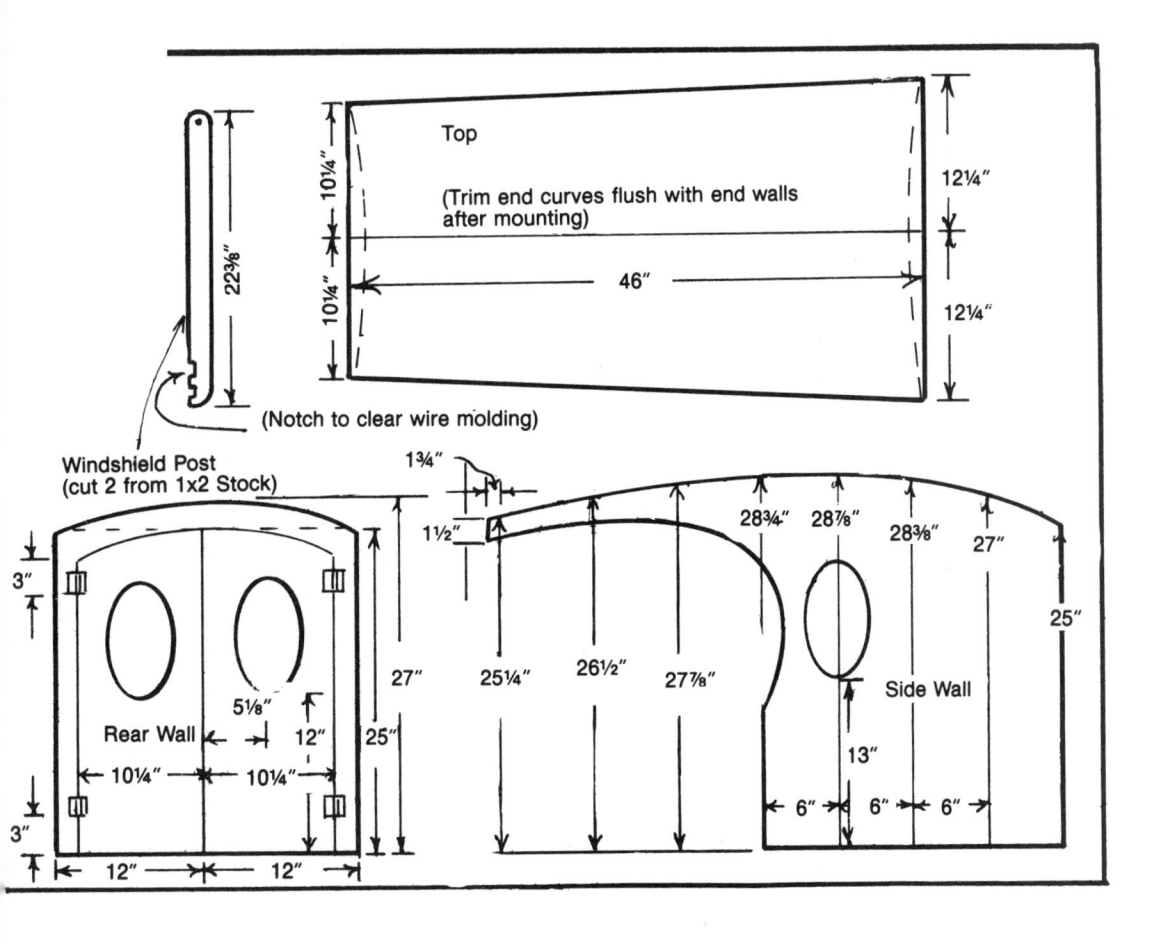

Top

(Trim end curves flush with end walls after mounting)

10¼"

10¼"

12¼"

12¼"

46"

22⅜"

(Notch to clear wire molding)

Windshield Post
(cut 2 from 1x2 Stock)

1¾"

1½"

3"

3"

27"

25"

27"

25"

Rear Wall

5⅛"

12"

10¼"

10¼"

12"

12"

28¾"

28⅞"

28⅜"

27"

25"

25¼"

26½"

27⅞"

Side Wall

13"

6"

6"

6"

1" scrap stock (Fig. 12–13). Screw the bed front to the bed bottom, spacing screws about 4" apart and sinking pilot holes into the center grain of the bed bottom. Use the same method to attach the lower sides to the bottom and bed front. Next, attach the braces to the lower sides with the center of the forward brace $2\frac{1}{4}$" back from the front of the bed and the others spaced 9" apart on center; their angled side should be aligned with the top of the lower side.

Cut the upper edges of the bottom sides with the blade set at 15 degrees and place them against the inside angled edges of the braces and the outside of the bed front. Drive screws into the edge of the bed front and braces to mount the upper sides.

Place the bed on the rear deck up against the seat back and centered. Then place 3" butt hinges with removable pins against the rear of the deck and bottom of the bed. The heads of the hinge pins should point outward to allow tipping of the bed as well as easy removal.

□ The Van Back

After cutting the bottom, top, front wall, rear wall, and sides from $\frac{1}{4}$" plywood (Fig. 12–14), mark the windows and doors and drill a $\frac{1}{4}$" hole inside the oval window shapes as a starter hole. Cut out the windows with a saber saw. Plunge-cut the rear doors with the circular saw across the top, then rip it out.

Use $\frac{3}{4}$"-square pine molding and 1" screws to join the panels at the corners, as shown in Figure 12–14. First, attach the gussets to the unfinished side of the front wall, flush at all four sides, noting the notches at top and bottom corners. Draw a line squarely across the top side of the box bottom $\frac{1}{2}$" back from the front

edge. Then tilt the bottom up on one side edge and align the bottom side of the front wall with its front against this line. Drive screws through the bottom to attach the front wall to the bottom.

Next, attach gussets to the top of the bottom piece (flush at the sides) from the front wall to $\frac{3}{4}$" forward of the rear edge. Screw the side pieces to the front wall (keeping it held squarely to the bottom) and to the bottom. Attach $1\frac{1}{2}$" × $\frac{3}{4}$" gussets to the inboard surface of the sides, flush at the rear, and attach the rear wall, with the wide sides facing to the rear.

Cut gussets to fit along the curved top line of the sides and kerf them every 3" by cutting into them about $\frac{3}{8}$" deep. Attach them to the sides facing center, spacing the screws every 3", starting at the back and working forward; push down on the gussets to pull down at the next screw mark before drilling and driving the screws. Be careful at the front not to put too much side load on the arms sticking forward). Top side gussets should be trimmed back $\frac{3}{4}$" to $\frac{7}{8}$" from the front end of the panel arm.

To mount the top panel, push down on the two rear corners to gauge the placement, then drive in screws about midpoint, working out toward both ends one screw at a time, then across the back. Next, mount the angled and curved-out edge of the roof-front visor by driving 1" screws down through the top and into the edge, as well as one 1" screw in through the side panel and into the end grain. Cut a curved-edge top gusset for the rear and mount it to the front of the rear wall, flush at the top.

Screw a length of 1 × 2 to the rear of the left door; the edge of the door lying along the center line of the 1 × 2 will act as a stop for the right door. Next, mount ornamental brass butterfly hinges to the

rear wall and sides of the doors, 3″ up from the bottom and 3″ down from the top, driving the screws into the corner gussets and in through the $\frac{1}{4}$″ doors. Nip screw tips on the insides of the doors with wire cutters and grind them flat with a grinder-wheel drill attachment. Mount a twist latch (like the one used for the door) to the doors about halfway up; screw a barrel-bolt sliding lock to the vertical 1×2 and drill a $\frac{5}{16}$″ hole in the floor of the van so the left door can be locked shut when the bolt is slipped down into the hole.

Drill two $\frac{5}{16}$″ mount holes through the van floor, as shown in Figure 12–14. With the van back in place against the seat back and centered on the rear deck, drill through these holes through the deck top and bolt the van to the rear deck with two $\frac{5}{16}$″ $\times$ $1\frac{1}{2}$″ roundhead bolts with wing-nuts and wide washers.

For a front mount, cut two 1×2s as shown in Figure 12–14, drill as noted with a $\frac{5}{16}$″ bit, countersinking the top holes flush and the bottom holes to a depth of about $\frac{3}{4}$″. Screw these windshield posts to the rear of the top visor with their outer side edges $\frac{5}{8}$″ in from the outside of the side wall panel. Place the bottom ends in position against the body sides at the front, drill a pilot hole, and secure it with a $1\frac{1}{2}$″ screw.

Round off the top corners and edges of the van with the Surform wood shaper. Then drape the top with a $2\frac{1}{2}'$ $\times$ $4'$ piece of stretchable vinyl upholstery material. Staple it in the center of the rear wall about $\frac{3}{4}$″ down from the top, then pull the material tight from the center of the front and staple it in the center as before. Then, smoothing and working along both sides out from the center to the corners and pulling tight as you progress, tuck and fold the corners to staple them

neatly. Cut off the free edges of the material with a pair of scissors about $\frac{1}{4}$″ below the staples. Then lay down a bead of molding (made from the electric cable in the Materials List) over the staples and tack in place, covering the edge of the material.

■ FINISHING

Round off all exposed edges with the Surform wood shaper and fill all gaps, splits and holes with catalyzed polyester autobody putty. Lay a bead of putty into the joint at the rear of the hood and front of the dashboard, smoothing it with your thumb. Smooth plenty of putty over the fender screws (it's much easier to remove the fenders for finishing and painting). If you have a belt sander, smoothing the fenders will be a lot easier. Another help is to remove, recountersink, and redrive (one at a time) any screw heads that appear above the surface at the initial gluing.

After you have puttied, scraped, sanded, and finish-sanded the body, paint it with three coats of oil-base gloss enamel. It's almost useless to pass the word (we never paid any attention to it either until we got tired of learning the hard way), but it *does* take less actual work time to put on many thin coats of paint than it does to put on several thick, runny coats that never quite dry. After painting the body, give the interior a few coats of a dark brick red semigloss.

Paint the wheels the base color. Then mount a bolt in the vise to use as a temporary axle and spin the wheels on this as a pivot while you paint on the white-walls. Use an El Marko marking pen (the only one we've found that's weather-resistant) to put on the wheel stripes. We

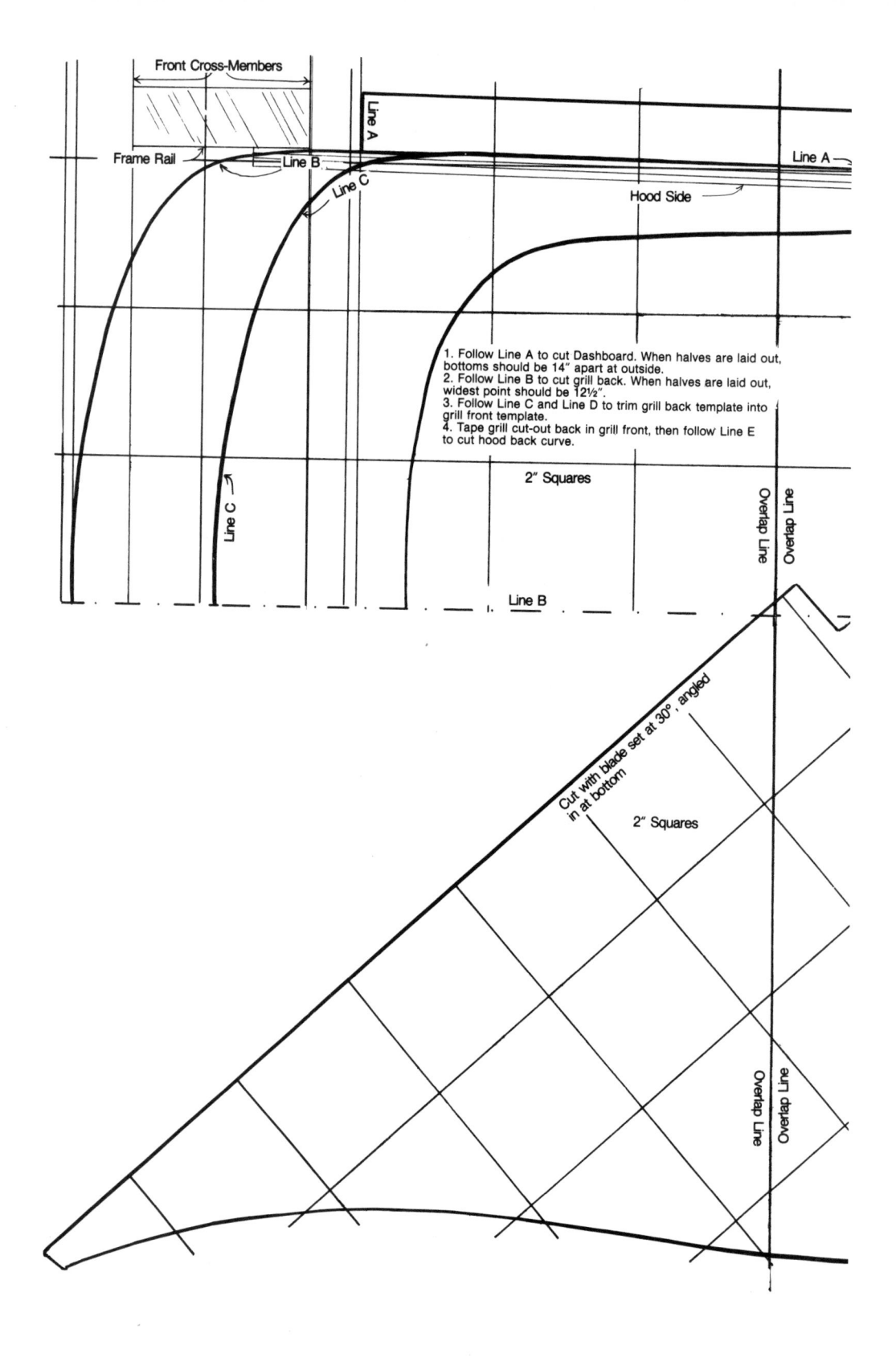

Front Cross-Members

Frame Rail

Line A

Line B

Line C

Hood Side

Line A

1. Follow Line A to cut Dashboard. When halves are laid out, bottoms should be 14″ apart at outside.
2. Follow Line B to cut grill back. When halves are laid out, widest point should be 12½″.
3. Follow Line C and Line D to trim grill back template into grill front template.
4. Tape grill cut-out back in grill front, then follow Line E to cut hood back curve.

2″ Squares

Line C

Overlap Line

Overlap Line

Line B

Cut with blade set at 30°, angled in at bottom

2″ Squares

Overlap Line

Overlap Line

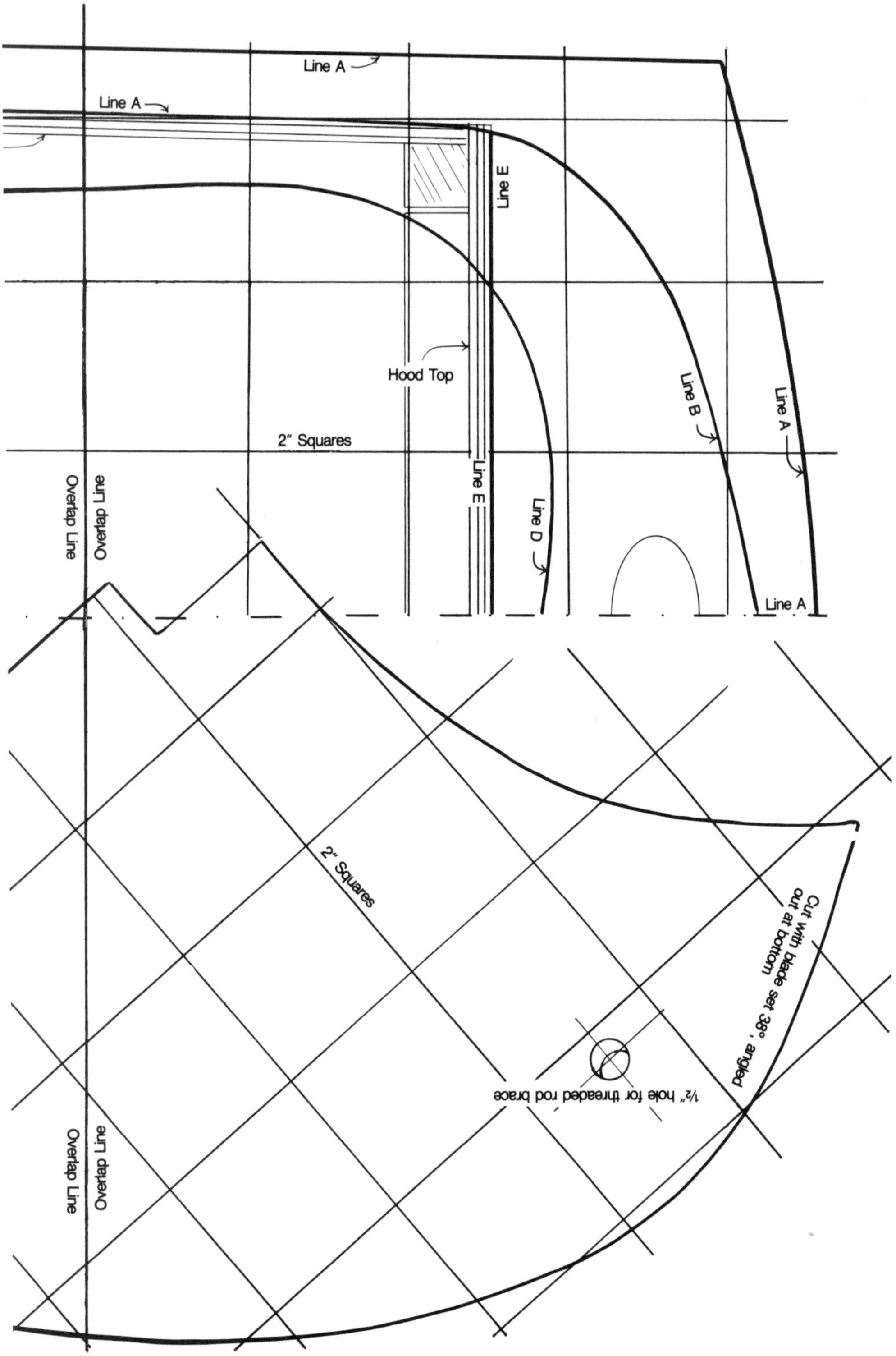

Line A

Line A

Line E

Hood Top

2" Squares

Line E

Overlap Line

Overlap Line

Line B

Line A

Line D

Line A

2" Squares

Cut with blade set 36° angled out at bottom

½" hole for threaded rod brace

Overlap Line

Overlap Line

FIGURE 12–15 *Patterns for cutting the dashboard and grill and the front fender valance. Enlarge onto a grid with 2" squares.*

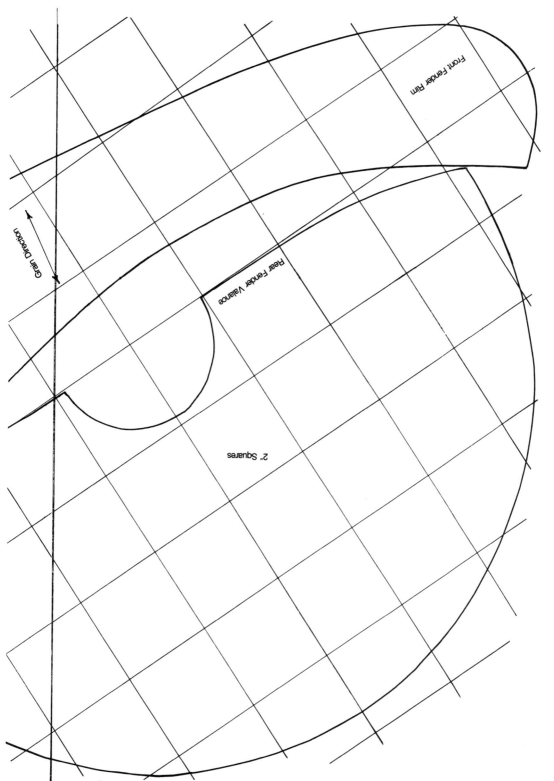

Front Fender Rim

Rear Fender Valance

Grain Direction

2" Squares

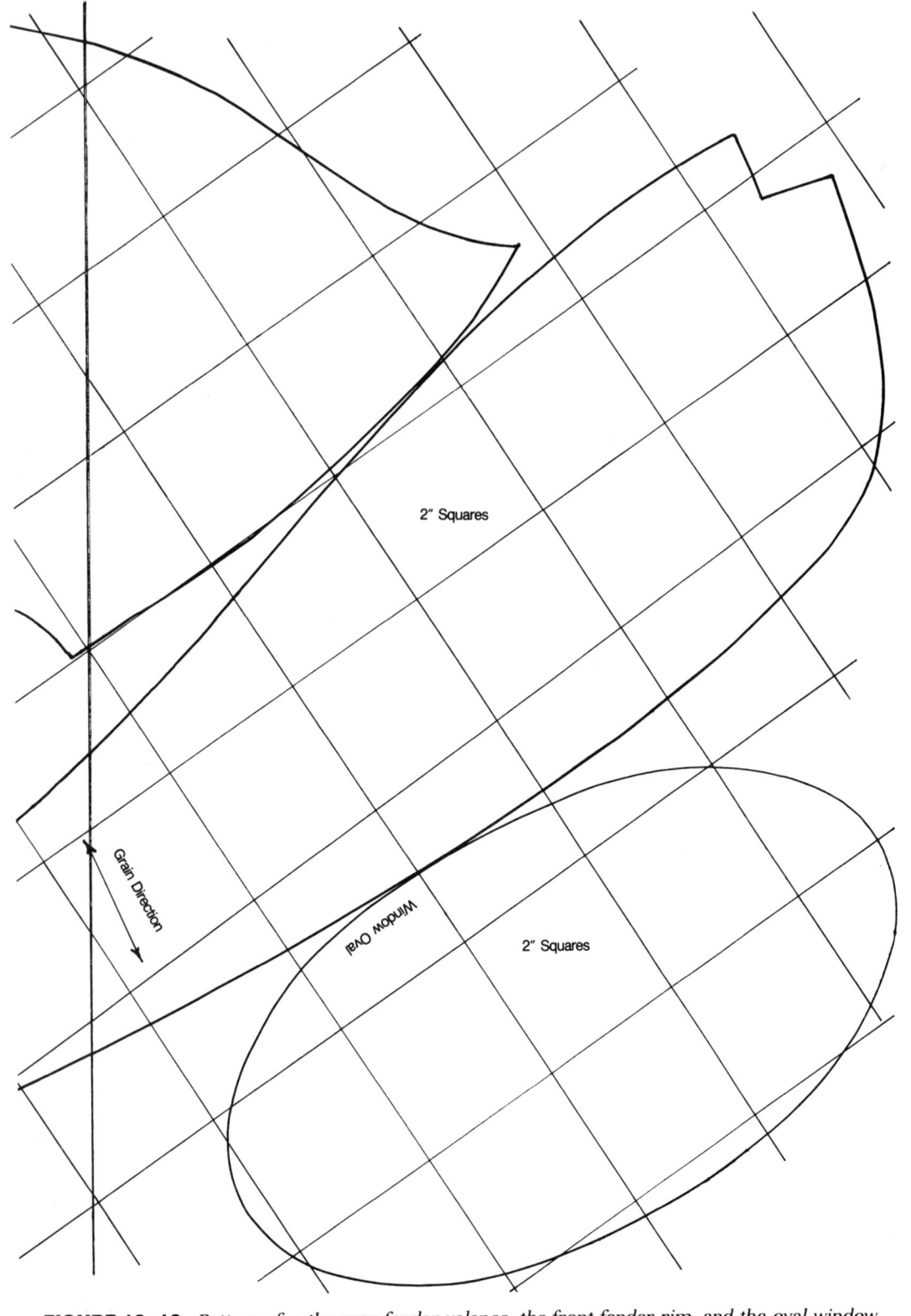

FIGURE 12–16 *Patterns for the rear fender valance, the front fender rim, and the oval window. Enlarge onto a grid with 2" squares.*

did the "blackwalls" inside with barbeque black semigloss. All suspension parts and drive-train parts were also painted semigloss black, as well as the inside of the grill back at the front.

To decorate the grill, cut a piece of expanded aluminum (although any expanded metal or plastic grillwork will probably look similar), staple it in place, and touch up the staples to match the black. Cover the outside of the grill shell with chrome-metal tape, starting a horizontal strip across the front sticking about 1″ up above the top. Cut down at the center point with scissors about 1″ and carefully smooth the tape over the curved top.

We kept adding horizontal strips across with the top edge of each strip butted up against the bottom of the last strip, laid down and smoothed on to about 1″ over the front. Then we cut a 15″ length of tape, trimmed it to $1\frac{1}{4}$″ wide, cut an indent in the center of the rear (uncut)

edge to clear the radiator cap, and carefully laid it down over the top of the radiator, forming its rear edge down to the moldings on the side of the hood. We applied more $1\frac{1}{4}$″ wide strips along the sides of the hood. We then applied $\frac{3}{8}$″ wide strips over the folded-over parts of the horizontal strips applied to the front. This provided a smoother, more regular-looking interior to the radiator-shell cutout. For trim on the van back and dump back, apply $\frac{1}{2}$″ plastic tape about 1″ in from all edges.

Mount bike reflectors on the rear deck. We made the lights from 4″-diameter plastic, self-contained, battery-powered closet ceiling lights clamped to the $\frac{1}{2}$″ threaded rod with plastic $\frac{5}{8}$″ half-round garden-hose clamps. The battery mounts for these lights aren't made for the road jolts you get in a truck, so you could simply use any 4″-diameter stainless pan, plastic-pipe end cap, or brass lamp bezel for an ornamental effect.

13

THE EMPORIUM

■ MATERIALS LIST

Four 4' × 8' ACX plywood panels, $\frac{3}{8}$"
thick
Two 4' × 8' ACX plywood panels, $\frac{1}{4}$"
thick
Three 8' lengths of fir 2 × 2 stock
Two 10' lengths of fir 2 × 2 stock
Four 8' lengths of fir 1 × 3 stock
Three 8" lengths of #2 pine 1 × 12
stock
Six 8' lengths of fir 1 × 2 stock
Five 8' lengths of #2 pine 1 × 6 stock
One 4' length #2 pine 1 × 10 stock
One hundred $1\frac{1}{2}$" #8 flathead wood
screws
One pound of 3" galvanized finishing
nails

☐ *See color insert for completed project.*

The idea behind the Emporium was that
playhouses are fun, but once you've ar-
ranged the furniture, you may want more
action than just having friends over for
tea. So we designed an all-purpose mer-
cantile establishment for playing store, or
really selling produce and products to
passersby.

■ CUTTING AND ASSEMBLY

Cut the front, rear, and end walls and the
roof panels from $\frac{3}{8}$" plywood; cut the flat
roof panel from $\frac{1}{4}$" plywood ($\frac{1}{2}$" plywood is
stronger but costs more, so we used the
lighter weight and made sure all panels
were well braced with decorative framing). Front and side views are shown in
Figures 13–1 and 13–2, measurements in
Figure 13–3.

Mark the door and window openings.
(Note that the doors and windows can be
placed anywhere you like with this type
of construction.) To loft the top curve of
the windows, drive nails in at the top
outside corners and top center position.
Take a batten about the size of a yardstick and push it evenly against the bottom side of the three nails. Mark the
curve made by the bent batten on its up-
per side. Drill a $\frac{1}{2}$" hole inside the window
outline, then cut out the shape with a saber saw.

To conserve plywood and make a set of
shutters at the same time, draw a center
line on the window and plunge-cut the
window outline with the blade of a Skilsaw set to cut through the plywood only
about $\frac{1}{8}$", holding the blade guard up and

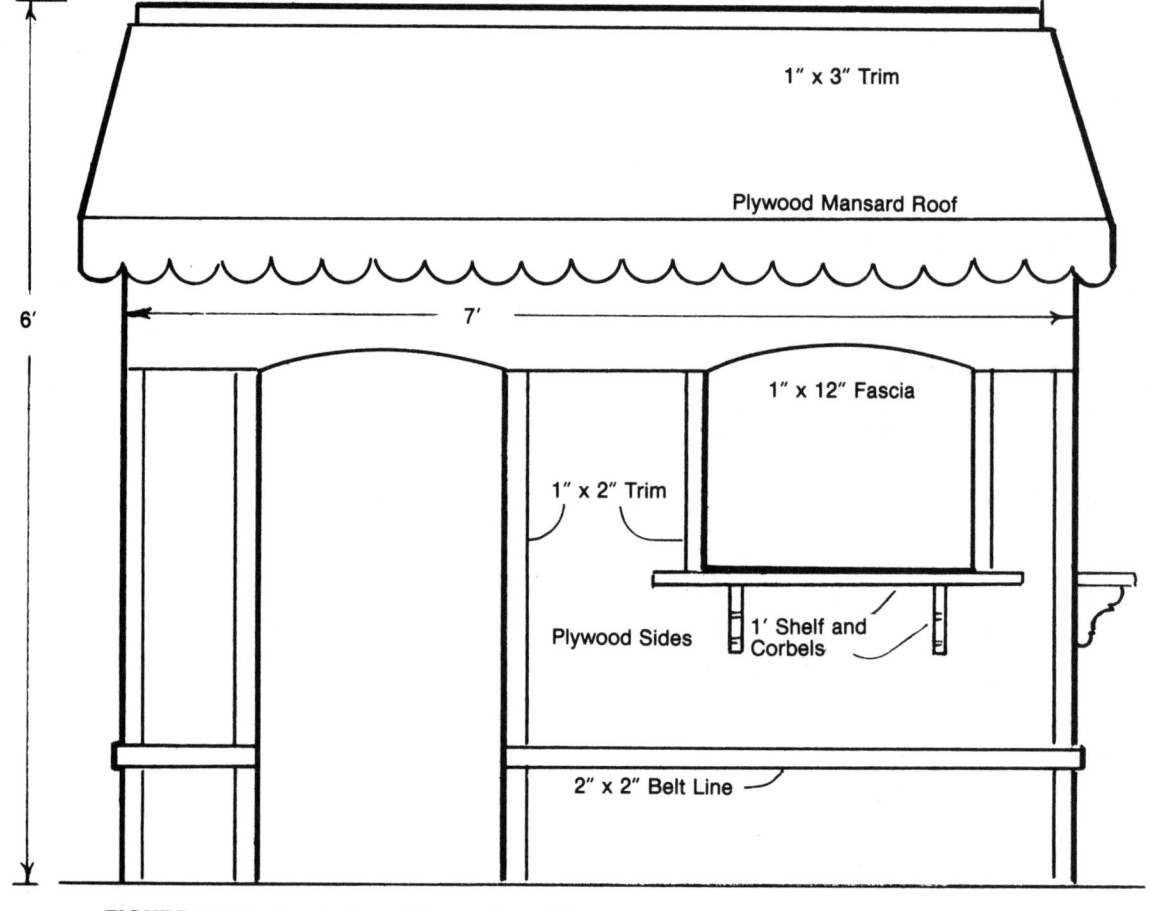

FIGURE 13–1 *Front view of Emporium with measurements.*

The following labels appear in the figure:
- 1" x 3" Trim
- Plywood Mansard Roof
- 6'
- 7'
- 1" x 12" Fascia
- 1" x 2" Trim
- Plywood Sides
- 1' Shelf and Corbels
- 2" x 2" Belt Line

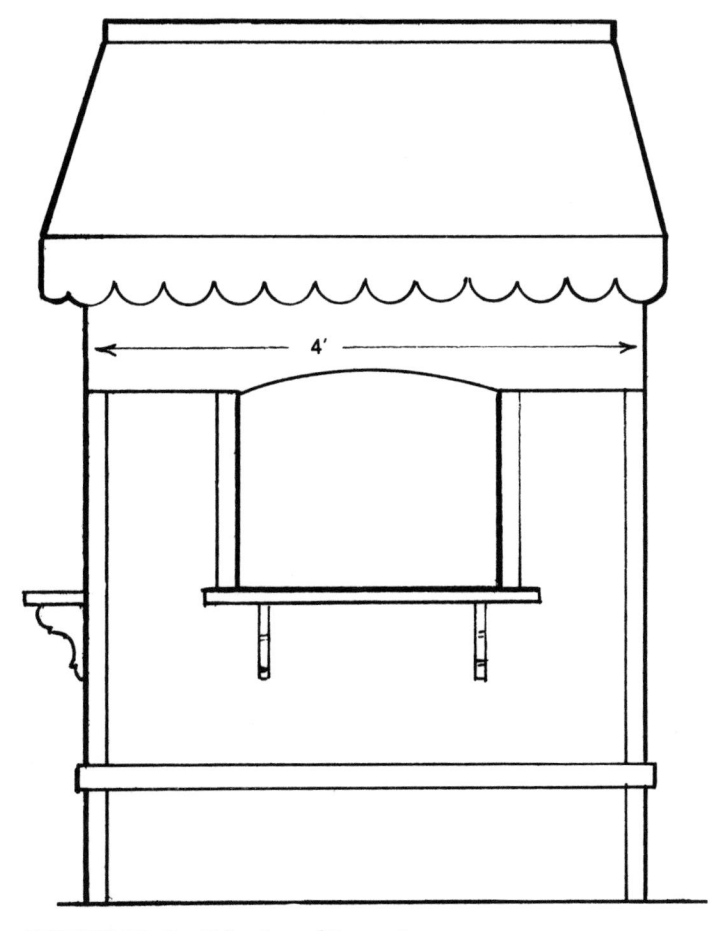

FIGURE 13–2 *Side view of Emporium.*

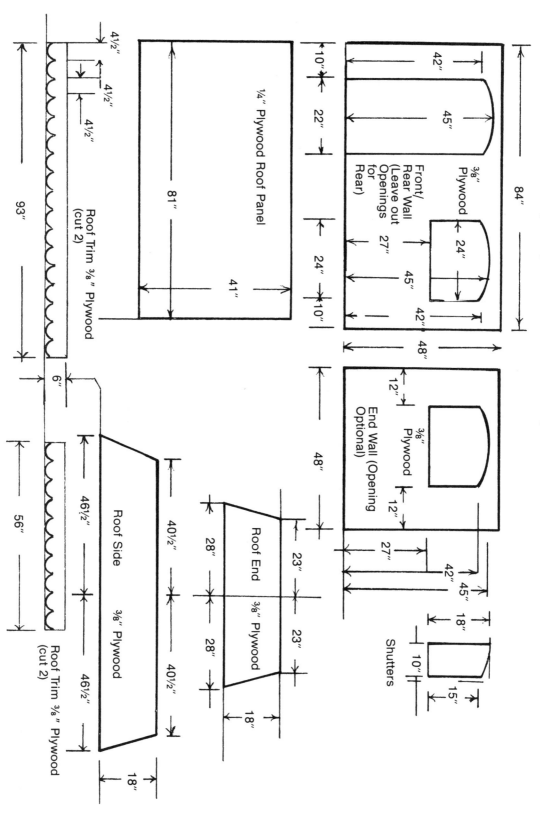

FIGURE 13–3 Measurements for the front and end walls and the roof and trim.

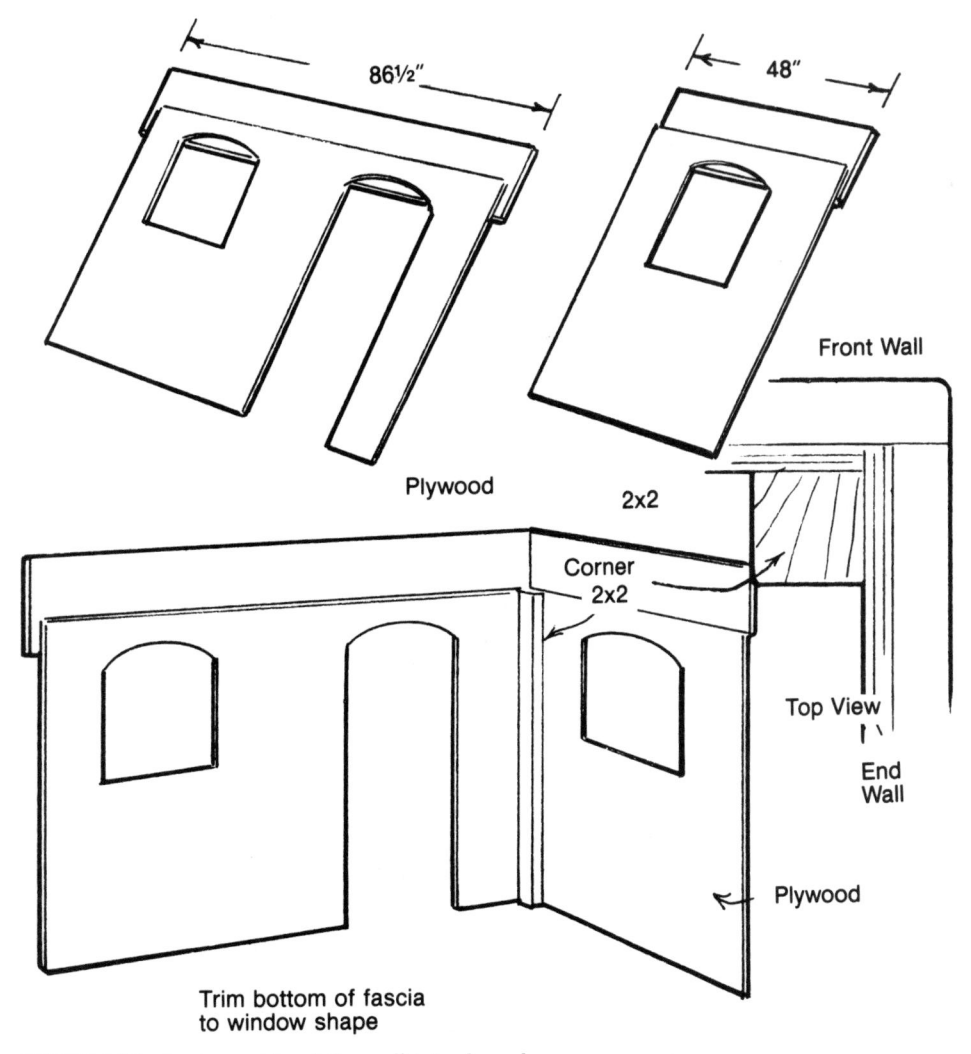

86½"

48"

Front Wall

Plywood

2x2

Corner
2x2

Top View

End
Wall

Plywood

Trim bottom of fascia
to window shape

FIGURE 13–4 *Assembly of the wall-trim boards.*

THE EMPORIUM   **173**

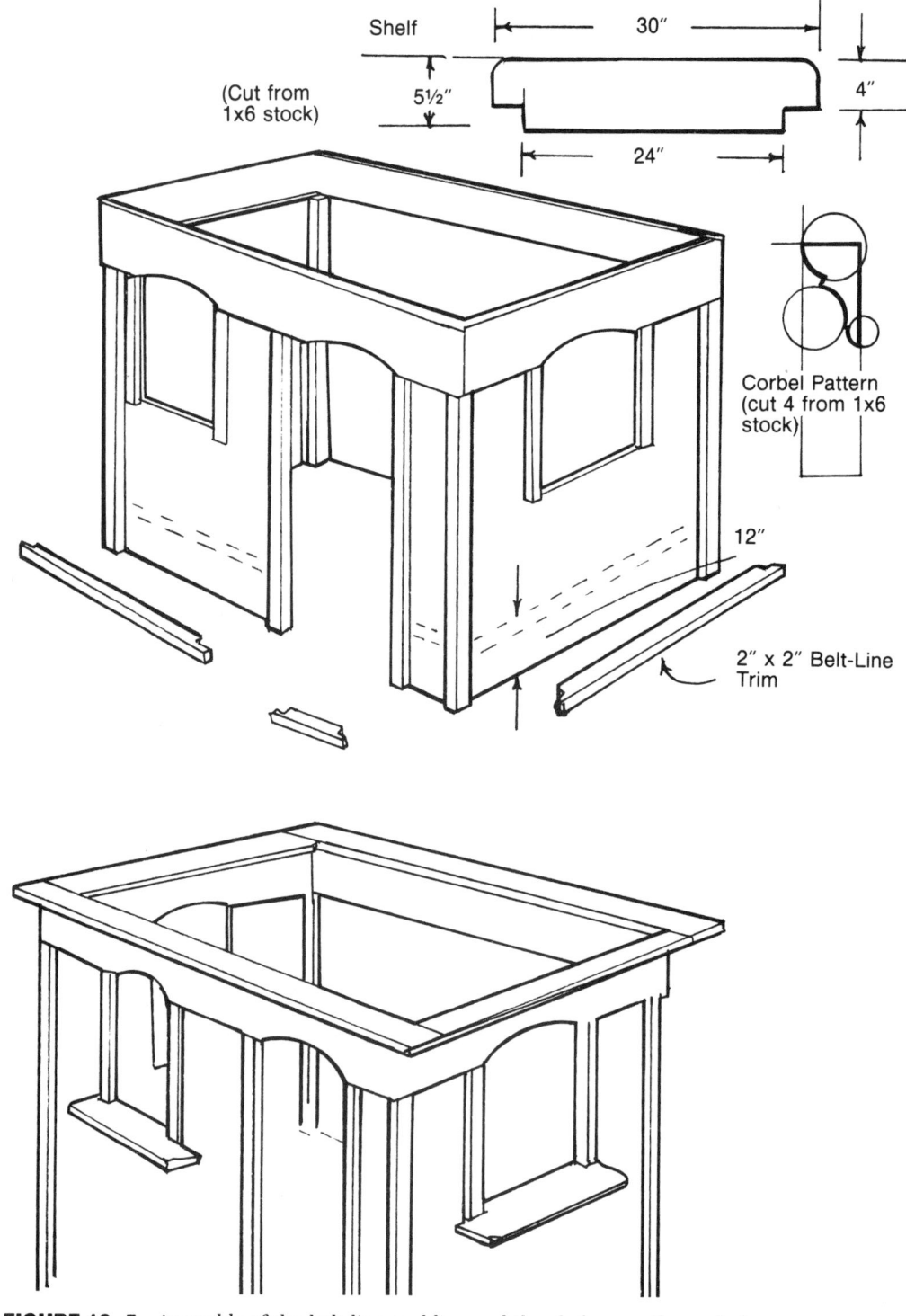

Shelf

(Cut from 1x6 stock)

5½"

30"

24"

4"

Corbel Pattern (cut 4 from 1x6 stock)

12"

2" x 2" Belt-Line Trim

FIGURE 13–5 *Assembly of the belt-line molding and the shelves on the corbels.*

cutting carefully along the window out-line and up the center line. The unfin-ished corner cuts can be made with a sa-ber saw or hand saw. After cutting the windows and door on the first side and end-wall panels, place them over the re-maining panels to use as a pattern to mark any more openings you may want.

Next, cut the mansard roof side and end panels as shown in Figure 13–3. Then rough-cut the roof trim side and end strips to size and use a $4\frac{1}{2}''$ can or dish to mark the scalloped bottom edges. If needed, the last arc on each strip can be slightly shortened to provide a fairly even spacing of the scallops to the overall dimensions shown.

The next step is to cut and attach the top wall-trim boards to the outside of the four walls, as shown in Figure 13–4. Use 1″ #8 plated flathead wood screws to at-tach the boards to the wall face. Drill pilot holes with a combination counter-sink/drill bit from the rear side of each wall, spacing the screws about 8″ apart. Next, cut lengths of 2×2 fir to fit from the wall bottom to the top of the plywood panel. Attach the wall panels together at the corners by driving screws through them and into the 2×2 stock on the in-side as shown in Figure 13–4. Use $1\frac{1}{2}''$ screws to join the $1'' \times 2''$ corner wall trim.

Cut the arches over the windows into the wall-top trim board using a saber saw; then cut and attach the 2×2 belt-line molding, $1'' \times 2''$ window solid trim, $1'' \times 6''$ window shelves, and $1'' \times 6''$ cor-bels under the shelves with screws (see Fig. 13–5). Attach the shelves to the cor-bels with $1\frac{1}{2}''$ screws.

Cut and nail the horizontal $1'' \times 6''$ bases for the mansard roof onto the tops of the wall-top trim boards, flush at the inside (Fig. 13–6). Screw the scalloped

roof bottom trim to the front face of these base boards on all four sides, spacing the screws about 6″ apart. Next, nail the flat roof panel to the edges of the 1×3s ex-tending around its four sides, flush at the outside.

The four tapered mansard roof panels were joined at the four corners 1″ down from the top with screws driven in through the roof sides. Carefully lift this delicate assembly onto the tops of the horizontal roof supports and align it with the bottom edges of the roof panels, flush with the face of each scalloped roof-bot-tom trim strip. Angle the screws down through these panels about 10″ apart near their bottom edge so that they reach down into the top surface of the horizon-tal roof boards. Countersink each pilot hole deeply so that they can be puttied over later on. Next, the flat roof panel with the 1×3 edge trim is simply lowered into place between the upper edges of all four tapered roof panels to rest on the wood corner braces near the top of the roof (see Fig. 13–6).

■ FINISHING

Smooth all edges with a shaper and sand before painting. Cut and sand all window and door lintels and nail them over the arched openings as shown in Fig. 13–6.

Roll the walls with semigloss canary yellow and paint all trim with semigloss white. Sand the shutters and paint them flat olive green. Nail them in place next to the windows.

To provide a "canopy" look to the roof, paint the panels and scalloped bottom trim white. When this is dry, mask off ver-

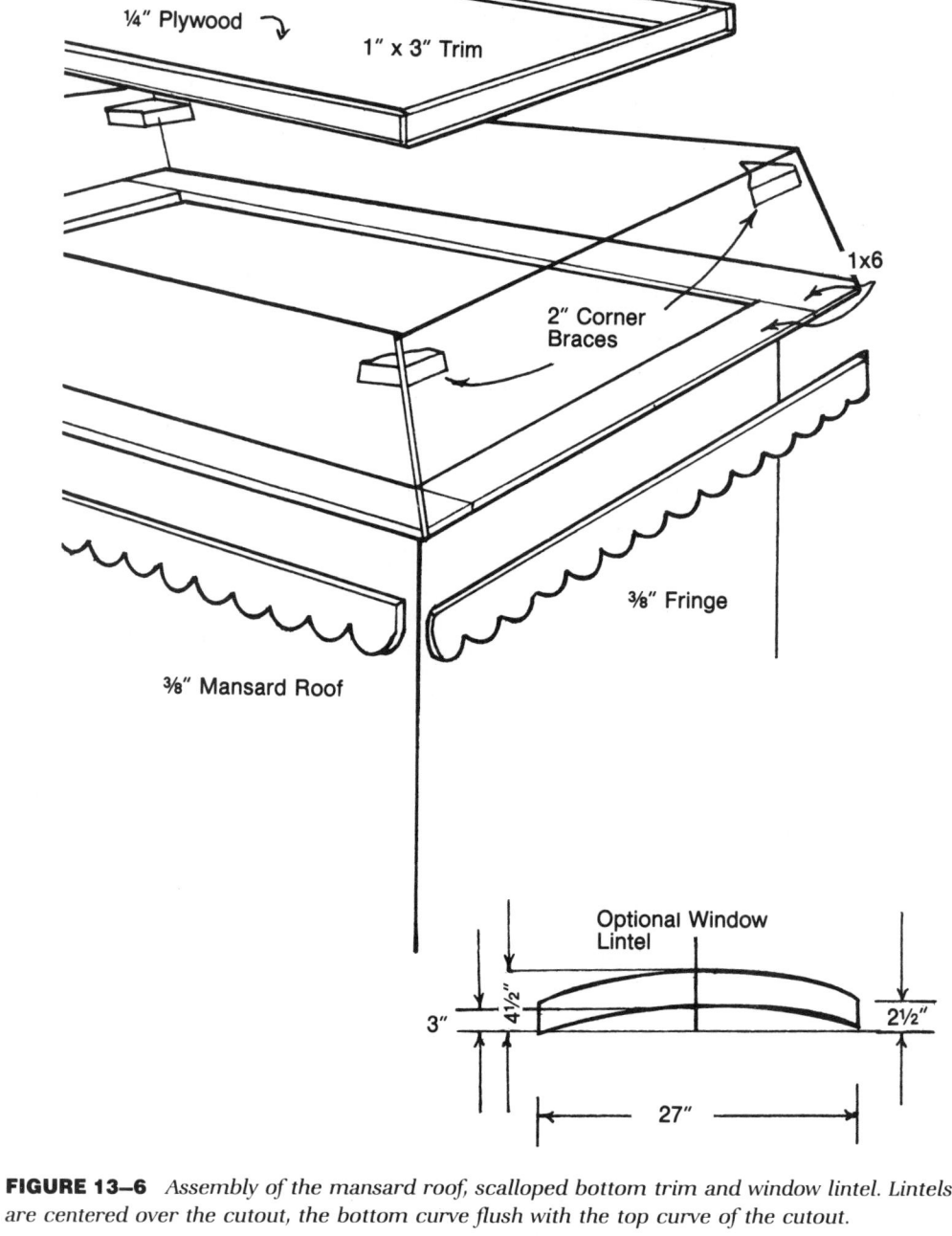

FIGURE 13–6 *Assembly of the mansard roof, scalloped bottom trim and window lintel. Lintels are centered over the cutout, the bottom curve flush with the top curve of the cutout.*

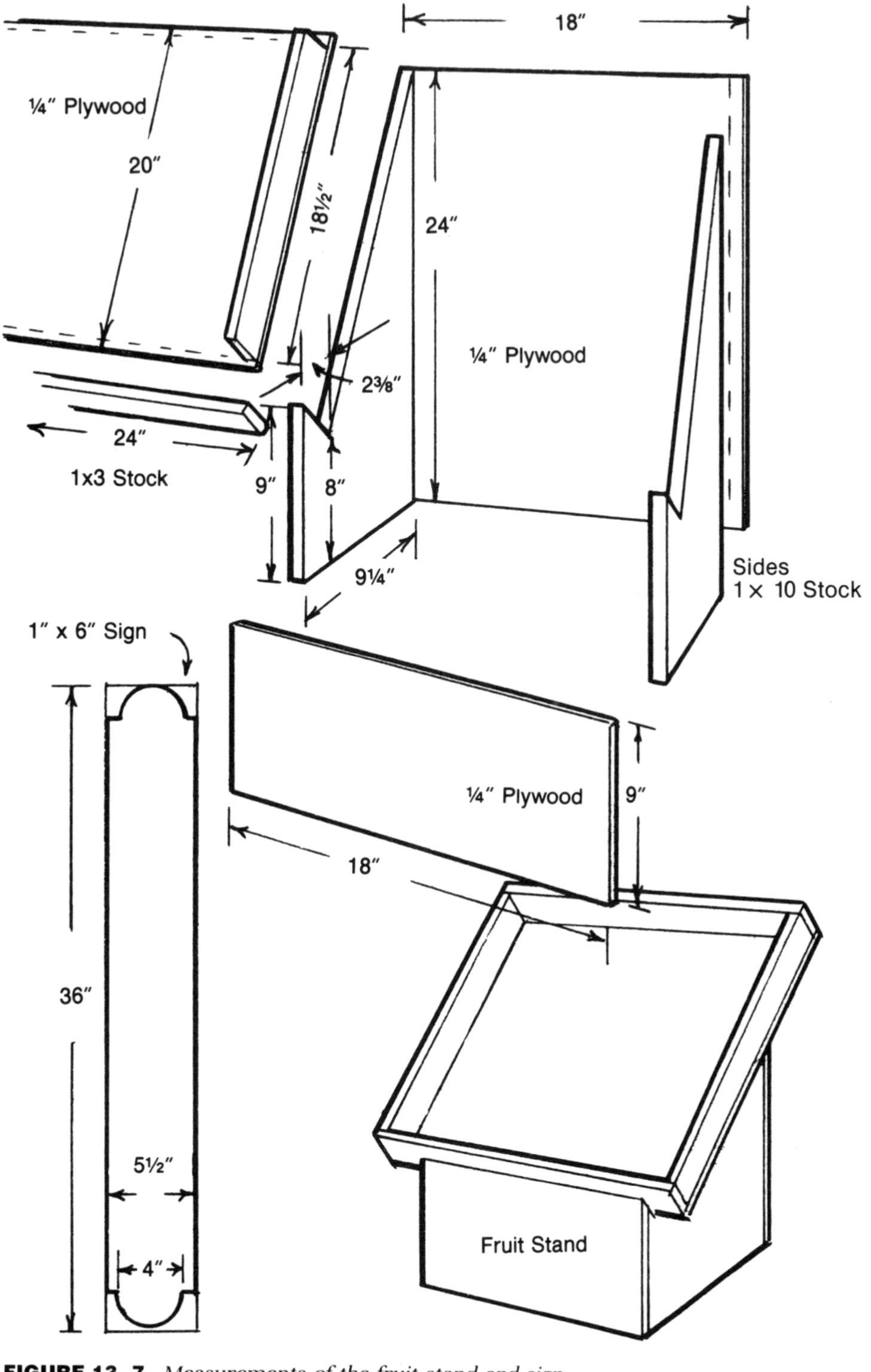

FIGURE 13–7 *Measurements of the fruit stand and sign.*

¼" Plywood
20"
18½"
18"
24"
¼" Plywood
2⅜"
24"
1x3 Stock
9"
8"
9¼"
Sides
1 × 10 Stock
1" × 6" Sign
36"
5½"
4"
¼" Plywood
18"
9"
Fruit Stand

tical stripes at each arc and paint between the tapes, alternating orange and red. Trim the shutters and sign (see Fig. 13–7) with $\frac{1}{8}''$ plastic auto trim pin-stripe tape. We cut shutter locks (optional) from plywood with the saber saw, sanded them, painted them white, and nailed them in place. We painted the sign white, then marked backward letters onto the back of contact adhesive paper and smoothed them onto the sign.

For more permanent installation, the wall bottoms can be set down onto rough redwood 1 × 4s laid down flat on the ground to provide some rot protection on bare earth.

☐ The Fruit Stand

Cut the sides of the base for the fruit stand from the 1″ × 10″ piece of pine. Nail the $\frac{1}{4}''$ plywood front and rear panels into place, flush at the sides (Fig. 13–7). Cut the box from $\frac{1}{4}''$ plywood and frame it with 1″ × 3″ stock. Drive 1$\frac{1}{2}''$ nails through the plywood back and into the edges of the 1 × 3s (which were also nailed together at the corners). Paint the base and the box.

Add some curtains, maybe some drawers or shelf units inside, and you're about ready to put on an apron, warm up the cash register, and open shop.

THE FIREHOUSE

■ MATERIALS LIST

Five 4′ × 4′ ACX plywood panel, $\frac{1}{2}$″ thick
One 4′ × 8′ ACX plywood panel, $\frac{3}{8}$″ thick
Ten 8′ lengths of fir 2 × 2 stock
Two 11′ lengths of fir 2 × 10 stock
6′ length of fir 1 × 2 stock
10′ length of #2 pine 1 × 8 stock
Two 8′ lengths of #2 pine 1 × 6 stock
Two 8′ lengths of #2 pine 1 × 4 stock
1′ length of #2 pine 1 × 12 stock
3′ length of 1″ dowel
Two 4′ lengths of $1\frac{3}{8}$″ dowel
$1\frac{1}{4}$″ wooden drawer-pull knob
20″ × 120″ roll of aluminum flashing
One hundred $1\frac{1}{2}$″ #8 plated flathead wood
    screws
One hundred 1″ #8 plate flathead wood
    screws
Six $3\frac{1}{2}$″ roundhead $\frac{3}{8}$″ bolts, nuts, and
    washers
One pound of 2″ galvanized finishing
    nails

☐ *See color insert for completed project.*

The Firehouse is sort of a generic tower than can be used for everything from a tower in Camelot to Fort Apache to Checkpoint Charlie, depending on the vintage of your imagination that day. Below is a storage enclosure, which also just happens to fit the fire truck. Above is the lookout porch that doubles as a platform for the slide down one side. A built-in ladder on the opposite side provides access to the top of the tower.

■ CUTTING AND ASSEMBLY

☐ The Walls and Floor

Begin by cutting the $\frac{1}{2}$″ plywood panels for the front wall, rear wall, ladder wall, slide wall, tower floor, and four triangular roof sides (Figs. 14–1 and 14–3). Next, cut the 2″ × 2″ pieces of fir framing. Use $1\frac{1}{2}$″ #8 plated flathead wood screws to attach the side panels to the vertical and horizontal frames so that the panels can be disassembled at the corners and the structure knocked down and stored flat. Use a combination countersink/drill bit to drill pilot holes for each screw.

Mount the vertical 2 × 2s on the ladder wall and slide wall flush with the side edges so that the front and rear walls can

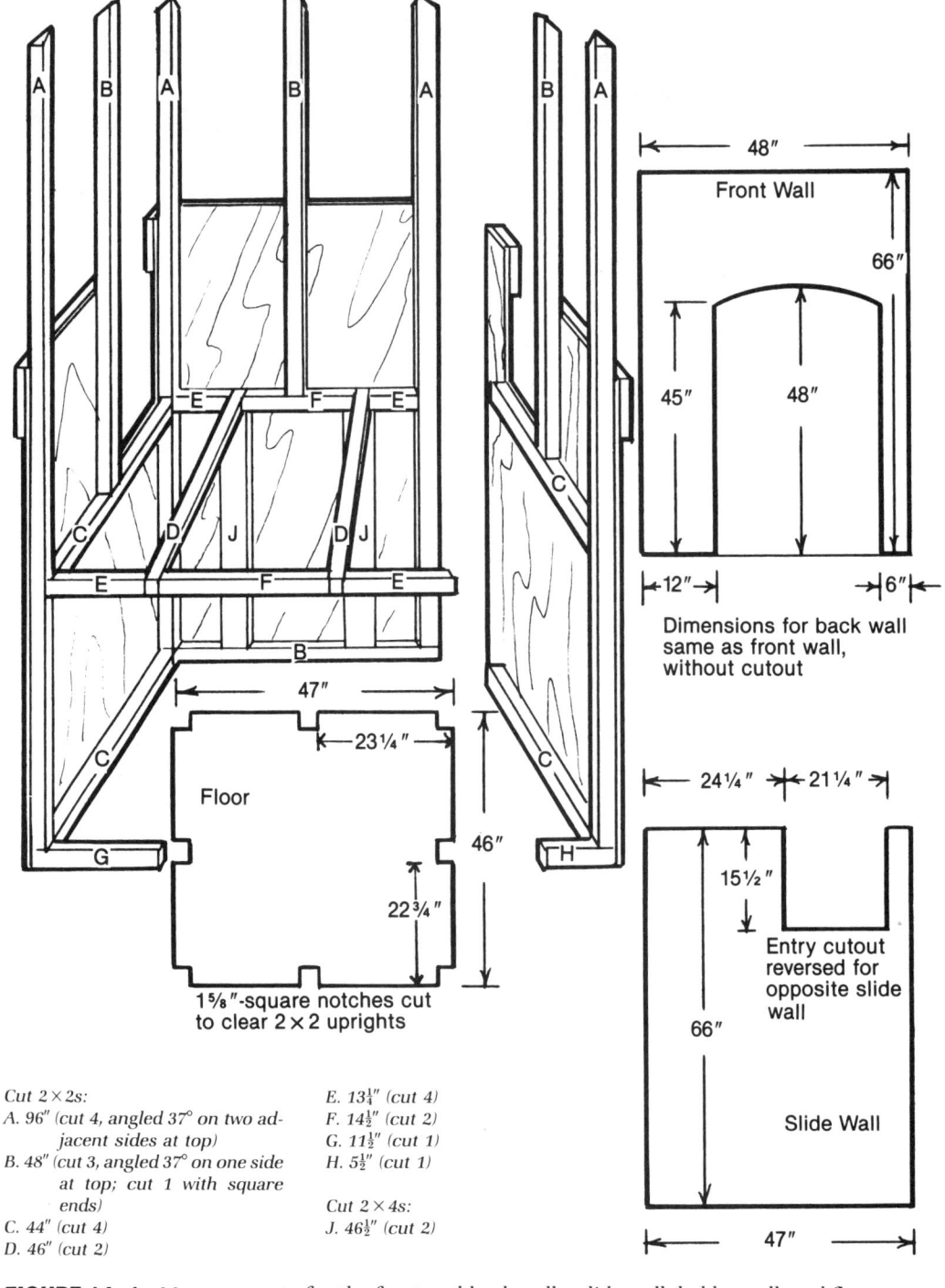

FIGURE 14—1 *Measurements for the front and back walls, slide wall, ladder wall, and floor.*

Front Wall

48″

66″

45″

48″

Dimensions for back wall
same as front wall,
without cutout

12″

6″

47″

23¼″

Floor

46″

22¾″

1⅝″-square notches cut
to clear 2 × 2 uprights

24¼″   21¼″

15½″

Entry cutout
reversed for
opposite slide
wall

66″

Slide Wall

47″

Cut 2 × 2s:
A. 96″ (cut 4, angled 37° on two ad-
    jacent sides at top)
B. 48″ (cut 3, angled 37° on one side
    at top; cut 1 with square
    ends)
C. 44″ (cut 4)
D. 46″ (cut 2)

E. 13¼″ (cut 4)
F. 14½″ (cut 2)
G. 11½″ (cut 1)
H. 5½″ (cut 1)

Cut 2 × 4s:
J. 46½″ (cut 2)

be mounted to cover the edge grain of the other two walls at the corners (see Fig. 14–1).

After attaching the frames and joining the walls at the corners, position the cross-frames for the tower flooring on top of the shorter frames attached to the sides; then drive screws in through the sides and into the ends of the cross-frames. Slip the flooring panel into place from above and screw it to the cross-frames.

Cut the sides of the ladder from the 1″ × 8″ piece of pine and drill holes for the $1\frac{3}{8}$″-diameter dowel rungs (Fig. 14–2). Cut the rungs to length, insert them in the holes, and drive $1\frac{1}{2}$″ screws through the edge of the ladder side and into the rungs, making sure that they are flush with the sides of the ladder. Place the ladder in position against the ladder wall (the insides of the ladder should be flush with the insides of the ladder-wall opening), and drive screws out through the walls and into the edges of the ladder sides, spacing the pilot holes about 8″ apart down the sides. Attach the ladder with white glue.

Cut the 1″ × 6″ rim boards to go around the top of all four walls, then drive screws out through the walls and into the 1 × 6s about 10″ apart (Fig. 14–2). Cut the "lintel" board over the door to the louver area from scrap plywood. Glue and nail it in place with 1″ brads.

□ The Roof

The first step in making the roof is to rip the angled edge on the sides (but not the base) of the roof panels at a 37° angle (Fig. 14–3). Then cut the 1″ × 4″ square border frames and screw them together at the corners with $1\frac{1}{2}$″ screws.

Next, hold one of the triangular roof sides roughly at the angle shown in Figure 14–3 and drive screws through the roof panel near the bottom edge and into the top edge of the border frame. Then screw the adjacent roof panel to the top of the border frame under it. Position the beveled flagstaff base up under the two roof panels so that the corners are flush with the sides of the panels. Screw the other two roof panels in place.

Cut the flagpole staff from the 3′ piece of 1″-diameter dowel. Drill and nail the drawer-pull knob to the top before slipping the pole through the opening in the top of the roof and into the hole in the beveled flagstaff base screwed to the inner sides of the roof panels.

□ The Slide

The slide is made from 2″ × 10″ pieces of fir. Its bottom is $\frac{3}{8}$″ plywood covered with aluminum flashing for a slippery surface (Figs. 14–4 through 14–6). The two basic rules we've found for building fun slides are (1) make sure there are no potential splinters, and (2) set the angle of the slide so that it is fast enough, but not too fast for the age group using it. The slide side boards can be cut with an upward curve to their bottom edges to provide a little "bump" to the ride, or they can be left straight.

The first step in making the slide is to cut the sides from 2″ × 10″ fir, as shown in Figure 14–5. Next, cut the plywood bottom panels so that the grain of the shorter panel runs across the direction of the slide (see Fig. 14–6).

Unroll a 10′ length of 20″-wide aluminum flashing and, with the two sides of the slide sitting on their upper edges and positioned side by side 20″ apart at their outer sides, tack the aluminum onto the bottom edges of the sides (flush at the

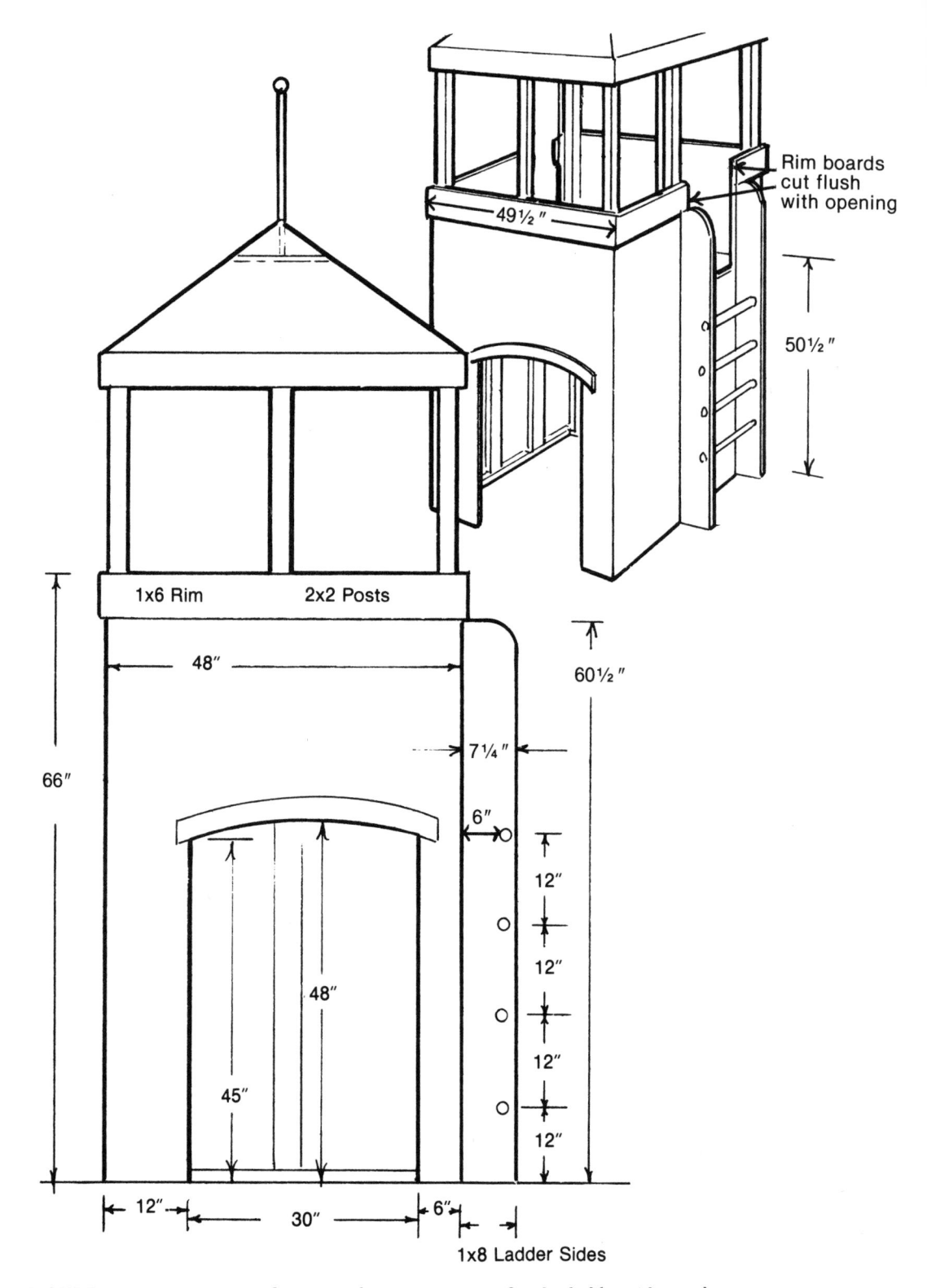

Rim boards
cut flush
with opening

49½"

50½"

1x6 Rim   2x2 Posts

48"

60½"

66"

7¼"

6"

12"

12"

48"

12"

45"

12"

12"   30"   6"

1x8 Ladder Sides

182   **FIGURE 14–2** *Front view of tower with measurements for the ladder sides and rungs.*

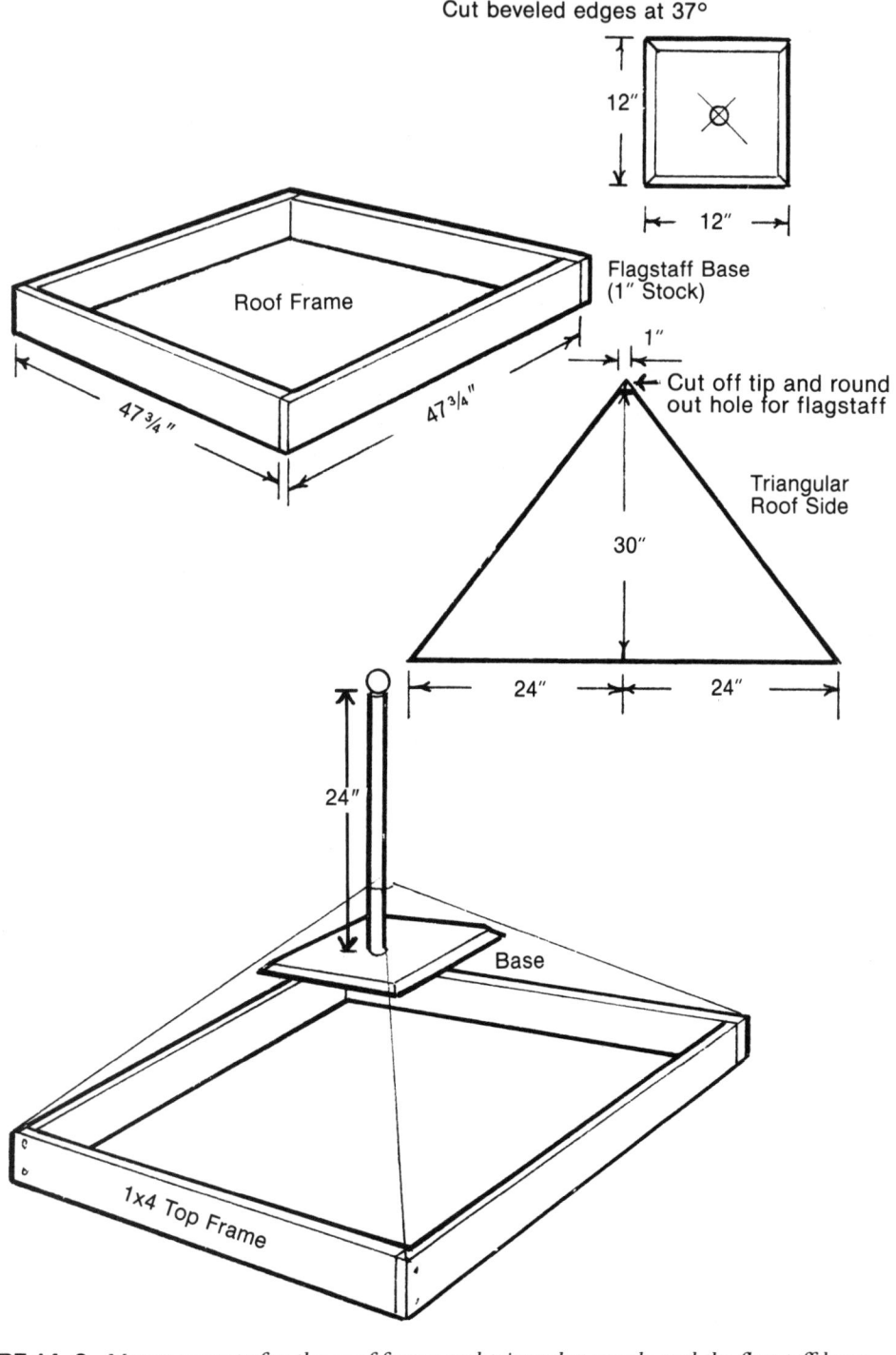

Cut beveled edges at 37°

12"

12"

Flagstaff Base
(1" Stock)

1"

Cut off tip and round
out hole for flagstaff

Roof Frame

47 3/4"

47 3/4"

Triangular
Roof Side

30"

24"

24"

24"

Base

1x4 Top Frame

FIGURE 14–3 *Measurements for the roof frame and triangular panels and the flagstaff base.*

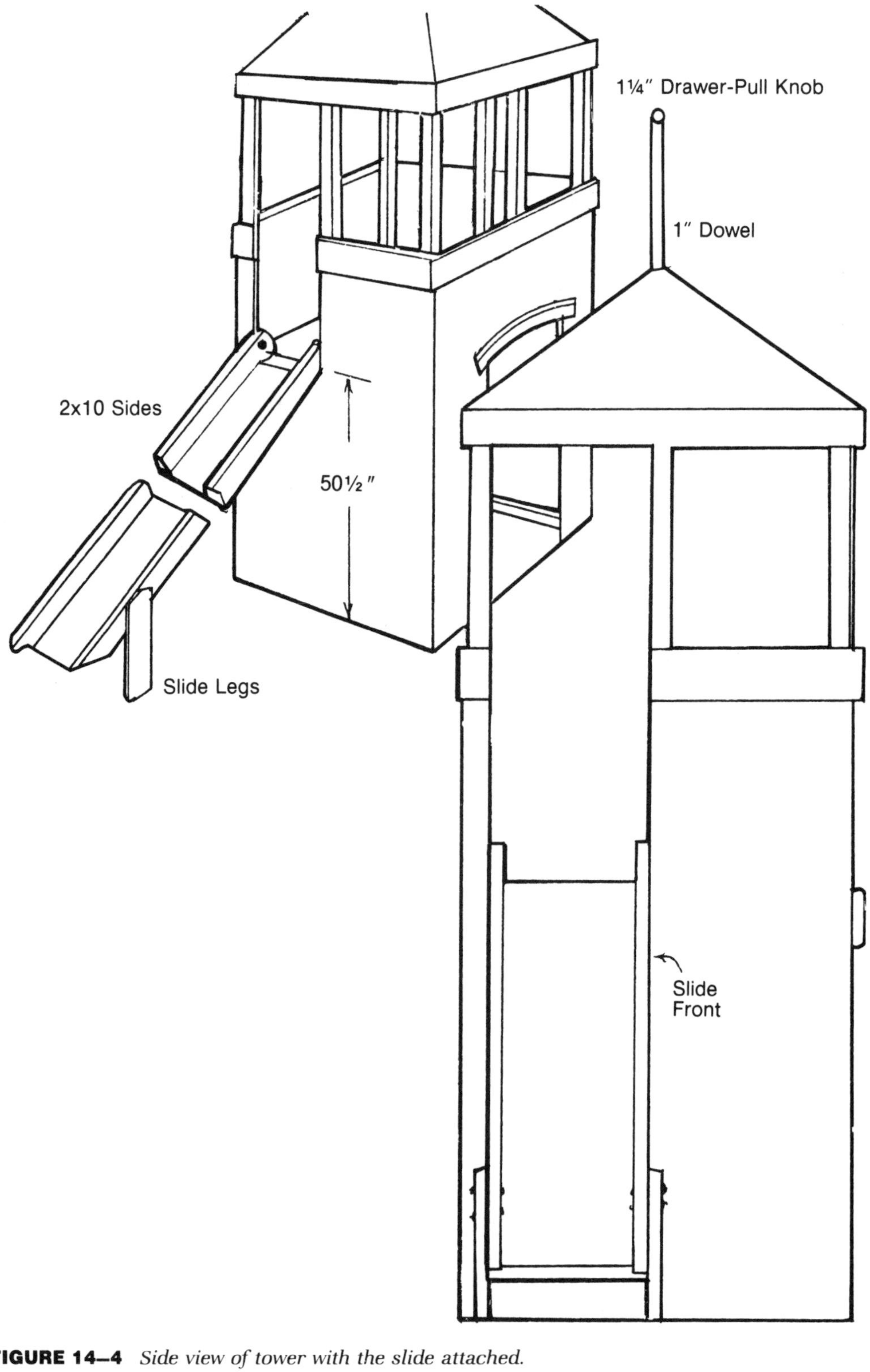

FIGURE 14—4 *Side view of tower with the slide attached.*

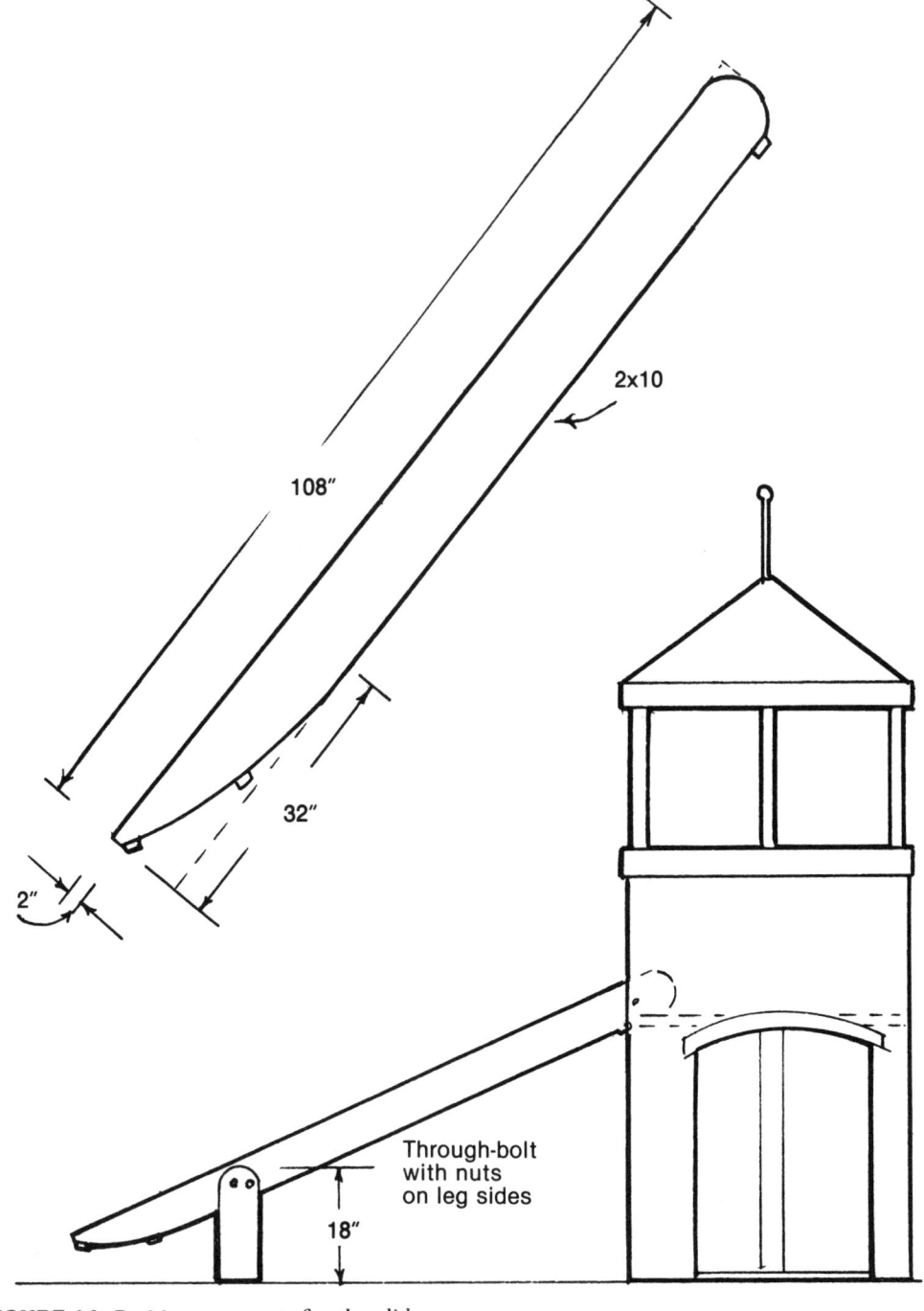

108"

2x10

32"

2"

Through-bolt
with nuts
on leg sides

18"

FIGURE 14—5 *Measurements for the slide.*

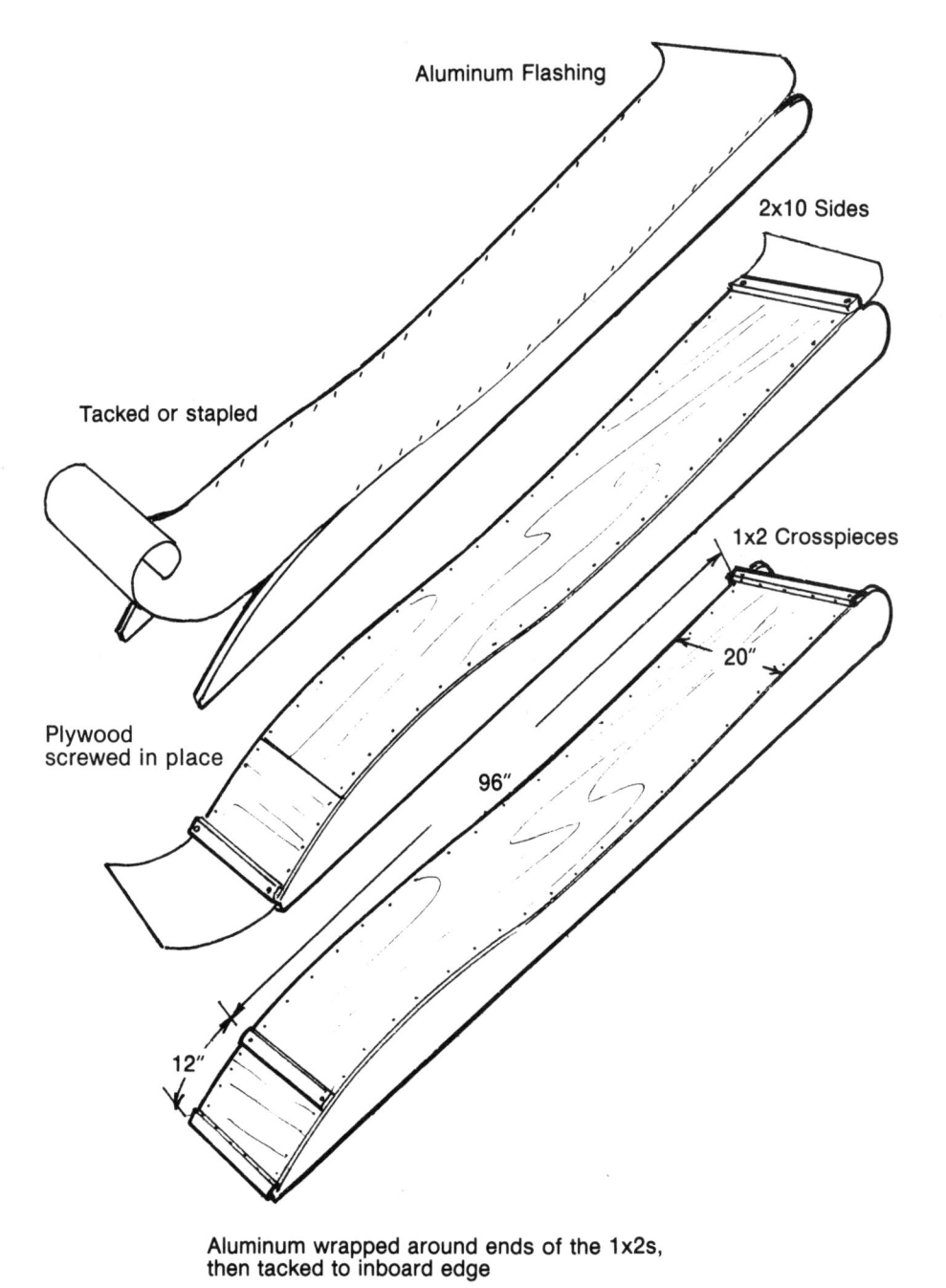

Aluminum Flashing

2x10 Sides

Tacked or stapled

1x2 Crosspieces

20"

Plywood
screwed in place

96"

12"

Aluminum wrapped around ends of the 1x2s,
then tacked to inboard edge

FIGURE 14—6 *Assembly of the aluminum flashing on the slide.*

outsides) with 2″ galvanized box nails or staples (Fig. 14-6). Before attaching the aluminum, use a carpenter's square to make sure the ends of the parallel sides of the side are aligned. Attach the aluminum so that a roughly equal amount extends out on either end.

Next, screw the plywood panels to the aluminum, driving the screws through the plywood and aluminum and into the edge of the 2 × 10s. Apply some glue and screw the 1″ × 3″ fir cross-frames to the plywood, driving the screws into the side frames. Place one cross-frame at each end of the plywood panels, then place one directly over the butt joint of the two panels near the bottom end of the slide.

With the cross-frames in place, bend the aluminum around the end frames and trim it about $3\frac{3}{4}$″ up from the bend. The trimmed ends of the aluminum can be bent so that they wrap around the end cross-frames. Then tack or staple them to the side of each cross-frame facing the middle of the slide.

The slide is held to the 2 × 2 frames on both sides of the slide opening on the slide wall with $3\frac{1}{2}$″ × $\frac{3}{8}$″ roundhead bolts extending through holes drilled through the sides of the slide and on through the 2 × 2 frames. Roundhead bolts were tapped into the wood to provide an inside surface on the sides of the slide that wouldn't catch clothing.

Cut the legs at the bottom end of the slide from the 2″ × 10″ stock. Bolt them to the sides of the slide with two $3\frac{1}{2}$″ × $\frac{3}{8}$″

roundhead bolts inserted out through holes in the sides and legs with nuts on the outside. Round off all exposed edges of the slide and sand all surfaces thoroughly.

■ FINISHING

We gave the sides of the slide, the legs, the wood trim, the ladder, and the flagstaff several coats of gloss white paint. The walls were rolled with one coat of white enamel.

Use $\frac{3}{4}$″-wide masking tape to mask off horizontal stripes around the walls, leaving $2\frac{1}{2}$″ between the stripes. Marks made $3\frac{1}{4}$″ apart up each corner will show how to stretch the tape between the corners. Place vertical stripes of tape between the horizontal stripes, leaving an 8″ space between vertical stripes to form "brick" shapes. Stagger the placement of the vertical stripes between alternate layers of horizontal stripes to provide a brick-wall look.

Mix several quarts of flat rust-red or brick-red primer paint with granulated paint-texturing material. With a roller, paint over the masking tape on the four walls up to the bottom of the white top trim. (Make sure all tape is firmly smoothed down onto the white paint below before rolling.) As soon as the brick-red paint is tacky, pull off all masking tape to reveal the brick pattern.

15

THE LOG CABIN

■ MATERIALS LIST

Fifty 8′ × 4″ × 6″ landscaping timbers
    (peeler logs)
Twelve 8′ lengths of rough redwood,
    2 × 4 stock
Four 6′ lengths of rough redwood, 2 × 4
    stock
Two 4′ × 8′ ACX plywood panels, $\frac{3}{4}$″ thick
Three 4′ × 8′ T–1–11 textured plywood
    panels, $\frac{5}{8}$″ thick
Three 10′ lengths of rough redwood or
    cedar, 1 × 6 stock
Roll of tarpaper roofing
Three bundles of cedar shake shingles
Four 10′ lengths of rough redwood or
    cedar, 1 × 6 stock
Four 6′ lengths of rough redwood, 1 × 4
    stock
Four 10′ lengths of rough redwood,
    1 × 4 stock
Four 3″ butt hinges
Barrel bolt lock
4′ × 4′ ACX plywood panel, $\frac{1}{2}$″ thick
2′ × 4′ sheet of clear Plexiglas, $\frac{1}{8}$″ thick
Two 8′ lengths of rough redwood, 2 × 6
    stock
Fifty feet of $\frac{3}{8}$″ to $\frac{1}{2}$″ hemp rope
Two 6′ lengths of rough redwood, 2 × 3
    or 2 × 4 stock

One pound 4″ galvanized box nails
One pound 3″ galvanized box nails
Five pounds 1″ roofing nails
Eight 1$\frac{1}{2}$″ butt hinges
Fifty $\frac{7}{8}$″ brads
Ten cartridges of brown caulking
    compound

☐ *See color insert for completed project.*

The idea for the Log Cabin grew out of a
pile of landscape timbers stacked at the
lumberyard. They seemed too good just
to use as fence posts or retaining walls.
And there was potential in those modi-
fied plywood peeler logs, with their rough
texture but reasonably uniform sizing. Of
course, if you can't find peeler logs or
landscape timbers (peeler logs that have
been milled flat on two sides), the project
is pretty much out of the question. The
cabin is included here, even though these
logs may not be universally available, because it's so much fun to build.

    Peeler logs are what's left over after a
tree has been cut to 8′ lengths and its
wood has been peeled off in a sheet as
the log is spun to make 4″ × 8″ panels of
plywood. So 8′ is the maximum length we
have to work with in building the cabin.

After the logs have been cut, the assembly is exactly like working with a full-size Lincoln Logs set. So we did all the cutting and original stacking of the logs in the most convenient place we could find, then disassembled the walls, carried them to the building site, and assembled the cabin.

The first step is to level off a flat site for the cabin. One of the charms of building log cabins is that your work can be a little sloppy and it just adds to the rustic charm. Once you begin to realize there are few mistakes you can make when building log cabins, the tense precision we've maintained with the other toys dissipates and the project becomes relaxing fun—and a great excuse to get young builders in on some memorable building afternoons. You can relax and make this a great collaborative project between kids and grownups. And this relaxation starts with the first step. If the floor foundation turns out to be a little off and twisted, a whole corner of the cabin can be levered up with a crowbar and filled in to true things up just before the roof panels are attached. If logs are cut to slightly off-standard length around the windows and doors, a final trim with the hand saw will fix all that.

■ CUTTING AND NOTCHING

After flattening off an area about 10′ × 10′, cut the rough redwood 2 × 4s to the lengths shown in Figure 15–2. Nail two 4′ × 8′ panels of $\frac{3}{4}$″ plywood onto these 2 × 4s, with both panels attached to the top edge of the same center 2 × 4, butting the panels side by side against each other. Use 3″ nails to fasten the panels onto the top edges of the 2 × 4s. Rough redwood 2 × 4s are used because redwood won't rot or be gobbled up by bugs. (If redwood isn't available, treated Wolmanized foundation lumber can be used.)

The next step is to begin cutting the logs and notching them near the ends. You sometimes have a choice about what kind of basic log wall you want. Peeler logs are round, so they present the same look no matter where you begin to notch them. One drawback is that they vary considerably in width, whereas landscaping timbers that have been flattened off on two sides provide a rough 4″ × 6″ cross section. These 4 × 6s can be notched on their wider sides, which provides a rounded look to the exposed face of the logs and a wider, flat-bearing surface between logs. But notching the logs so they lie flat on their wider sides will mean that one-half again more logs have to be bought, notched, and hauled to the site. We like the rough-hewn look of the flattened sides when they're exposed, so this is how we notched them. (The notching process is easier if you cut into the narrower side.)

The basic tools needed for the notching are a chain saw or circular saw, a hand saw, a framing hammer (with a claw end that's a little straighter than the usual household claw hammer), and a small carpenter's square. Mark the first cut for the notch 2″ in from one end of the log, and the second cut 6″ in from the end. With the saw blade set to a depth of about $1\frac{1}{2}$″, make two cuts at the sides of the notch, following the lines marked across the logs with the square. To cut away the wood inside the notched area, sharpen the claws of a claw hammer and use it as an axe blade. Lay the log on its flat side, sticking out about 10″ from the edge of the workbench or sawhorse. Then begin making vertical chops with the claws, removing about $\frac{1}{4}$″ of the log within

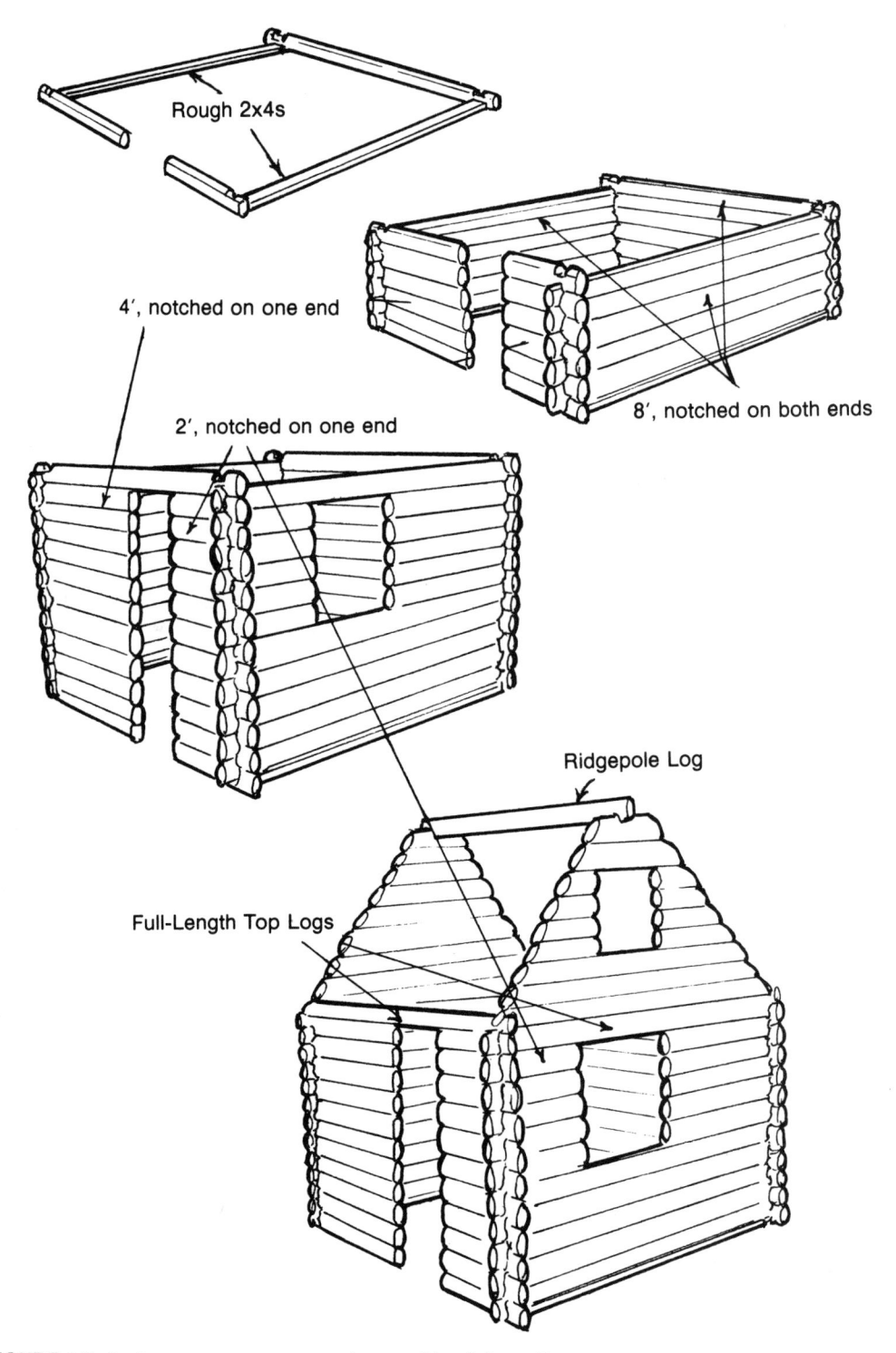

Rough 2x4s

4', notched on one end

2', notched on one end

8', notched on both ends

Ridgepole Log

Full-Length Top Logs

FIGURE 15–1 *Log measurements and assembly of the walls.*

the notch with each chop. If there are no knots within the notch, it should take only about eight to 10 chops to clean out the notch. (Whenever we ran into knots, we cleaned out the notch as best we could with the claw, then used a hammer and wood chisel to cut out the harder knot wood.)

The sharpened claw hammer also makes a perfect mini-adz to cut back the sides of any logs that have too much bow to them. But like an adz or an axe, or even a chisel, they are dangerous and you have to stay awake while operating one. After a few notches, the process begins to speed up (and your right arm starts to grow noticeably larger), and the idea of notching the logs is no longer such a formidable proposition.

First, notch the logs for the rear, front, and side walls up to the roof line. Notch four 8', two 4', and two 2' logs on one side only. (Note that the offset spacing of the windows and doors was done on purpose to get maximum use from the 8' logs.) Whenever cutting off a short log, draw the cut on both sides with the square, then cut on both sides with the circular saw, completing any final cuts remaining between these cuts with a hand saw.

To cut the gabled tops of the side walls, lay the logs side by side and mark the diagonal cuts. This allows you to save as much remaining log as possible for the opposite wall (Fig. 15–4). We found that an upper-story window was needed on one side wall next to the loft bunk to brighten things up after the roofing was attached, so do this now rather than cutting the window after the walls are up (as we did).

To keep the count straight, stack the logs up in walls as you cut them and do any custom fitting of the notching as the logs are stacked up to the bottom of the roof line. Then number the logs and dismantle the walls for assembly at the site.

■ ASSEMBLY

□ The Walls and Floor

Cut two redwood 2 × 4s to 84" to fit between the notches of the full-length logs. Lay the one 8' log with notches in its top edge only along the rear edge of the plywood floor. Then align the two 2 × 4s parallel to the side edges of the floor (see Fig. 15–1). Their center lines should lie along the centers of the notches in the log at the rear floor edge. Nail these boards with 4" nails to the sides of the foundation.

Place one 2' log and one 4' log (both notched only on the top edge and at one end) parallel to the front edge of the foundation and butted against the front ends of the 2 × 4s. Drive 4" nails at an angle through the unnotched ends at the door opening and into the foundation. Next, lay a full-length log onto the notches at the ends of the front and rear logs. Drive a 4" nail into the center of every notch lying down over another notch at each corner to help hold the corners together in final assembly. Lay a 2' log and a 4' log with notches at one end only onto the front notches of the side-wall logs; lay down a full-length notched log at the rear wall.

Toenail the ends of the 2' and 4' logs to the ends of the short logs below them, leaving about $\frac{1}{2}$" of the nail head showing temporarily. From now on, the four walls will be nailed at the corners and toenailed at the sides of the door and windows (leaving $\frac{1}{2}$" of nail exposed) until there are eleven rows of front, short logs.

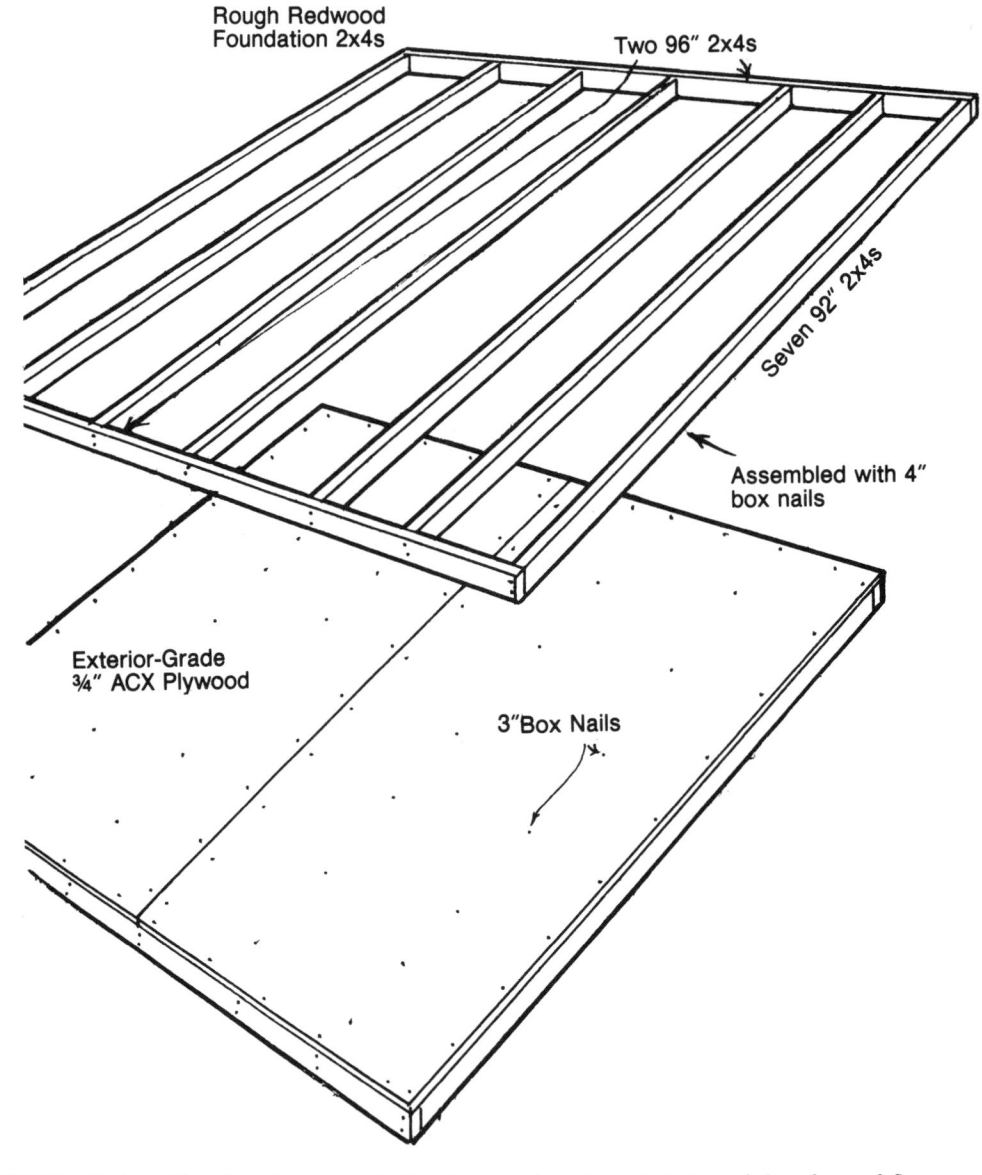

Rough Redwood Foundation 2x4s

Two 96" 2x4s

Seven 92" 2x4s

Assembled with 4" box nails

Exterior-Grade ¾" ACX Plywood

3"Box Nails

FIGURE 15–2 *Cabin foundation, including the rough redwood 2 × 4s and the plywood floor.*

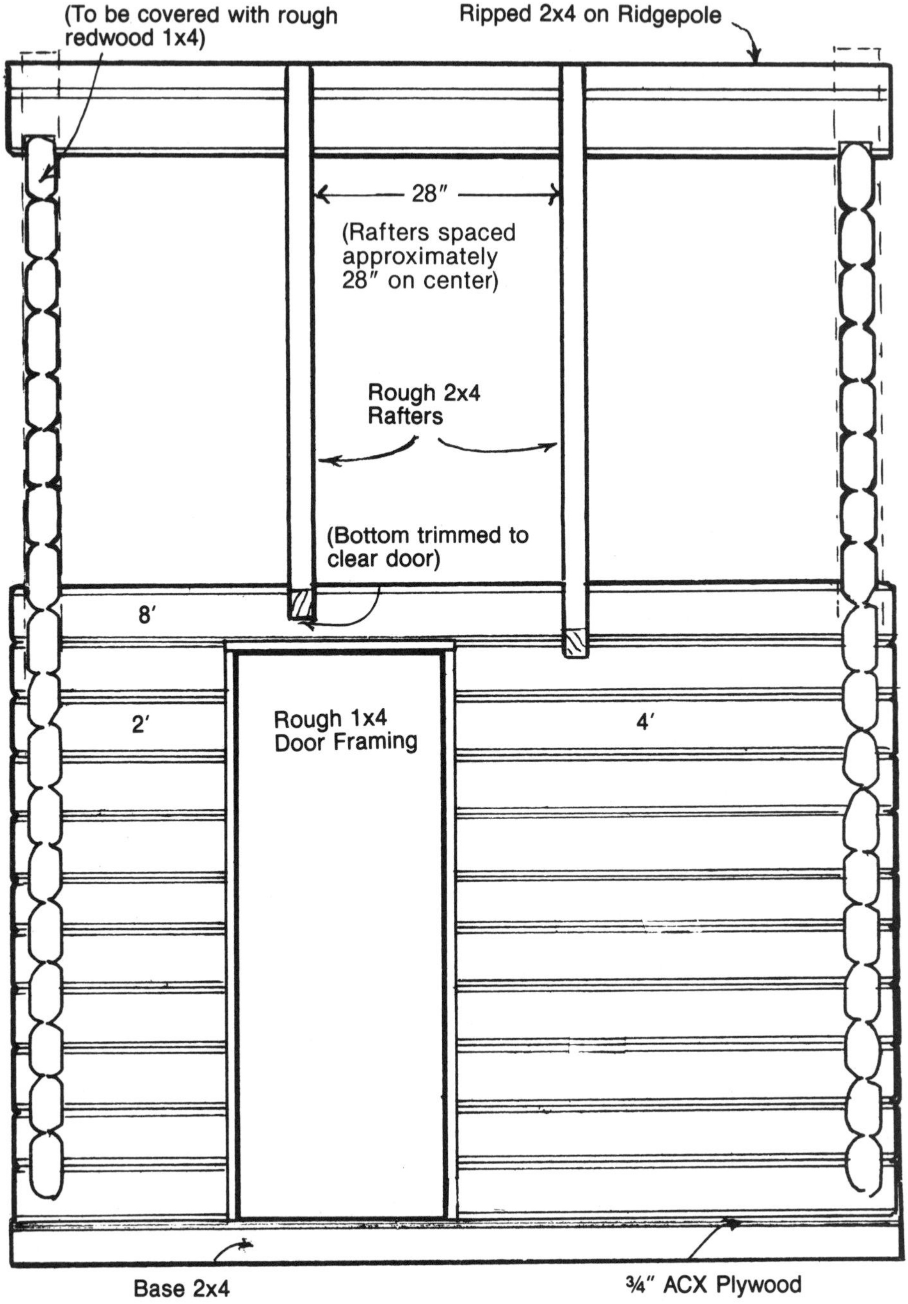

(To be covered with rough redwood 1x4)

Ripped 2x4 on Ridgepole

← 28" →

(Rafters spaced approximately 28" on center)

Rough 2x4 Rafters

(Bottom trimmed to clear door)

8'

2'

Rough 1x4 Door Framing

4'

Base 2x4

¾" ACX Plywood

FIGURE 15–3 *The front wall assembled on the foundation.*

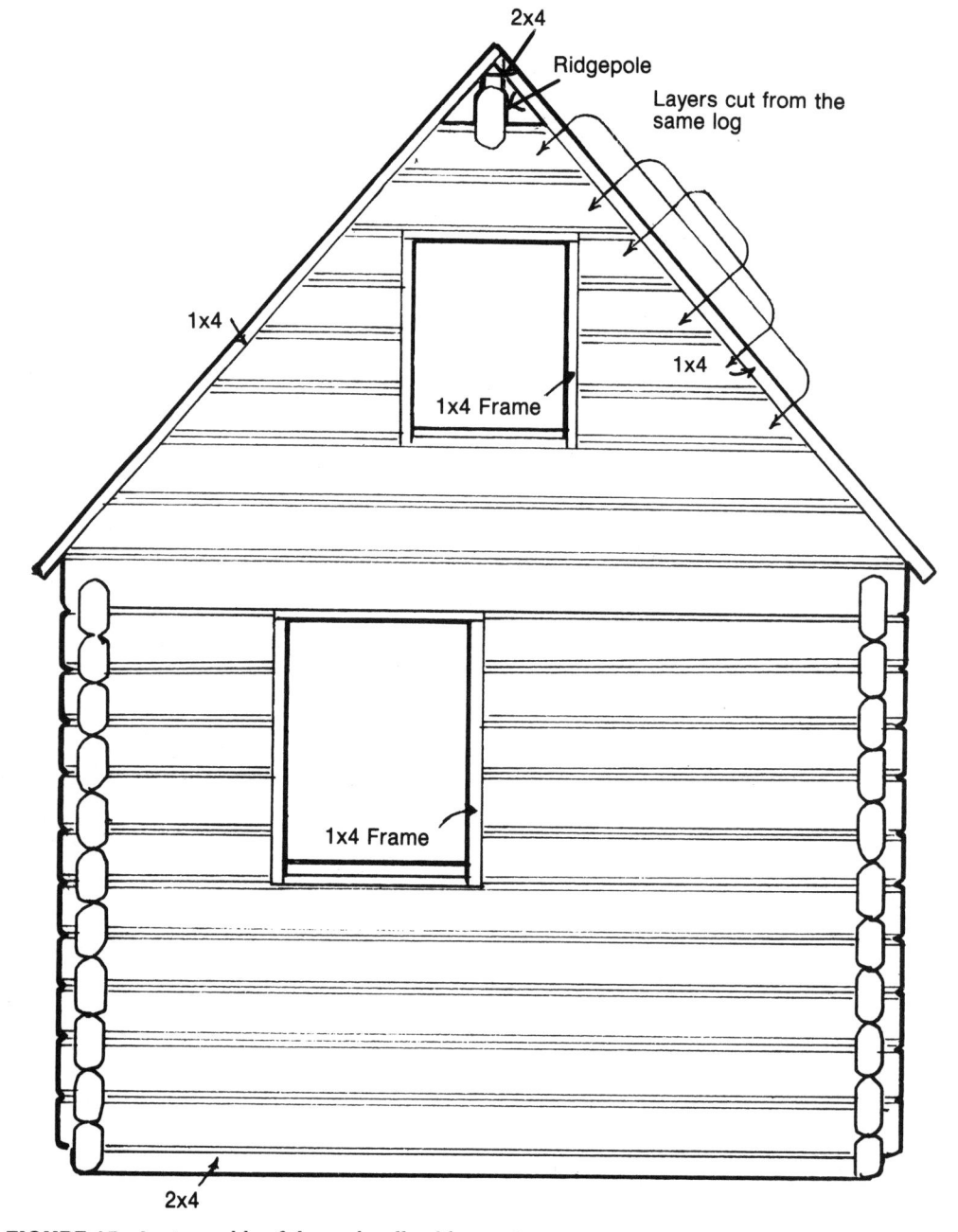

2x4

Ridgepole

Layers cut from the same log

1x4

1x4

1x4 Frame

1x4 Frame

2x4

FIGURE 15—4 *Assembly of the end-wall gables.*

Then lay a full-length log onto the tops of the front and rear log and nail it down.

□ The Gables

At this point, the tapered logs cut for the end-wall gables can be nailed on (Fig. 15–4). In final assembly, drive two 4″ nails into each beveled end about $1\frac{1}{2}″$ from each tip and angled back slightly toward the center at the bottom. About $\frac{1}{8}″$ of these nails should be visible from the bottom of the log. Then lift the first tapered log onto the top side-wall log, center it, and finish driving the nails into the log below. Nail, position, and attach the next tapered log to the log below in the same way. The end gables will be very fragile and probably uneven, wobbling in and out at the top until the top ridgepole log is attached and the 1″ × 4″ gable edges and top panels are in place; then the whole structure will become a rigid unit.

After nailing the second gable end on the opposite side wall, span a full-length log notched only on its bottom side on top of each upper-most tapered gable logs and toenail it in place. This is the ridgepole log seen in Figure 15–1. Next, lay a 6′ rough redwood (or cedar) 1 × 4 on top of the beveled ends of one side of one of the gables, with the top end of the 1 × 4 aligned with the angled cuts of the other side of the gable when viewed from the point of the roof. Drive 2″ nails through the 1 × 4 and into the beveled end of the bottom gable log. Align the 1 × 4 with the sides of the next log up and drive in a nail. Pull the 1 × 4 to align it with the next log up before driving in the next nail, and so on. In other words, pull or push the 1 × 4 to align it with the logs to straighten out the gable ends when viewed from the front. Nail a 1 × 4 along the other gable side in the same

way, aligning it flush with the top side of the first 1 × 4 to set the peak of the roof. Repeat these steps to straighten the opposite gable.

Cut a rough redwood 2 × 4 to sit on top the ridgepole between the gables (see Figs. 15–4 and 15–5). When this is in place, mark where the tops of the 1 × 4 on the gables hit the ends of the 2 × 4 lying on edge on top of the ridgepole. Mark these points, draw a straight line between them, and rip the 2 × 4 to this width before toenailing it on top of the ridgepole, with its top edge aligned with the top edges of the 1 × 4s (Fig. 15–5).

□ The Rafters

Cut the rafters from rough 2 × 4s as shown in Figure 15–5 and nail them to the ridge pole and to the top full-length logs on the front and rear walls with 4″ nails. Next, rip a 4″ × 8″ panel of $\frac{5}{8}″$ T–1–11 textured plywood with grooves 8″ on center right down the middle the long way. Nail these (with the textured sides facing down), to the tops of the gable 1 × 4s, the rafters, and the ridgepole 2 × 4. The cut edges of the panels should be butted along the ridge of the roof; gable overhang should be equal at both ends. Next, slide the remaining two 4′ × 8′ panels of plywood so their grooved side edges slip into the grooved edges of the 2′ × 8′ panels just nailed and align at the ends, textured sides face down. Nail these panels to the gable 1 × 4s and the rafters with $1\frac{1}{2}″$ nails.

□ The Windows and Door

Use rough redwood or cedar 1 × 4s to make the window and door frames. First, even out the ends of the logs at each opening. Some logs can simply be drifted

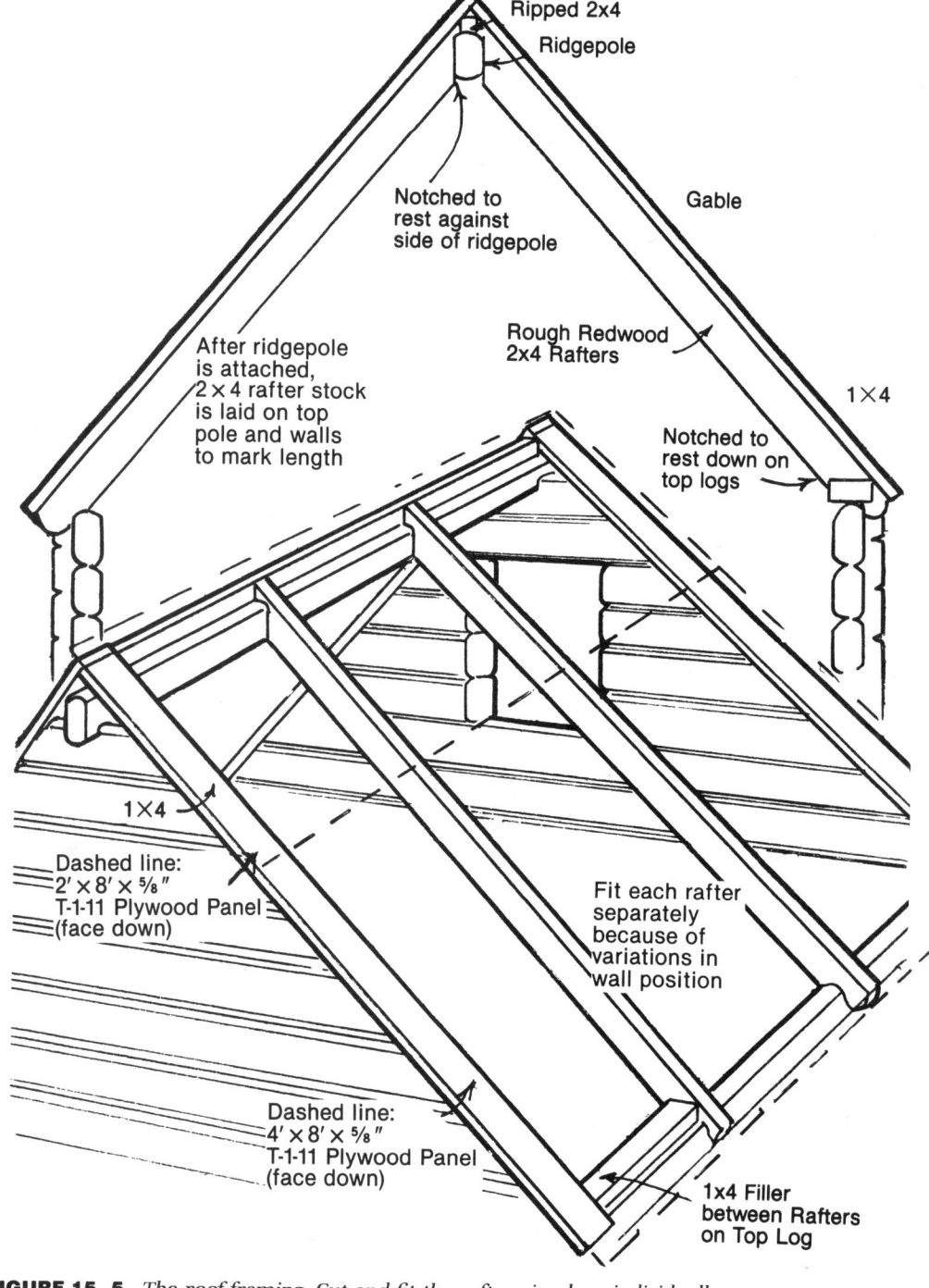

Ripped 2x4
Ridgepole

Notched to
rest against
side of ridgepole

Gable

After ridgepole
is attached,
2 × 4 rafter stock
is laid on top
pole and walls
to mark length

Rough Redwood
2x4 Rafters

Notched to
rest down on
top logs

1×4

1×4

Dashed line:
2' × 8' × ⅝"
T-1-11 Plywood Panel
(face down)

Fit each rafter
separately
because of
variations in
wall position

Dashed line:
4' × 8' × ⅝"
T-1-11 Plywood Panel
(face down)

1x4 Filler
between Rafters
on Top Log

FIGURE 15–5 *The roof framing. Cut and fit the rafters in place individually.*

over toward the opening center or away from it if you tap them on the ends with a hammer. If any stick out so far into the opening that drifting them won't remedy the situation, trim them by pulling out the toenail (that's why they aren't driven all the way in) and cutting them flush with a hand saw; then redrive the toenail.

Lateral placement of the log ends can be set once the 1″ × 4″ framing is in and can hold the log ends in place with nails driven through. To frame an opening, cut a 1 × 4 to fit across the top of the opening and nail it in place along the center line with 2″ nails (see Figs. 15–3 and 15–4). Then cut 1 × 4s to fit from the bottom of this board to the top of the log forming the bottom of the opening (or with the door, down to the plywood flooring). Drive 2″ nails through these side frames to align the log ends with the sides of the 1 × 4s. Finally, cut 1 × 4s to fit across the bottom of the opening between the side frames.

On the windows, slant the frame bottoms slightly downward to allow rain to drain off. (A bottom frame, or threshold, for the door is optional. It's something to trip over in an already small door opening, and it makes sweeping more difficult. But then, it helps to keep dirt from getting in in the first place.)

For window and door seals, rip 1″ × 1″ stringers from the rough redwood stock and nail them around all four sides of the windows with 2″ nails. Their outside edges should lie along the center line of the frames at each opening. (We did not use a bottom seal at the door.)

Make the door from rough 1″ × 6″ stock (Fig. 15–6). First, rip a 4′ length to about 2″ and 4″ wide with a Skilsaw. Then cut four 1 × 6s about $\frac{3}{8}$″ shorter than the door-opening height. (Our door opening

was a little out of square, so we marked the angled trim cut needed along one side and ripped this.) Next, lay down the 1 × 6s and cut the 2″ and 4″ cross-frames to length. Nail the 4″ cross-frames flush at the top and bottom of the door and at the side edge that opens out. To make a dutch door, nail the 2″ cross-frame across the door about 30″ from the bottom. Then nail the other 2″ cross-frame across (with two nails for every board) with its bottom $\frac{1}{8}$″ above the top of the cross-frame that you just nailed in place.

Cut the door in two, running the saw blade between the two 2″ cross-frames. The door can be hung with 3″ butt hinges countersunk into the edge of the door and fastened with $1\frac{1}{2}$″ screws. Or use ornamental, wrought-iron hinges mounted to the door front with 1″ screws. We used a barrel bolt mounted vertically on the inside of the door to lock the top of the door to the bottom. Then we screwed a wrought-iron garden-gate latch to the door.

To make scaled-down wooden casement windows, first cut $\frac{1}{2}$″ plywood shapes slightly oversized for each of the lower window openings (Fig. 15–7). The upper window does not have to open and can be glazed with a single piece. We happened to find an old leaded window at an antique warehouse that fit reasonably closely, then built the framing to fit it.

Hold each rough-cut plywood panel up to its opening and mark the exact side cuts needed for the panel to fit against the 1″ × 1″ stringers nailed in for window "stops." With these marked and labeled to show the positioning of the window— which side faces out and which way is up—cut these panels to fit. Then cut a second set of $\frac{1}{2}$″ plywood panels. Mark a center line along each panel (marking

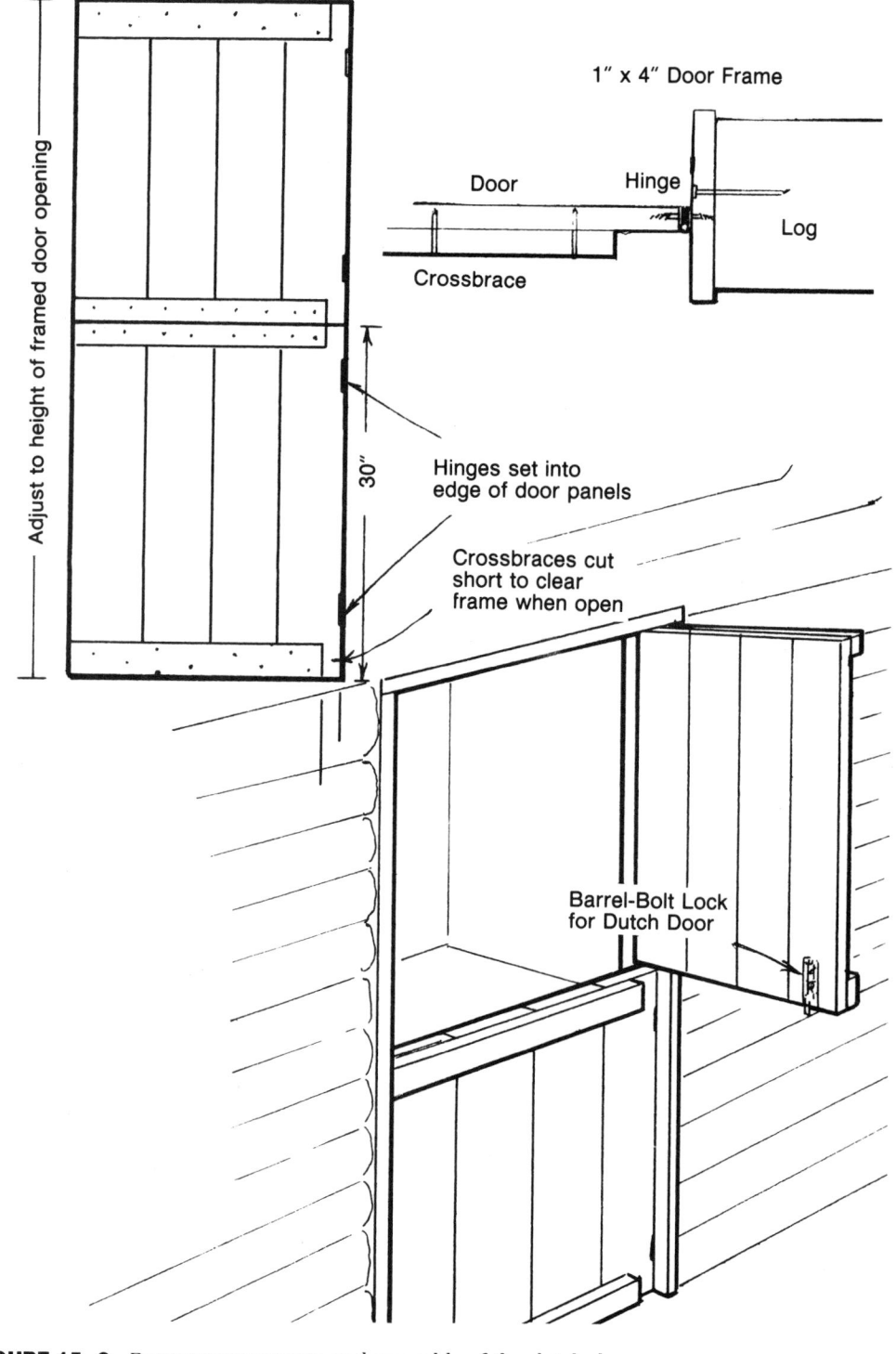

FIGURE 15–6 *Door measurements and assembly of the dutch door.*

The following labels appear in the figure:

Adjust to height of framed door opening

1″ x 4″ Door Frame

Door

Hinge

Log

Crossbrace

30″

Hinges set into edge of door panels

Crossbraces cut short to clear frame when open

Barrel-Bolt Lock for Dutch Door

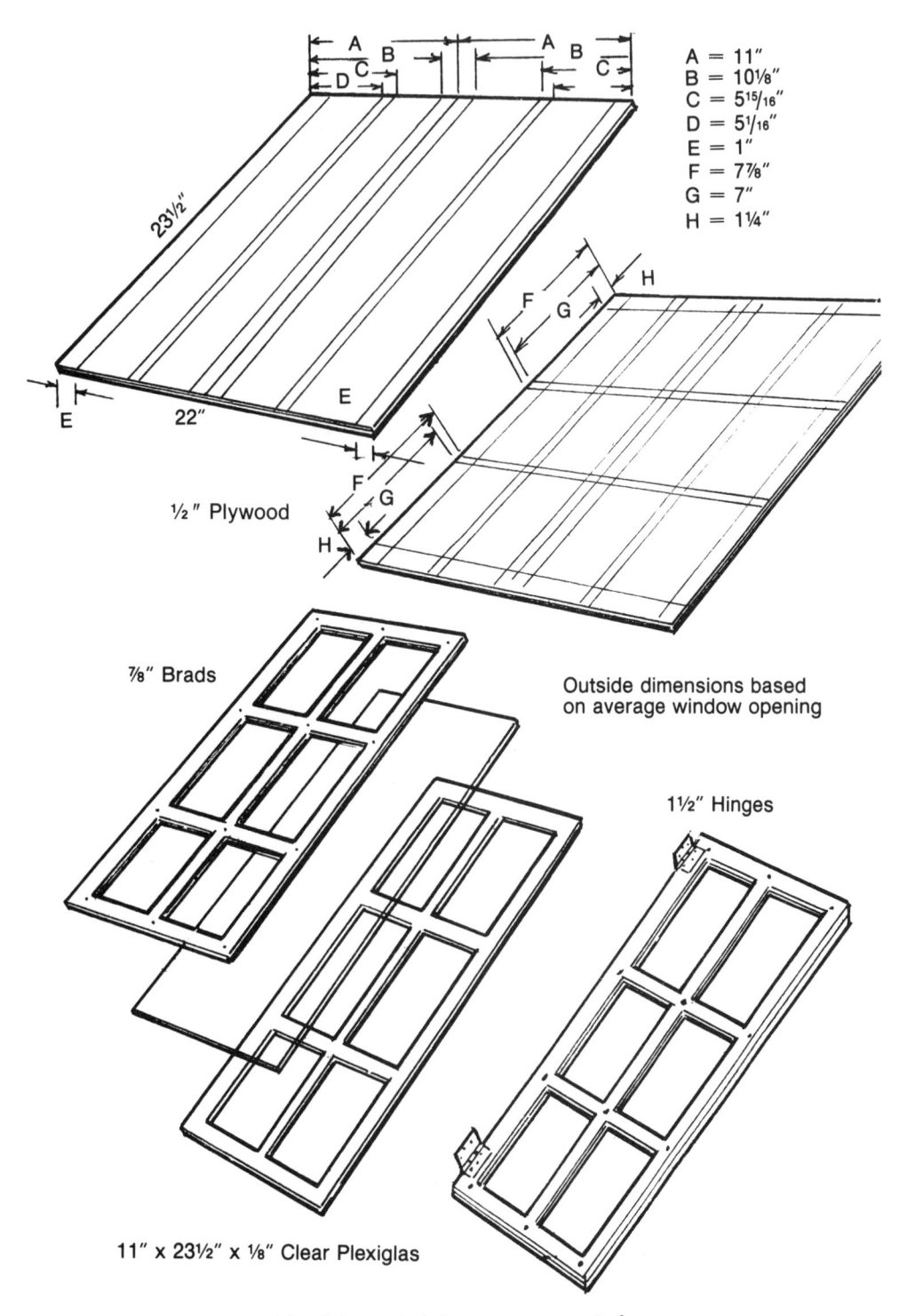

A = 11"
B = 10⅛"
C = 5¹⁵/₁₆"
D = 5¹/₁₆"
E = 1"
F = 7⅞"
G = 7"
H = 1¼"

23½"

22"

½" Plywood

⅞" Brads

Outside dimensions based on average window opening

1½" Hinges

11" x 23½" x ⅛" Clear Plexiglas

FIGURE 15–7 *Assembly of the sealed-down casement windows.*

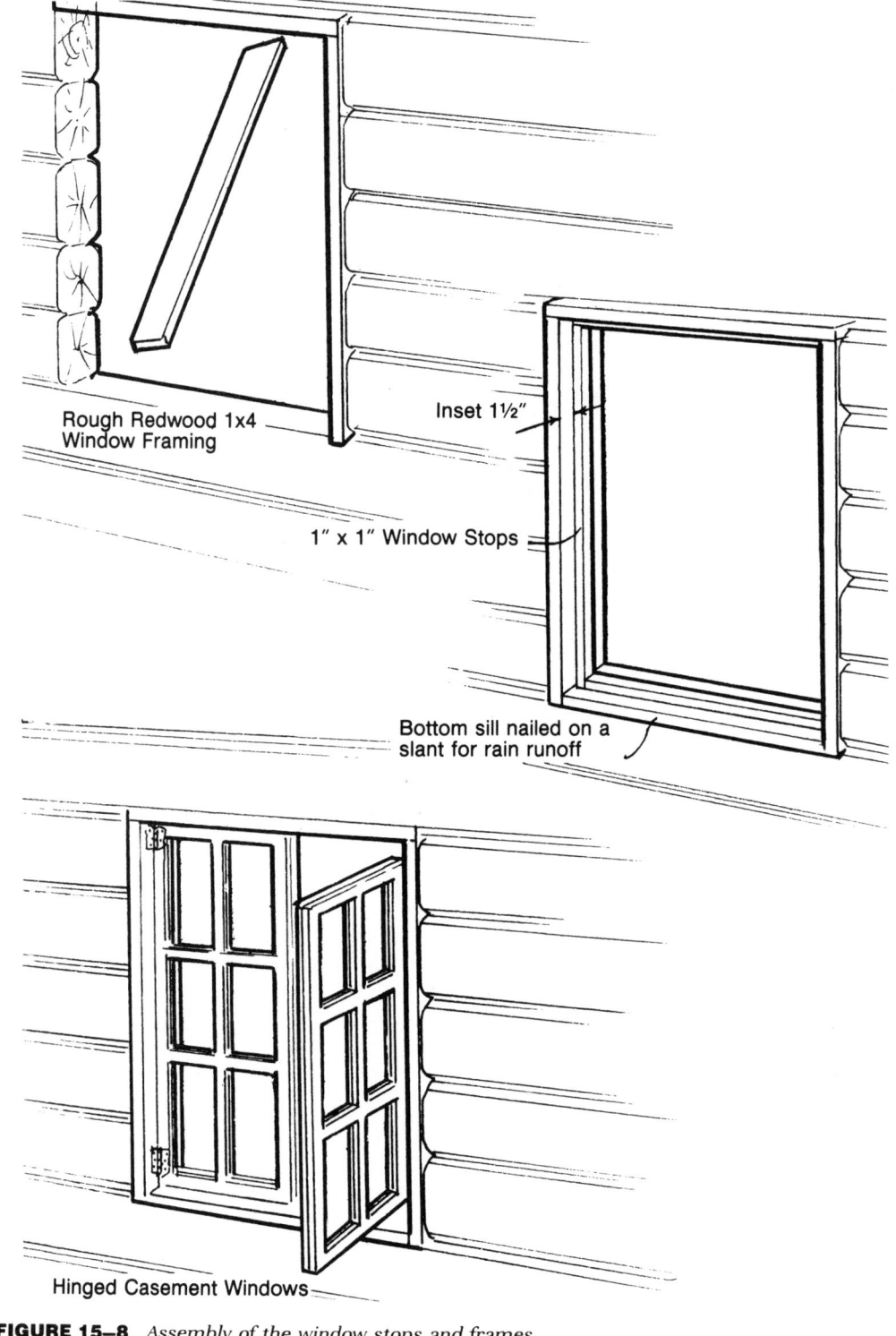

Rough Redwood 1x4
Window Framing

Inset 1½"

1" x 1" Window Stops

Bottom sill nailed on a
slant for rain runoff

Hinged Casement Windows

FIGURE 15—8 *Assembly of the window stops and frames.*

which half goes with which) and stack the pairs of identical panels. Cut them along the vertical center line.

Next, place a right and left plywood panel down over $\frac{1}{8}''$ clear Plexiglas and mark its shape. Cut the Plexiglas with a band saw, or use a hacksaw blade in a saber saw (but protect the Plexiglas from the bottom skid of the saw and go slowly).

Put aside one identical set of plywood window panels and mark the other with rectangles that leave approximately $1\frac{1}{2}''$ borders at the top and bottom of the panels, $\frac{7}{8}''$ borders between the rectangles, and about 1″ borders at the sides, as shown in Figure 15–7.

To cut out each rectangular window-pane opening, carefully make plunge cuts with a Skilsaw, pulling back the blade guard while slowly lowering the spinning blade onto the wood aligned with the sides of the rectangles. It's not possible to cut right up to the corners with a circular blade, so after making all the plunge cuts, cut out the corners with a saber saw. (You can cut out the rectangles using a $\frac{1}{2}''$ or larger starter hole and cutting from this point inside each pane with the saber saw, but it's hard to get a clean cut when cutting across the plywood grain.) When all the rectangles are cut out, place each window onto its identical twin panel, align them at the sides, mark the rectangular cutout panes onto the panels below, and repeat the cutting steps for another set of windows. Sand smooth both sets of window panels and remove all splinters.

To assemble the windows, place the Plexiglas cut to the same shape on top of the window frame, then place the twin plywood window frame on top of these. Align the three-panel sandwich at the sides and drill down through the top

panel and Plexiglas with a $\frac{1}{16}''$ drill bit. Insert a 1″ finishing nail and gently tap it in flush with the panel front. Repeat this at each corner of the window and at each place on the side frame where a horizontal frame meets the side frame. Drill the Plexiglas gently, and make sure there is no dirt or obstructions between it and the plywood to create a specific pressure point.

Hang the windows along the side frames of the window openings with small ornamental brass hinges (Fig. 15–8). Casement-window latches can be used as locks. To glaze the fixed upper-story window, run a bead of seam sealer along the outside of the 1″ × 1″ window stops. Push the glazing material (plastic, glass, or leaded glass) against the sealer, working out any air bubbles around all edges. Run another bead of sealer along the outside of the window around the edges, cut another set of 1″ × 1″ window stops and pre-nail 2″ finishing nails into them about 6″ apart. Push the stops against the sealer on the outside of the window and drive the nails into the framing (purposely sliding the side of the hammer firmly against the glass so that it can't bang into it by accident and crack it).

Making the casement windows is time-consuming, but it's virtually impossible to find scaled-down ready-made windows to fit. Larger panes are inappropriate, and custom-made (or even ready-made) casement windows are astronomically priced. And besides, making windows with milled frames the old-fashioned way is a good way to become a recluse before you even have the cabin to retreat to.

☐ The Roof (Fig. 15–9)

We used standard, medium-thickness cedar-shake shingles to roof the cabin, with

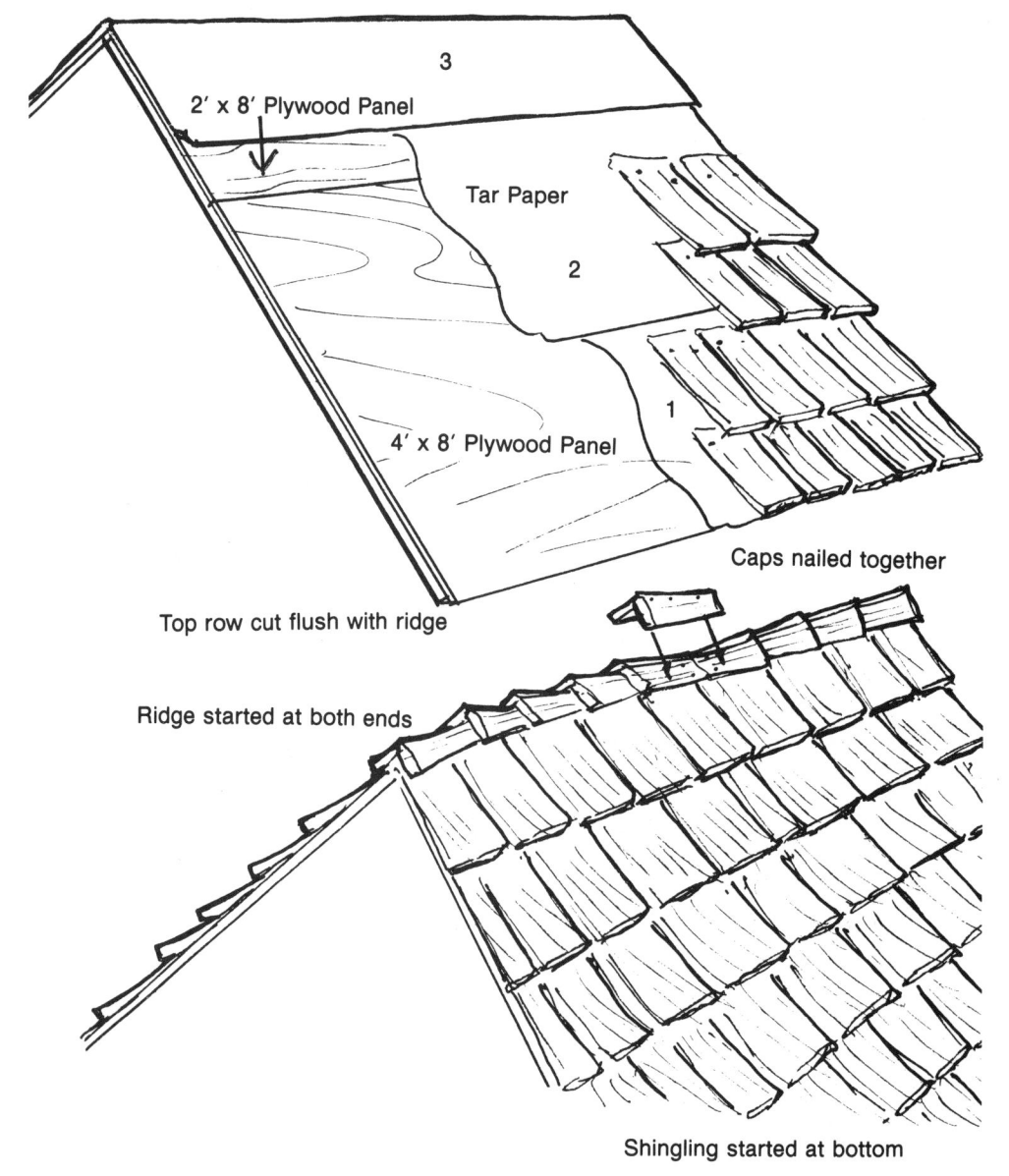

3

2' x 8' Plywood Panel

Tar Paper

2

4' x 8' Plywood Panel

1

Caps nailed together

Top row cut flush with ridge

Ridge started at both ends

Shingling started at bottom

FIGURE 15—9 *Roofing sequence.*

a layer of 90-pound tar paper underneath for sure weatherproofing. The roll of tar paper came with a set of instructions for lapping a layer of paper under each row of shingles, which works well for larger roofs. But for the small area to be covered here, we simply unrolled a layer and tacked it to the roof panels at the gable 1 × 4s along the bottom edge of the front and rear roof panel. Then we unrolled and cut off another 8' length to lay over the top ridge of the roof, overlapping the first layers. We tacked them with 1" roofing nails onto the gable 1 × 4s as before.

Use 1" roofing nails to fasten the first row of shingles with their fat ends roughly aligned with the bottom edge of the roof panels (Fig. 15–9). Drive the nails through about 4" to 6" down from the top of the shingle so that about $\frac{5}{8}''$ of nail pokes through into the roof panels. Shingle roofs shouldn't be completely straight and lined up, so you can work slightly haphazardly in the vertical positioning of the shingles to create a rustic look.

Continue to nail on rows of shingles, working up toward the top. At the top, saw off the shingle tops so that they will be flush with the roof ridge. Next, split the shingles to about 4" to 5" wide and, starting at the ends of the ridge and working toward the middle, lay these small shingles horizontally and nail them to the top row on each side of the ridge, mounted vertically. At the center, nail a pair of small shingles over the last two butted head-to-head pairs that you nailed onto the top-row shingles. Even though we *did* nail through the tar paper, in contradiction to the instructions, the pitch of the roof is sufficient to prevent leaks.

□ **Sealing the Walls**

We tried a number of methods for caulking between the logs to keep wind and wildlife out. Plaster and plaster-mix concrete were inexpensive but too messy and brittle. Latex glazing putty can be rolled into "snakes" in your hands and stuffed into the cracks, but it's also messy and not that inexpensive. For a little more money, we invested in architectural-quality seam caulk in cartridge form. It was quick and probably the least messy to work with.

Begin by spreading a bead of caulk along the base of the bottom 2 × 4s of the side walls and the bottom logs of the front and rear logs on both sides. Whenever laying down a bead of caulk from the cartridge gun, run your thumb along the bead to smooth it and force it into the cracks along the joint. We used dark brown caulk because it was unobtrusive.

From the first row up, apply caulk along the joints between logs (and at the notched end joints) on the outside only, spreading the caulk well onto both logs at each joint with your fingers. You can cut small, wedge-shaped scraps of 2 × 4s to fill in between the ridgepole log, the top gable log, and the bottom of the gable 1 × 4s at both sides of both ends of the ridgepole log.

Cut the lengths of rough 2 × 4 to fit on top of the front- and rear-wall logs between the rafters. Nail them down on top of the logs with prenailed 4" box nails and caulk to seal around edges.

■ **CONSTRUCTION NOTES**

Remember that in a cabin, where kerosene lamps and pot-bellied stoves are often used, proper ventilation is a must. After you've done your best to seal up the cabin into a draft-free, bug-free house, you must take precautions to make sure a window is left open or a vent is built in to ensure that a supply of fresh air is

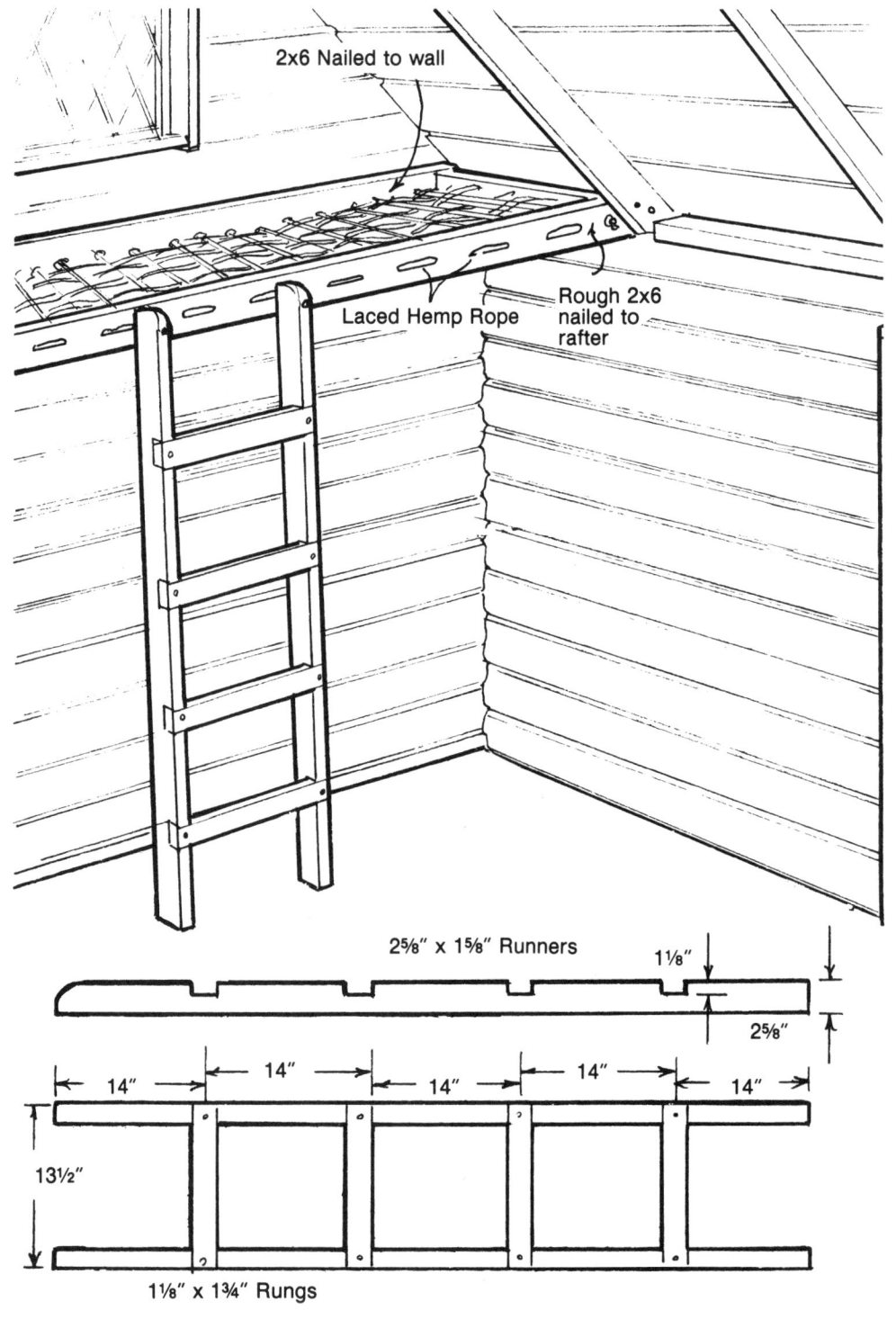

2x6 Nailed to wall

Laced Hemp Rope

Rough 2x6 nailed to rafter

2⅝" x 1⅝" Runners

1⅛"

2⅝"

14" 14" 14" 14" 14"

13½"

1⅛" x 1¾" Rungs

FIGURE 15–10 *Measurements of the loft bed and the ladder leading to it. The ladder can be bolted to the 2 × 6 and the gap filled with 1 × 4s or with screening for ventilation.*

maintained on chilly nights. Never use a charcoal heater in a cabin as small as this one.

Speaking of small, once we started to move in furniture and hang Currier and Ives prints on the walls, it became obvious that there just wouldn't be enough space for a nice living room if a bed were included. So we decided to try a loft bed. We cut and drilled the 2×4s, as shown in Figure 15–10, set the inboard 2×4 on the top logs of the front and rear walls and nailed it to the outboard side of the rafters with 4″ box nails. Then we set the outboard 2×4 in place on the top logs near the wall and strung the $\frac{3}{8}$″ hemp rope bed "springs" through the $\frac{1}{2}$″ holes back and forth between the 2×4s.

Next, we nailed the outboard 2×4 securely to the side-wall log with 4″ nails spaced about 9″ apart. Short lengths of 2×4 were cut and drilled for the bed frame ends, and 4″ nails were driven in at an angle through the end 2×4s and into the side 2×4s. More hemp rope was threaded through the end 2×4 holes, weaving the rope through the cross-ropes threaded through the side 2×4s. A lawn chaise pad makes a perfect mattress, although you can use a sleeping bag.

To get up to the loft, we made a ladder, ripping and notching rough 2×4s and cutting the rungs from 1″ × 6″ redwood stock. We simply nailed the rungs into the notches in the uprights with 3″ galvanized box nails.

The pioneers were a tough, hardy bunch. But even they might have winced at the conditions of the inaugural slumber party in the cabin, when more noisy young weekend pioneers than we care to think about somehow jammed into the shelter for an all-night gigglethon.

INDEX